Millard Fillmore

Millard Fillmore. (Photograph courtesy of the Buffalo and Erie County Historical Society)

Millard Fillmore

A BIBLIOGRAPHY

Compiled by

John E. Crawford

Foreword by Arthur Schlesinger, Jr.

Bibliographies of the Presidents of the United States,
Number 13
Mary Ellen McElligott, Series Editor

Greenwood Press
Westport, Connecticut • London

Library of Congress Cataloging-in-Publication Data

Crawford, John E., 1946–.
   Millard Fillmore: a bibliography / John E. Crawford ; foreword by Arthur Schlesinger, Jr.
      p. cm.—(Bibliographies of the presidents of the United States, ISSN 1061–6500 ; no. 13)
   Includes index.
   ISBN 0–313–28171–8 (alk. paper)
   1. Fillmore, Millard, 1800–1874—Bibliography.   2. United States—Politics and
government—1845–1861—Bibliography.   I. Title.   II. Series.
Z9205.9
[E427]
016.9736′4′092—dc21   2002022806

British Library Cataloguing in Publication Data is available.

Library of Congress Catalog Card Number: 2002022806
ISBN: 0–313–28171–8
ISSN: 1061–6500

First published in 2002

Greenwood Press, 88 Post Road West, Westport, CT 06881
An imprint of Greenwood Publishing Group, Inc.
www.greenwood.com

Printed in the United States of America

The paper used in this book complies with the
Permanent Paper Standard issued by the National
Information Standards Organization (Z39.48–1984).

10 9 8 7 6 5 4 3 2 1

Copyright Acknowledgment

The author and publisher gratefully acknowledge permission from the Buffalo and Erie County
Historical Society for use of the photograph of Millard Fillmore.

*In memory of my parents, Olive and Edgar Crawford
and
friend, Paul Westmuller*

Contents

.

Foreword

Nothing in the American constitutional order continues to excite so much scholarly interest, debate, and controversy as the role of the presidency. This remains the case in spite of the complaint, so common in the historical profession a generation ago, about the tyranny of "the presidential synthesis" in the writing of American history.

This complaint had its point. It is true enough that the deep currents in social, economic, and intellectual history, in demography, family structure, and collective mentalities, flow on without regard to presidential administrations. To deal with these underlying trends, the "new history" began, in the 1950s and 1960s, to reach out beyond traditional history to anthropology, sociology, psychology, and statistics. For a season social-science history pushed politics and personalities off the historical stage.

But in time social-science history displayed its limitations. It did not turn out to be, as its apostles had promised, a philosopher's—or historian's—stone. "Most of the great problems of history," wrote Lawrence Stone, himself a distinguished practitioner of the new history, "remain as insoluble as ever, if not more so." In particular, the new history had no interest in public policy—the decisions a nation makes through the political process—and proved impotent to explain it. Yet one can reasonably argue that, at least in a democracy, public policy reveals the true meaning of the past, the moods, preoccupations, values, and dreams of a nation, more clearly and trenchantly than almost anything else.

The tide of historical interest is now turning again—from deep currents to events, from underlying trends to decisions. While the history of public policy requires an accounting of the total culture from which national decisions emerge, such history must center in the end on the decisions themselves and on the people who make (and resist) them. Historians today are returning to the insights of classical history—

to the recognition that the state, political authority, military power, elections, statutes, wars, the ideas, ambitions, delusions and wills of individuals make a difference to history.

This is far from a revision to "great man" theories. But it is a valuable corrective to the assumption, nourished by social-science history, that public policy is merely a passive reflection of underlying historical forces. For the ultimate fascination of history lies precisely in the interplay between the individual and his environment. "It is true," wrote Tocqueville, "that around every man a fatal circle is traced beyond which he cannot pass; but within the wide range of that circle he is powerful and free; as it is with man, so with communities."

The *Bibliographies of the Presidents of the United States* series therefore needs no apology. Public policy is a powerful key to an understanding of the past; and in the United States the presidency is the battleground where issues of public policy are fought out and resolved. The history of American presidents is far from the total history of America. But American history without the presidents would leave the essential part of the story untold.

Recent years have seen a great expansion in the resources available for students of the presidency. The National Historical Publications Commission has done superb work in stimulating and sponsoring editions, both letterpress and microform, of hitherto inaccessible materials. "Documents," as President Kennedy said in 1963, "are the primary sources of history; they are the means by which later generations draw close to historical events and enter into the thoughts, fears and hopes of the past." He saluted the NHPC program as "this great effort to enable the American people to repossess its historical heritage."

At the same time, there has been a rich outpouring of scholarly monographs on presidents, their associates, their problems, and their times. And the social-science challenge to narrative history has had its impact on presidential scholarship. The interdisciplinary approach has raised new questions, developed new methodologies, and uncovered new sources. It has notably extended the historian's methodological arsenal.

This profuse presidential literature has heretofore lacked a guide. The *Bibliographies of the Presidents of the United States* series thus fills a great lacuna in American scholarship. It provides comprehensive annotated bibliographies, president by president, covering manuscripts and archives, biographies and monographs, articles and dissertations, government documents and oral histories, libraries, museums, and iconographic resources. The editors are all scholars who have mastered their presidents. The series places the study of American presidents on a solid bibliographical foundation.

In so doing, it will demonstrate the wide sweep of approaches to our presidents, from analysis to anecdotes, from hagiography to vilification. It will illustrate the rise and fall of presidential reputations—fluctuations that often throw as much light on historians as on presidents. It will provide evidence for and against Bryce's famous proposition "Why Great Men Are Not Chosen Presidents." It will remind us that superior men have somehow made it to the White House but also that, as the Supreme Court said in *ex parte Milligan*, the republic has "no right to expect that it will always have wise and humane rulers, sincerely attached to the principles of the Constitution. Wicked men, ambitious of power, with hatred of liberty and contempt of law, may fill the place once occupied by Washington and Lincoln."

Above all, it will show how, and to what degree, the American presidency has been the focus of the concerns, apprehensions, and aspirations of the people and the times. The history of the presidency is a history of nobility and of pettiness, of courage and of cunning, of forthrightness and of trickery, of quarrel and of consensus. The turmoil perennially swirling around the White House illuminates the heart of American democracy. The literature reflects the turmoil, and the *Bibliographies of the Presidents of the United States* supply at last the light that will enable scholars and citizens to find their way through the literature.

Arthur Schlesinger, Jr.

Editor's Preface

Individuals who rise to the highest elected office offered by the American people hold a special fascination. Their backgrounds, their philosophies over time, the way they "rise" are matters of enduring observation, commentary, and analysis. The *Bibliographies of the Presidents of the United States*, splendidly begun by the late Carol Fitzgerald in 1988, provides to both the specialist and generalist a comprehensive guide to every aspect of those unique individuals.

Each volume records the mundane and the critical—from early education, to contemporary news and political analysis, family reminiscences, scholarly analysis and revision, partisan attacks, official papers, personal manuscripts, visual records, and, for administrations of our day, the film and video record.

The Greenwood series offers the possibility of complete access to every instant of the Chief Executive's career or preparation. Taken together, the volumes provide chronological, precise, and detailed accounts of how each President has risen, administered, and withdrawn—and how scholars, pundits, and the American people have weighed that progress.

Mary Ellen McElligott
Series Editor

Introduction and Acknowledgments

Two episodes at the end of Millard Fillmore's administration are representative of his hopes for the nation. On February 24, 1853, just days before leaving office, President Fillmore and his guests toured the ship *Ericsson* at Alexandria, Virginia. He and President-elect Franklin Pierce sat amidships and rode the huge pistons up and down to the amusement of themselves and everyone on board. Fillmore enjoyed the day and appeared content with the end of his administration. He could reflect on the quieted sectional disputes over slavery, the prospering national economy, and the respect for the country by other nations.

The *Ericsson* was a paddlewheeler featuring experimental engines designed to use less coal at speeds efficient for ocean commerce. The new powerful pistons symbolized the intelligence and inventiveness of the American people and the potential material progress of the nation. Fillmore hoped the ship's builder, engineer John Ericsson, could get federal support to continue his improvements. Fillmore believed federal support for inventions and other internal improvements would power the expansion of railroads, canals, and industries across the country and bind a nation in economic development and material progress.

Days later Fillmore's friends presented him with a lifetime membership in the American Colonization Society. Fillmore believed the Society's goals could relieve the country of slavery and remove the former slaves to Africa. The Society's philanthropy and federal subsidies would purchase slaves and help the south divest its capital from slavery without loss. The south would accept this plan as it began to appreciate the material progress of internal improvements, a diverse economy, and free labor. Meanwhile the transportation of former slaves to Africa would relieve the country, and African Americans, from the virulent racism he knew existed. He believed the plan offered a rational solution to the emotional and disreputable problem of slavery that was interfering with the nation's expansion and progress. He said so in his last presidential address. However, at the request of his cabinet, he deleted that section in order to maintain the sectional calm that many believed was the major success of his administration.

Fillmore's economic goals were classic American Whig proposals. The colonization plan was gathering a renewed following at mid-century and had the support of historically important Whig figures: Henry Clay, Daniel Webster, Edward Everett, John Crittenden, and Abraham Lincoln.

However, in less then a decade Fillmore's hopes collapsed. The *Ericsson* never received federal support nor did colonization inspire national backing. Ericsson's paddlewheeler was replaced by his new, government supported, screw propelled, ironclad warship the *Monitor.* Colonization was superseded by the Emancipation Proclamation. Even Fillmore's way of conducting politics was dismissed. Debate and compromise were replaced by renewed sectional hostility, then Civil War and unconditional surrender. Like the *Ericsson*, colonization, and sectional compromise, Fillmore too was dismissed to the margins of American history. Even before the Civil War Fillmore was exiled from public memory. By 1860 he told a friend that he was a forgotten man. He remained a forgotten man for the next century and a half.

Millard Fillmore led an exceptional life for a poor farmer's son born in a log cabin. He worked hard and combined self education, pluck, and luck into a legal career by the early 1820s in Buffalo, New York. In 1823 he moved to the nearby village of East Aurora and started his own legal practice. In 1826 he married Abigail Powers and began a family. He moved back to a thriving Buffalo in 1830, now powered by the commerce of the Erie Canal. He started another successful law firm and established himself as one of the city's reputable men.

He was active in local politics. He was a first-rate organizer for the National Republican party and the Antimasonic party in the late 1820s, and for the Whig party in the 1830s and 40s. In 1828 he successfully ran for the state assembly and was reelected twice. In 1832 he was elected Whig congressman from western New York. With one hiatus he continued in congress until 1842, the last two years as chairman of the House Ways and Means Committee. During this time he helped western New York become the "faithful west" for the New York Whig party. In 1844 he lost the Governor's race but became the first elected Comptroller of New York state in 1847. One year later he was Zachary Taylor's running mate. Elected Vice President in November 1848, he was inaugurated on March 9, 1849. As president of the senate he was commended for preserving its decorum during the debates on the Compromise of 1850. At mid-century he was a successful politician with a regional following who could get out the vote, ably perform his public service, and be available. On the negative, he appeared to lack the drive and cunning to be a national leader.

When President Taylor died, Fillmore assumed the Presidency on July 10, 1850. He immediately helped Congress reorganize and pass the acts known as the Compromise of 1850. At the apex of his public service, his signature on these laws effectively cut short his political career. For signing and enforcing the Fugitive Slave Law he drew the wrath of abolitionists, antislavery politicians, and rivals in his own party.

At this time he was not a marginal figure. He was the chief executive of the nation willing to use military force to execute the laws of the land. Antislavery politicians moved against him. Charles Sumner stated, "Better for him had he never been born; better for his memory, and for the good name of his children, had he never been President." Abolitionists Theodore Parker, Wendell Phillips, and William Lloyd Garrison joined the call. Later, Ralph Waldo Emerson and Henry Thoreau added their protests against the act and its supporters. They were further enraged by their inability to organize against the Fugitive Slave Law. It must be remembered that the Compromise did calm sectional debates. Abolitionists were tormented by their inability to excite public outrage. Thomas Higginson walked around with a Fillmore presidential address in his pocket to remind him how ineffectual his small movement was. Wendell Philllips publicly asked how to bribe Americans into protest. Pre-war abolitionists were frustrated over Fillmore's and the public's accommodation to slavery and their resignation at the "abductions" of African Americans back into bondage. Abolitionists were still prophets in the early 1850s; they were years away from being history's heroes.

However, the controversy led the Whigs to deny Fillmore's nomination to a second term in 1852. Four years later he hoped to use the American party and its Know-Nothing contingent to regain the Presidency and somehow repair the growing sectional divide. He came in third in a three-way race. Many blamed him for the defeat of the Republican party's first presidential candidate. Afterward, Republican newspaperman William Cullen Bryant dismissed Fillmore to "obscurity and contempt." By the end of the decade Fillmore was already a fugitive in the public's mind and exiled to the margins of American history.

Even in death Fillmore was shunned from national memory. As Buffalo mourned his death in March 1874, Senator Charles Sumner died. First elected by running against Fillmore's Compromise he had been a national figure for twenty-five years. The national tributes to Sumner overshadowed the local ceremonies for Fillmore. Garrison, eulogizing Sumner, restated the Senator's earlier curse: Fillmore deserved to be buried "unwept, unhonored and unsung." He remained unsung. And no small measure of his dismissal from history derived from the stature and the writings of abolitionists and antislavery politicians, the victory of their just cause to abolish slavery, and their resonance into the present.

One would think history would notice a man with such enemies. But other circumstances added to the obscurity of Fillmore. For instance, The Albany *Argus* apologized for any missing information in its memorial biography of Fillmore because it was looking back "in the dim light of his own time." The murky barrier to the past was a compound of the drama, violence, and magnitude of the Civil War, followed by the political combat of Reconstruction, and the factory haze of the new urban-industrial age. The recent and present, like the framed reality of the new photography, engrossed the reflective mind and dimmed public memory. Later, national public history would enshrine Lincoln's Presidency and leave antebellum Presidents to the dim recollections of their hometowns, the jeers of pundits, and indifference of most historians.

Even more important to Fillmore's faint image in history was his reticence to insist himself into its written record. The nineteenth century filled library shelves with political and war memoirs. The abolitionists, their colleagues, and Fillmore's colleagues, left volumes of words for generations to debate their ideas, ideals, passions, and political behavior. Fillmore left very little to enter these debates. This reticence to argue publicly before and after the Civil War was part of his personality and public character. As a lawyer he had valued the resolution of differences in his office while leaving his partners to contend in the courtroom. As President he negotiated with politicians and avoided public oratory. He censored himself on slavery issues to ease the rhetoric of sectional debate.

Historians rely on the written record and value those who write volumes. Fillmore did not publish his papers. Nor did his friends write a narrative around his correspondence, as was fashionable in the nineteenth century. Not until 1907 did an incomplete set of his papers appear. Other than his presidential addresses, Fillmore did not publicly explain his actions to contemporaries, nor did he write for posterity. Consequently, he made himself vulnerable to the uncontested jibes of his enemies and the forgetfulness of later generations.

For much of the twentieth century Fillmore attracted little attention from historians. They used the two-volume *Millard Fillmore Papers* to glean material for their own projects. Knowing little about him they readily gave him below-average ratings as President. Even Robert J. Rayback's 1957 biography, *Millard Fillmore*, came about because of his original interest in the Whig party. But that biography made a difference. It finally profiled Fillmore in a scholarly manner. Apropos, it remained the only modern biography of Fillmore until Robert J. Scarry's just published work. However there were formidable hints that he was worth further study. Holman Hamilton's *Prologue to Conflict* in 1964 and David Potter's *The Impending Crisis* in 1976 suggested Fillmore should claim more of our attention.

Clio, the muse of history, was listening. In the late 1960s, a cache of Fillmore papers thought destroyed became available and was housed at the State University College of New York at Oswego. These papers were merged with collections at the Buffalo and Erie County Historical Society and papers from other collections. In 1975 these collated materials were processed onto sixty-eight rolls of microfilm. Thus a major resource on Fillmore's life and the antebellum era became available. Belatedly scholars reclaimed a forgotten President. They found his administration significant to antebellum history and his earnest efforts to quiet sectional disputes both interesting and a little praiseworthy. By the end of the century President Millard Fillmore was back from the margins of American history. Although not a spirited restoration, it is nevertheless a satisfactory reintroduction of a forgotten man into the debates of his era.

Early use of the new Fillmore papers and reappraisal of his career appeared in works by Elbert Smith, Benson Lee Grayson, and Robert C. Schelin. But foremost are three virtuosi works on antebellum history: Mark J. Stegmaier's *Texas, New Mexico, and the Compromise of 1850* (1996); Michael J. Holt's *The Rise and Fall of the American Whig Party* (1999); and William E. Gienapp's *The Origins of the Republican Party, 1852–1856* (1987). These works introduce us to a new Fillmore. He plays a decisive role quelling the Texas-New Mexico border dispute immediately after taking office. He helps maneuver passage of the Compromise of 1850. He is heroic trying to save his Whig party while frustratingly temperate toward his political enemies. He is both sympathetic and pitiable when campaigning to save the nation through the American party in the election of 1856. And in a complimentary collection of letters, *The Lady and the President* (1975) edited by Charles M. Snyder we find a decent and gracious man of friendships, personal decorum, and loyalty to his hometown. He is a loving husband and father, and later a widower mourning the deaths of his wife and daughter. Collectively these works portray a Whig President and a considerate man seeing reason in compromise with the slave south. He may have been deliberate and precedent minded, but he worked energetically and decisively to bring his strengths to save the nation and his party. The authors convey respect for his political competence, administrative abilities, public dignity, and personal behavior. Most important, they admit him to the history of his administration and into the events of his time.

A significant portion of this bibliography deals with Fillmore's support for the Fugitive Slave Law. Scholars investigating his appeasement to southern slavery will find a decent man signing a bill that terrorized a segment of the American population. Despite his antislavery sentiments he sacrificed the hopes of fugitive slaves, jeopardized the liberty of free African Americans, and sanctioned the future of slavery. Anyone studying Fillmore finds this proposition awkward and haunting. How could a man hoping for charitable policies toward African Americans sign laws coercing them? Context can help us. Fillmore's enforcement of the fugitive law was accepted by a large public—whether indifferent or approving—and the law was tolerated well into Lincoln's administration. Fillmore's appeasement, it can be argued, represented the American public's relationship to African Americans at that time. He and a large American public were willing to sacrifice a segment of the American population for sectional peace, a secure nation, and their own continued pursuit of happiness.

Fillmore's future in American history may revolve around analysis of this dilemma. In an odd sense Fillmore will have proven Albert J. Von Frank's proposition in *The Trials of Anthony Burns*, that "what is marginalized is always secretly at the center." Von Frank applied the insight to the neglected importance of African-American history. Likewise, after the Civil War, Fillmore was marginalized because he represented the unacceptable proposition that in the recent past most Americans were willing to sacrifice African Americans for their own continued security. A proposal at the center of antebellum politics but unacceptable in the post-Civil War era.

Today Fillmore is reemerging as historians put slavery and the politics of slavery at the center of antebellum sectionalism and the Civil War. They are recruiting

Fillmore from the margins of American history and finding a featured role for him in the central issues of antebellum America. He seems to be emerging as a representative figure of the public's acceptance of slavery and perhaps an archetype of the compromiser willing to forfeit others for what he perceived as a greater good. Many can even see Fillmore's dilemma as an episode in a central theme of American history: tolerating injustice in order to engage problems perceived more important by an apparently more worthy segment of the nation. One can even imagine Fillmore's dilemma echoing into our generation's current examination of inequalities. In which case he will have come from the margins of American history into the center of national debate.

I hope this bibliography offers students and scholars the materials to study the historical Fillmore. Thanks to recent scholarship and library technology he is in his time again and the materials are at hand to investigate his life, his administration, and his era. And perhaps he and his era can add perspective to our own debates and compromises on America's future.

I would like to thank the librarians of the University at Buffalo, particularly the departments of Interlibrary Loan, Reference, Government Documents, and Rare Book Room. Special appreciation is due the library clerks at the Lockwood, Undergraduate, Health Science, and Architecture libraries. They were always courteous when I took out books, renewed books, returned books, and paid fines for overdue books.

Other libraries extended their help and courtesy: the Special Collections department of the Penfield Library at the State University College of New York at Oswego; the Rush Rhies Library at the University of Rochester, the Powers Library in Moravia, New York; the Interlibrary Loan and the Rare Book departments at the Buffalo and Erie County Downtown Library. The past and current staff at the Buffalo and Erie County Historical Society were especially helpful, particularly former staff members Art Detmars, Herman Sass, and Scott Eberle, who thought I might be interested in this project. The Roswell Park Cancer Institute's Mirand Library staff shared with me their reference and computer skills.

I'd like to acknowledge my appreciation to the Graduate Student Association of the University at Buffalo for a research grant that enabled me to view the original Millard Fillmore Papers at the State University College at Oswego.

The History Department of the University at Buffalo introduced me to the research techniques that have proved essential to this work. Particular credit belongs to historian Richard E. Ellis, who is an exemplar of the earnest and dedicated researcher.

I wish to thank Greenwood Publishing Group for its commitment to the *Bibliographies of the Presidents of the United States* series and allowing me to be associated with two remarkable editors who went beyond the call of duty to assist in this bibliography. I want to remember my original editor Carol B. Fitzgerald, who laughed at my fears and encouraged me to follow my own interests. And special thanks to my current editor Mary Ellen McElligott for her patience, sense of humor, and more patience.

Chronology

1832	March 27. Daughter, Mary Abigail Fillmore, is born
	April. Forms law firm of Clary & Fillmore
	Published critique of religious oaths for witnesses in court. Used the pseudonym "Juridicus"
	November. Elected representative to the Twenty-Third Congress
1833	December 2. Takes seat in House of Representatives
1834	Forms law firm of Fillmore & Hall with former student Nathan K. Hall
	Law firm employed by the Holland Land Company
	Declines Whig renomination to Congress fearing his work for the Company will take votes from the new Whig party
1836	January 10. Forms law firm of Fillmore, Hall & Haven with new partner Solomon Haven
	October 4. After two-year absence he is renominated to the House of Representatives
	November. Reelected Whig congressman to the Twenty-Fifth Congress
1838	Reelected to the Twenty-Sixth Congress
1840	Reelected to the Twenty-Seventh Congress, chairman of the Ways and Means Committee
1842	June 9. Makes his well-received tariff speech in the House
	Declines renomination to Congress
1844	May. Unsuccessful candidate for Vice President at the Whig National Convention, Baltimore
	September 11. Receives Whig nomination for governor of New York
	November. Defeated for governor by Democrat, Silas Wright
1846–47	First chancellor of the University of Buffalo. Remained chancellor until his death
1847	Millard Powers Fillmore attends Harvard and Mary Abigail attends finishing school in Massachusetts
	October 6. Nominated for New York State comptroller at the Whig convention in Syracuse
	November 2. First elected New York State comptroller
1848	January 1. Assumes office as comptroller
	June 1. Nominated for Vice President at the Whig national convention
	November. Elected Vice President
1849	February 20. Resigns as New York State comptroller
	March 4. Inaugurated Vice President
1849–50	As president of the Senate he presides over the debates on the Compromise of 1850
1850	July 10. Takes oath of office as President of the United States, after the death of President Taylor

August 6. Sends message to Congress proposing to protect New Mexico's eastern boundary from Texan incursions

September 9. Signed the act admitting California as a free state

Signed the Texas boundary and New Mexico Territory Act

Signed the Utah Territory Act

September 18. Signed the Fugitive Slave Law

September 20. Signed the act abolishing the slave trade in the District of Columbia

September 26. Fillmore's "silver grays" bolt from New York State Whig convention when it approved William Seward's position against the Compromise Acts

December 2. First annual message

1851   February 18. Proclamation calling on civil and military officers and citizens of Massachusetts to enforce the Fugitive Slave Law

April 25. Proclamation warning the public against participation in the armed intervention (the Lopez expedition) against Cuba

May. Attends opening celebration of the New York and Erie Railroad

June. Administration formalizes plans to undertake mission to Japan to open trade and secure friendly harbors for Pacific trade routes

July 4. Lays the cornerstone to the extension of the Capital building

September. Attends Boston celebration for the opening of railroad link between the United States and Canada

October 22. Proclamation warning the public against participation in an armed intervention against Mexico

December 2. Second annual message

1852   June 16–21. Loses Whig presidential nomination to Winfield Scott

June 29. Executive Order announcing the death of Henry Clay

October 25. Executive Order announcing the death of Secretary of State Daniel Webster

November 19. Administration instructs Commodore Matthew C. Perry to proceed on mission to Japan

December 6. Third annual message

1853   March 4. Attends Franklin Pierce's inaugural and retires from the presidency. Abigail becomes sick after the ceremony from standing in the cold and damp weather

March 30. Death of Abigail Fillmore in Washington

1854   March–May. Tours the South with John P. Kennedy, his former Secretary of the Navy

July 26. Death of daughter Mary Abigail Fillmore from cholera

1855   May 17. Sails to Liverpool for tour of Europe and the Middle East

1856   February 22. While on tour he receives nomination for president by the American party

May 21. Writes acceptance of his nomination from Paris

June 22. Arrives in New York City and makes speeches along the route to Buffalo that are printed for the American party campaign

November. Defeated in the election

1858   February 10. Marries widow Mrs. Caroline C. McIntosh of Albany

1860   Supports the Constitutional Union party during the presidential campaign

1861   February. President-elect Abraham Lincoln is guest of Fillmore in Buffalo while on his way to Washington

1862   Chairman, Buffalo Committee of Public Defense in the Civil War

One of the founders of the Buffalo Fine Arts Academy

May 20. President and founding member of the Buffalo Historical Society

1863   May 28. Fillmore's father, Nathaniel, dies

1864   Delivers speech critical of the war

Supports General George B. McClelland for president

1865   April. Chairman of the delegation meeting Lincoln's funeral train

December 8. Executes his last will and testament (codicils dated September 19, 1868 and April 28, 1873)

1866   Spring–Summer. Visits Europe with his wife

August. Heads Buffalo delegation meeting President Andrew Johnson

1867–68   First president of the Buffalo Club

1870   President, Buffalo General Hospital

1870–74   Trustee, Grosvenor Library, Buffalo

1871   Writes short autobiography of his youth and young adulthood

1874   February 13. Suffers first stroke causing paralysis

March 8. Following a second stroke he dies in his home

1881   August 11. Caroline, Fillmore's second wife, dies

1889   November 15. Son Millard Powers Fillmore dies

Chapter 1

Manuscripts and Archival Sources

A. UNPUBLISHED PERSONAL AND ADMINISTRATIVE PAPERS OF MILLARD FILLMORE

1. Fillmore, Millard. Papers. Buffalo and Erie County Historical Society, Buffalo, NY. Major collection of presidential correspondence and public papers. This collection contains 8,400 letters received in the period 1849 to 1853, and a smaller number of letters and speeches written by Fillmore throughout his career.

2. ———. Papers. New-York State Historical Society, Albany. 43 items of political correspondence on the Whig and American parties.

3. ———. Papers. State University College of New York at Oswego. Substantial collection of correspondence to Fillmore and a smaller number from Fillmore. This collection contains legal, political, and family papers. However, there are only a small number of papers from the presidential period.

4. ———. Papers of the State University of New York at Buffalo Archives. 25 items from 1849 to 1850. There is a draft of a letter to Secretary Webster on using force in Texas to settle the Texas–New Mexico boundary dispute.

5. Smith, Lester W. "Research Collection-Manuscripts." *Niagara Frontier* 9 (Summer–Autumn 1962): 48–51. Reviews major acquisitions of Fillmore papers and the publication of the two-volume *Millard Fillmore Papers*.

6. Smith, Lester W., and Arthur C. Detmers. *Guide to the Microfilm Edition of the Millard Fillmore Papers*. Buffalo: Buffalo and Erie County Historical Society,

1975. An exhaustive collection gathered and microfilmed on 68 rolls. The *Guide* annotates each roll and gives a history of the acquisitions. The core of the collection are the 25 rolls of correspondence during the presidential years.

7. Snyder, Charles M. "Forgotten Fillmore Papers Examined." *American Archivist* 32 (January 1969): 11–14. Describes the loss of a major collection of Fillmore papers and its recovery in the 1960s.

B. PUBLISHED COMPILATIONS OF FILLMORE'S PERSONAL AND ADMINISTRATIVE PAPERS

8. Boykin, Edward, ed. *State of the Union.* New York: Funk & Wagnalls Company, Inc., 1963. Excerpts from Fillmore's three messages highlight his desire to settle the sectional crises, reform naval discipline, and expand the U.S. role in world commerce.

9. "Documents of Early Days." *Publications of the Buffalo Historical Society, Volume 25.* Buffalo: Buffalo Historical Society, 1921. 369–80. In an 1865 letter, Fillmore gave advice on success: high standards, no bad habits, industry, honesty, and perseverance.

10. Farrell, John J., ed. *Zachary Taylor 1784–1850 / Millard Fillmore 1800–1874.* Dobbs Ferry, NY: Oceana Publications, 1971. The book contains seven excerpts from major addresses and messages by Fillmore.

11. "Foreign Policy of the Presidents." *Current History* 7 (November 1944): 367–73. Reprints Fillmore's foreign policy statement on nonintervention from his third Message to Congress.

12. Frost, Elizabeth, ed. *The Bully Pulpit, Quotations from American Presidents.* New York: New England Publishing Associates Book, 1988. Contains 19 Fillmore quotations on various political themes, and a disparaging Truman quote about Fillmore's presidency.

13. Frost-Knappman, Elizabeth, ed. *The World Almanac of Presidential Quotations: Quotations from American Presidents.* New York: Pharos Books, 1993. Republication of item **12**.

14. Hamlin, L. B., ed. "Selections from the Follett Papers, IV." *Quarterly Publication of the Historical and Philosophical Society of Ohio* 11 (January–March 1916): 5–35. One 1834 letter on presidential prospects for 1836, and another against President Jackson's national banking policy.

15. Hibbard, George, ed. "The Fillmore Correspondence." *Grosvenor Library Bulletin* 3 (December 1920): 1–13. Letters on presidential diplomacy, Daniel Webster, and his 1855–1856 European tour.

16. Israel, Fred L., ed. *The State of the Union Messages of the Presidents, 1790–1966.* 3 vols. New York: Chelsea House Publishers, 1966. Volume One contains Fillmore's three Annual Messages to Congress.

17. "Millard Fillmore." *Collector: A Magazine for Autograph and Historical Collectors* 62 (May 1949): 97–101. Contains three letters from 1860 relating his unhappy and rebellious apprenticeship as a 14-year-old cloth dresser.

18. "Millard Fillmore." *Harper's Encyclopedia of United States History: From 458 A.D. to 1909.* New York: Harper & Brothers Publishers, 1905. 10 vols. 3: 360–66. Reprints Fillmore's August 6, 1850, letter to Congress on the Texas–New Mexico border issue.

19. Morris, Richard B., ed. *Great Presidential Decisions, State Papers that Changed the Course of History.* New York: J. B. Lippincott Company, 1967. Reprints the special message to Congress on the Texas–New Mexico boundary dispute and his letter to the Emperor of Japan.

20. Park, Julian, ed. "Inaugural Address of Honorable Millard Fillmore as President of the Buffalo Historical Society, July 1, 1862." *Niagara Frontier* 9 (Summer–Autumn 1962): 29–33. Abridged address with comments.

21. Podell, Janet, and Steven Anzovin, eds. *Speeches of the American Presidents.* New York: H. W. Wilson Company, 1988. Excerpts from Fillmore's first Annual Message on his noninterventionist foreign policy and arguments for accepting the Compromise of 1850.

22. "President Fillmore to the Sultan of Muscat." *Golden Book Magazine* 16 (August 1932): 164–65. In this May 1851 letter, Fillmore requests that the Sultan honor a treaty by reopening his ports to American shipping.

23. "The President Reads a New Biography: 1851." *Maryland Historical Magazine* 46 (December 1951): 297–99. Reprints Fillmore's letter to John P. Kennedy acknowledging receipt of his biography of William Wirt, and recounting his brief acquaintance with Wirt.

24. Richardson, James D., comp. *A Compilation of the Messages and Papers of the Presidents of the United States, 1789–1897.* 20 vols. New York: Bureau of National Literature Inc., 1897–1917. Volume Six contains Fillmore's Annual Messages to Congress, proclamations, and important executive orders.

25. Severance, Frank H., ed. *Millard Fillmore Papers, Publications of the Buffalo Historical Society, Vol. 10.* Buffalo: Buffalo Historical Society, 1907. The first volume of the published Fillmore papers. Contains letters and addresses from pre-presidential political career. The Presidential years include a calendar of messages and proclamations plus the suppressed portion of his third Annual Message regarding slavery and race. It also includes post-presidential addresses; a genealogy; an autobiography of Fillmore's early years; a biography, and portraits of Fillmore and his family.

26. ———, ed. *Millard Fillmore Papers, Publications of the Buffalo Historical Society, Vol. 11.* Buffalo: Buffalo Historical Society, 1907. Second volume of papers contains speeches given during the 1856 presidential campaign; correspondence from 1821 to 1874; an 1873 interview with the New York *Herald;* Fillmore's will; and a 1907 bibliography.

27. Snyder, Charles M., ed. *The Lady and the President: Letters of Dorothea Dix and Millard Fillmore.* Lexington: University of Kentucky Press, 1975. Separate discoveries of letters from Dix and Fillmore reveal a special friendship between the humanitarian and the President. The letters cover political, social, and personal subjects from 1850 to 1869.

28. "Then and Now." *Grosvenor Library Bulletin* 5 (March 1923): 10–12. An excerpt from Fillmore's 1871 Annual Report for the Grosvenor Library, Buffalo.

29. Thomas, Maurice J., comp. *Presidential Statements on Education, Excerpts from Inaugural and State of the Union Messages, 1789–1967.* Pittsburgh: University of Pittsburgh Press, 1967. Fillmore praises common schools for spreading intelligence, promoting progress, and laying the foundation for prosperity.

30. "Two Fillmore Documents." *Grosvenor Library Bulletin* 6 (December 1923): 10–13. Contains an 1828 proposal for a law partnership, which he turned down, and an 1830 Erie County certificate of election to the state assembly.

31. "Two Fillmore Documents." *Grosvenor Library Bulletin* 7 (December 1924): 27–29. An inexplicable reprint of item **30**.

32. "Two Letters of Millard Fillmore." Massachusetts Historical Society, *Proceedings* 63 (1931): 122–23. In March 1861, he described the impropriety of his recommending patronage claims to Lincoln. In July of 1861 he described his wife Caroline's painful riding fall.

C. UNPUBLISHED PERSONAL AND ADMINISTRATIVE PAPERS OF FILLMORE'S ASSOCIATES

Daniel D. Barnard, Diplomat

33. Barnard, Daniel D. Papers. Library of Congress, Washington. Barnard family papers (1714–1901). 1,100 items.

34. ———. Papers. New York Historical Society, New York. 21 items (1828–1858).

35. ———. Papers. New York State Library, Albany. Correspondence, diaries (1850–1853), scrapbooks, dispatch books (1850–1853), photographs, and other papers. Provides a picture of diplomatic life in mid-nineteenth-century Berlin and Europe.

Daniel Moreau Barringer, Diplomat

36. Barringer, Daniel Moreau. Papers. University of North Carolina, Southern Historical Collection, Chapel Hill. 2,300 items (1797–1873). Family, business, and political papers and correspondence. Unpublished guide in library.

Thomas Corwin, Secretary of the Treasury

37. Corwin, Thomas. Papers. Library of Congress, Washington. 21 containers with an index (1850–1853).

38. ———. Papers. Ohio Historical Society, Columbus. 1 foot of letters and papers relating to state issues (1825–1859).

39. ———. Papers. Warren County Historical Society, Lebanon, OH. Miscellaneous letters include Whig leaders writing to Corwin.

John J. Crittenden, Attorney General

40. Crittenden, John J. Papers. Duke University Library, Durham, NC. 1,055 items and 3 volumes (1786–1932). Family and political correspondence, scrapbooks, letterbook, speeches, and a portrait. Many extracts of this correspondence were published in the *Life of John J. Crittenden,* edited by his daughter, Mary Ann Butler Coleman.

41. ———. Papers. Filson Club, Louisville, KY. One half foot of items. Personal, business, and congressional papers. Other letters in the Orlando Brown Papers, Charles Lanmam Collection, J. M. Clayton Papers, and Henry Clay Papers.

42. ———— . Papers. Kentucky Department for Libraries and Archives, Frankfort. 3.5 cubic feet of items (1848–1850). Gubernatorial papers.

43. ———— . Papers. Kentucky Historical Society, Frankfort. Items from 1816 to 1863. Also items in the Harry I. Todd Papers and the Orlando Brown Papers.

44. ———— . Papers. Library of Congress, Washington. 2,600 items (1782–1888). Correspondence, legal papers, speeches, and state papers. Published calendar. Correspondence covers his term as Fillmore's Attorney General and includes political relationships with leading Whigs.

45. ———— . Papers. New-York Historical Society, New York. 16 letters (1817–1863).

46. ———— . Papers. Pierpont Morgan Library, New York. 4 items (1814–1851).

47. ———— . Papers. University of Kentucky, Lexington. 52 items (1814–1861).

48. ———— . Papers. Western Kentucky University, Kentucky Library and Museum, Bowling Green. 10 items (1825–1853). Correspondence and business papers.

Edward Everett, Secretary of State

49. Allis, Frederick S., Jr. *Guide to the Microfilm Edition of the Edward Everett Papers.* Boston: Massachusetts Historical Society, 1972. A guide to the 54 rolls of microfilm.

50. Everett, Edward. Papers. Massachusetts Historical Society, Boston. A lifetime of correspondence, letterbooks, and diaries collected and organized in 279 volumes by Everett himself. Administration papers cover letters to Everett and letterbooks of his correspondence to others, plus diaries and official state papers.

William A. Graham, Secretary of the Navy

51. Graham, William Alexander. Papers. Boston Public Library, Boston. 6 items.

52. ———— . Papers. Duke University, Durham, NC. 58 items (1841–1896). Family correspondence.

53. ———— . Papers. Library of Congress, Washington. 1 letter from 1852.

54. ———— . Papers. North Carolina Department of Archives and History, Raleigh. 2,050 items (1779–1918). Includes governor's papers.

55. ———— . Papers. University of North Carolina, Southern Historical Collection, Chapel Hill. 7 feet including 17 volumes (1750–1927). Political, legal, business, family, and plantation papers. Additional material in other collections at the University.

Samuel D. Hubbard, Postmaster General

56. Hubbard, Samuel D. Papers. Connecticut Historical Society, Hartford. 1 box (1822–1843).

John Pendleton Kennedy, Secretary of the Navy

57. Griffin, Lloyd W. "The John Pendleton Kennedy Papers." *Maryland Historical Magazine* 48 (December 1953): 327–36. Reviews the large manuscript collection at the Peabody Institute where Kennedy was its first President.

58. Kennedy, John Pendleton. Papers. Boston Public Library, Boston. 34 letters.

59. ———— . Papers. Columbia University Rare Book and Manuscript Library, New York. Two official letters (January 7 and 10, 1853) in the Adelman Collection. 172 letters (1813–1863) in the Philip C. Pendleton Papers.

60. ———— . Papers. Johns Hopkins University, George Peabody Library, Baltimore. 130 volumes (1812–1870) of correspondence, journals, manuscripts, scrapbooks, and memoranda (some while Secretary of the Navy).

61. ———— . Papers. Library of Congress, Washington. 1 container of items (1822–1870).

62. ———— . Papers. Maryland Historical Society, Baltimore. 35 items (1763–1856).

63. ———— . Papers. New-York Historical Society, New York. 13 items of personal correspondence (1823–1869).

64. ———— . Papers. Johns Hopkins University, Peabody Institute Archives, Baltimore. 17 feet of letters, journals, manuscripts, lectures, and scrapbooks (1812–1870).

65. ———— . Papers. University of Maryland, McKeldin Library, College Park. 1 foot of items in the Charles Lanman Papers (1823–1868).

66. ———— . Papers. Virginia Historical Society, Richmond. 79 items of correspondence and genealogical material in Kennedy family papers (1813–1884).

67. ———— . Papers. West Virginia University Library, Morgantown. 3 items and two reels of microfilm from originals in Peabody Institute Library and Library of Congress.

Abbott Lawrence, Minister to Great Britain

68. Lawrence, Abbott. Papers. Boston Public Library, Boston. 11 letters.

69. ———— . Papers. Harvard University, Houghton Library, Cambridge, MA. 9 volumes. (1849–1852). Correspondence and dispatches, chiefly from his diplomatic service in London, and personal account books (1841–1855). Unpublished guide in library.

Alexander H. H. Stuart, Secretary of the Interior

70. Stuart, Alexander Hugh Holmes. Papers. Library of Congress, Washington. 33 items (1790–1868).

71. ———— . Papers. University of Virginia Library, Charlottesville. 500 items (1791–1928). Includes family correspondence and material relating to the Department of the Interior and political parties. 4,500 items (1742–1865) in papers of Archibald Stuart and Brisco G. Baldwin.

72. ———— . Papers. Virginia Historical Society, Richmond. 131 items (1831–1927) in the McCue and Robertson family papers. 1,233 items (1757–1888), in the Stuart family papers.

73. ———— . Papers. Virginia State Library and Archives, Archives Branch, Richmond. 650 items (1768–1912). Personal and business papers. Some copies of originals at Mary Baldwin College. 4,700 items and 14 volumes in the Tazewell family papers (1780–1867). Personal and business papers and correspondence. 1,000 items in the Vanmeter family papers (1773–1855). Personal papers and correspondence. 37 items in Washington and Lee University miscellaneous manuscript collection (1777–1869).

Daniel Webster, Secretary of State

74. Webster, Daniel. Papers. Boston Public Library, Boston. 92 items.

75. ———— . Papers. Brandeis University, Waltham, MA. 5 feet of items, chiefly correspondence (1840–1843).

76. ———— . Papers. Columbia University, New York. 29 items (1828–1837).

77. ———— . Papers. Dartmouth College, Hanover, NH. 1,800 items (1800–1852). Microfilm edition available on 41 reels with published guide and index. Collection includes photographs, portraits, and memorabilia.

78. ———— . Papers. Harvard University, Houghton Library, Cambridge, MA. 500 items (1805–1874).

79. ———— . Papers. Library of Congress, Washington. 16 containers of correspondence, scrapbooks, speeches, clippings, etc., (chiefly 1824 to 1852) with index and register. Available on 8 roles of microfilm.

80. ———— . Papers. Maryland Historical Society, Baltimore. 60 items (1814–1891). Includes letters on politics, drafts of speeches, correspondence, and family papers.

81. ———— . Papers. Massachusetts Historical Society, Boston. 1,200 items (1800–1865). Includes letters, speeches, invitations, receipts, notebooks, photographs, and portraits.

82. ———— . Papers. New Hampshire Historical Society, Concord. 6 feet of items including correspondence relating to political, social, business, and personal life.

83. ———— . Papers. Phillips Exeter Academy, Exeter, NH. 100 items. Correspondence relating to politics, business, and personal affairs.

84. ———— . Papers. Pierpont Morgan Library, New York. 23 items (1808–1852).

85. ———— . Papers. University of Virginia, Alderman Library, Charlottesville. 130 items (1800–1852).

Other Associates

86. Beekman, James William. Papers. New York Historical Society, New York. 5 ft. of correspondence and papers (1834–1877). Numerous letters pertaining to state Whig politics.

87. Dix, Dorothea L. Papers. Harvard College Library, Cambridge, MA. Correspondence, miscellaneous papers, and notebooks including recently discovered Fillmore material.

88. ———— . Massachusetts Historical Society, *Proceedings* 55 (1923): 3. Society received a Bible previously presented by Fillmore to Dorothea Dix on December 1, 1850. He hoped she would accept it because of his esteem for her humanitarianism. There is also a gold clasp inscribed "MF to Miss Dix, 1851."

89. ——— . Papers. New-York Historical Society, New York. Contains her letters from the Civil War.

90. ——— . Papers. Boston Public Library, Boston. Miscellaneous collection.

91. Fish, Hamilton. Papers. Library of Congress, Washington. 60,000 items (1732–1914). Correspondence, journals, diaries, and scrapbooks which include material pertaining to his terms as Whig governor and senator from New York during Fillmore's administration.

92. Granger, Francis. Papers. Boston Public Library, Boston. 1 item.

93. ——— . Papers. Library of Congress, Washington. 276 items in the Francis and Gideon Granger papers (1800–1864). Includes correspondence on the Antimasonic and Whig parties.

94. ——— . Papers. New-York Historical Society, New York. 52 items (1820–1854). Includes items on state and national politics.

95. Greeley, Horace. Papers. Library of Congress, Washington. 4 ft. (1826–1928). Correspondence, autobiography, speeches, and articles by and about Greeley. Guide available.

96. ——— . Papers. New-York Historical Society, New York. 105 items (1839–1872). 25 letters to Thurlow Weed on the Whig party and national politics.

97. Hammond, Jabez Delano. Papers. New-York Historical Society, New York. 50 items (1818–1853). 24 letters between 1849 and 1852 pertain to state politics and his political history of New York state.

98. Hard, Gideon. Papers. New-York Historical Society, New York. Autobiography. Writes about his dispute with Thurlow Weed during the Fillmore-Seward state leadership controversy.

99. Haven, Solomon George. Papers. New-York Historical Society, New York. 14 items (1839–1856). Includes 10 letters about the American party from Fillmore's friend and political colleague.

100. Hunt, Washington. Papers. New York State Library, Albany. 42 items (1848–1862). Also 120 items (1845–1961) in the Henry Wyckoff Papers. New York governor during Fillmore's administration.

101. ——— . Papers. Library of Congress, Washington. 2 letters, 1850 and 1858.

102. Marcy, William Learned. Papers. New-York Historical Society, New York. 50 items (1824–1856).

103. ———. Papers. New York State Library. Albany. 4,000 items (1837–1860). Account books, correspondence, and papers, many dealing with his term as a Democratic governor while the Whig party developed in western New York.

104. ———. Papers. Library of Congress, Washington. 15,000 items (1806–1857). Correspondence, diary (1831–1857), draft of autobiography, and diplomatic messages. Material covers his state and national Democratic political career.

105. ———. Papers. Rutgers University, New Brunswick, NJ. 69 items (1832–1853). Correspondence when governor of New York (1833–1839), and Secretary of War (1845–1849).

106. Patterson, George Washington. Papers. University of Rochester, Rochester, NY. 8,200 items (1827–1879). Correspondence covers political career as a western New York Whig. These letters can be used in conjunction with the Weed and Seward papers also at the University of Rochester.

107. Pearce, James A. Papers. Boston Public Library, Boston. 2 letters.

108. ———. Papers. Maryland Historical Society, Baltimore. 162 items of correspondence relating to politics and contemporary issues.

109. Seward, William H. Papers. Essex Institute, Salem, MA. One folder in the George Manchester Correspondence (1852–1857).

110. ———. Papers. Goshen Library and Historical Society, Goshen, NY. 96 items on family and business; 135 items of correspondence on business, Anti-Masonic party papers, and 2 items on his support for the Republican party.

111. ———. Papers. Library of Congress, Washington. 40 items plus photographs (1834–1866).

112. ———. Papers. New York State Library, Albany. Miscellaneous correspondence (1828–1868) and 85 items including governor's material (1838–1883).

113. ———. Papers. New-York Historical Society, New York. 90 items (1832–1870). Correspondence on state politics plus photographs and portraits.

114. ———. Papers. Syracuse University, Syracuse, NY. 30 letters (1842–1857). Some letters in the Gerrit Smith Papers.

115. ———. Papers. University of Rochester, Rochester, NY. 150,000 items (chiefly 1830–1872). Includes photographs, correspondence, diaries, notebooks, speeches, reports. The bulk of the correspondence concerns political affairs. The material can be enhanced when used in conjunction with the Weed and Patterson papers also at the University of Rochester. Microfilm available.

116. Seymour, Horatio. Papers. New-York Historical Society, New York. 440 items (1840–1883). Some correspondence pertains to Democratic activities in the early and middle 1850s.

117. Tracy, Albert Haller. Papers. New York State Library, Albany. 254 items (1815–1851). Correspondence from Fillmore's first political mentor concerning the Antimasonic and Whig parties.

118. Ullman, Daniel. Papers. New-York Historical Society, New York. 2,000 items (1832–1885). Contains material on his association with New York City Whigs and the American Party.

119. Van Buren, Martin. Papers. Library of Congress, Washington. 6,000 items (1787–1868). Most of the correspondence concerns his leadership of the state and national Democratic party. Also available on 34 rolls of microfilm.

120. Weed, Thurlow. Papers. Library of Congress, Washington. 3 boxes (1823–1894) including political correspondence.

121. ———. Papers. New-York Historical Society, New York. 190 items (1818–1882). Many items pertain to Antimasonry, the Whig party, and abolitionism.

122. ———. Papers. University of Rochester, Rochester, NY. 14,000 items (1816–1882). Major source for Weed's political correspondence with state and national Antimasons, Whigs, and Republicans. This material can be augmented with the Seward and Patterson papers also at the University of Rochester.

123. Wright, Silas. Papers. New York Historical Society, New York. 17 items (1828–1847).

D. PUBLISHED COMPILATIONS OF PERSONAL AND ADMINISTRATIVE PAPERS OF FILLMORE'S ASSOCIATES

Daniel D. Barnard, Diplomat

124. Barnard, Daniel D. "The Social System." In *The American Whigs: An Anthology,* ed. Daniel Walker Howe. New York: John Wiley & Sons, Inc., 1973. Describes

the interdependence of classes, regions, and interest groups which promote national unity and social harmony.

Charles Magill Conrad, Secretary of War

125. Bartlett, Ruhl J., ed. *The Record of American Diplomacy: Documents and Readings in the History of American Foreign Relations.* New York: Alfred A. Knopf, 1964. Chapter 16 reprints Acting Secretary of State Conrad's instructions for the Perry expedition.

126. Cooling, Benjamin Franklin, ed. *The New American State Papers, Military Affairs.* Wilmington, DE: Scholarly Resources, Inc., 1979. 19 vols. Contains administrative reports to and from Conrad including correspondence in volumes: 2, 3 *(Policy)*; 4, 5, 7, 8, 9, 10 *(Combat)*; 11, 12, 13, 14 *(Military Society)*; 15, 16, 18, 19 *(National Development).*

Thomas Corwin, Secretary of the Treasury

127. Corwin, Thomas. "On the Mexican War." In *The American Whigs: An Anthology,* ed. Daniel Walker Howe. New York: John Wiley & Sons, Inc., 1973. Did not support the war against Mexico.

128. Hamlin, L. Belle, ed. "Selections from the Follett Papers, 2." *Quarterly Publications of the Historical and Philosophical Society of Ohio* 9 (July–September 1914): 70–100. Among letters of Whig partisanship are three letters when Secretary.

129. ――――. "Selections from the William Green Papers, 1." *Quarterly Publications of the Historical and Philosophical Society of Ohio* 13 (January–March, 1918): 3–38. Contains correspondence when he was governor of Ohio, 1841–1842; U.S. senator, 1845–1850; and Secretary of the Treasury, 1850–1853.

130. Morrow, Josiah. *Life and Speeches of Thomas Corwin, Orator, Lawyer and Statesman.* Cincinnati: W. H. Anderson & Co., 1896. A lifetime of speeches printed in newspapers and revised by Corwin.

131. Strohm, Isaac. *Speeches of Thomas Corwin, With a Sketch of His Life.* Dayton: Wm. F. Comly & Co., Publishers, 1859. Long extract from his 1850 Treasury report.

John J. Crittenden, Attorney General

132. *Calendar of the Papers of John Jordan Crittenden.* Washington: Government Printing Office, 1913. An annotated chronology of correspondence and speeches held by the Library of Congress.

133. Coleman, Mrs. Chapman, ed. *The Life of John J. Crittenden with Selections from His Correspondence and Speeches.* 2 vols. Philadelphia: J. B. Lippincott & Co., 1871. Memorial biography by his daughter using copious excerpts from Crittenden's papers.

134. Hall, Benjamin F. *Official Opinions of the Attorneys General of the United States, Advising the President and Heads of Departments in Relation to Their Official Duties.* Washington: Published by Robert Farnham, 1856. 5. Contains Crittenden's advice to Fillmore and cabinet including his opinion endorsing the Fugitive Slave Bill.

135. Powell, H. Jefferson. *The Constitution and the Attorneys General.* Durham: Carolina Academic Press, 1999. Reprints Crittenden's opinion on the constitutionality of the Fugitive Slave Law and lists his other opinions on the constitution.

Edward Everett, Secretary of State

136. Edward Everett. *Correspondence on the Proposed Tripartite Convention Relative to Cuba.* Boston: Little, Brown and Company, 1853. In the name of the President, Everett informed England and France that the U.S. was unable to participate in or support the proposed compact to oversee Cuba.

137. ———— . *Orations and Speeches.* Boston: Little, Brown and Company, 1892. 4 vols. Volume Three covers the 1850s and includes his address at the 1851 Boston Railroad Jubilee and memorials for Daniel Webster (1852) and Abbott Lawrence (1855).

138. ———— . "The Promise of Industrialization." In *The American Whigs: An Anthology,* ed. Daniel Walker Howe. New York: John Wiley & Sons, Inc., 1973. Uses Lowell textile mills as an example of opportunity for both workers and owners.

William A. Graham, Secretary of the Navy

139. Bauer, K. Jack, ed. *The New American State Papers, Naval Affairs.* 10 vols. Wilmington: Scholarly Resources Inc., 1981. Graham's reports and correspondence are in volumes: 1 *(Policy)*; 2, 3 *(Diplomatic Activities)*; 6 *(Administration)*; 7 *(Personnel)*; 8 *(Social History and Science)*; 9 *(Science)*; 10 *(Vessels)*.

140. Hamilton, J. G. DeRoulhac, Max R. Williams, and Mary Reynolds, eds. *Papers of William A. Graham.* Raleigh: North Carolina State Department of Archives and History, 1957–1992. 8 vols. Volumes three and four contain his correspondence as Secretary of the Navy. Volumes five through eight contain correspondence with Nathan K. Hall referring to Fillmore's retirement.

John P. Kennedy, Secretary of the Navy

141. Bauer, K. Jack, ed. *The New American State Papers, Naval Affairs.* 10 vols. Wilmington: Scholarly Resources Inc., 1981. Kennedy's reports and correspondence are in Volumes: 1 *(Policy)*; 2, 3 *(Diplomatic Activities)*; 6 *(Administration)*; 7 *(Personnel)*; 8 *(Social History & Science)*; 9 *(Science)*; 10 *(Vessels)*.

142. Kennedy, John P. *The Collected Works.* New York: G. Ulms, 1969 [1871–1872]. 10 vols. Collection of his major fiction and political writings including his 1844 *Defense of the Whigs.*

143. ——— . *Defense of the Whigs.* New York: Harper, 1844. Summary of Whig policies and defense of Whig opposition to President Tyler.

144. ——— . "The Whig Interpretation of History: John Pendleton Kennedy, The Defense of the Whigs." In *The American Whigs: An Anthology,* ed. Daniel Walker Howe. New York: John Wiley & Sons, Inc., 1973. Selection from *Defense of the Whigs.* Whigs stand on a Madisonian interpretation of government: national, American, liberal and honorable.

145. ——— . *Political and Official Papers.* New York: Putnam, 1872. Contains an excerpt from his report on naval explorations and surveys.

Abbott Lawrence, Minister to Great Britain

146. Hill, Hamilton Andrews. *Memoir of Abbott Lawrence.* Cambridge: J. Wilson and Son, 1883. Includes letters and reports from England to Secretaries of State Clayton and Webster.

Daniel Webster, Secretary of State

147. Shewmacker, Kenneth E., and Kenneth R. Stevens, eds. *The Papers of Daniel Webster, Diplomatic Papers.* 2 vols. Hanover, NH: University Press of New England, 1983–1987. Volume Two contains the definitive set of published papers and correspondence pertaining to his second term as Secretary of State, 1850–1852.

148. Van Tyne, C. H., ed. *The Letters of Daniel Webster.* New York: Haskell House Publishers, 1969 [1902]. Contains many letters to Fillmore and five letters from the President. Includes correspondence on Webster's pursuit of the presidency in 1852.

149. Webster, Daniel. *The Great Speeches and Orations of Daniel Webster.* Boston: Little, Brown & Co., 1886. Reprints the March 7, 1850, speech supporting the Compromise, and the Hülsemann letter supporting republican governments in Europe.

150. Webster, Fletcher, ed. *The Private Correspondence of Daniel Webster.* Boston: Little, Brown and Company, 1857. 2 vols. Volume Two contains many letters to Fillmore on politics and diplomacy.

151. Wiltse, Charles M., ed. *The Papers of Daniel Webster, Correspondence.* 7 vols. Hanover, NH: University Press of New England, 1974–1986. Definitive published collection of Webster's correspondence. Volume Seven contains substantial administrative correspondence between Webster and Fillmore. Volumes have references to Fillmore letters not published in the set.

152. ———— . *The Papers of Daniel Webster, Speeches and Formal Writings.* 2 vols. Hanover, NH: University Press of New England, 1988. Volume Two contains Webster's speeches supporting the Compromise of 1850, and its Fugitive Slave Law.

E. CONTEMPORARY NEWSPAPERS

153. *Albany Argus*, Democrat

154. *Albany Evening Journal*, Whig

155. *Albany New York State Register*, Whig

156. *Alton* (IL) *Telegraph*, Whig

157. *Augusta* (GA) *Chronicle and Sentinel*, Whig

158. *Baltimore Sun*, Independent pro South

159. (Baltimore) *American and Commercial Daily Advertiser*, Whig

160. *Baton Rouge Gazette*

161. *Boston Atlas*, Whig

162. *Boston Courier*, Whig

163. *Boston Post*, Democrat

164. *Brooklyn Eagle*, Democrat

165. *Buffalo Commercial Advertiser*, Fillmore Whig paper

166. *Buffalo Express*, Seward Whig paper

167. *Buffalo Republican*, Democrat

168. (Burlington) *Iowa Territorial Gazette*, Democrat

169. *Charleston Mercury*, Democratic pro South

170. *Chicago Daily Journal*, Whig

171. *Chicago Democrat*, Democrat

172. *Cincinnati Daily Enquirer*, Democrat

173. *Cleveland Plain Dealer*, Democrat

174. *Concord* (NH) *Statesman*, Whig

175. *Delaware State Journal* (Wilmington) Whig

176. *Detroit Daily Advertiser*, Whig

177. *Detroit Free Press*, Democrat

178. *Eastern Argus* (ME), Democratic

179. *Elmira* (NY) *Daily Republican*, Whig

180. *Frankfort* (KY) *Commonwealth*, Whig

181. Frederick Douglass's Paper (Rochester), Abolitionist

182. (Galena) (IL) *Weekly Northwest Gazette*, Whig

183. *Harold of Freedom* (NH), Abolitionist

184. *Harrisburg* (PA) *State Journal*, Whig

185. *Hill's Patriot* (Concord NH), Democratic

186. (Huntsville) *Southern Advocate*, Whig

187. (Iowa City) *Iowa Republican*, Whig

188. *Jackson Mississippian*, Democrat

189. (Jacksonville) *Florida News*, Democratic

190. (Jacksonville) *Florida Republican*, Whig

191. (Jefferson City) (MO) *Jefferson Inquirer*, Democrat

192. *Knoxville* (TN) *Whig*, Whig

193. *Lancaster* (PA) *Examiner and Herald*, Whig

194. *Lexington* (KY) *Observer and Reporter*, Whig

195. *Liberator* (Boston), Abolitionist

196. *Little Rock* (AR) *Whig*, Whig

197. (Little Rock) (AR) *True Democrat*, Democrat

198. (Little Rock) *Arkansas State Gazette*, Democrat

199. *Louisville Journal*, Whig

200. *Louisville Daily Courier*, Whig

201. *Louisville Times*, Democrat

202. *Memphis Daily Eagle and Enquirer*, Whig

203. (Milledgeville) (GA) *Southern Recorder*, Whig

204. *Milwaukee Free Democrat*, Democrat

205. (Milwaukee) *Weekly Wisconian*, Democrat

206. *Minneapolis Democrat*, Democrat

207. *Mobile Daily Advertiser*, Whig

208. *Nashville Banner*, Whig

209. *Nashville True Whig*, Whig

210. *Natchez* (MS) *Courier*, Whig

211. *National Anti-Slavery Standard* (NY), Abolitionist

212. *New Hampshire Patriot* (Concord), Democrat

213. *New Hampshire Sentinel* (Keene), Whig

214. *New Orleans Commercial Bulletin,* Whig

215. *New Orleans Delta*, Democrat

216. *New Orleans Picayune*, Unionist

217. *New York Express*, Whig

218. *New York Journal of Commerce*, pro-Fillmore Whig

219. *New York Post*, Democrat

220. *New York Tribune*, Whig

221. *North Carolina Standard* (Raleigh), Democrat

222. *Ohio State Journal* (Columbus), Whig

223. *Pensacola* (FL) *Gazette*, Whig

224. *Philadelphia Daily News*, Whig

225. *Philadelphia Daily Sun*, Fillmore Whig

226. *Philadelphia North American*, Whig

227. (Philadelphia) *Pennsylvanian*, Democratic

228. *Pittsburgh Gazette*, Whig

229. (Portland) *Oregonian*, Whig

230. *Racine* (WI) *Advocate*, Democrat

231. *Richmond Daily Whig*, Whig

232. *Richmond Enquirer*, Democratic

233. *Rochester* (NY) *Advertiser*, Democrat

234. *Rochester* (NY) *American*, Whig

235. (Salem) *Oregonian Statesman*, Democrat

236. *San Antonio* (TX) *Ledger*, Democratic

237. *Savannah Georgian*, Democrat

238. (Springfield) *Illinois State Register*, Democrat

239. *St. Lawrence* (NY) *Republican*, Democrat

240. (St. Louis) *Daily Missouri Republican*, Whig

241. (St. Paul) *Minnesota Chronicle*, Whig

242. (St. Paul) *Minnesota Democrat*, Democrat

243. (Tallahassee) *Floridian and Journal*, Democratic

244. *Vicksburg* (MS) *Weekly Sentinel*, Democratic

245. *Vicksburg* (MS) *Whig*, Whig

246. (Washington) *National Era*, Abolitionist

247. *Washington National Intelligencer*, Whig

248. *Washington Southern Press*, Sessionist

249. *Washington Union*, Democrat

250. *Wheeling* (VA) *Intelligencer*, Whig

251. *Wilmington* (NC) *Journal*, Democrat

252. *Wisconsin Statesman* (Madison), Whig

Chapter 2

Published Writings of
Millard Fillmore

253. Juridicus. *An Examination of the Question, Is It Right to Require Any Religious Test as a Qualification to be a Witness in a Court of Justice.* Buffalo: Charles Faxon, 1832. Under the pseudonym, Fillmore argued against using the religious oath at trials to determine the competency of witnesses. Fillmore wrote the argument in response to trials on the abduction of William Morgan. They excluded important testimony from a witness to the abduction because he was an atheist.

254. *Speech of Mr. Fillmore, of New York, on the Bill to Suspend Payment of the Fourth Installment of the Surplus Revenue to the States. Delivered in the House of Representatives, September 25, 1837.* Washington: Gales & Seaton, 1837. Fillmore opposed the bill to postpone payment to the states. He regarded the bill as a breach of contract by the Democratic administration. It would further disrupt the financial operations of the country which needed currency during the depression.

255. *Address and Suppressed Report of the Minority of the Committee on Elections on the New Jersey Case. Presented to the House of Representatives, March 10, 1840, Together with the Remarks of Mr. Fillmore.* Washington: Printed at the Madison Office, 1840. Fillmore protested the Democratic majority withholding confirmation of New Jersey Whigs because of disputed state elections. He argued for his right to speak on the subject and against the Democratic majority that silenced him.

256. *Speech of Mr. Fillmore, of New York, on the Revenue Bill. Delivered in the House of Representatives, July 24, 1841.* Washington: n.p., 1841. Fillmore spoke for the bill after a lengthy critique of Tyler's fiscal policies.

257. *Speech of Mr. Fillmore, of New York, on the Tariff Bill. Delivered in the Committee of the Whole, House of Representatives, June 9, 1842.* Washington: National Intelligencer Office, 1842. As Chairman of the House Ways and Means Committee, he reported the bill to meet the emergency of a bankrupt treasury. He explains why the current bill is only a revenue bill to collect needed income for the treasury. The bill was vetoed by President Tyler.

258. "Annual Report of the Comptroller." *Documents of the Assembly of the State of New York, Seventy-Second Session, 1849.* Albany: Weed, Passon & Co. Public Printers, 1849. Vol. 1, document 5. His ideas on banking and national currency in this report persisted through the 1850s and influenced Republican fiscal policy.

259. *Message from the President of the United States, to the Two Houses of Congress, at the Commencement of the Second Session of the Thirty-First Congress, December 2, 1850.* Washington: Printed for the Senate, 1850.

260. *Message from the President of the United States, to the Two Houses of Congress, at the Commencement of the First Session of the Thirty-Second Congress, December 2, 1851.* Washington: Printed by A. Boyd Hamilton, 1851.

261. *The Suppressed Portion of President Fillmore's Annual Message to Congress, on the 6th December, 1852, Relating to Slavery.* Buffalo: Thomas, Typographer, *n.d.* Fillmore expressed the American Colonization Society's standard appeal for gradually emancipating slaves and removing them from the United States by founding colonies. He believed former slaves could not live in America because of race prejudice that would probably culminate in the violent extinction of African Americans.

262. *Fillmore on the Great Questions of the Day: The Arrival, Reception, Progress and Speeches of Millard Fillmore.* New York: R. M. De Sitt, 1856. Fillmore arrived in New York City from his European tour in June, 1856. On his way to Buffalo he gave a number of speeches. They are part of his American Party campaign.

263. *Mr. Fillmore at Home: His Reception at New York and Brooklyn and Progress through the State, etc.* Buffalo: Thomas & Lathrop, 1856. Popular reprint of his American party campaign speeches.

264. *Buffalo General Hospital Dedicatory Exercises, June 24th 1858.* Buffalo: Courier Steam Printing House, 1858. As Chairman of the event, he gave a brief address on the necessity for the hospital in Buffalo.

265. *Great Central Fair. Ex-President Fillmore's Address, Anson G. Chester's Poem, David Gray's Poem, Together with Washington's Farewell Address.* Buffalo: Joseph Warren & Co., Publisher, 1864. Fillmore urged the defeat of the Confederacy

but asked forgiveness for Confederates. Later he surmised the conduct of the war was too destructive to encourage a fraternity between the North and South after the war. He was criticized for these remarks.

266. "Inaugural Address of the Hon Millard Fillmore." *Publications of the Buffalo Historical Society, Volume 1.* Buffalo: Buffalo Historical Society, 1879. 1: 1–15. As president of the Society he opened its first meeting on July 1, 1862 by defining its purpose and describing the origin of the city's name.

267. "The Early History of Hon. Millard Fillmore. Written by Himself." *Publications of the Buffalo Historical Society, Volume 2.* Buffalo Historical Society, 1880. 2: 375–87. Written in 1871 for the Buffalo Historical Society, it was first published in the second volume of the Society's Publications in 1880. Approximately 20 pages in length covering his hard rural childhood, adolescent ambitions for a legal career, his removal to Buffalo, passage into the legal community, and family life in East Aurora, New York in the late 1820s.

268. *The Early Life of Millard Fillmore: A Personal Reminiscence.* Buffalo: Salisbury Club, 1958. Reprint of *267*, the "Early History" published in Volume 2 of the *Publications of the Buffalo Historical Society.*

Chapter 3

Biographical Publications

A. GENERAL COMPILATIONS

269. Anbinder, Tyler. "Fillmore, Millard." In *American National Biography,* ed. John A. Garraty and Mark C. Carnes. New York: Oxford University Press, 1999. 24 vols. 7: 910–12. Political biography.

270. Carruth, Gorton. *The Encyclopedia of American Facts & Dates.* 8th ed. New York: Harper & Row, 1987. Chronologically arranged with a brief Fillmore biography.

271. Cluskey, M. W. *Political Text Book or Encyclopedia, Containing Everything Necessary for the Reference of the Politicians and Statesmen of the United States.* Philadelphia: James B. Smith & Co., 1858. Excerpts from Fillmore's letters.

272. Congressional Quarterly. *American Leaders, 1789–1987: A Biographical Summary.* Washington: Congressional Quarterly, 1987. Concise biographies of Presidents and other national leaders.

273. Coryell, Janet L. "Millard Fillmore (1800–1874)." In *Political Parties & Elections in the United States: An Encyclopedia.* New York: Garland Publishing Inc., 1991. 2 vols. 1: 371–72. Thoughtful, sympathetic summary of his political career.

274. Drake, Francis S. *Dictionary of American Biography.* Boston: James R. Osgood and Company, 1872. Sketch of his political career.

275. "Fillmore, Millard (1800–1874)." In *Who Was Who in the Civil War,* ed. Stewart Sifakes. New York: Facts on File Publications, 1988. 218. Reviews Fillmore's growing disillusionment with the conduct of the Civil War.

276. Fitch, Charles Elliott. *Encyclopedia of Biography of New York: A Life Record of Men and Women of the Past.* New York: American Historical Society, 1916. 3 vols. In Volume One, Fillmore's biography is marred by inaccuracies.

277. Gale, Robert L. *A Cultural Encyclopedia of the 1850s in America.* Westport, CT: Greenwood Press, 1993. This valuable resource contains brief biographies of Millard and Abigail Fillmore.

278. Gienapp, William E. "Fillmore, Millard." In *The Reader's Companion to American History*, ed. Eric Foner and John A. Garraty. Boston: Houghton Mifflin Company, 1991. Captures Fillmore's national influence in a few paragraphs.

279. Hamilton, Holman. "Fillmore, Millard." In *Encyclopedia of American Biography,* ed. John A. Garraty. New York: Harper & Row Publishers, 1974. 351–52. Fillmore was a bland man and a natural compromiser.

280. Harrison, Frederick G. "Millard Fillmore." In *Biographical Sketches of Preëminent Americans.* Boston: Consolidated Book Company, 189?[sic]. Competent, sympathetic biography. No pagination, documentation or index.

281. Johnson, Rossiter, and John Howard Brown. *The Twentieth-Century Biographical Dictionary of Notable Americans.* Boston: Biographical Society, 1904. 10 vols. Volume 4 contains a good factual biography and portrait.

282. Johnson, Thomas H. *The Oxford Companion to American History.* New York: Oxford University Press, 1966. Surveys Fillmore's political career.

283. Lalor, John J. *Cyclopedia of Political Science, Political Economy and of the Political History of the United States.* Chicago: Melbert B. Cary & Company, 1881, 1883, 1884. 3 vols. Brief political biography.

284. Lanman, Charles. "Millard Fillmore." *Biographical Annals of the Civil Government of the United States, During Its First Century.* Detroit: Gale Research Company, 1976 [1876]. 145–46.

285. MacDonald, William. "Millard Fillmore." In *Cyclopedia of American Government,* ed. Andrew C. McLaughlin and Albert Bushnell Hart. New York: Peter Smith, 1930 [1914]. 3 vols. 1: 731–32. Highlights his signing the Fugitive Slave Law on the recommendations of Daniel Webster and John J Crittenden.

286. Meerse, David E. "Fillmore, Millard, Administration." In *The Encyclopedia of Southern History,* ed. David C. Roller and Robert W. Twyman. Baton Rouge: Louisiana State University Press, 1979. 433–34.

287. "Millard Fillmore." *Harper's Encyclopedia of United States History: From 458 A.D. to 1909.* New York: Harper & Brothers Publishers, 1905. 10 vols. 3: 360–66 Biographical review concludes that he left office with the country at peace and industry flourishing.

288. "Millard Fillmore—13th President of the United States." *Compton's Pictured Encyclopedia and Fact Index.* Chicago: F. E. Compton & Company, 1962. 15 vols. 5: 111–14.

289. Morris, Richard B. *Encyclopedia of American History, Bicentennial Edition.* New York: Harper & Row Publishers, 1976. 1029.

290. Nelson, Michael, ed. *The Presidency A to Z: A Ready Reference Encyclopedia.* In *CQ's Encyclopedia of American Government.* vol. 11. Washington: Congressional Quarterly Inc., 1992. 177–78. Short survey of Fillmore's life and administration. Contains list of Cabinet members and congressional party affiliations.

291. O'Brian, John Lord. "Fillmore, Millard." *Encyclopaedia Britannica.* Chicago: William Benton, Publisher, 1968. 9: 267–68. Biography and review of administration. Fillmore is commended for his integrity and devotion to the Union but censured for his poor judgment in participating in the intolerant Antimasonic and Know-Nothing movements.

292. Peterson, Robert C. "Millard Fillmore." In *Great Lives From History: American Series,* ed. Frank N. Magill. Pasadena: Salem Press, 1987. 5 vols. 2: 792–96. Reviews his administration and explains his Know-Nothing candidacy as a principled conservative trying to preserve the Union.

293. Pratt, Julius. "Fillmore, Millard." *DAB* (1960), 3, pt. 2: 380–82. Excellent summary of political career highlighted by Fillmore's "cool-headed" concern to settle the sectional disputes with the Compromise of 1850. That action damned him with abolitionists and with history for fifty years.

294. Richards, Donald. "Millard Fillmore 1800–1874." In *Research Guide to American Historical Biography,* ed. Robert Muccigrosso. Washington: Beacham Publishing, 1988. 5 vols. 1: 499–503. Sympathetic political biography with annotated bibliography.

295. Schlesinger, Arthur M., Jr. *The Almanac of American History.* New York: G. P. Putnam's Sons, 1983. Chronological reference contains an even-handed sketch.

296. Smith, Elbert B. "Fillmore, Millard." In *The Encyclopedia of the United States Congress*. ed. Bacon, Donald C., et al. New York: Simon & Shuster, 1995. 4 vols. 2: 835–36.

297. White, Truman C., ed. *Our Country and Its People: A Descriptive Work on Erie County, New York*. Boston: Boston History Company, Publishers, 1898. 2 vols. 2: 5–8

298. Wilson, James Grant, and John Fiske, eds. *Appleton's Cyclopedia of American Biography*. New York: D. Appleton and Company, 1887. Volume Two contains an essay written by Wilson, who credits Fillmore as a hardworking, safe, and sagacious President.

B. PRESIDENTIAL COMPILATIONS

299. Armbruster, Maxim E. *The Presidents of the United States, and Their Administrations from Washington to Ford*. 6th ed. New York: Horizon Press, 1975. Balanced assessment.

300. Austerman, Wayne R. "Millard Fillmore, 1850–1853." In *The American Presidents: The Office and the Man*, ed. Frank N. Magill and John L. Loos. Pasadena: Salem Press, 1986. 3 vols. Volume One has a sympathetic chapter on Fillmore's political career and administration.

301. Beard, Charles. *The Presidents in American History, Brought Forward Since 1948 by William Beard*. New York: Julian Messner, 1977. Brief description of Fillmore and his administration.

302. Boller, Paul F. *Presidential Anecdotes*. New York: Oxford University Press, 1981. One mention of Fillmore: "His Accidency."

303. Bruce, David K. E. *Sixteen American Presidents*. New York: Bobbs-Merrill Co. Inc., 1962 [1942]. A dated reprint containing more about national politics than Fillmore.

304. Connelly, Thomas L., and Michael D. Senecal, eds. *Almanac of American Presidents*. New York: Manly, Inc., 1991. Assesses Fillmore's administration as honorable. Contains three portraits plus a good sketch of his post-presidential years.

305. Cooke, Donald E. *Atlas of the Presidents*. Maplewood, NJ: Hammond Inc., 1985. Biographical sketch marred by inaccuracies.

306. DeGregorio, William A. *The Complete Book of U.S. Presidents.* New York: Dembner Books, 1984. Synopsis of Fillmore's family, political career, and administration.

307. Diller, Daniel C., and Stephen L. Robertson. *The Presidents, First Ladies, and Vice Presidents.* Washington: Congressional Quarterly Inc., 1989. Short biography of Fillmore and his family. Reprints Mathew Brady photograph of Fillmore.

308. Durant, John. *The Sports of Our Presidents.* New York: Hastings House Publishers, 1964. Fillmore was exceptional by not participating in boyhood sports and games. His father's disapproval of games and constant farmwork deprived him of childhood entertainments.

309. Freidel, Frank. *Our Country's Presidents.* Washington: National Geographic Society, 1969. Contains reprint from the January 1965 *National Geographic.*

310. ———— . "Profiles of the Presidents: Part 11, A Restless Nation Moves West." *National Geographic* (January 1965): 80–122. Illustrated three-page biography of Fillmore and a summary of the Compromise of 1850.

310a. Holt, Michael F., "Millard Fillmore: 1850–1853." In *The Reader's Companion to the American Presidency.* ed. Alan Brinkley and Davis Dyer. Boston: Houghton Mifflin Company, 2000. Distilled from Holt's major work on the Whig party. It is a fresh, informative review of Fillmore's administration, its successes, and his failures.

311. Kane, Joseph Nathan. *Facts About the Presidents: A Compilation of Biographical and Historical Information.* New York: H. W. Wilson Company, 1981. Biographical and political information, including a section comparing presidents.

311a. Kunhardt, Philip B., Jr. and Philip B. Kunhardt III, Peter W. Kunhardt. *The American President.* New York: Riverhead Books, 1999. Brief, informative, fair review of administration dominated by the Compromise of 1850. Lavishly illustrated.

312. Miers, Earl Schenck. *America and Its Presidents.* New York: Tempo Books, 1964. Complimentary sketch.

313. Morgan, James. *Our Presidents: Brief Biographies of Our Chief Magistrates from Washington to Eisenhower, 1789–1958.* New York: Macmillan Company, 1966. Belittles Fillmore.

314. Riccards, Michael P. *The Ferocious Engine of Democracy: A History of the American Presidency. Volume One, From the Origin Through William McKinley.*

Lanham, MD: Madison Books, 1995. Complimentary review of Fillmore and his administration during very troubled times.

315. Smith, Elbert. "Millard Fillmore." In *Encyclopedia of the American Presidency*, ed. Leonard W. Levy and Louis Fisher. 4. vols. New York: Simon & Schuster, 1994. 2: 622–26. Complimentary synopsis of Fillmore's public life and thorough review of his administration, concluding that he was a responsible and highly effective President.

316. Sobel, Robert, ed. *Biographical Directory of the United States Executive Branch, 1774–1977.* Westport, CT: Greenwood Press, 1977. Political biographies of Presidents, Vice Presidents, and Cabinet Secretaries.

317. Stoddard, William O. *The Lives of the Presidents: Zachary Taylor, Millard Fillmore, Franklin Pierce and James Buchanan.* New York: Frederick A. Stokes & Brothers, 1888. A sympathetic 66-page biography. It contains some chronological errors and no documentation.

318. Taylor, Tim. *The Book of Presidents.* New York: Arno Press, 1972. A unique genealogical and chronological account.

319. Whitney, David C. *The American Presidents: Biographies of the Chief Executive from Washington Through Carter.* Garden City, NY: Doubleday & Company Inc., 1978. Biographical sketch and short administrative history with information on elections, Cabinets, and Congress.

320. Wilson, James Grant, ed. *The Presidents of the United States, 1789–1900.* New York: D. Appleton and Company, 1900. 4 vols. The Fillmore chapter is a reprint of Wilson's complimentary essay in *Appleton's Cyclopedia of American Biography* (see **298**).

C. BIOGRAPHIES OF MILLARD FILLMORE

321. Bailey, Howard. "Millard Fillmore: The Forgotten President." *American History Illustrated* 6 (June 1971): 26–35. An illustrated survey of Fillmore's political career and family.

322. Barre, W. L. *The Life and Public Services of Millard Fillmore.* Buffalo: Wanzer, McKim & Co., 1856. An American Party campaign biography emphasizing Fillmore's Unionism and promoting him as a model of conduct, enterprise, and public service for American young men.

323. Condon, George E. *Stars in the Water, the Story of the Erie Canal.* New York: Doubleday & Company, Inc., 1874. Devotes a chapter to Fillmore. Uses secondary sources to review his life and association with Buffalo.

324. "Forgotten Man of the White House." *Senior Scholastic* (teacher's ed.) 85 (January 7, 1965): 5. Brief biographical article.

325. Griffis, William Elliot. *Millard Fillmore: Constructive Statesman, Defender of the Constitution, President of the United States.* Ithaca: Andrus & Church, 1915. A dated, undocumented, but very sympathetic biography and review of his administration and foreign policy.

326. Horton, John T. "Millard Fillmore." In *Adventures in Western New York, Volume 2.* Buffalo: Buffalo and Erie County Historical Society, 1960. An illustrated pamphlet highlighting his many civic contributions to Buffalo. Includes family portraits.

327. Hosmer, G. W. "Life of Millard Fillmore." *New England Historical and Genealogical Register* 31 (January 1877): 9–16. Thoughtful essay by a friend who disagreed with Fillmore's enforcement of the Fugitive Slave Law.

328. *Life of Millard Fillmore.* New York: R. M. DeWitt, 1856. Thirty-two-page American Party campaign biography. Stresses his Unionism over nativism and applauds his public service and recent administration. Includes a biography of Fillmore's running mate, Andrew J. Donelson.

329. Rayback, Robert J. *Millard Fillmore, Biography of a President. Publications of the Buffalo Historical Society, Volume 40.* Buffalo: Buffalo Historical Society, 1959. A sound scholarly biography and sympathetic description of his administration. It is still the only major published work on Fillmore and his presidency.

329a. Scarry, Robert J. *Millard Fillmore.* Jefferson: McFarland & Company, Inc., Pubishers, 2001. Sound, sympathetic biography. It highlights Fillmore's family relationships and the use of the recently recovered Fillmore papers in the political narrative.

330. Schelin, Robert C. "Millard Fillmore, Anti-Mason to Know-Nothing: A Moderate in New York Politics, 1828–1856." Ph.D. diss., State University of New York at Binghamton, 1975. Attempts to describe Fillmore's political motives and frustrations in his later Whig and Know-Nothing years. Uses recently recovered Fillmore papers.

Chapter 4

Childhood and Early Development

331. Baker, Oneta M. *History of the Town of Clarence.* Clarence Center, NY: Diane C. Baker, 1983. Fillmore's cousin Glezen Fillmore was a well-known Methodist preacher who rode circuit in Erie County for years.

332. Burke's Peerage. *Burke's Presidential Families of the United States of America.* London: Burke's Peerage Limited, 1975. Genealogy and biography.

333. Conable, F. W. *History of the Genesee Annual Conference of the Methodist Episcopal Church.* New York: Nelson & Phillips, 1876. Features a portrait of Glezen Fillmore showing a remarkable resemblance to his cousin Millard. Includes extracts from Glezen's circuit book describing the area he covered in Erie County.

334. Conzen, Kathleen Neils. "A Saga of Families." In *The Oxford History of The American West,* ed. Clyde A. Milner, Carol A. O'Connor, and Martha A. Sandweiss. New York: Oxford University Press, 1994. 315–57. Integrates eight generations of Fillmores into the westward expansion over North America. The President's family was typical of migrating families in the nineteenth century.

335. Cutter, William Richard. *Genealogical and Family History of Western New York.* 3 Vols. New York: Lewis Historical Publishing Company, 1912. 2: 806–12. Vital records of his ancestors and immediate family with a good biography.

336. Faber, Doris. *The Presidents' Mothers.* New York: St. Martin's Press, 1978 [1968]. Little is known about Phoebe Millard Fillmore except that she lived a hard rural life while raising nine children.

337. Fillmore, Charles L. *So Soon Forgotten: Three Thousand Fillmores.* Rutland, VT: Daamen, Inc., 1984. This extraordinary genealogical record places Fillmore in the fifth generation and follows the family into the current generation.

338. Fillmore, Millard. "Fillmore Genealogy." *Grosvenor Library Bulletin* 3 (March 1921): 24–25. Notes from a Fillmore memo book regarding the genealogy of his mother's family.

339. Hodge, William. "The William Hodge Papers." *Publications of the Buffalo Historical Society, Volume 26.* Buffalo: Buffalo Historical Society, 1922. 26: 169–314. Fillmore was a teacher during his early years in Buffalo.

340. Hollcroft, Temple R. "Walter Wood, Maker of a President." *Transactions—The American Lodge of Research* 9 (1964): 222–26. A brief biography of Fillmore's first mentor in the law. Fillmore worked in Wood's law and land office in Montville, Cayuga County, from 1819 to 1821. Also mentions Fillmore's first July 4th speech at Montville, New York, in 1821.

341. Hosmer, George W. *An Address Delivered at the Funeral of Nathaniel Fillmore Esq. of Aurora, Erie County New York on Tuesday, March 31, 1863.* Buffalo: Franklin Steam Printing House, 1863. Recounts Fillmore's father's hard rural life, temperate behavior, physical strength, and sense of humor. Nathaniel was not inclined to any religious sect but admired the teachings of Christ.

342. Hunt, Sandford. *Methodism in Buffalo: From Its Origins to the Close of 1892.* Buffalo: H. H. Otis & Sons, 1993. Fillmore's cousin Glezen Fillmore was considered the founder of Methodism in Buffalo. He preached on the Niagara Frontier for years before Millard settled in Buffalo.

343. Lord, Rev. John C. "Annual Address." *Publications of the Buffalo Historical Society, Volume 1.* Buffalo: Buffalo Historical Society, 1879. 1: 113–29. Recalls Fillmore's teaching days in Buffalo in the early 1820s.

344. "Millard Fillmore." *Memorial and Family History of Erie County.* 2 vols. New York: Genealogical Publishing Company, 1906–1908. 1: 49–51.

345. Pessen, Edward. *The Log Cabin Myth: The Social Backgrounds of the Presidents.* New Haven: Yale University Press, 1984. Unlike most Presidents, Fillmore's early life did fit the myth. However, he followed the typical presidential pattern of elite conservatism once he began his legal career.

346. Scarry, Robert J. *Millard Fillmore, the Forgotten President.* Moravia, NY: Scarry, 1973. Describes Fillmore's parents settling in Cayuga county and the

locations of the family's farms and houses. Biography and summary of political career.

347. Smith, H. Perry. *History of the City of Buffalo and Erie County.* Syracuse: D. Mason & Co., Publishers, 1889. 2 vols. Volume One contains many references to relatives who lived in Erie County before Fillmore moved there. Chapter Twenty-One establishes the family in Erie County with descriptions of his father Nathan, his uncle Calvin, his uncle Simeon, and their public services.

348. Steele, Oliver G. "The Buffalo Common Schools." *Publications of the Buffalo Historical Society, Volume 1.* Buffalo Historical Society, 1879. 1: 405–32. Fillmore taught school in Buffalo in 1822 and 1823, and was a deputy postmaster.

349. *A True Account of the Singular Sufferings of John Fillmore, and Others on Board a Noted Pirate Ship, with an Account of Their Daring Enterprise, and Happy Escape from the Tyranny of the Desperate Crew by Capturing Their Vessel. To Which Is Added a Brief Biography of Hon. Millard Fillmore of Buffalo.* Utica, NY: Russell Potter, 1851. Narrative of heroic acts by Fillmore's great-grandfather, a record of Fillmore's lineage, plus a partisan biography of Fillmore.

350. Turner, O. *Pioneer History of the Holland Land Purchase of Western New York.* Buffalo: Geo. H. Derby and Co., 1850. 546–47. Rev. Glezen Fillmore was the first Methodist minister licensed on the Purchase around 1809. He established a long, active, and well-regarded ministry.

351. Woodward, Ashbel. "Memoir of Captain John Fillmore." *New England Historical & Genealogical Register and Antiquarian Journal* 11 (January 1857): 61–66. Synopsis of Fillmore's great grandfather's 1724 abduction by pirates and the heroic mutiny he organized to capture and return them for trial.

352. Young, Jeff C. *The Fathers of American Presidents: From Augustus Washington to William Blythe and Roger Clinton.* Jefferson, NC: McFarland & Company, Inc., Publishers, 1997. Nathaniel Fillmore was the first father to visit his son in the White House. No other President's father had a longer life and few had a harder one.

Chapter 5

Early Career

A. LAWYER

353. Bryan, George J. "Life of Attorney General George P. Barker." In *Biographies and Journalism*. Buffalo: Courier Company, Printers, 1886. 9–131. Mentions Fillmore's early career at the bar. Relates his later defense of a midshipman who shot at the publisher of the Buffalo *Commercial Advertiser.*

354. Bunn, Mathew. "Narrative of Mathew Bunn." *Publications of the Buffalo Historical Society, Volume 7*. Buffalo: Buffalo Historical Society, 1904. 7: 377–436. As a commissioner of Erie County in 1826, Fillmore signed an affidavit that Mathew Bunn declared his narrative a true story of his life.

355. Chester, Alden. *Courts and Lawyers of New York: A History, 1609–1925.* 3 vols. New York: American Historical Society, Inc., 1925. 3: 1269, 1275. Mentions Fillmore's contributions to the Erie County Bar.

356. ———. *Legal and Judicial History of New York.* 3 vols. New York: National Americana Society, 1911. 3: 351–82. Mentions Fillmore in a review of Erie County lawyers.

357. "A Famous Old Law Office." *Publications of the Buffalo Historical Society, Volume 14.* Buffalo: Buffalo Historical Society, 1924. Reports the continuity of the law firm founded by Fillmore, Nathan K. Hall, and Solomon G. Haven with a picture of their office building.

358. Farrison, William E. "William Wells Brown in Buffalo." *Journal of Negro History* 39 (October 1954): 298–314. Abolitionist recalled that Fillmore was retained as counsel for alleged fugitive slaves in the late 1830s or early 1840s.

359. McAdam, David, et al., eds. *History of the Bench and Bar of New York.* 2 vols. New York: New York History Company, 1897. 1: 326–28. Fillmore was a lawyer of thorough learning and sound qualities.

360. "Obituary Notes: William Shannon Bissel." *Publications of the Buffalo Historical Society, Volume 7.* Buffalo: Buffalo Historical Society, 1904. 7: 488–90. Mentions Fillmore's legal offices.

361. Politzer, Geneva B. "A Presidential Gazetteer." *American History Illustrated,* April 1989, 43–52. A guide to presidential homes, museums, and libraries. Includes Fillmore's East Aurora home where he began his family, established his legal career, and won his first election. The home, southeast of Buffalo, is now the Millard Fillmore Museum.

362. Proctor, L. B. *The Bench and Bar of New York.* New York: Diossy & Company, 1870. 35–36, 704. He was deliberate and plain speaking with an unshakable logic in front of a jury.

363. Smith, H. Perry. *History of the City of Buffalo and Erie County.* Syracuse: D. Mason & Co., Publishers, 1889. 2 vols. Volume One contains many references to Fillmore with a tribute from his legal peers. Chapter Fifty contains a unique sketch of Fillmore's life in East Aurora in the late 1820s.

364. ———. "Millard Fillmore." In *History of the City of Buffalo and Erie County.* 2 vols. Syracuse: D. Mason & Co. Publishers, 1884. 2: 466–67. Sketch of legal career where he gained distinction and wealth as an office lawyer.

365. Smith, Lyman Morris. *Pictorial and Historical Review: East Aurora and Vicinity.* Holland, NY: History Recording Association, 1940. Contains a picture of Fillmore's East Aurora home.

365a. "To Our Mechanics . . . 'Come Let Us Reason Together.' " *Scientific American* 6 (May 17, 1851): 277. The editorial said former journeymen like Fillmore had to become lawyers to gain high positions in society.

366. Watson, Bob. "Fillmore, Hall & Haven." *Buffalo Magazine,* January 6, 1985, 12–15. A Buffalo *News* Sunday supplement article on the best-known law partnership in western New York. Formed in 1836, the partnership of Fillmore, Nathan K. Hall, and Solomon Haven combined law, politics, and friendship. Contains photographs of the three men.

367. Welch, Samuel M. *Home History: Recollections of Buffalo During the Decade from 1830 to 1840, or Fifty Years Since.* Buffalo: Peter Paul & Bro., 1891. Fillmore was a highly regarded lawyer and local citizen.

368. White, Truman C. *Our County and Its People, A Descriptive Work on Erie County.* New York: Boston History Company, 1898. 2 vols. Political and social history with many references to Fillmore and his contemporaries.

369. Winner, Julia Hull ed. "A Journey Across New York State in 1833." *New York History* 46 (January 1965): 60–78. George Johnson studied law under Fillmore, courted his sister, and worked for the Holland Land Company.

370. Witmer, Tobias. *Deed Tables in the County of Erie, N.Y. as Sold by the Holland Land Company, the Farmer's Loan and Trust Company, and the State of New York.* Buffalo: Clapp, Mathews & Co., 1859. Records the land holdings of Fillmore family members and the holdings of Fillmore and Hall in the 1830s.

B. HOLLAND LAND COMPANY

371. Bingham, Robert Warwick. *Holland Land Company's Papers, Reports of Joseph Ellicott. Publications of the Buffalo Historical Society, Vol. 32, 33.* Buffalo: Buffalo Historical Society, 1937, 1941. Yearly reports on company policy, land, and financial assets. It is a primary source on the company and the unrest on the company's land in the 1830s.

372. Evans, Paul D. *The Holland Land Company. Publications of the Buffalo Historical Society, Volume 28.* Buffalo: Buffalo Historical Society, 1924. Fillmore was involved in evicting debtors from the company's land in the 1830s while defending the company's original land claims. He later defended settlers against company policies.

373. *Proceedings of the Meeting Held at Lockport on the 2d and 3d of January 1827 and of the Convention of Delegates from the Several Counties on the Holland Purchase, Held at Buffalo on the 7th and 8th of February 1827.* Buffalo: Day & Follett, 1827. As a delegate from Aurora, Erie County, Fillmore endorsed the settlers' appeal to the Company for more investment in local improvements to attract settlers.

374. Winner, Julia Hull. "George Washington Johnson, Lawyer, and the Holland Land Company Office in Buffalo." *Niagara Frontier* 10 (Summer 1963): 56–61. Johnson was Fillmore's law student. Both worked in the company's Buffalo office in the early 1830s.

Chapter 6

Mature Years: Political Career

A. THE SECOND AMERICAN PARTY SYSTEM

375. Baker, Jean H. *Affairs of Party: The Political Culture of Northern Democrats in the Mid-Nineteenth Century*. Ithaca: Cornell University Press, 1983. Studies the nationalizing effect of the Democratic partisan culture.

376. Benson, Lee. *The Concept of Jacksonian Democracy: New York as a Test Case.* Princeton: Princeton University Press, 1961. Regards Fillmore as a major Whig political figure.

377. Benson, Lee, Joel H. Silbey, and Phyllis Field. "Toward a Theory of Stability and Change in American Voting Patterns: New York State, 1792–1970." In *The History of American Electoral Behavior*, ed. Joel H. Silbey, Allan G. Bogue, and William H. Flanigan. Princeton: Princeton University Press, 1978. Proposes a unique New York State cycle of three political party systems, including a stable second cycle from 1820 to 1892.

378. Chambers, William Nisbet. "Party Development and the American Mainstream." In *The American Party Systems: Stages of Political Development*, ed. William Nisbet Chambers and Walter Dean Burnham. New York: Oxford University Press, 1975. 3–32. The period from 1828 to 1860 is signified by a large voting population and their mobilization by political party structures.

379. Chambers, William N., and Philip C. Davis. "Party, Competition and Mass Participation: The Case of the Democratizing Party System, 1824–1852." In *The History of American Electoral Behavior*, ed. Joel H. Silbey, Allan G. Bogue, and

William H. Flanigan. Princeton: Princeton University Press, 1978. Indicates a strong relationship between party organization, increase in electoral turnout, and party competition.

380. Huston, James L. *Securing the Fruits of Labor: The American Concept of Wealth Distribution, 1765–1900.* Baton Rouge: Louisiana State University Press, 1998. Middle chapters discuss the Whig and Democratic principles on the tariff, a national bank, and their different consequences for equalizing income.

381. Krout, Alan M. "Partisanship and Principles: The Liberty Party in Antebellum Political Culture." In *Crusaders and Compromisers: Essays on the Relationships of the Antislavery Struggle to the Antebellum Party System,* ed. Alan M. Krout. Westport, CT: Greenwood Press, 1983. 71–99. Examines the party's contribution to the antislavery debate, elections, and the end of the second party system.

382. McCormick, Richard L. *The Party Period and Public Policy: American Politics from the Age of Jackson to the Progressive Era.* New York: Oxford University Press, 1986. Chapter Four surveys the Whig and Democratic parties.

383. McCormick, Richard P. "Political Development in the Second Party System." In *The American Party Systems: Stages of Political Development*, ed. William Nisbet Chambers and Walter Dean Burnham. New York: Oxford University Press, 1975. 90–116. From 1824 to 1850 there was an increased nationalization of political identity within political parties.

384. ———. *The Second American Party System: Party Formation in the Jacksonian Era.* Chapel Hill: University of North Carolina Press, 1973 [1963]. Standard state-by-state survey of the new party formations.

385. McGee, Patricia E. "Issues and Factions: New York State Politics from the Panic of 1837 to the Election of 1848." Ph.D. diss., St. Johns University, 1970. Describes changing party factions and realignments.

386. Meyers, Marvin. *The Jacksonian Persuasion: Politics and Belief.* Stanford: Stanford University Press, 1960 [1957]. Analyzes the appeal of Andrew Jackson and the Democratic party.

387. Pessen, Edward. *Jacksonian America: Society, Personality, and Politics.* Homewood, IL: Dorsey Press, 1969. Attempt at a comprehensive synthesis. Pessen derides the Antimasons as conceived in hysteria and later manipulated into the Whig party.

388. ———. *Jacksonian America: Society, Personality, and Politics.* Homewood, IL: Dorsey Press, 1978. 2d ed. Pessen uses new sympathetic studies on Antimasonry

and Whigs for a more balanced description of the origins and politics of Antimasonry.

389. Remini, Robert V. *Andrew Jackson.* New York: Harper & Row, Publishers, 1977–1984. 3 vols. Modern definitive biography of the Democratic figure who dominated national politics when Fillmore entered public life.

390. Remini, Robert V., and Robert O. Rupp. *Andrew Jackson: A Bibliography.* Westport: Meckler, 1991. This annotated bibliography is a great resource for the second American party system. Special attention to Antimasonic and Whig parties.

391. Schlesinger, Arthur M., Jr. *The Age of Jackson.* Boston: Little, Brown and Company, 1945. Classic work portraying the heroic ideology and politics of the Democratic party.

392. Silbey, Joel H. " 'The Salt of the Nation': Political Parties in Antebellum America." In *Political Parties and the Modern State,* ed. Richard L. McCormick. New Brunswick: Rutgers University Press, 1984. Whig and Democratic parties were responsive to their constituencies while stimulating loyalty to party leaders and programs.

393. Van Deusen, Glyndon G. *The Jacksonian Era, 1828–1848.* New York: Harper & Row, Publishers, 1959. Political history of the era.

394. ———. *The Rise and Decline of Jacksonian Democracy.* Huntington, NY: Robert E. Krieger, 1979. Survey of national politics from 1824 to 1856.

395. Varon, Elizabeth R. "Tippecanoe and the Ladies, Too: White Women and Party Politics in Antebellum Virginia." *Journal of American History* 82 (September 1995): 494–521. The Whigs were the first party to give women a public presence in election activities. Their moral beneficence, fused with Whig principles, would display integrity to the voters. Bibliography on antebellum women's activities.

B. THE ANTIMASONIC PARTY

396. Baldasty, Gerald J. "The New York State Political Press and Antimasonry." *New York History* 64 (July 1983): 261–79. The new party system allowed editors to gain power as they bridged the gap between candidate and voter.

397. Blakeslee, George Hubbard. "The History of the Antimasonic Party." Ph.D. diss., Harvard University, 1903. The Antimasonic uprising was a sensible movement considering the local disturbing activities of Masonry. Claims Fillmore was an active political leader but with "distinctly inferior" talents.

398. Brackney, William H. "Morgan, William." In *American National Biography*, ed. John A. Garraty and Mark C. Carnes. New York: Oxford University Press, 1999. 24 vols. 15: 857–58. His abduction for exposing the secrets of Masonry began the antimasonic movement.

399. ———. "Religious Antimasonry: The Genesis of a Political Party." Ph.D. diss., Temple University, 1976. The original fervor for Antimasonry took the character of contemporary regional religious crusades. Later, it was engineered to promote the new party.

400. Brown, Henry. *A Narrative of the Antimasonic Excitement in the Western Part of the State of New York, During the Years 1826, 7, 8 and a Part of 1829.* Universal Masonic Library, Vol. 28. New York: Jno. W. Leanard & Co., 1856 [1829]. Early Masonic history of the abduction of William Morgan, which precipitated Antimasonry. It was dedicated to Martin Van Buren, which confirmed for Antimasons the existence of a corrupt coalition between Masonry and Democrats.

401. Bryant, George J. *Life of George P. Barker.* Buffalo: Oliver G. Steele, 1849. Biography of Buffalo Democrat who had a rough time campaigning against rural Antimasons.

402. Cross, Whitney R. *The Burned-Over District: The Social and Intellectual History of Enthusiastic Religion in Western New York, 1800–1850.* New York: Harper & Row Publishers, 1950. Primary social history of the area where the Antimasonic movement originated.

403. Davis, David Brion. "Some Thoughts of Counter-Subversion: An Analysis of Anti-Masonic, Anti-Catholic, and Anti-Mormon Literature." *Mississippi Valley Historical Review* 48 (September 1960): 205–24. Seminal article stating that Antimasonry consisted of imagined threats to American institutions by subversive means. The article stimulated counter arguments that Masonry was a real threat.

404. Formisano, Ronald P. "Political Character, Antipartyism and the Second Party System." *American Quarterly* 21 (Winter 1969): 683–709. Antimasonry emitted the strongest antiparty feeling of any political movement in the United States. This caused trouble for politicians like Fillmore who directed the party into the new Whig party.

405. Formisano, Ronald P., and Kathleen Smith Kutolowski. "Antimasonry and Masonry: The Genesis of Protest, 1826–1827." *American Quarterly* 29 (Summer 1977): 139–65. Antimasonry began as a reasonable protest against real Masonic activities that undermined local law enforcement in western New York.

406. Goodman, Paul. *Towards a Christian Republic: Antimasonry and the Great Transition in New England, 1826–1836.* New York: Oxford University Press, 1988. Sympathetic reexamination of the social and ideological context of the Antimasonic movement and political party.

407. Gribbon, William. "Antimasonry, Religious Radicalism, and the Paranoid Style of the 1820s." *History Teacher* 7 (February 1974): 239–54. This reassessment claims that scholars used opponents' rhetoric to describe the Antimasonic movement which shared a paranoid style expressed throughout antebellum politics.

408. Griffin, Leland. "The Antimasonic Persuasion: A Study of Public Address in the American Antimasonic Movement, 1826–1838." Ph.D. diss., Cornell University, 1950. This massive study contains original reports alleging Masonry's influence in judicial and political corruption. Fillmore is depicted as one of Antimasonry's leading young men.

409. Gunn, L. Ray. "The New York State Legislature: A Developmental Perspective, 1777–1846." *Social Science History* 4 (August 1980): 267–94. Analysis of the New York Assembly, where Fillmore spent three years as an Antimasonic assemblyman.

410. Haigh, Elizabeth Bruchholz. "New York Antimasons, 1826–1833." Ph.D. diss., University of Rochester, 1980. Argues that Antimasonry was not a religious movement but a civic movement concerned with the values of a changing republican society. This allowed it to be politicized by politicians like Fillmore.

411. Hamilton, Milton W. "Anti-Masonic Newspapers, 1826–1834." *Papers of the Bibliographical Society of America, 1938 no. 32.* Lists location of papers, editors, and number of issues.

412. H[amlin], L. B. "Follett Papers, I." *Quarterly Publication of the Historical and Philosophical Society of Ohio* 5 (April–June 1900): 33–76. A Buffalo editor comments on the growth and triumph of political Antimasonry.

413. Hammond, Jabez D. *The History of Political Parties in the State of New York: From the Ratification of the Federal Constitution to December 1840.* Albany: C. Van Benethuysen, 1842. 3 vols. Volume 2 is the standard reference on the importance of western New York to the rise of Antimasonry and the Whig party. That section was written with the help of Frederick Whittlisey, an Antimason and colleague of Fillmore.

414. Kruschke, Earl R. "Antimason." *Encyclopedia of Third Parties in the United States.* Santa Barbara: ABC-CLIO, 1991. Review of New York beginnings and attempt at a national party. Bibliography.

415. Kutolowski, Kathleen Smith. "Antimasonry Reexamined: Social Bases of the Grass Roots Party." *Journal of American History* 71 (September 1984): 269–93. Important demographic analysis overturning the former stereotype of Antimasons as unreasonable populists.

416. ———. "Freemasonry and Community in the Early Republic: The Case for Antimasonic Anxieties." *American Quarterly* 34 (Winter 1982): 543–61. Antimasons were intimately aware of Masonic interests in local business and politics. They easily accepted indictments of judicial and political corruption against Masonry.

417. Lewis, Clarence O. *The Morgan Affair.* Lockport, NY: Niagara County Court House, 1966. Thirty-two-page history of William Morgan's abduction by Masons and the judicial cover-up that began the Antimasonic uprising. Includes details of local trials.

418. McCarthy, Charles M. "The Antimasonic Party: A Study of Political Anti-Masonry in the United States, 1827–1840." *American Historical Association Annual Report* 2 (1902): 365–574. Washington: Government Printing Office, 1903. First state-by-state survey of political Antimasonry. Local influences sparking the movement were ill defined but the outrage quickly focused into an effective political party.

419. Rupp, Robert O. "Parties and the Public Good: Political Antimasonry in New York Reconsidered." *Journal of the Early Republic* 8 (Fall 1988): 253–79. Antimasonry challenged the electoral supremacy of New York Democrats and changed the model of a political party.

420. Spencer, Ivor Debenham. *The Victor and the Spoils, A Life of William L. Marcy.* Providence: Brown University Press, 1959. Marcy was the Democratic governor of New York during the rise of political Antimasonry and was accused of aiding Masonry.

421. Vaughn, William Preston. *The Antimasonic Party in the United States, 1826–1843.* Lexington: University of Kentucky Press, 1983. Survey of political Antimasonry using recently recovered Fillmore papers to describe his role in the party and its transition to the Whig party.

422. ———. "An Overview of Pre and Post–Civil War Antimasonry." *Historian* 49 (August 1987): 494–507. Survey of the successful and later unsuccessful phases of Antimasonry in the 19th century.

C. THE WHIG PARTY

423. "The American Whig Party." *Whig Almanac, 1838.* New York: New York Tribune, 1838. 3. Outline of the party's formation and principles.

424. Ashworth, John. *'Agrarians' & 'Aristocrats,' Party Political Ideology in the United States, 1837–1846.* London: Royal Historical Society, 1983. Highlights Whig and Democratic political characteristics.

425. Boritt, G. S. *Lincoln and the Economics of the American Dream.* Memphis: Memphis State University Press, 1978. Excellent analysis of Whig political economy.

425a. Brown, Thomas. *The Politics of Statesmanship: Essays on the American Whig Party.* New York: Columbia University Press, 1985. Ideological history of the Whig party with attention to leadership, sectional divisions, and its demise following the Compromise of 1850 and the election of 1852.

426. Carroll, Malcolm E. *Origins of the Whig Party.* Durham, NC: Seeman Printing Inc., 1925. Early national study.

427. Crawford, John E. "The Importance of Millard Fillmore and Antimasonry to the New Whig Party in 1834." *Studies in History, SUNY at Buffalo* 3 (1981–1982): 15–32. Fillmore did not run for reelection to Congress because he feared his association with the Holland Land Company made him a liability to the imminent success of the new Whig party.

428. Dubofsky, Melvin. "Daniel Webster and the Whig Theory of Economic Growth: 1828–1848." *New England Quarterly* 42 (December 1969): 551–72. The Whigs articulated insights on advanced commercial and industrial economy.

429. Fox, Dixon Ryan. "The Economic Status of the New York Whigs." *Political Science Quarterly* 33 (December 1918): 501–18. A dated study proposing a class relationship between Whigs and city wards with substantial property.

430. Friedman, Jean E. *The Revolt of the Conservative Democrats: An Essay on American Political Culture and Political Development, 1837–1844.* Ann Arbor: UMI Research Press, 1979. Fillmore and western New York Whigs resented a coalition with conservative Democrats, rightly fearing that political offices would go to candidates never loyal to Whig principles.

431. Gerber, David A. *The Making of an American Pluralism: Buffalo, New York 1825–60.* Urbana: University of Illinois Press, 1989. Parts One and Two describe

Buffalo's antebellum commercial economy and the formation of a Protestant elite that included Fillmore and his Whig cohorts.

432. Gerring, John. *Party Ideologies in America, 1828–1996.* New York: Cambridge University Press, 1998. Historical synthesis of Whig-Republican ideology from the 1830s to Reaganism.

433. "The Grounds of Difference Between the Contending Parties." *Whig Almanac, 1843.* New York: New York Tribune, 1843. 16–17. Description of principles that distinguished Whigs from Democrats.

434. Hamlin, L. Belle. "Selections from the Follett Papers, 3." *Quarterly Publication of the Historical and Philosophical Society of Ohio* 10 (January–March 1915): 2–33. Newspaper editor Oran Follett advised Henry Clay to alter his 1844 statement on Texas annexation and let Fillmore make it public.

434a. Hauptman, Laurence M. *Conspiracy of Interests: Iroquois Dispossession and the Rise of New York State.* Syracuse: Syracuse University Press, 1999. Fillmore was associated with New York Whigs looking to obtain Indian lands around Buffalo to expand its boundaries and secure its prosperity.

435. Horton, John Theodore. "Erie County." In *History of Northwest New York.* 3 Vols. New York: Lewis Historical Publishing Company, Inc., 1947. 1: 9–489. Chapters Five and Six offer an excellent local context for Fillmore's legal and political career.

436. Howe, Daniel Walker, ed. *The American Whigs: An Anthology.* New York: John Wiley & Sons, Inc., 1973. Introduction to Whig principles and prominent Whigs. Five Whigs in this book were in Fillmore's administration: Edward Everett, Daniel Webster, John Pendleton Kennedy, Daniel D. Barnard, and Thomas Corwin.

437. ——— . "The Evangelical Movement and Political Culture in the North during the Second Party System." *Journal of American History* 77 (March 1991): 1216–39. Insightful study proposing the evangelicals' new vision of a moral, disciplined, and organized society pioneered the systematic improvement of government advocated by Whigs and Republicans.

438. ——— . *The Political Culture of the American Whigs.* Chicago: University of Chicago Press, 1979. Thoughtful appraisal of the Whig vision for America. Fillmore is portrayed as a colorless, career politician and does not compare well with "Conscience" Whigs like William Seward.

439. Matthews, J. V. " 'Whig History': The New England Whigs and a Usable Past." *New England Quarterly* 51 (June 1978): 193–208. Whigs held a perception of history based on reason, restraint, and resistance to conflict.

440. Morris, John. "The New York State Whigs, 1834–1842." Ph.D. diss., University of Rochester, 1970. Examination of party principles and political development in which Fillmore played a leading role as a regional and state organizer.

441. Muntz, Ernest G. "The First Whig Governor of New York, William Henry Seward, 1838–1842." Ph.D. diss., University of Rochester, 1960. Fillmore played a prominent role organizing western New York for Whig electoral campaigns.

442. Poage, George Rawlings. *Henry Clay and the Whig Party.* Chapel Hill: University of North Carolina Press, 1936. Clay and Fillmore were acquainted at the beginning of the Whig party. Clay later supported Fillmore's 1852 presidential nomination.

443. Reed, John Julius. "The Emergence of the Whig Party in the North: Massachusetts, New York, Pennsylvania and Ohio." Ph.D. diss., University of Pennsylvania, 1953. Analysis of the New York State coalition of Antimasons and National Republicans into the Whig party. The study relies on sources from William Seward and Thurlow Weed with little mention of Fillmore.

444. Richards, Donald Joseph. "A Study in Persuasion: New York City Whigs View the Issues, 1834–1844." Ph.D. diss., University of Notre Dame, 1984. Extracts of Whig sentiments and political policies from city newspapers and manuscript collections.

445. Schouler, James. "Whig Party." In *Cyclopedia of American Government,* ed. Andrew C. McLaughlin and Albert Bushnell Hart. New York: Peter Smith, 1930 [1914]. 3 vols. 3: 80–85. Reviews the national party.

446. Smith, H. Perry. *History of the City of Buffalo and Erie County.* 2 vols. Syracuse: D. Mason & Co. Publishers, 1884. In Volume One, Chapters Twenty-one through Twenty-three narrate Buffalo's political history with many references to Fillmore as an Antimason, Whig, and President.

447. Titus, W. A. "A Bit of New York History and an Unpublished Letter of Henry Clay." *Wisconsin Magazine of History* 7 (December 1923): 214–18. Thurlow Weed's campaign to appease conservative Democrats offended loyal western New York Whigs like Fillmore.

448. Watson, Harry L. *Liberty and Power: The Politics of Jacksonian America.* New York: Hill and Wang, 1990. In 1840, Fillmore wondered if the Whig party could

supersede the old anti-Jackson coalition and win a broad spectrum of popular support.

D. CONGRESSMAN

449. Becker, Ronald L. "A Bibliography Relating to the Broad Seal War in New Jersey, 1830–1840." *Journal of the Rutgers University Library* 44 (1982): 35–51. Seventy-six annotated sources on the contested 1838 New Jersey elections, including Fillmore's minority report.

450. Corey, Albert B. *The Crisis of 1830–1842 in Canadian-American Relations*. New Haven: Yale University Press, 1941. During the Canadian rebellion and border hostilities with western New York, Fillmore urged a subdued diplomacy with Great Britain while lobbying for a stronger military defense.

451. Edmonds, John B., Jr. *Frances W. Pickens and the Politics of Destruction*. Chapel Hill: University of North Carolina Press, 1986. Fillmore introduced a resolution that all diplomatic correspondence concerning Canadian hostilities be made public.

452. Frank, Douglas. "The Canadian Rebellion and the American Public." *Niagara Frontier* 16 (Winter 1969): 96–104. Highlights Buffalo's sympathies for the Canadian rebels.

453. Guillet, Edwin C. *The Lives and Times of the Patriots: An Account of the Rebellion in Upper Canada, 1837–1838, and the Patriot Agitation in the United States, 1837–1842*. Toronto: University of Toronto Press, 1963.

454. Jennings, R. Y. "The *Caroline* and McLeod Cases." *American Journal of International Law* 32 (January 1938): 82–99. Examines the diplomatic discussions and the claims resulting from the American-Canadian border dispute.

455. Johnson, Arthur L. "The New York State Press and the Canadian Rebellion, 1837–1838." *American Review of Canadian Studies* 14 (Fall 1984): 279–90. Like Fillmore, the press and public favored the Canadian rebellion but urged diplomatic caution.

456. Jones, Howard. "The *Caroline* Affair." *Historian* 38 (May 1976): 485–502. History of the burning of the ship *Caroline* on the American side of the Niagara River by Canadian loyalists, which inflamed American citizens on the Niagara frontier.

457. ———— . *To the Webster-Ashburton Treaty: A Study in Anglo-American Relations, 1783–1843*. Chapel Hill: University of North Carolina Press, 1977. The

Caroline affair was the most serious diplomatic problem with Britain since the war of 1812. Congressman Fillmore advocated more military defense along the border while hoping to find a diplomatic compromise to settle border animosities.

458. Jones, Howard, and Donald A. Rakestraw. *Prologue to Manifest Destiny: Anglo-American Relations in the 1840s.* Wilmington: Scholarly Resources Inc., 1997. Fillmore worked behind the scenes to calm anti-British feelings following the failure of the patriots' revolt in Canada.

459. Manley, Henry S. "Buying Buffalo from the Indians." *New York History* 28 (July 1947): 313–29. In 1838, Fillmore urged a decision on a treaty with the Seneca that was obtained by discreditable means. He made no public statement, but he desired a treaty to expand the boundaries of Buffalo.

460. Miller, William Lee. *Arguing About Slavery: The Great Battle in the United States Congress.* New York: Alfred A. Knopf, 1996. Fillmore was an astute parliamentarian, who tried to deflect Congress away from the slavery debate.

461. Russo, David J. "The Major Political Issues of the Jacksonian Period and the Development of Party Loyalty in Congress, 1830–1840." *Transactions of the American Philosophical Society 62, Pt. 5, May 1972.* Philadelphia: American Philosophical Society, 1972. Investigates the variation of party loyalty on major partisan issues.

462. Severance, Frank H., ed. *Millard Fillmore Papers, Volume 1, Publications of the Buffalo Historical Society. Volume 10.* Buffalo Historical Society, 1907. Section titled "Speeches and Debates as Representative in Congress" uses excerpts from his debates and speeches, including those supporting New Jersey Whig representatives, the Canadian border conflict, and the tariff debates during Tyler's administration.

463. Shortridge, Wilson Porter. "The Canadian-American Frontier During the Rebellion of 1837–1838." *Canadian Historical Review* 7 (March 1976): 13–26. Reviews American-Canadian border hostilities and the sensible diplomacy that prevented an Anglo-American war.

464. Stevens, Kenneth R. *Border Diplomacy: The* Caroline *and McLeod Affairs in Anglo-American-Canadian Relations, 1837–1842.* Tuscaloosa: University of Alabama Press, 1989. Describes events leading to strained British-American relations. Fillmore urged more border defenses while working in Congress to suppress hostilities.

E. CHAIRMAN, HOUSE WAYS AND MEANS COMMITTEE

465. Bolles, Albert S. *The Financial History of the United States from 1789 to 1860.* New York: Augustus M. Kelly, Publishers, 1969 [1894]. Mentions Fillmore's role in the tariff controversy with President Tyler.

466. Chitwood, Oliver Perry. *John Tyler, Champion of the Old South.* New York: D. Appleton-Century Company, 1939. Fillmore considered it unwise for the Whig Cabinet to resign in protest over President Tyler's policies. The author does not continue the citation where Fillmore still approved the resignations.

467. Gantz, Richard A. "Henry Clay and the Harvest of Bitter Fruit: The Struggle with John Tyler, 1841–1842." Ph.D. diss., Indiana University, 1986. Mentions Fillmore's work on the tariff of 1842.

468. "History of the Tariff." *Whig Almanac, 1844.* New York: New York Tribune, 1844. 5–6. Concise description of the 1842 tariff. Fillmore moved that the President's tariff proposals be given to the Committee on Manufactures.

469. Kennon, Donald R., and Rebecca M. Rogers. *The Committee on Ways and Means: A Bicentennial History, 1789–1989.* Washington: Government Printing Office, 1989. Fillmore won praise for his banking and protective tariff legislation. He energetically pursued a stringent oversight of government appropriations and administered the everyday work of the committee.

470. Lambert, Oscar Doane. *Presidential Politics in the United States, 1841–1844.* Durham: Duke University Press, 1936. Mentions Fillmore's work on the 1842 tariff bill.

471. Maness, Lonnie, and Richard D. Chesteen. "The First Attempt at Presidential Impeachment: Partisan Politics and Intra-Party Conflict at Loose." *Presidential Studies Quarterly* 10 (Winter 1980): 51–62. Tyler's vetoes of the Fillmore tariff added incentive to Whig arguments for impeachment.

472. McKinley, William. *The Tariff in the Days of Henry Clay and Since.* New York: Kraus Reprint Co., 1970 [1896]. Soon to be President, McKinley examines the 1842 tariff.

473. Mushkat, Jerome. *Fernando Wood, A Political Biography.* Kent: Kent State University Press, 1990. Fillmore's tariff sent shivers through the New York shipping community as it made foreign goods too costly to import.

474. Shields, Johanna Nicol. *The Line of Duty: Maverick Congressmen and the Development of American Political Culture, 1836–1860.* Westport, CT: Greenwood

Press, 1985. Fillmore probably did more to lead House Whigs than did the maverick Speaker of the House, John White.

475. Stephenson, George M. *The Political History of the Public Lands from 1840 to 1862: From Pre-Emption to Homestead.* New York: Russell & Russell, 1967 [1917]. Fillmore's introduction of the 1842 "Little Tariff" added to Tyler's political trials.

476. "The Tariff Question." *Whig Almanac, 1846.* New York: New York Tribune, 1846. 5–9. Fillmore is given partial credit for the intelligent handling of the passage of the 1842 tariff.

477. Tyler, Lyon G. *The Letters and Times of the Tylers.* New York: DaCapo Press, 1970 [1884–1896]. 3 vols. Volume Two refers to Fillmore's congressional maneuvers to upset Tyler's administration. Volume Three contains a reminiscence by First Lady Julia Tyler, where she remembers a handsome though somewhat vain Fillmore.

478. White, Leonard D. *The Jacksonians: A Study in Administrative History, 1829–1861.* New York: Macmillan Company, 1954. Mentions Fillmore's scrutiny of departmental budgets. Reviews his concern for the disparity of low state employee salaries compared to higher federal salaries, causing inordinate loss of good state workers to the national government.

F. GUBERNATORIAL CAMPAIGN, 1844

479. Adams, Henry. "Charles Francis Adams Visits the Mormons in 1844." Massachusetts Historical Society, *Proceedings* 68 (1947): 267–300. Adams heard from Whig delegates to the National Convention that Fillmore was a potential candidate for Vice President.

480. Christman, Henry. *Tin Horns and Calico: A Decisive Episode in the Emergence of Democracy.* Cornwallville, NY: Hope Farm Press, 1978 [1945]. Both Fillmore and Silas Wright were mute about the eastern New York farmers' revolt against their antiquated leaseholds.

481. Garraty, John Arthur. *Silas Wright.* New York: Columbia University Press, 1949. Fillmore ran against the state's most popular Democrat in 1844.

482. Glashan, Ray R. *American Governors and Gubernatorial Elections, 1775–1978.* Westport, CT: Meckler Books, 1979. Useful guide to the 1844 election.

483. Hammond, Jabez D. *Political History of the State of New York.* Syracuse: L. W. Hall, 1852. 3 vols. Volume Three describes Fillmore losing the nomination for

Whig Vice President then loyally accepting to run against the popular Silas Wright for governor. Good profiles of Fillmore and Wright.

484. Jenkins, John S. *Lives of the Governors of the State of New York.* Auburn: Derby and Miller, 1851. 795–815. Mentions Fillmore's loss of the Whig gubernatorial nomination in 1846, when his name was proposed against his wishes.

485. Kallenback, Joseph E., and Jessamine S. Kallenback. *American State Governors, 1776–1976.* Dobbs Ferry, NY: Oceana Publications, Inc., 1977. 3 vols. Contains 1844 election results.

486. "The Past and the Future." *Whig Almanac, 1846.* New York: New York Tribune, 1846. 4–6. The Whigs renewed their claim of Democratic voting frauds in the national and state elections of 1844 but vowed to continue fighting for their principles.

487. Peterson, Norma Lois. *The Presidencies of William Henry Harrison & John Tyler.* Lawrence: University Press of Kansas, 1989. Many Whigs regretted sacrificing Fillmore to the nationally popular Wright while others were disappointed that Fillmore, with only a local following, was running at all.

488. Roach, George W. "The Presidential Campaign of 1844 in New York State." *New York History* 19 (April 1938): 153–72. The popular Silas Wright campaigned against Fillmore in order to bolster New York's chances to elect Polk and defeat Clay.

489. Shaw, Ronald E. *Erie Water West: A History of the Erie Canal, 1792–1854.* Lexington: University of Kentucky Press, 1966. New York internal improvement was an important issue in the race between Fillmore and Wright.

490. Sheldon, Marion. "Wright, Silas." *DAB* (1964), 10, pt. 2: 565–67. Highlights his Jacksonian politics with brief reference to his 1844 election.

491. Sobel, Robert, and John Raimo, eds. *Biographical Directory of the Governors of the United States, 1789–1978.* Westport, CT: Meckler Books, 1978. 4 vols. 3: 1079. Brief political biography of Silas Wright.

492. Stringham, James. "Early Days of the Buffalo *Courier.*" *Publications of the Buffalo Historical Society. Volume 19.* Buffalo Historical Society, 1915. 161–65. Colorful story of a railroad conductor's signal informing Buffalo of Wright's victory and the contrasting way both parties received the news.

493. "Wright, Silas, Jr." In *Encyclopedia of Biography of New York.* ed. Charles Elliott Fitch. Boston: American Historical Society, Inc., 1916. 3 vols. 3: 251–53.

Highlights Wright's defeat of Fillmore by a 10,000-vote plurality while Polk defeated Clay by only a 5,000-vote plurality.

G. STATE COMPTROLLER, 1847–1849

494. Hammond, Bray. *Banks and Politics in America from the Revolution to the Civil War.* Princeton: Princeton University Press, 1957. This classic work uses Fillmore's 1849 comptroller's report to define "free banking."

495. Redlich, Fritz. *The Molding of American Banking: Men and Ideas.* New York: Johnson Reprint Corporation, 1968 [1947]. While Comptroller and the incumbent Vice President, Fillmore worked on a national banking plan based on a national currency secured by United States stocks. The plan remained in circulation throughout the 1850s and influenced the new banking structure that financed the Civil War.

496. Roberts, James A. *A Century in the Comptroller's Office, State of New York.* Albany: James B. Lyon, Printer, 1897. Fillmore was the first statewide-elected comptroller.

497. Robertson, Ross M. *The Comptroller and Bank Supervision: A Historical Appraisal.* Washington, DC: McCall Printing Co., 1968. Fillmore was a free banking advocate. However he urged the adoption of a national currency to displace the individual issues from state banks.

498. Severance, Frank H., ed. *Millard Fillmore Papers, Volume 1, Publications of the Buffalo Historical Society. Volume 10.* Buffalo Historical Society, 1907. Section titled "As Comptroller of New York State" includes letters and his report on banks. Volume's chronology reports his election to office on November 2, 1847. He resigned February 20, 1849.

499. Shade, William Gerald. *Banks or No Banks: The Money Issue in Western Politics, 1832–1865.* Detroit: Wayne State University Press, 1972. Fillmore's Comptroller's report favoring a national currency echoed into Republican party fiscal policy.

Chapter 7

Vice Presidency

A. THE 1848 CAMPAIGN

500. Hamilton, Holman. "Election of 1848." In *History of American Presidential Elections, 1789–1968*. ed. Arthur M. Schlesinger, Jr., Fred L. Israel, and William P. Hansen. New York: Chelsea House Publishers, 1971. 4 vols. 2: 865–918. Substantial review plus election documents.

501. Serio, Anne Marie. *Political Cartoons in the 1848 Election Campaign*. Smithsonian Studies in History and Technology, No. 14. Washington: Smithsonian Institution Press, 1972. Contains one cartoon with Fillmore.

502. Troy, Gil. "1848." In *Running for President: The Candidates and Their Images*, ed. Arthur M. Schlesinger, Jr. New York: Simon and Shuster, 1994. 2 vols. 1: 185–203. Contains remarkable color reproductions of campaign posters, books, ribbons, and medals that reproduce Fillmore's image.

B. THE WHIG CAMPAIGN

503. Bauer, K. Jack. *Zachary Taylor: Soldier, Planter, Statesman of the Old South*. Baton Rouge: Louisiana State University Press, 1985. Scholarly biography tracing the experiences that shaped Taylor's nationalism and his inclination to limit slavery.

504. Boucher, Chauncey, and Robert P. Brooks. "Correspondence Addressed to John C. Calhoun, 1837–1849." *Annual Report of the American Historical Association 1929: One Volume and a Supplement Volume.* Washington: Government

Printing Office, 1930. 1: 125–570. Southerners appraised Fillmore as a Wilmot Proviso man detrimental to their interests.

505. Brauer, Kinley J. "The Webster-Lawrence Feud: A Study in Politics and Ambititon." *Historian* 29 (November 1966): 34–59. Rivalry for the Massachusetts Whig leadership indirectly led to Fillmore's Vice Presidential nomination.

506. Congleton, Betty Carolyn. "Contenders for the Whig Nomination in 1848 and the Editorial Policy of George D. Prentice." *Register of the Kentucky Historical Society* 67 (April 1969): 119–33. In 1847 and 1848 this former Clay supporter turned to Taylor.

507. "The Election of 1848." *Whig Almanac, 1849.* New York: New York Tribune, 1849. 4–9. Endorsements for Taylor and Fillmore, with an analysis of the Democratic and Free Soil parties.

508. Gatell, Frank Otto. " 'Conscience and Judgment'; The Bolt of the Massachusetts Conscience Whigs." *Historian* 21 (November 1958): 18–45. Conscience Whigs turned the Vice Presidential nomination away from Abbott Lawrence allowing an opportunity for Fillmore's nomination.

509. Graebner, Norman A. "1848: Southern Politics at the Crossroads." *Historian* 25 (November 1962): 14–35. Taylor's election resulted in increased sectionalism.

510. Hatch, Louis Clinton. *A History of the Vice Presidency of the United States.* New York: American Historical Society, Inc., 1934. Biographical material on Fillmore and his role in the 1848 campaign.

511. Lavender, David. "How to Make It to the White House Without Really Trying." *American Heritage,* June 1967: 22–23, 80–86. Being a successful general, circumstance, and luck led to Taylor's presidency.

512. Lorant, Stefan. *The Glorious Burden, The American Presidency.* New York: Harper & Row, Publishers, 1968. Review of Taylor's administration with photographs of Taylor, Fillmore, and their political contemporaries.

513. "Military Presidents." *U. S. Magazine and Democratic Review* 26 (June 1850): 481–98. Democratic assessment of Taylor and his cabinet but no mention of Fillmore.

514. Rayback, Joseph G. "Who Wrote the Allison Letters: A Study in Historical Detection." *Mississippi Valley Historical Review* 36 (June 1949): 51–72. Supports the claim that Fillmore and Thurlow Weed wrote the second Allison letter, which quieted fears that Taylor had no attachment to the Whig party.

515. Walton, Brian G. "The Elections for the Thirtieth Congress and the Presidential Candidacy of Zachary Taylor." *Journal of Southern History* 35 (May 1969): 186–202. Claims that the 15-month extended congressional elections assisted Taylor's nomination.

C. THE DEMOCRATIC CAMPAIGN

516. Donovan, Herbert D. A. *The Barnburners: A Study of the Internal Movements in the Political History of New York State and of the Resulting Changes in Political Affiliation, 1830–1852.* Philadelphia: Porcupine Press, 1974 [1925]. Pioneering study on the Democratic schism that helped elect Taylor and Fillmore.

517. Klunder, Willard Carl. *Lewis Cass and the Politics of Moderation.* Kent: Kent State University Press, 1996. Democrats denounced Fillmore as the abolition candidate.

518. Morrison, Chaplin W. *Democratic Politics and Sectionalism: The Wilmot Proviso Controversy.* Chapel Hill: University of North Carolina Press, 1967. Consequences of the Proviso on 1848 election.

519. National Democratic Republican Committee. *Millard Fillmore, Proved to be an Abolitionist! General Taylor, Probably Pledged to the Whigs of the North, in Favor of the Wilmot Proviso.* Washington, D.C., 1848. Declared Fillmore ready to liberate slaves.

520. Stevens, Walter W. "Lewis Cass and the Presidency." *Michigan History* 49 (June 1965): 123–34. Reviews Cass's presidential nomination in 1848.

D. THE FREE SOIL CAMPAIGN

521. Duberman, Martin. *Charles Francis Adams, 1807–1886.* Stanford: Stanford University Press, 1961. Former conscience Whig was the Free Soil vice presidential nominee in 1848.

522. Foner, Eric. "Racial Attitudes of the New York Free-Soilers." *New York History.* 46 (October 1965): 311–29. Racism determined that the Free Soilers were the first antislavery party to disregard the issue of equal rights for free African Americans in its national platform.

523. Gardiner, O. C. *The Great Issue: Or, The Three Presidential Candidates; Being a Brief Historical Sketch of the Free Soil Questions in the United States, from the Congresses of 1774 and 87 to the Present Time.* New York: Wm. C. Bryant & Co., 1848. Campaign material supporting Martin Van Buren for President.

524. Niven, John. *Martin Van Buren: The Romantic Age of American Politics.* New York: Oxford University Press, 1983. Modern political biography of the former Democratic President who ran as the Free Soil candidate in 1848.

525. Rayback, Joseph G. *Free Soil, the Election of 1848.* Lexington: University of Kentucky Press, 1970. Refers to the dilemma for Southern Whigs when Democrats claimed Fillmore was an abolitionist.

526. ———— . "Martin Van Buren's Break with James K. Polk: The Record." *New York History* 36 (January 1955): 51–62. The road to Van Buren's Free Soil campaign began with his estrangement from Polk over federal patronage in New York.

E. THE VICE PRESIDENCY

527. Alotta, Robert I. *A Look at the Vice Presidency.* New York: Julian Messner, 1981. Analysis of the office with bibliography.

528. Alvarez, Joseph. *Vice-Presidents of Destiny.* New York: G. P. Putnam's Sons, 1969. Little on Fillmore's Vice Presidency but praise for his later administration.

529. Benson, Adolph B. *America of the Fifties: Letters of Fredrika Bremer.* New York: American-Scandinavian Foundation, 1924. While touring Washington, Bremer was impressed by Fillmore's manly countenance in the Senate and his ability to shine in personal conversation. She reports that Fillmore looked more Presidential than Taylor.

530. Borzman, Sol. *Madmen & Geniuses: The Vice Presidents of the United States.* Chicago: Follett Publishing Company, 1974. Neither madman nor genius, Fillmore was just lucky to get nominated.

531. Carman, Harry J., and Reinhard H. Luthin. "The Seward-Fillmore Feud and the Crisis of 1850." *New York History* 24 (April 1943): 163–84. Examines the escalating rivalry for Taylor's favor and Fillmore's loss of federal patronage in New York.

532. Clapp, Margaret. *Forgotten First Citizen: John Bigelow.* Boston: Little, Brown and Company, 1947. In 1849, Bigelow reported how Thurlow Weed and William Seward eclipsed Fillmore's influence in Taylor's administration and acquired the state's federal patronage.

533. Curtis, Richard, and Maggie Wells. *Not Exactly a Crime: Our Vice Presidents from Adams to Agnew.* New York: Dial Press, 1972. Superficial biographical sketches.

534. DiSalle, Michael V., and Lawrence G. Blackman. *Second Choice.* New York: Hawthorn Books, Inc., 1966. A former governor of Ohio, DiSalle writes thoughtfully on the Vice Presidency and Fillmore's inability to reconcile sectionalism.

535. Dorman, Michael. *The Second Man: The Changing Role of the Vice President.* New York: Delacorte Press, 1968. Critical of Taylor's ill use of Fillmore during the Compromise of 1850.

536. Gara, Larry. "Who Was an Abolitionist?" In *The Antislavery Vanguard: New Essays on the Abolitionists,* ed. Martin Duberman. Princeton: Princeton University Press, 1965. Prior to the Compromise of 1850, Fillmore's enemies accused him of being an abolitionist. His supporters denied it, saying he was antislavery but not fanatical.

537. Hamilton, Holman. "Zachary Taylor and Minnesota." *Minnesota History* 30 (June 1949): 97–110. Fillmore could not appoint his former law partner Nathan K. Hall to the governorship of Minnesota Territory because of Seward's interference.

538. ———. *Zachary Taylor, Volume 2: Soldier in the White House.* Hamden, CT: Archon Books, 1966 [1951]. Fair description of Fillmore's Vice Presidential nomination, campaign, patronage problems, and his succession to the Presidency after Taylor's death.

539. Healy, Diana Dixon. *America's Vice Presidents: Our First Forty-Three Vice Presidents and How They Got to Be Number Two.* New York: Athenaeum, 1984.

540. Hoopes, Ray. *The Changing Vice Presidency.* New York: Thomas Y. Crowell, 1981.

541. Johnston, Richard Malcolm and William Hand Browne. *Life of Alexander H. Stephens.* Philadelphia: J. B. Lippincott, 1878. Described Vice President Fillmore's appearance as striking, his expression open and bland, and one knew he was far above the average.

542. Learned, Henry Barrett. "Casting Votes of the Vice Presidents, 1789–1915." *American Historical Review* 20 (April 1915): 571–76. Fillmore is recorded on three unimportant procedural votes in the Senate.

543. *Niles National Register.* March 14, 1849. Describes the inauguration of Taylor and Fillmore. Fillmore's brief address referred to America's peaceful presidential change compared to Europe's violent revolutions.

544. Paullin, Charles O. "The Vice President and the Cabinet." *American Historical Review* 29 (April 1924): 496–500. Reviews the precedents for Taylor excluding Fillmore from his Cabinet.

545. Poore, B: Perley "The Way to Washington, No. IV.*" Gleason's Pictorial Drawing-Room Companion,* 25 Dec. 1852. Recalls meeting Fillmore on his way to Washington in 1849. He was a burly gentleman with a carpet bag and a pleasant disposition.

546. Smith, Elbert B. *The Presidencies of Zachary Taylor & Millard Fillmore.* Lawrence: University Press of Kansas, 1988. Sympathetic review of Fillmore's early career and tenure as Vice President during the Compromise debates.

547. Stephens, Alexander H. *A Constitutional View of the War Between the States; Causes, Character, Conduct and Results, Presented in a Series of Colloquies at Liberty Hall.* Philadelphia: National Publishing Company, 1870. 2 vols. 2: 198. Stephens remembered Fillmore as a dignified and guileless Vice President who kept the Senate debates on a high plain.

548. Swisshelm, Jane Grey. *Half a Century.* New York: Source Book Press, 1970 [1880]. During the Compromise debates, Fillmore reluctantly allowed her to be the first woman journalist ever seated in the Senate press gallery.

549. Tally, Steve. *Bland Ambition: From Adams to Quayle—The Cranks, Criminals, Tax Cheats, and Golfers Who Made It to Vice President.* New York: Harcourt Brace Jovanovich, Publishers, 1992. Sophomoric humor.

550. Williams, Irving G. *The Rise of the Vice Presidency.* Washington: Public Affairs Press, 1956. Short, informative, and even handed description of Fillmore during the Compromise debates and his later presidential support for the bills.

551. Witcover, Jules. *Crapshoot: Rolling the Dice on the Vice Presidency.* New York: Crown Publishers, Inc., 1992. Mentions Fillmore presiding over the Senate Compromise debates. Regards him as an ineffective President.

F. SUCCESSION TO THE PRESIDENCY

552. "Clues to Mr. Truman's Future: 6 Who 'Inherited' Presidency." *U.S. News & World Report,* 16 July 1948, 11–13. Truman's succession was much like Fillmore's. They contended with a growing split in their party and congressional pressure to control policy.

553. Cunliffe, Marcus. *The Presidency.* 3d ed. Boston: Houghton Mifflin Company, 1987. More Presidential hopefuls should have tried for the Vice Presidency considering there were four successions in 40 years during the 19th century.

554. Ettinger, Amos A. "H. L. Bulwer on the Death of President Taylor, 1850." *American Historical Review* 32 (April 1927): 553–54. The British envoy in Washington informs Britain's Foreign Secretary about the little-known new President, Millard Fillmore.

555. Feerick, John D. *From Failing Hands: The Story of Presidential Succession.* New York: Fordham University Press, 1965. The succession was without incident and a credit to Fillmore. However he surprised everyone by accepting the resignations of Taylor's Cabinet. Good bibliography on the history of succession.

556. ———. *The Twenty-Fifth Amendment: Its Complete History and Earliest Applications.* New York: Fordham University Press, 1976. Points out that after Fillmore's succession the next in line for the presidency was a Senate Democrat.

557. Harding, Warren G., II, and J. Mark Stewart. *Mere Mortals: The Lives and Health Histories of American Presidents.* Worthingham, OH: Renaissance Publications, 1992. 61–65. Taylor's death was diagnosed as cholera morbus and treated with opium and brandy. The study reviews other possible causes of death. It includes a report on the 1992 exhumation of Taylor's body to learn if he was poisoned. It was determined he died of natural causes.

558. Levin, Peter R. *Seven By Chance: The Accidental Presidents.* New York: Farrar, Straus and Company, 1948. A disparaging assessment of Fillmore.

559. Lindop, Edmund. *Presidents By Accident.* New York: Franklin Watts, 1991. Reports the ease of succession and Fillmore's request of the Senate to fill its president pro tempore position to provide a successor should something happen to him.

560. Milkis, Sidney M., and Michael Nelson. *The American Presidency, Origins and Development, 1776–1990.* Washington: Congressional Quarterly Inc., 1990. Refers to the precedent of Tyler's succeeding Harrison, which allowed Fillmore an easy succession.

561. "Monthly Record of Current Events." *Harper's Monthly* 1 (August 1850): 416. Item on Fillmore's assumption of the Presidency and his Cabinet selections.

562. Plesur, Milton. "The Heartbeat in the White House." *American History Illustrated,* 5 April 1970, 38–48. Taylor's death is described as a typhoid-like fever.

563. Rosenberg, Charles E. *The Cholera Years: The United States in 1832, 1849, and 1866.* Chicago: University of Chicago Press, 1962. Part Two narrates the spread, tragedy, and social consequences of cholera from 1849 to 1854. However, the work does not mention Taylor's death by a cholera-related disease.

564. Sherman, W. T. *Memoirs of General W. T. Sherman.* New York: Charles L. Webster & Company, 1891. 2 vols. 1:113. Sherman saw Fillmore take the oath of office and remembered his splendid appearance. He reports the South feared the start of a new antislavery crusade.

565. Silva, Ruth C. *Presidential Succession.* Westport, CT: Greenwood Press, 1968. [1951]. Fillmore's uncontested confirmation followed the precedent set by Tyler's succession in 1841.

566. Smith, Grace. *High Crimes and Misdemeanors: The Impeachment and Trial of Andrew Johnson.* New York: William Morrow and Company, Inc., 1977. In 1865, Chief Justice Chase read the presidential oath to Johnson only after confirming the precedents of succession established by Tyler and Fillmore.

567. Stathis, Stephen W. "John Tyler's Presidential Succession: A Reappraisal." *Prologue* 8 (Winter 1976): 223–36. Although Tyler's succession was characterized by political manipulation, it set the precedent for Fillmore's easy confirmation.

568. Stegmaier, Mark J. "Zachary Taylor versus the South." *Civil War History* 33 (September 1987) 219–41. Investigates the contemporary allegations that Taylor's death was hastened by meetings with hostile southern congressmen as he lay sick in the White House.

569. "The Thirty-first Congress." *U.S. Magazine and Democratic Review* 28 (April 1851): 289–98. Claimed Fillmore's succession and the Compromise deflated the issues of the Free Soil movement and brought back old party issues.

Chapter 8

The Fillmore Administration

A. THE ADMINISTRATION

570. Bryant, William Cullen, and Sydney Howard Gay. *A Popular History of the United States*. New York: Charles Scribner's Sons, 1881. 4 vols. 4: 401–3. Fillmore's administration won credit for its conduct of national affairs. The exception was his enforcement of the Fugitive Slave Law in the North where many never forgave him.

571. "Fillmore, Millard." In *Dictionary of American Foreign Affairs*, ed. Stephen A. Flanders and Carl N. Flanders. New York: Macmillan Publishing Company, 1993. Standard survey of Fillmore's administration with a separate entry on the Treaty of Kanawaga with Japan.

572. *Gleason's Pictorial Drawing-Room Companion*, July 26, 1851. Illustration of Fillmore with comments on his competent handling of the Compromise and the current prosperity of the country.

573. Graebner, Norman A. "Zachary Taylor/Millard Fillmore." In *The Presidents, A Reference History*, ed. Henry F. Graff. New York: Charles Scribner's Sons, 1984. Survey essay and bibliography.

574. Grayson, Benson Lee. *The Unknown President: The Administration of President Millard Fillmore*. Washington, DC: University Press of America, Inc., 1981. Features the decency of Fillmore's foreign policy and insists he directed its administration.

575. Griffis, William Elliot. "Millard Fillmore's Forgotten Achievements." *Harper's Monthly* 122 (May 1911): 943–49. Bold effort to reacquaint the general public with Fillmore's appreciable efforts to save the Union and open trade with Japan.

576. Griswold, R. W. "Millard Fillmore, Thirteenth President of the United States." *Sartain's Union Magazine of Literature and Art,* September, 1850: 177–80. Biography of the new President.

577. Holt, Michael F. *The Rise and Fall of the American Whig Party: Jacksonian Politics and the Onset of the Civil War.* New York: Oxford University Press, 1999. Major study of the Whig party and mid-century politics with substantial attention given to Fillmore's administration. Includes his political efforts to suppress sectionalism by imposing the Compromise of 1850 while forwarding traditional Whig economic programs.

578. Irelan, John Robert. *The Republic; or, a History of the United States of America in the Administrations, from the Monarchic Colonial Days to the Present Time. Volume 13, History of the Life, Administration, and Times of Millard Fillmore, Thirteenth President of the United States.* Chicago: Fairbanks and Palmer Publishing Co., 1888. 18 vols. A little-known but very favorable biography and administrative history. Includes three presidential messages and other documents.

579. Lunt, George. *The Origins of the Late War, Traced from the Beginnings of the Constitution to the Revolt of the Southern States.* New York: D. Appleton and Company, 1866. This state's rights interpretation of American history praises Fillmore for his patriotic conservatism, honorable administration, and leaving office with prosperity at home and respect abroad.

580. MacDonald, William. *From Jefferson to Lincoln.* New York: Henry Holt and Company, 1913. His principles led him to uphold the laws rather than promote change through moral leadership.

581. McMaster, John Bach. *A History of the People of the United States: From the Revolution to the Civil War.* New York: D. Appleton and Company, 1885–1938. 8 vols. Volume 8 contains a fair assessment of Fillmore's actions during the Compromise, and his neutrality in foreign affairs.

582. "Millard Fillmore." *Whig Almanac, 1851.* New York: New York Tribune, 1851. 8. Concise biography of the new President who desired to "conciliate the warring sections and restore harmony to the Union."

583. Morris, Richard B., ed. *Encyclopedia of American History: Bicentennial Edition.* New York: Harper & Row, Publishers, 1976. 250–57. Chronological review of Fillmore's administration.

584. Nelson, Michael, ed. *Guide to the Presidency.* Washington, DC: Congressional Quarterly Inc., 1996. 2 vols. Volume Two has a brief biography of Fillmore and both volumes have references to different aspects of his Presidency.

585. Nevins, Allan. *Ordeal of the Union, Volume 1: Fruits of Manifest Destiny, 1847–1852.* New York: Charles Scribner's Sons, 1947. Fillmore is presented as a steady and principled Vice President and President.

586. [Parmelee, T. N.] "Recollections of an Old Stager." *Harper's New Monthly Magazine* 47 (September 1873): 586–90. Fillmore's administration was generally successful. He was an experienced public servant who surrounded himself with good men and stayed away from extreme courses.

587. Poore, Ben: Perley. *Perley's Reminiscences of Sixty Years in the National Metropolis.* Philadelphia: Hubbard Brothers, Publishers, 1886. 2 vols. 1: 376–424. Sympathetic toward Fillmore. Highlights the national policies and social life in Washington, DC while emphasizing Webster's obsession to be president.

588. Potter, David. *The Impending Crisis, 1848–1861,* completed and edited by Don E. Fehrenbacher. New York: Harper & Row Publishers, 1976. Standard survey of the period gives Fillmore credit for his adroit, though historically unrecognized, settling of the Compromise.

589. Rayback, Robert J. "Millard Fillmore: The Politics of Compromise." In *Six Presidents from the Empire State,* ed. Harry J. Sievers. Tarrytown: Sleepy Hollow Restorations, 1974. A compelling argument for Fillmore's political acumen and for his reasoned and responsible administration.

590. Rhodes, James Ford. *History of the United States from the Compromise of 1850.* New York: Harper & Brothers Publishers, 1896–1919. 7 vols. Volume One records the struggle to enforce the Fugitive Slave Law for which Fillmore's reputation was unjustly blighted. Fillmore was industrious, honest, and followed his Whig principles by executing the laws passed by Congress.

591. Ridpath, John Clark. *The New Complete History of the United States of America. Volume 11, Slavery and the Territories.* Washington, DC: Ridpath History Company, 1907. 15 vols. Credits Fillmore for reaching beyond the expected and ably executing measures for peace and prosperity.

592. ———. *A Popular History of the United States of America, from the Aboriginal Times to the Present Day.* New York: Nelson and Phillips, 1879. Signing the Compromise was fatal to Fillmore's career.

593. Sargent, Nathan. *Public Men and Events, From the Commencement of Mr. Monroe's Administration to the Close of Mr. Fillmore's Administration, in 1853.* Philadelphia: J. B. Lippincott & Co., 1875. 2 vols. 2: 371–98. Fillmore led the country with a steady hand, and left office to the plaudits of the people and press.

594. Schouler, James. *History of the United States of America under the Constitution.* New York: Dodd, Mead & Company, 1880–1897. 6 vols. Volume Five commends Fillmore as a wise and upright statesman, though under the sway of Clay and Webster. The Compromise was in keeping with his approach to governing by allaying excitement. It was sustained by the people.

595. Smith, Elbert B. *The Presidencies of Zachary Taylor & Millard Fillmore.* Lawrence: University Press of Kansas, 1988. Important reappraisal of Fillmore and his administration. He was a conscientious President who deserves a better reputation.

596. Smith, Theodore Clark. *Parties and Slavery, 1850–1859.* New York: Harper & Brothers Publishers, 1906. The Compromise of 1850 and economic prosperity brought a second "era of good feelings" during Fillmore's administration. His tenure was respectable but without prestige nor did he develop a personal following.

597. Spencer, J. A. *History of the United States: From the Earliest Period to the Administration of James Buchanan.* New York: Johnson, Fry, and Company, 1858. 3 vols. 3: 471–98. Fillmore maintained national honor with foreign powers while promoting harmony and attachment to the Union for which he was praised everywhere.

598. Thompson, Richard W. *Recollections of Sixteen Presidents.* Indianapolis: Bowen-Merrill Company, 1894. 2 vols. In Volume Two, Fillmore is praised for his actions during the Compromise, negotiations with Japan, and interdiction against Cuban filibusters.

599. Von Holst, Hermann E. *Constitutional History of the United States.* Chicago: Callaghan and Company, 1876–92. 8 vols. Volume Three portrays Fillmore as a little-known but conscientious politician who laid aside his support for the Wilmot Proviso to follow a conservative course during the Compromise and as President.

600. Willard, Emma. *History of the United States, or Republic of America.* New York: A. S. Barnes & Co., 1852. The education reformer believed Fillmore was intelligent, moral, and physically fit for the presidency. The Compromise quieted the sectional storm while many Northern men looked to a modification of the Fugitive Slave Law to settle any lingering animosity.

601. Young, Andrew W. *The American Statesman: A Political History.* New York: Derby & Jackson, 1856. A popular mid-century work describes Fillmore's successful measures against Texas encroachment into New Mexico and his signing of the Compromise bills.

B. GENERAL WORKS

602. Beardsley, Levi. *Reminiscences, Personal and Other Incidents; Early Settlements of Otsego County, etc.* New York: Charles Vinten, 1852. New York Democrat applauded Fillmore's enforcement of the Compromise laws.

603. Berwanger, Eugene H. *The Frontier Against Slavery: Western Anti-Negro Prejudice and the Slavery Extension Controversy.* Urbana: University of Illinois Press, 1967. Analysis of statutes and social prejudice excluding slaves and free African Americans. Also mentions debates on excluding the new Chinese immigrants in California.

604. Billington, Ray Allen. *The Far Western Frontier: 1830–1860.* New York: Harper & Row, Publishers, 1956. Surveys western settlement with chapters on the Mormons and the California gold rush.

605. Brock, William R. *Parties and Political Conscience: American Dilemmas, 1840–1856.* Millwood, NY: KTO Press, 1979. Fillmore showed political sense during the Compromise by joining Northern conservatives and winning Southern support. However, the Compromise proved unsuccessful because it accepted sectionalism without debating the future of slavery.

606. Brown, Thomas J., ed. *American Eras: Civil War and Reconstruction, 1850–1877.* Detroit: Gale Research, 1997. References to Fillmore's role in the Compromise and the Fugitive Slave Law.

607. Calhoun, Richard James. "Literary Criticism in Southern Periodicals During the American Renaissance." *E S Q: Journal of the American Renaissance* 55 (Spring 1969): 76–82. Southern literary critics protected their region from Northern antislavery propaganda.

608. Chase, Henry, and C. H. Sandborn. *The North and the South: Being a Statistical View of the Condition of the Free and Slave States.* Westport, CT: Negro Universities Press, 1970 [1857]. Comparison of sections using the 1850 Census as compiled by J. D. B. De Bow.

609. Christian, Charles M. *Black Saga: The African American Experience.* Boston: Houghton Mifflin Company, 1995. Reference work chronicles the African-American perspective on their free and slave experiences in the 1850s.

610. Clark, Norman H. "Prohibition and Temperance." In *Encyclopedia of American Political History: Studies of the Principal Movements and Ideas,* ed. Jack P. Greene. New York: Charles Scribner's Sons, 1984. 3 vols. 3: 1005–17. The Maine Law of 1851 to suppress drinking inspired temperance workers into politics. However, Whigs could not capitalize on its energy because their party was dissolving over slavery.

611. Cooper, William J., Jr. *The South and the Politics of Slavery, 1828–1856.* Baton Rouge: Louisiana State University Press, 1978. Southern Whigs praised President Fillmore's performance.

612. Craven, Avery O. *Civil War in the Making, 1815–1860.* Baton Rouge: Louisiana State University Press, 1959. The rational and democratic process of the 1850 Compromise was overwhelmed by sectional hatred following the Kansas-Nebraska Act.

613. ———. *The Growth of Southern Nationalism, 1848–1861.* Baton Rouge: Louisiana State Press, 1953. Examines the evolution of sectionalist attitudes toward national events.

614. Davis, David Brion. *Antebellum American Culture: An Interpretive Anthology.* University Park: Pennsylvania State University Press, 1979. Numerous selections with extensive analytic introductions on the ideals and reality of antebellum life.

615. ———. *The Slave Power Conspiracy and the Paranoid Style.* Baton Rouge: Louisiana State University Press, 1969. The 1850s transmuted the sectional rhetoric of the North and South into palpable, mutually menacing forces.

616. Donald, David Herbert. *Liberty and Union: The Crisis of Popular Government, 1830–1890.* Boston: Little, Brown and Company, 1978. Sympathetic toward Fillmore's support for the Compromise but the transient majorities for each of the bills demonstrated its weakness.

617. DuBois, Ellen Carol. *Feminism and Suffrage: The Emergence of an Independent Women's Movement in America, 1848–1869.* Ithaca: Cornell University Press, 1978. Describes feminism's inseparable development with the antislavery movement and the use of abolitionist strategies to make their own appeal for emancipation.

618. Durden, Robert F. *The Self-Inflicted Wound: Southern Politics in the Nineteenth Century.* Lexington: University Press of Kentucky, 1985. Follows the South's transition from nationalism to aggrieved sectionalism.

618a. Engerman, Stanley L., and Robert E. Gallman. *The Cambridge Economic History of the United States.* Cambridge: Cambridge University Press, 1996–2000. 3 vols. Volume Two covers the nation's rapid economic expansion between 1789 and 1914.

619. Evans, Sara. *Born for Liberty: A History of Woman in America.* New York: Free Press, 1989. Chapter Five is a broad review of women in mid-nineteenth-century America and the women's rights movement.

620. Faust, Drew Gilpin. "The Peculiar South Revisited, White Society, Culture, and Politics in the Antebellum Period, 1800–1860." In *Interpreting Southern History: Historiographical Essays in Honor of Sanford W. Higginbotham,* ed. John B. Boles and Evelyn Thomas Nolen. Baton Rouge: Louisiana State University Press, 1987. Review of studies on the antebellum South.

621. ———. *A Sacred Circle: The Dilemma of the Intellectual in the Old South, 1840–1860.* Baltimore: Johns Hopkins University Press, 1977. History of an informal association of pro-slavery, secessionist writers who countered Northern antislavery arguments while criticizing Southern unionists.

622. Filler, Louis. *The Crusade Against Slavery, 1830–1860.* New York: Harper & Row, Publishers, 1960. Chapter Nine describes the consequences of the Compromise of 1850 for abolitionists, anti-slavery politicians, and party politics.

623. Flexner, Eleanor. *Century of Struggle: The Woman's Rights Movement in the United States.* New York: Athenaeum, 1971 [1959]. Women's rights conventions in the early 1850s brought the movement and its leaders into national prominence.

624. Floan, Howard R. *The South in Northern Eyes, 1831 to 1861.* Austin: University of Texas Press, 1958. Critical of New England writers who stereotyped all Southerners as brutal slaveholders. Finds New York writers more sympathetic to variations in Southern geography and social stratification.

625. Foner, Philip S. *Business & Slavery: The New York Merchants & the Irrepressible Conflict.* Chapel Hill: University of North Carolina Press, 1941. Many merchants publicly supported the Compromise and Fillmore in order to stabilize commerce. Extensive use of the published Fillmore papers.

626. Forgie, George B. *Patricide in the House Divided: A Psychological Interpretation of Lincoln and His Age.* New York: W. W. Norton & Company, 1979. Fillmore's political generation measured itself against the legacy of the Founding Fathers.

627. Franklin, John Hope. *From Slavery to Freedom: A History of Negro America.* New York: Alfred A. Knopf, 1967. Chapters 14 and 15 review the African-American experience in the 1850s and their resistance to laws of exclusion and humiliation.

628. Freehling, William W. *The Road to Disunion, Volume 1: Secessionists at Bay, 1776–1854.* New York: Oxford University Press, 1990. Excellent political and social study of Southern regional differences toward slavery, the expansion of slavery, manumission, and secession.

629. Gale, Robert L. *A Cultural Encyclopedia of the 1850s in America.* Westport, CT: Greenwood Press, 1993. Valuable resource for biographies of politicians, writers, and other prominent men and women. It also describes political events, social movements, published works, the visual arts, and influential ideas. Includes chronology, bibliography, and indexes.

630. Gara, Larry. "Antislavery Congressmen, 1848–1856: Their Contributions to the Debate Between Sections." *Civil War History* 32 (September 1986): 197–207. They gave national attention and respectability to moderate abolitionism.

631. Ginzberg, Lori D. " 'Moral Suasion Is Moral Balderdash': Women, Politics, and Social Activism in the 1850s." *Journal of American History* 73 (December 1986): 601–22. The decade saw more women working to acquire the vote, pass reform legislation, and establish urban institutions for humanitarian reforms.

632. Heale, M. J. The *Presidential Quest: Candidates and Images in American Political Culture, 1787–1852.* New York: Longman Inc., 1982. Fillmore was caught in two Whig contradictions: personal leadership vs. a restrained presidency, and party principles vs. the era's anti-partyism.

633. Holt, Michael F. *The Political Crisis of the 1850s.* New York: John Wiley & Sons Inc., 1978. Hoping to keep a united national party, Fillmore used patronage and persuasion to impose the Compromise on the Whig party.

634. Howe, Daniel Walker. *Making the American Self: Jonathan Edwards to Abraham Lincoln.* Cambridge: Harvard University Press, 1997. Describes an American moral philosophy fundamental to mid-century discussions on politics, reform movements, and religion. Outlines contemporary self definitions of Democrat and Whig.

635. Isenberg, Nancy. *Sex and Citizenship in Antebellum America.* Chapel Hill: University of North Carolina Press, 1998. Chapter Five reviews women's civic marginality by analyzing their feminist arguments on national issues and civil law.

636. Johnson, Paul. *A History of the American People.* New York: Harper Collins Publishers, 1997. Mistakenly refers to Taylor and Fillmore as Democrats and inexplicably states Fillmore was an "experienced New York Tweed machine-man."

637. Krammer, Aaron. *The Prophetic Tradition in American Poetry, 1835–1900.* Rutherford: Fairleigh Dickinson University Press, 1968. Major poets condemned the Fugitive Slave Law through prose.

638. Litwack, Leon F. *North of Slavery: The Negro in the Free States, 1790–1860.* Chicago: University of Chicago Press, 1961. Describes pervasive statutory and social prejudice against African Americans. Mentions Fillmore's endorsement of the American Colonization Society because he believed that African Americans would never secure equal rights in the United States.

639. McCormick, Richard P. "The Jacksonian Strategy." *Journal of the Early Republic* 10 (Spring 1990): 1–17. Whigs in the 1850s were adopting the Jacksonian strategy of depoliticizing the slavery issue to sustain the Union.

640. McPherson, James M. *Battle Cry of Freedom: The Civil War Era.* New York: Oxford University Press, 1988. Describes Fillmore as an active participant in the passage of the Compromise of 1850. The early chapters are an informative introduction to the 1850s.

641. Meinig, D. W. *The Shaping of America: A Geographical Perspective on 500 Years of History: Volume 3, Transcontinental America, 1850–1915.* New Haven: Yale University Press, 1998. Describes the new territorial and Californian articulation with continental America. Maps.

642. Merk, Frederick. *History of the Westward Movement.* New York: Alfred A. Knopf, 1978. Concludes that the sectional crisis and Compromise of 1850 were the result of overindulgence in territorial expansion.

643. Merriam, Louise A., and James W. Oberly. *United States History: A Bibliography of the New Writing on American History.* Manchester, NY: Manchester University Press, 1995. Sections 5 and 6 annotate political and social sources covering the 1850s published after 1980.

644. Miller, Randall M. "Slavery." In *Encyclopedia of African-American Culture and History,* ed. Jack Salzman, Davis Lionel Smith, and Cornel West. New York: Simon & Schuster Macmillan, 1996. 5 vols. 5: 2454–69. Good introduction to a large subject. The 1850s saw the South marketing a Christian, civilized image of slavery, while disapproving the North's brutal wage slavery.

644a. Minicucci, Stephen D. "Finding the 'cement of interest': Internal Improvements and American Nation-Building, 1790–1860." Ph.D. diss., Massachusetts Institute of Technology, 1998. Evidence supports success in the north for regional economic planning but it never occurred within the south or between the north and south.

645. Nichols, Roy F. *A Historian's Progress.* New York: Alfred A. Knopf, 1968. Reviews his published work on politics in the 1850s and reveals his genealogical relationship to Fillmore.

646. O'Connor, Thomas H. *The Disunited States: The Era of Civil War and Reconstruction.* 2d ed. New York: Harper & Row Publishers, 1978. Highlights the economic interests promoting sectional peace through compromise.

647. ———. *Lords of the Loom: The Cotton Whigs and the Coming of the Civil War.* New York: Charles Scribner's Sons, 1968. Massachusetts industrialists warmed to Fillmore as they believed the Compromise made their commerce safe from secession.

648. Pattee, Fred Lewis. *The Feminine Fifties.* New York: D. Appleton-Century Company, 1940. Entertaining study of the decade's literature. It highlights the many popular female writers and the influence of female readers on writers.

649. Pike, James S. *First Blows of the Civil War: The Ten Years of Preliminary Conflict in the United States from 1850 to 1860.* New York: American News Company, 1879. Reprints articles belittling Fillmore and Webster.

650. *The Pro-Slavery Argument; as Maintained by the Most Distinguished Writers of the Southern States.* New York: Negro Universities Press, 1968 [1852]. Important defense of Southern slavery by five writers with secessionist sentiments.

651. Ransom, Roger L. *Conflict and Compromise: The Political Economy of Slavery, Emancipation, and the American Civil War.* New York: Cambridge University Press, 1989. Despite averting a constitutional crisis, Fillmore was vilified for enforcing the Compromise.

652. Reid, Brian Holden. *The Origins of the American Civil War.* New York: Longman, 1996. Considers the Compromise of 1850 a truce between politicians rather than an armistice between fervid sectional masses.

653. Reynolds, David S. *Beneath the American Renaissance: The Subversive Imagination in the Age of Emerson and Melville.* Cambridge: Harvard University Press, 1988. Describes the influences of reform materials and popular culture on the major literary works of the 1850s.

654. Rose, Anne C. *Voices of the Marketplace: American Thought and Culture, 1830–1860.* New York: Twayne Publishers, 1995. Introduction to the public interplay of religion, democracy, the marketplace, and regionalism in the 1850s. Informative bibliographic essay.

655. Ryan, Barbara. *The Women's Movement: References and Resources.* New York: G. K. Hall & Co., 1996. Annotations on recent scholarship.

656. Saum, Lewis. *The Popular Mood of Pre–Civil War America.* Westport, CT: Greenwood Press, 1980. Believes ordinary people were less enthusiastic about politics than historians claim.

657. Sewell, Richard H. *A House Divided: Sectionalism and Civil War, 1848–1865.* Baltimore: Johns Hopkins University Press, 1988. Points to slavery as the root cause of sectional discord. Bibliographic essay.

658. Sherman, Joan R. *African-American Poetry of the Nineteenth Century.* Urbana: University of Illinois Press, 1992. Contains many antislavery poems. Bibliography on contemporary African-American literature.

659. Shi, David E. *Facing Facts: Realism in American Thought and Culture, 1850–1920.* New York: Oxford University Press, 1995. Part One is an introduction to the changing culture influencing the 1850s.

660. Silbey, Joel H. *The American Political Nation, 1838–1893.* Stanford: Stanford University Press, 1991. Reviews the partisan organizations, elections, and core assumptions of the Democratic, Whig, and Republican parties. Reviews recent interpretations of antebellum politics and electoral scholarship.

661. ———. *The Transformation of American Politics, 1840–1860.* Englewood Cliffs, NJ: Prentice-Hall, Inc., 1967. Silbey's interpretive essay discusses 35 contemporary documents on slavery extension, sectional conflict, and political parties.

662. Smith, Page. *The Nation Comes of Age: A People's History of the Ante-Bellum Years.* New York: McGraw-Hill Book Company, 1981. Saga of the middle period with standard references on Fillmore.

663. Spiller, Robert E., et al. *Literary History of the United States.* New York: Macmillan Company, 1948. 3 vols. Volume One contains sections on the published debate over slavery. Volume Three is an annotated bibliography on mid-nineteenth-century literature and the slavery debate.

664. Stanton, Elizabeth Cady, Susan B. Anthony, and Matilda Joselyn Gage. *History of Woman Suffrage*. New York: Source Book, 1970 [1881–1902]. 4 vols. Volume One describes the 1848 Seneca Falls Women's Rights Conference plus many other conventions, speeches, and letters of support in the early 1850s.

665. Sydnor, Charles S. *The Development of Southern Sectionalism, 1819–1848.* Baton Rouge: Louisiana State University Press, 1948. Examines Southern patriotism and its later perception of itself as a beleaguered minority in the nation.

666. Taylor, William R. *Cavalier & Yankee: The Old South and American National Character.* New York: Harper Torchbooks, 1969 [1957]. This sociological review of Southern fiction highlights the benign portrayal of slavery and the arguments against Northern antislavery ideas.

667. Tyler, Alice Felt. *Freedom's Ferment: Phases of American Social History from the Colonial Period to the Outbreak of the Civil War.* New York: Harper & Row Publishers, 1962 [1944]. Still an informative survey on reform movements during the middle period.

668. Unruh, John D., Jr. *The Plains Across: The Overland Emigrants and the Trans-Mississippi West, 1840–1860.* Urbana: University of Illinois Press, 1979. Recounts the westward movement of a quarter million people and their effect on the country and government. Extensive bibliography with historiographic survey.

668a. Wells, Jonathan Daniel. "The Origins of the Southern Middle Class: Literature, Politics, and Economy, 1820–1880." Ph.D. diss., The University of Michigan, 1998. Though small in number, they pushed economic development in every southern state. They voiced their agenda through the Whig party but were never persuaded to abandon slavery.

669. Wiecek, William M. " 'The Blessings of Liberty': Slavery in the American Constitutional Order." In *Slavery and Its Consequences: The Constitution, Equality, and Race,* ed. Robert A. Goldwin and Art Kaufman. Washington, DC: American Enterprise Institute for Public Policy Research, 1988. Proposes that a majority of Americans felt slavery was regrettable but necessary and constitutional.

669a. Williams, George W. *History of the Negro Race in America from 1619 to 1880: Negroes as Slaves, as Soldiers, and as Citizens.* New York: G. P. Putnam's Sons, 1883. 2 vols. Classic work on African American contributions and oppression in America along with their visions and programs to make a better North America and Africa.

670. Wyatt-Brown, Bertram. "Slavery, Sectionalism, and Secession." In *Encyclopedia of American Political History: Studies of the Principal Movements and Ideas,*

ed. Jack P. Greene. New York: Charles Scribner's Sons, 1984. 3 vols. 3: 1160–86. Review of slavery and its consequences. Fillmore's signing of the Compromise yoked the Whig party to laws his colleagues could not endorse. The breakup of the Whig party followed.

671. Yellin, Jean Fagin. *Woman & Sisters: The Antislavery Feminists in American Culture.* New Haven: Yale University Press, 1989. Imaginative blend of antislavery iconography and literature that charts the rise of public feminism. Informative bibliography on feminist and abolitionist literature.

C. COMPROMISE OF 1850

1. General Works

672. Albreckt, Frank M. "Georgia Platform." In *The Encyclopedia of Southern History,* ed. David C. Roller and Robert W. Twyman. Baton Rouge: Louisiana State University Press, 1979. 540–41. The Georgia legislature's support for the Compromise ended effective Southern opposition.

673. Alexander, Thomas B. *Sectional Stress and Party Strength: A Study of Roll-Call Voting Patterns in the United States House of Representatives, 1836–1860.* Nashville: Vanderbilt University Press, 1967. The sectional debates and votes of 1850 previewed patterns in the 1860 Presidential election.

674. Ames, Herman V., ed. *State Documents on Federal Relations: The States and the United States.* No. 6, *Slavery and the Union, 1845–1861.* Philadelphia: University of Pennsylvania, 1906. A guide to state and sectional reaction to the Wilmot Proviso and the Compromise of 1850.

675. Barnwell, John D. "Compromise of 1850." In *Dictionary of Afro-American Slavery,* ed. Randall M. Miller and John David Smith. Westport, CT: Greenwood Press, 1988. 135. Its failure was foreshadowed by the maneuvers necessary to enact it.

676. Clark, John G. "The Compromise of 1850." In *Great Events from History: American Series,* ed. Frank N. Magill. Englewood Cliffs, NJ: Salem Press Incorporated, 1975. 3 vols. 2: 854–58. Reviews the political conflict over the Mexican land cession and slavery extension.

677. "Compromise of 1850." In *The African American Encyclopedia,* ed. Michael W. Williams. New York: Marshall Cavendish, 1993. 5 vols. 2: 369.

678. "Compromise of 1850." In *Documents of American History,* ed. Henry Steele Commager. New York: Appleton-Century-Crofts, Inc., 1958. Text of the Compromise with a short introduction.

679. "Congress in 1850." *Whig Almanac, 1851.* New York: New York Tribune, 1851. 10–11. Reviews the Compromise and the reception of Fillmore's first Annual Message.

680. Finkelman, Paul. "Compromise of 1850." In *Encyclopedia of African-American Culture and History,* ed. Jack Salzman, Davis Lionel Smith, and Cornel West. New York: Simon & Schuster Macmillan, 1996. 5 vols. 2: 628. The compromise was a failure. It exacerbated sectional tension and showed the inability of the political process to solve the slavery issue.

681. Gardner, John Cooper. "Winning the Lower South to the Compromise of 1850." Ph.D. diss., Louisiana State University and Agricultural and Mechanical College, 1974. 2 vols. Southern nationalists convinced the electorate that the Compromise did not threaten white supremacy.

682. Hamilton, Holman. " 'The Cave of the Winds' and the Compromise of 1850." *Journal of Southern History* 23 (August 1957): 331–53. Narrates the emotional and political trials of the 31st Congress.

683. ———. "Compromise of 1850." In *The Encyclopedia of Southern History,* ed. David C. Roller and Robert W. Twyman. Baton Rouge: Louisiana State University Press, 1979. 264–65. Informative summary.

684. ———. "Democratic Senate Leadership and the Compromise of 1850." *Mississippi Valley Historical Review* 41 (December 1954): 403–18. The votes of Democratic senators were more important to the passage of the Compromise than the personalities of Clay and Webster.

685. ———. *Prologue to Conflict: The Crisis and Compromise of 1850.* New York: W. W. Norton & Company, 1966. The standard work on the Compromise with voting data and bibliography.

686. Hart, Albert Bushnell. "Compromise of 1850." In *Cyclopedia of American Government,* ed. Andrew C. McLaughlin and Albert Bushnell Hart. New York: Peter Smith, 1930 [1914]. 3 vols. 1: 366–67. Summary of territorial controversies involved.

687. Hart, Charles Desmond. " 'The National Limits of Slavery Expansion': The Mexican Territories as a Test Case." *Mid-America* 52 (April 1970): 119–31. Presents the congressional arguments and votes for and against slavery expansion between 1846 and 1850.

688. "Is Southern Civilization Worth Preserving?" *Southern Quarterly Review* 3 (January 1851): 189–225. The government is antislavery and the Compromise is

treacherous toward the South. Fillmore would never have threatened the use of federal troops against Northern states as he did against Texas.

689. Knupfer, Peter B. *The Union As It Is: Constitutional Unionism and Sectional Compromise, 1787–1861.* Chapel Hill: University of North Carolina Press, 1991. Fillmore wanted the Compromise to mend the slavery controversy in the Whig party so it could remain a national party while subduing sectional discontent.

690. Lamar, Howard Roberts. *The Far Southwest, 1846–1912: A Territorial History.* New Haven: Yale University Press, 1966. Fillmore was considered a hero by residents in the new Utah and New Mexico territories.

690a. Leonard, Glen M. "Southwestern Boundaries and the Principles of Statemaking." *Western Historical Quarterly* 8 (January 1977): 39–53. Historical background on the boundaries set by the Compromise of 1850.

691. McLaughlin, Andrew C. *A Constitutional History of the United States.* New York: D. Appleton-Century Company, 1935. Reviews the constitutional and political aspects of the Compromise.

692. Mendelson, Wallace. "Dred Scott's Case-Reconsidered." *Minnesota Law Review* 38 (December 1952): 16–28. In reality, the Compromise left the question of the extension of slavery to federally appointed judges in the territories and to the Supreme Court.

693. Norton, L. Wesley. "The Religious Press and the Compromise of 1850: A Study of the Relationship of the Methodist, Baptist, and Presbyterian Press to the Slavery Controversy, 1846–1851." Ph.D. diss., University of Illinois, 1959. Southern religious editors supported the Compromise. Their Northern counterparts denounced the Fugitive Slave Law but rarely counseled overt resistance and generally settled for passive obedience.

694. Phillips, Ulrich Bonnell. *The Course of the South to Secession.* New York: D. Appleton-Century Company, 1939. The compromise gave the South a gesture of hope that sectional arguments would cease.

695. "Policy of the Nation in Regard to Slavery and Its Extension.*"American Whig Review* 27 (March 1850): 219–29. Reviews the arguments against the extension of slavery and advises no congressional action.

696. Quaife, Milo Milton. *The Doctrine of Non-Intervention with Slavery in the Territories.* Chicago: Mac C. Chamberlin Co., 1910. The territorial acts in the Compromise clearly establish that Congress refrained from making a decision on slavery in the territories.

697. Rozwenc, Edwin C., ed. *The Compromise of 1850: Problems in American Civilization.* Boston: D. C. Heath and Company, 1957. Collection of contemporary pronouncements and historical assessments on the Compromise.

698. Russell, Robert R. "The Issues in the Congressional Struggle over the Kansas-Nebraska Bill, 1854." *Journal of Southern History* 39 (May 1963): 187–210. The territorial measures in the Compromise of 1850 influenced the Kansas-Nebraska Bill.

699. ———— . "What Was the Compromise of 1850?" *Journal of Southern History* 22 (August 1956): 292–309. Examines the slavery provisions in the acts organizing the New Mexico and Utah territories.

700. Schouler, James. "Whig Party." In *Cyclopedia of American Government,* ed. Andrew C. McLaughlin and Albert Bushnell Hart. New York: Peter Smith, 1930 [1914]. 3 vols. 3: 80–85. Fillmore was a sound, honest, principled Whig who believed in the Compromise which proved to be a glorious illusion.

701. Shryock, Richard Harrison. *Georgia and the Union in 1850.* Durham: Duke University Press, 1926. Georgia Whigs and Unionist politicians played an important role in the passage and acceptance of the Compromise.

702. Wilson, Major L. *Space, Time and Freedom: The Quest for Nationality and the Irrepressible Conflict, 1815–1861.* Westport, CT: Greenwood Press, 1974. Chapter Seven portrays Webster and Fillmore as men respecting the Union's progress over time through public debate and compromise.

2. California

703. Bancroft, Hubert Howe. *Annals of the California Gold Rush Era: Being that Part of the Author's Series on the History of California Concerning the Gold Discovery Period of 1848–1859.* New York: Bancroft Company, 188?. Senator Gwin screened Fillmore's appointments to the 1851 Land Commission determining the validity of Spanish and Mexican land claims.

704. Berwanger, Eugene H. "Western Prejudice and the Extension of Slavery." *Civil War History* 12 (September 1966): 197–212. Despite statutes prohibiting slavery, it was accepted in California because white settlers did not demand enforcement. Records the anti-Negro bias in state antislavery movements.

705. "California in 1851." *Whig Almanac, 1852.* New York: New York Tribune, 1852. 19. Describes the rapid increase in state population, mining, and crime.

706. Ellison, Joseph. "The Mineral Land Question in California, 1848–1866." In *The Public Lands, Studies in the History of the Public Domain,* ed. Vernon Caratensen. Madison: University of Wisconsin Press, 1968. Fillmore laid aside a plan to sell small tracts of federal land in the goldfields because of state opposition.

707. Finkelman, Paul. "The Law of Slavery and Freedom in California, 1848–1860." *California Western Law Review* 17 (1981): 437–64. The buying and selling of slaves continued in California throughout most of the 1850s. In 1852, the legislature passed a law approving the federal Fugitive Slave Law and ordered local officials to help enforce it.

708. Gates, Paul W. "The California Land Act of 1851." *California Historical Quarterly* 50 (December 1971): 395–430. Fillmore appointed a commission to unravel the confusion of title claims.

709. Gibson, Patricia. "California and the Compromise of 1850." *Journal of the West* 8 (October 1969): 578–91. Introduction to California's application and admittance as a state.

710. Lapp, Rudolph M. *Blacks in Gold Rush California.* New Haven: Yale University Press, 1977. California's own 1852 Fugitive Slave Law allowed the rendition of fugitives. However, urban African American resistance saved many men and women from abduction. Abolitionists repealed the law in 1855.

711. Paul, Rodman W. "The Origins of the Chinese Issue in California." *Mississippi Valley Historical Review* 25 (September 1938): 181–96. After 1849 the Chinese were a growing, visible minority willing to work for low wages. Debates on their exclusion or use as indentured labor coincided with debates on excluding slavery and free African Americans.

712. Pitt, Leonard. *The Decline of the Californios: A Social History of the Spanish Speaking Californians, 1848–1890.* Berkeley: University of California Press, 1966. Statehood and the rearrangement of land claims to accommodate new settlers proved detrimental to the status of native Californians.

713. Saxton, Alexander. *The Indispensable Enemy: Labor and the Anti-Chinese Movement in California.* Berkeley: University of California Press, 1971. Chinese exclusion codes duplicated actions already taken against African Americans, which were modeled on Black Codes used in the midwestern states.

714. Stephenson, Nathaniel Wright. "California and the Compromise of 1850." *Pacific Historical Review* 4 (June 1935): 114–22. When denied slavery in southern California, the South renewed its activities to expand slavery into the Caribbean and South America.

715. Taylor, Bayard. *Eldorado, or, Adventures in the Path of Empire.* New York: George P. Putnam, 1850. 2 vols. Widely read account of his journey from New York to California and back. Its record of the gold rush and the immediate need for federal control in the region helped the acceptance of statehood. Volume Two includes an official report on California by T. Butler King to Secretary of State Clayton.

716. Thrope, Francis Newton. *A Constitutional History of the American People, 1776–1859.* New York: Harper & Brothers Publication, 1898. 2 vols. Volume Two makes extensive use of California's debate over the exclusion of free African Americans and slaves to maintain a "white man's government."

717. ———— , comp. *The Federal and State Constitutions, Colonial Charters, and Other Organic Laws of the States, Territories, and Colonies.* Buffalo: William S. Hein & Co., Inc., 1993 [1909]. 7 vols. 1: 377–89, Treaty of Guadalupe Hidalgo where Mexico ceded California; 1: 391–407, Constitution of California, 1849; 1: 390, Act for Admission of California, 1850.

718. Woolsey, Ronald C. "A Southern Dilemma: Slavery Expansion and the California Statehood Issue in 1850—A Reconsideration." *Southern California Quarterly* 65 (Summer 1983): 123–44. The southern split vote on the admittance of California revealed the variety and fragmented nature of the pro-slavery defense.

3. Texas-New Mexico Border Dispute

719. A. J. "The Rights of the Slave States." *Southern Quarterly Review* 3 (January 1851): 101–45. Attacks Fillmore's discreditable "war message" to Texas and the government's dismemberment of Texas in the Compromise of 1850.

720. Binkley, William C. *The Expansionist Movement in Texas, 1836–1850.* New York: Da Capo Press, 1970 [1925]. Fillmore portrayed the boundary dispute as a crisis requiring Congress to act on the Compromise.

721. ———— . "The Question of Texan Jurisdiction in New Mexico Under the United States, 1848–1850." *Southwestern Historical Quarterly* 26 (July 1920): 1–38. Describes Texas-New Mexico tensions before and during the Compromise.

722. Campbell, Randolph B. "Antebellum Texas: From Union to Disunion, 1846–1861." In *A Guide to the History of Texas,* ed. Light Townsend Cummins and Alvin R. Bailey, Jr. Westport, CT: Greenwood Press, 1988. Bibliographic essay covering Texas, New Mexico, Indians, and Mexico.

723. Fehrenback, T. R. *Lone Star: A History of Texas and the Texans.* New York: Macmillan Company, 1968. Fillmore was prepared to use force against Texas to protect New Mexico's border claims.

724. Hamilton, Holman. "Texas Bonds and Northern Profits: A Study in Compromise, Investment, and Lobby Influence." *Mississippi Valley Historical Review* 43 (March 1957): 579–94. Identifies lobbyists who promoted federal payments to cover the Texas bond debt as part of the Compromise.

725. "Monthly Record of Current Events." *Harper's Monthly* 1 (September 1850): 562. Contains Fillmore's tough message on the Texas-New Mexico boundary dispute.

726. Morris, Richard B., ed. *Great Presidential Decisions: State Papers that Changed the Course of History.* New York: J. B. Lippincott Company, 1967. Reprints Fillmore's August 6, 1850, special message to Congress. His tough stance against Texas was critical to the passage of the Compromise bills.

727. Neighbours, Kenneth F. "The Taylor-Neighbors Struggle over the Upper Rio Grande Region of Texas in 1850." *Southwestern Historical Quarterly* 61 (April 1958): 431–63. Texas employed Neighbors to organize eastern New Mexico into its own western counties, but the Compromise denied them to Texas.

728. Ramsdell, Charles William. "Bell, Peter Hansborough." *DAB* (1955), 1. pt. 2: 160–61. Texas Governor who threatened to use force to secure the Texas land claim in New Mexico.

729. Stegmaier, Mark J. *Texas, New Mexico, and the Compromise of 1850: Boundary Dispute & Sectional Crisis.* Kent, OH: Kent State University Press, 1996. Fundamental study on the border conflict and its relation to the Compromise. Fillmore receives high marks for thwarting the boundary war and assisting the passage of the Compromise. The study relies on a close reading of regional materials, the *Congressional Record*, and manuscript sources. Includes maps and bibliography.

730. Taylor, Morris F. "Spruce McCoy Baird: From Texas Agent to New Mexico Official, 1848–1860." *New Mexico Historical Review* 53 (January 1978): 39–58.

4. New Mexico Territory

730a. Carson, Wm. G. B. "William Carr Lane, Diary." *New Mexico Historical Review* 39 (July 1964): 181–234. Fillmore appointed Lane territorial governor of New Mexico in July 1852.

731. Ganaway, Loomis Morton. *New Mexico and the Sectional Controversy 1846–1861.* Philadelphia: Porcupine Press, 1976 [1944]. Fillmore supported New Mexico boundaries but received no local support for his Southern federal appointees to the territory.

732. Larson, Robert W. *New Mexico's Quest for Statehood, 1848–1912.* Albuquerque: University of New Mexico Press, 1968. Fillmore delayed statehood and appointed its first two governors.

733. Thorpe, Francis Newton, comp. *The Federal and State Constitutions, Colonial Charters, and Other Organic Laws of the States, Territories, and Colonies.* Buffalo: William S. Hein & Co., Inc., 1993 [1909]. 7 vols. 5: 2615–22. The act to establish the Territorial Government of New Mexico, 1850.

5. Utah Territory

734. Arrington, Leonard J. *Brigham Young, American Moses.* New York: Alfred A. Knopf, 1985. Mormon leader appointed by Fillmore as first territorial governor of Utah.

735. Bancroft, Hubert Howe. *History of Utah: 1540–1887.* San Francisco: History Company, Publishers, 1890. Brigham Young chose the site for the capital of Utah Territory and named it Fillmore in honor of the President. Millard County also was named for the President.

736. Billington, Ray A. "Best Prepared Pioneers in the West." *American Heritage,* October 1956: 20–25, 116–17. Illustrated article on the Mormon migration and the establishment of Utah Territory.

736a. Crane, Angus E. "Millard Fillmore and the Mormons." *Journal of the West* 34 (January 1995): 70–76. Fillmore refused to oust Brigham Young as Utah territorial governor insuring self-government for Mormons.

737. Furniss, Norman F. *The Mormon Conflict, 1850–1859.* New Haven: Yale University Press, 1960. Fillmore gave the Mormons a respite from hostility by recalling his first antagonistic federal judges and appointing more sympathetic men.

738. Hinton, Wayne K. "Millard Fillmore, Utah's Friend in the White House." *Utah Historical Quarterly* 48 (1980): 112–28. Residents were grateful Fillmore signed Utah into a territory.

738a. Leonard, Glen M. "The Mormon Boundary Question in the 1849–50 Statehood Debates." *Journal of Mormon History* 18 (1992): 114–36. Utah territorial boundaries were set by the Compromise of 1850.

739. Lythgoe, Dennis L. "Negro Slavery in Utah." *Utah Historical Quarterly* 39 (Winter 1971): 40–54. Legal slavery existed after the Compromise. Slaveowners were chiefly Mormons from the South.

740. Morgan, Dale L. *The State of Deseret.* Logan: Utah State University Press, 1987. Mormons believed providence influenced Fillmore's signing the Utah Territory bill.

741. "The Mormons." *Harper's Monthly* 6 (April 1853): 605–22. Article suggests potential problems over polygamy, allegiance to the United States, and the appointment of federal officials.

742. Thorpe, Francis Newton, comp. *The Federal and State Constitutions, Colonial Charters, and Other Organic Laws of the States, Territories, and Colonies.* Buffalo: William S. Hein & Co., Inc., 1993 [1909]. 7 vols. 6: 3687–93. The act to establish the Territorial Government of Utah, 1850.

6. Abolition of the District of Columbia Slave Trade

743. Bancroft, Frederic. *Slave Trading in the Old South.* New York: Frederick Ungar Publishing Co., 1959 [1931]. Chapter Three is a review of D.C.'s slave trade and the efforts to end it.

744. Green, Constance McLaughlin. *The Secret City: A History of Race Relations in the Nation's Capital.* Princeton: Princeton University Press, 1967. Ending the slave trade in the District did not make it safe for African Americans. The Fugitive Slave Law increased efforts to capture Maryland and Virginia runaways in the capital.

745. ———. *Washington: Village and Capital.* Princeton: Princeton University Press, 1962. Washingtonians accepted the end of the slave trade as long as legislation did not free their slaves. They encouraged the Fugitive Slave Law to keep runaways from increasing the local African American population.

746. Horton, James Oliver. "The Genesis of Washington's African American Community." In *Urban Odyssey: A Multicultural History of Washington, D.C.*, ed. Francine Curro Cary. Washington, DC: Smithsonian Institution Press, 1996. Fearing abduction by the Fugitive Slave Law, free African Americans did not speak out against slavery but organized an important station on the Underground Railway.

747. Laprade, William T. "The Domestic Slave Trade in the District of Columbia." *Journal of Negro History* 11 (January 1926): 17–34. The Compromise only removed the slavetrading depot outside the District's boundaries. However it was Congress's first act against established slavery.

748. Robinson, Henry S. "District of Columbia, Slavery in the." In *Dictionary of Afro-American Slavery*, ed. Randall M. Miller and John David Smith. New York: Westport, CT: Greenwood Press, 1988. 192–93.

749. Tremain, Mary. *Slavery in the District of Columbia: The Policy of Congress and the Struggle for Abolition.* New York: Negro Universities Press, 1969 [1892]. Brief reference to the debates over the abolition of the slave trade in the District.

7. Fugitive Slave Law

750. Bestor, Arthur. "State Sovereignty and Slavery: A Reinterpretation of Proslavery Constitutional Doctrine, 1846–1860." *Journal of the Illinois State Historical Society* 54 (1961): 117–80. Clear exposition of the Fugitive Slave Law and its ramifications.

751. Burgess, John W. *The Middle Period, 1817–1858.* New York: Charles Scribner's Sons, 1897. As the Compromise of 1850 reduced sectional agitation, Congress sustained Fillmore's use of the military to enforce the Fugitive Slave Law.

752. Calhoun, Frederick S. *The Lawmen: United States Marshals and Their Deputies, 1789–1989.* Washington, DC: Smithsonian Institution Press, 1989. Fillmore used federal marshals to enforce the Fugitive Slave Law and against filibusters.

753. Campbell, Stanley W. "Fugitive Slave Laws." In *The Encyclopedia of Southern History,* ed. David C. Roller and Robert W. Twyman. Baton Rouge: Louisiana State University Press, 1979. 498–99. Review essay.

754. ———. *The Slave Catchers: Enforcement of the Fugitive Slave Law, 1850–1860.* Chapel Hill: University of North Carolina Press, 1968. Acknowledges Fillmore's fortitude to enforce the law and claims the law performed adequately despite resistance and contemporary claims of failure.

755. Coakley, Robert W. *The Role of Federal Military Forces in Domestic Disorders, 1789–1878.* Washington, DC: Center of Military History, United States Army, 1988. Fillmore set the precedent for claiming an inherent constitutional right to use federal forces to assist civilians executing federal laws.

756. Cover, Robert M. *Justice Accused: Antislavery and the Judicial Process.* New Haven: Yale University Press, 1975. Examines the legal philosophies of the judges who sustained the Fugitive Slave Laws and the abolitionist lawyers who defended alleged runaways. It reviews the important legal cases and also provides biographies of the judges who, like Fillmore, believed they were executing a law without moral prejudice.

757. Cummings, Homer, and Carl McFarland, *Federal Justice: Chapters in the History of Justice and the Federal Executive.* New York: Macmillan Company,

1937. Reviews the Fugitive Slave Law, Fillmore's concern that it conflicted with writs of *habeas corpus*, and Crittenden's opinion that it was constitutional.

757a. Fehrenbacher, Don E., *The Slaveholding Republic: An Account of the United States Government's Relations to Slavery*. New York: Oxford University Press, 2001. Devotes two informative chapters to the Fugitive Slave Laws. He assesses the 1850 law as the "the most intrusive action" by the government in support of slavery. And despite Fillmore's own repugnance of slavery, his administration was "directly and wholeheartedly involved" in recovering fugitive slaves.

758. Finkelman, Paul. "Fugitive Slave Laws." In *Encyclopedia of African-American Culture and History,* ed. Jack Salzman, Davis Lionel Smith, and Cornel West. New York: Simon & Schuster Macmillan, 1996. 5 vols. 2: 1070–72. Good review of the laws from the Articles of Confederation to their repeal in 1864.

759. ———. " 'The Law, and Not Conscience, Constitutes the Rule of Action': The South Bend Fugitive Slave Case and the Value of 'Justice Delayed.' " In *The Constitution, Law, and American Life: Critical Aspects of the Nineteenth Century Experience,* ed. Donald G. Nieman. Athens: University of Georgia Press, 1992. Analysis of Justice John McLean's interpretation of the Fugitive Slave Laws and then reviews abolitionist resistance tactics.

760. Fuess, Claude M. *The Life of Caleb Cushing.* New York: Harcourt, Brace and Company, 1923. 2 vols. In Volume Two, Pierce's Attorney General furthered the ability of federal marshals to enforce the law.

761. "Fugitive Slave Law." In *The African American Encyclopedia,* ed. Michael W. Williams. New York: Marshall Cavendish, 1993. 5 vols. 3: 633.

762. Gara, Larry. "The Fugitive Slave Law: A Double Paradox." *Civil War History* 10 (September 1964): 229–40. Despite its intention to moderate sectional disputes, the law recharged the slavery debate and helped bring on the Civil War.

763. ———. *The Presidency of Franklin Pierce.* Lawrence: University Press of Kansas, 1991. The Pierce administration strengthened the Fugitive Slave Law after the Kansas-Nebraska Act increased Northern resistance to it.

764. ———. "Slavery and the Slave Power: A Crucial Distinction." *Civil War History* 15 (March 1969): 5–18. The Fugitive Slave Law was pivotal in arousing Northern resentment against Southern political influence in Washington, real or imagined.

765. Hyman, Harold M., and William M. Wiecek. *Equal Justice Under Law: Constitutional Development, 1835–1875.* New York: Harper & Row, Publishers,

1982. Chapter Five reviews the legal arguments surrounding the law, particularly Fillmore's actions to protect those executing the law.

766. Jensen, Joan M. *Army Surveillance in America, 1775–1980.* New Haven: Yale University Press, 1991. Fillmore escalated the use of the military in civilian affairs when he used troops to support federal marshals detaining fugitive slaves after federal judges certified their need.

767. Johnson, Allen. "The Constitutionality of the Fugitive Slave Acts." *Yale Law Journal* 31 (December 1921): 161–81. Argues against the abolitionists' legal challenges and declares the Act's administrative powers were constitutional. He points out the precedent of the law for later non-jury administrative commissions, i.e., the Interstate Commerce Commission. Suggests that such usage will decrease the emotionalism attached to the Fugitive Slave Law of 1850.

768. Kallenback, Joseph E. *The American Chief Executive, the Presidency and the Governorship.* New York: Harper and Row, Publishers, 1966. Mentions Fillmore's policy to use federal force when necessary to execute federal laws.

769. Keller, Ralph A. "Extraterritoriality and the Fugitive Slave Debate." *Illinois Historical Journal* 78 (Summer 1985): 113–28. Some Southern arguments for remanding fugitive slaves by federal intervention theoretically jeopardized their state control of slave property.

770. Mohl, Raymond A. "Presidential Views of National Power, 1837–1861." *Mid America* 52 (July 1970): 177–89. It's ironic that Fillmore, who believed in a limited Executive, used federal force to protect slavery.

771. Randall, James G. *Constitutional Problems Under Lincoln.* New York: D. Appleton and Company, 1926. The Fugitive Slave Laws of 1793 and 1850 were repealed on June 28, 1864.

772. Rich, Bennett Milton. *The Presidents and Civil Disorder.* Washington, DC: Brookings Institute, 1941. Fillmore believed it was inappropriate to make military intentions known through proclamations since it would notify the adversary and possibly defeat the federal actions.

773. Shaw, Robert B. *A Legal History of Slavery in the United States.* Potsdam, NY: Northern Press, 1991. Chapter 15 scans the history of the Fugitive Slave Laws and the efforts to increase enforcement. Reviews the legal intricacies of the 1850 act.

774. Tushnet, Mark V. "Fugitive Slave Act of 1850." In *Dictionary of Afro-American Slavery,* ed. Randall M. Miller and John David Smith. Westport, CT: Greenwood Press, 1988. 276.

775. White, Leonard D. *The Jacksonians: A Study in Administrative History, 1829–1861.* New York: Macmillan Company, 1954. Claims Fillmore was on impregnable constitutional grounds when enforcing the Fugitive Slave Law. Fillmore understood the breakdown of Northern cooperation as a nullification of the Constitution.

776. Wilson, Frederick T. *Federal Aid in Domestic Disturbances, 1787–1903.* Washington, DC: Government Printing Office, 1903. Explains the laws allowing the president to use U.S. troops against those resisting federal laws. Reviews use of federal troops in Boston.

777. Yanuck, Julius. "The Fugitive Slave Law and the Constitution." Ph.D. diss., Columbia University, 1953. Review of the law from the Constitution to the Civil War.

8. Resistance to the Fugitive Slave Law

778. Adeleke, Tunde. *UnAfrican Americans: Nineteenth-Century Black Nationalists and the Civilizing Mission.* Lexington: University Press of Kentucky, 1998. The law convinced a number of free blacks of America's virulent racism, the necessity for African Americans to emigrate, and the need for a black nationalist state.

779. Aptheker, Herbert. *Abolitionism, A Revolutionary Movement.* Boston: Twayne Publishers, 1989. Reviews slave escapes and slave unrest in the 1850s.

780. ———. "Militant Abolitionism." *Journal of Negro History* 26 (October 1941): 438–84. Beginning in the 1850s, African American abolitionists preferred militant action to pacifist persuasion.

781. Bell, Howard H. "The Negro Emigration Movement, 1849–1854: A Phase of Negro Nationalism." *Phylon Quarterly* 20 (Summer 1959): 132–42. The law was another reason that free African Americans experimented with emigration.

782. Blight, David W. "They Knew What Time It Was: African-Americans and the Coming of the Civil War." In *Why the Civil War Came,* ed. Gabor Boritt. New York: Oxford University Press, 1996. The law stimulated an organized and violent African American resistance to slave catchers and their legal procedures. It was a rehearsal for the explosion of self-liberating slaves during the Civil War.

783. Brock, Peter. *Radical Pacifists in Antebellum America.* Princeton: Princeton University Press, 1968. Resistance to the law undermined the antebellum pacifist movement.

784. Catterall, Helen Tunnicliff, ed. *Judicial Cases Concerning American Slavery and the Negro.* New York: Octagon Books, Inc., 1968 [1926–36]. 5 vols. Volume 4 contains Fugitive Slave cases in the Northeast and Middle states, including the Jerry and Christiana rescues, plus the prosecution of Capt. Drayton for helping fugitive slaves on his vessel the *Pearl.*

785. Cheek, William F. "John Mercer Langston: Black Protest Leader and Abolitionist." *Civil War History* 16 (June 1970): 101–20. Organized freeman societies and conventions to protest slavery, racism, and the Fugitive Slave Law.

786. Cheek, William, and Aimee Lee Cheek. *John Mercer Langston and the Fight for Black Freedom, 1828–65.* Urbana: University of Illinois Press, 1989. Describes African American antislavery conventions and their black nationalist sentiments.

786a. Collison, Gary L. "Alexander Burton and Salem's 'Fugitive Slave Riot' of 1851." *Essex Institute Historical Collections* 128 (January 1992): 17–26. The false arrest demonstrates the mistakes made by the enforcers of the law and the peril to free African Americans.

787. Curry, Leonard P. *The Free Black in Urban America, 1800–1850: The Shadow of the Dream.* Chicago: University of Chicago Press, 1981. Free African Americans organized resistance to the fugitive law, hid runaways, and aided their escape.

788. Davis, Thomas J. "A Historical and Economic Opportunity: Class and Status Among Blacks in Buffalo." In *African Americans and the Rise of Buffalo's Post-Industrial City, 1940 to Present.* ed. Henry Louis Taylor, Jr. Buffalo: Buffalo Urban League, Inc., 1990. 2 vols. 2: 8–47. In the early 1850s the small community suffered from economic competition with immigrants and population loss as residents fled to Canada to escape the Fugitive Slave Law.

789. De Bow, J. D. B. "Fugitive Slaves." In *The Cause of the South: Selections from De Bow's Review, 1846–1867,* ed. Paul F. Paskoff and Daniel J. Wilson. Baton Rouge: Louisiana State University Press, 1982. The influential Southern editor believed the law would not be enforced and the South would be betrayed.

789a. Delany, Martin Robison. *The Condition, Elevation, Emigration, and Destiny of the Colored People of the United States.* New York: Arno Press and The New York Times, 1968 [1852]. Delany argued the impossibility of African Americans overturning or directly resisting the law. Only self-organized colonization outside the United States was an option.

790. Donald, Aida DiPace, ed. "The Diary of an Abolitionist: George W. Johnson." *Niagara Frontier* 4 (Summer 1957): 45–52. Highlights the passionate criticism of Fillmore by a Buffalo abolitionist and former friend of the President.

791. Finkelman, Paul. *Slavery in the Courtroom: An Annotated Bibliography of American Cases*. Washington, DC: Library of Congress, 1985. Extended annotations on 34 pamphlets about 21 cases of rendition.

792. Foner, Philip S. *History of Black America: From the Compromise of 1850 to the End of the Civil War.* Westport, CT: Greenwood Press, 1983. A study of African American resistance to the fugitive laws.

793. Fordham, Monroe. "Major Themes in Northern Black Religious Thought, 1800–1860." Ph.D. Diss., State University of New York at Buffalo, 1973. Every sizable African American community resisted the Fugitive Slave Law as an unholy humiliation at odds with God's universal equality.

794. Gara, Larry. *The Liberty Line.* Lexington: University of Kentucky Press, 1961. Claims the Underground Railroad was more important for propaganda than a help to self-liberating slaves.

795. ———. "The Professional Fugitive in the Abolitionist Movement." *Wisconsin Magazine of History* 48 (Spring 1965): 196–204. Former slaves gave authority to the cruelty of slavery and overturned the Southern myth of slave contentment.

796. Graf, Hildegard. "The Underground Railroad in Erie County." *Niagara Frontier* 1 (Autumn 1954): 69–71. Buffalo was a main terminus for slaves fleeing to Canada.

797. Harding, Vincent. *There Is a River: The Black Struggle for Freedom in America.* New York: Harcourt Brace & Company, 1981. Northern free African Americans organized conventions to resist the law and challenged Fillmore to kidnap them.

798. Hildreth, Richard. *Despotism in America: An Inquiry into the Nature, Results, and Legal Basis of the Slave-Holding System in the United States.* New York: Negro Universities Press, 1968 [1854]. The final section is a critique of the Fugitive Slave Law and particularly Daniel Webster's support of it.

799. Ilisevich, Robert D. *Galusha A. Grow: The People's Candidate.* Pittsburgh: University of Pittsburgh Press, 1988. Grow and others resisted a congressional movement to pledge no amendments to the law. He wanted an opportunity for change or repeal.

800. Landon, Fred. "The Negro Migration to Canada After the Passing of the Fugitive Slave Act." *Journal of Negro History* 5 (January 1920): 22–36. Uses contemporary newspapers to describe the exodus of fugitives and free African Americans to Canada. Canada allowed no extradition.

801. Levine, Bruce. *Half Slave and Half Free: The Roots of the Civil War.* New York: Hill and Wang, 1992. Lively review of the North's escalating resistance to the fugitive law.

802. Mabee, Carleton. *Black Freedom: The Nonviolent Abolitionists from 1830 through the Civil War.* London: Macmillan Company, 1970. Abolitionists vowed that Buffalo would never return fugitives to slavery.

803. *Massachusetts Anti-Slavery Society Annual Report, 1850–1853.* Westport: Negro Universities Press, 1970. Appendix A of the 1851 report claims that Fillmore could not induce Buffalo to obey the fugitive law nor could the entire Army enforce the law in western New York.

803a. McKivigan, John R. *History of the American Abolitionist Movement: A Bibliography of Scholarly Articles.* New York: Garland Publishing, Inc., 1999. 5 vols. Important collection of twentieth-century articles on antislavery campaigns up to the Civil War.

803b. McKivigan, John R., and Jason H. Silverman. "Monarchial Liberty and Republican Slavery: West Indies Emancipation Celebrations in Upstate New York and Canada West." *Afro-Americans in New York Life and History* 10 (January 1986): 7–18. Public freedom celebrations by free blacks renewed their community, continued calls for equality, and indicted white society's racism.

804. Merrill, Arch. *The Underground: Freedom's Road and Other Upstate Tales.* New York: American Book-Stratford Press Inc., 1963. Stories about western New York's aid to escaped slaves.

805. Morris, Thomas D. *Free Men All: The Personal Liberty Laws of the North, 1780–1861.* Baltimore: Johns Hopkins University Press, 1974. Describes the arguments for enforcing the Fugitive Slave Law while defending the primary thesis that all persons are born free and cannot be deprived of that freedom except by due process.

806. Pease, Jane H., and William H. Pease. "Confrontation and Abolition in the 1850s." *Journal of American History* 58 (March 1972): 923–37. The early violent resistance to the Fugitive Slave Law inspired abolitionists' tolerance for violence against slaveholders, slavecatchers, and their enforcing agencies.

807. ———. *They Who Would Be Free: Blacks Search for Freedom, 1830–1861.* New York: Atheneum, 1974. Chapter Ten reviews African American resistance to the Fugitive Slave Law with summaries of the Shadrach, Sims, Jerry, and Christiana cases. Good primary source bibliography.

808. Priebe, Paula J. "Central and Western New York and the Fugitive Slave Law of 1850." *Afro-Americans in New York Life and History* 16 (January 1992): 19–29. Describes resistance to the law.

809. Rhodes, Jane. *Mary Ann Shadd Cary: The Black Press and Protest in the Nineteenth Century.* Bloomington: Indiana University Press, 1998. A free woman of color escaped the threat of wrongful abduction and emigrated to Canada where she edited the antislavery *Provincial Freeman.*

810. Ripley, C. Peter, ed. *The Black Abolitionist Papers.* Chapel Hill: University of North Carolina Press, 1985–92. 5 vols. 4: 61–65. One African American clergyman was so disheartened by the law that he vowed to resist Fillmore himself if he tried to enslave him.

811. ———, ed. *Witness for Freedom: African American Voices on Race, Slavery and Emancipation.* Chapel Hill: University of North Carolina Press, 1993. Reprints selections from the *Black Abolition Papers.*

812. Rosenberg, Norman L. "Personal Liberty Laws and Sectional Crisis, 1850–1861." *Civil War History* 17 (March 1971): 25–44. Reviews the revival of Northern state liberty laws to frustrate the Fugitive Slave Law.

812a. Sernett, Milton C. " 'On Freedom's Trail': Researching the Underground Railroad in New York State." *Afro-Americans in New York Life and History* 25 (January 2001): 7–32. Good review of the literature, resource collections, and web-sites available to researchers.

812b. Simson, Rennie. "A Community in Turmoil: Black American Writers in New York State Before the Civil War." *Afro-Americans in New York Life and History* 13 (January 1989): 57–67. Describes articulate reaction to the Fugitive Slave Law in the writings of Frederick Douglass, James M. Whitfield and others.

812c. Smith, Robert P. "William Cooper Nell: Crusading Black Abolitionist." *Journal of Negro History* 55 (July 1970): 182–99. Besides actively resisting the law, Nell published his 1851 pamphlet on the *Services of Colored Americans in the Wars of 1776 and 1812* to gather appreciation for his race and to undo the harm being done by the law.

813. Sumner, Charles. "Freedom National, Slavery Sectional: Speech in the Senate, on a Motion to Repeal the Fugitive Slave Act, August 20, 1852." In *Charles Sumner: His Complete Works.* New York: Negro Universities Press, 1969 [1900]. 20 vols. 3: 257–366. Elaborate historical and constitutional argument against the law.

814. Takaki, Ronald T. *A Pro-Slavery Crusade: The Agitation to Reopen the African Slave Trade.* New York: Free Press, 1971. Northern aid to fugitives led to Southern arguments for renewing the African slave trade.

815. Trefousse, Hans L. *The Radical Republicans: Lincoln's Vanguard for Radical Justice.* New York: Alfred A. Knopf, 1969. When Fillmore signed the law, he unleashed a hostile opposition from antislavery congressmen.

816. Tyler, Ronnie C. "Fugitive Slaves in Mexico." *Journal of Negro History* 57 (January 1972): 1–12. Mexico had no extradition treaty and allowed thousands of fugitive slaves to find refuge there.

817. White, Arthur O. "School Segregation and Its Critics in a Northern City: A Case Study, Buffalo, New York, 1837–1880." Unpublished ms, State University of New York at Buffalo, Archives, n.d. Suggests the law contributed to the timidity of Negro protests against segregated public schools in Buffalo until after the Civil War.

818. Williams, Lillian Serece. *Strangers in the Land of Paradise: The Creation of an African American Community, Buffalo, New York, 1900–1940.* Bloomington: Indiana University Press, 1999. Chapter One reviews the early history of the small community, their efforts to gain civil rights, and their aid to fugitive slaves.

819. Yee, Shirley J. *Black Women Abolitionists: A Study in Activism, 1828–1860.* Knoxville: University of Tennessee Press, 1992. Examines efforts to end the Fugitive Slave Law and slavery while enduring racist, sexist, and class opposition.

D. ENFORCING DOMESTIC LAWS

1. Boston

820. Bearse, Austin. *Reminiscences of Fugitive Slave Law Days in Boston.* New York: Arno Press & The New York Times, 1969 [1880]. Participated in the Shadrach escape and Sims demonstrations.

821. Blue, Frederick J. *The Free-Soilers: Third Party Politics, 1848–1854.* Urbana: University of Illinois Press, 1973. Free-Soilers belittled Fillmore and believed his militaristic actions against the rescuers of fugitives were really aimed at defeating Charles Sumner for senator.

822. Bowditch, Vincent Y. *Life and Correspondence of Henry Ingersoll Bowditch.* Freeport NY: Books For Libraries Press, 1970 [1902]. 2 vols. Volume One contains letters and selections from a narrative describing Boston abolitionists' efforts to rescue the Crafts, Shadrach, and Sims.

823. Collison, Gary L. "The Boston Vigilance Committee: A Reconsideration." *Historical Journal of Massachusetts* 12 (June 1984): 104–116. The committee was a relief center, legal defense, and propaganda agency. It had little to do with the violent rescue of Shadrach by local African Americans. Fillmore followed that rescue with federal force and succeeded in rendering Thomas Sims back into slavery.

824. ————. *Shadrach Minkins: From Fugitive Slave to Citizen.* Cambridge: Harvard University Press, 1997. Fillmore's proclamation threatening to employ troops in response to Shadrach's escape was cautious compared to Webster's rage for immediate use of troops and treason indictments against the African American and white rescuers.

825. Craft, William. *Running A Thousand Miles For Freedom; Or, the Escape of William and Ellen Craft from Slavery.* Salem, NH: Ayer Company, Publishers, 1991 [1860]. Boston abolitionists were sure the government would use force to return the Crafts into slavery. Fillmore wrote their former owner that he would use the military to do so. The Crafts fled to Britain.

826. Edelstein, Tilden G. *Strange Enthusiasm: A Life of Thomas Wentworth Higginson.* New Haven: Yale University Press, 1968. Massachusetts abolitionist carried Fillmore's last annual message in his pocket to remind him that the country was not listening to them.

827. Finkelman, Paul. *Slavery in the Courtroom: An Annotated Bibliography of American Cases.* Washington, DC: Library of Congress, 1985. 86–88, 88–94. One pamphlet on the Shadrach escape. One pamphlet on the Sims case.

828. ————, ed. *Slavery, Race and the American Legal System, 1700–1872. 16 vols. Fugitive Slaves and American Courts: The Pamphlet Literature, Series 2.* New York: Garland Publishing, Inc., 1988. 4 vols. 1: 573–616; 617–63. Contains report of proceedings against those who helped Shadrach escape, and a report on the trial of Thomas Sims.

829. *Gleason's Pictorial Drawing-Room Companion,* May 3, 1851. Illustrations and comments on the Thomas Sims trial. Praises the local police for keeping order.

830. *Gleason's Pictorial Drawing-Room Companion,* May 10, 1851. Illustration and comments on the Boston Police conveying Thomas Sims to the ship *Acorn* and his return to slavery.

831. Goodheart, Lawrence B. *Abolitionist, Actuary, Atheist: Elizur Wright and the Reform Impulse.* Kent: Kent State University Press, 1990. Editor of Boston's Free-Soil newspaper the *Commonwealth.* He was arrested for helping Shadrach

escape. Some believed his arrest was Fillmore's attempt to hinder the Free-Soil election of Charles Sumner to the Senate.

832. Higginson, Thomas Wentworth. *Cheerful Yesterdays.* Cambridge: Riverside Press, 1898. Abolitionist recalls Boston's excitement during the Shadrach rescue and Sims' failed rescue.

833. Horton, James Oliver, and Lois E. Horton. *Black Bostonians: Family Life and Community Struggles in the Antebellum North.* New York: Holmes & Meier Publishers, Inc., 1979. Reviews the strategic African American participation in the fugitive escapes and the attempted escapes.

834. Horton, Lois E., and James Oliver Horton. "Power and Social Responsibility: Entrepreneurs and the Black Community in Antebellum Boston." In *Entrepreneurs: The Boston Business Community, 1700–1850,* ed. Conrad Edick Wright and Katheryn P. Viens. Boston: Massachusetts Historical Society, 1997. African American business people led protests against the Fugitive Slave Laws and comforted runaway slaves.

835. Jacobs, Donald M., ed. *Courage and Conscience: Black & White Abolitionists in Boston.* Bloomington: Indiana University Press, 1993. Ten informative essays on African American leadership and their participation in biracial abolitionism and fugitive slave rescues.

836. Levy, Leonard W. "Sims' Case: The Fugitive Slave Law in Boston." *Journal of Negro History* 35 (January 1950): 39–74. Describes the successful remanding of Thomas Sims to Georgia. It features the federal and local actions supporting the law under duress of local resistance.

837. Pease, Jane H., and William H. Pease. *The Fugitive Slave Law and Anthony Burns: A Problem in Law Enforcement.* Philadelphia: J. B. Lippincott Company, 1975. Good review of the law, the resistance to it, and Fillmore's efforts to enforce it. Includes excerpts demonstrating Fillmore's determination to execute the law. Bibliography.

838. Robbey, Stanley J., and Anita W. Robbey. "Lewis Hayden: From Fugitive Slave to Statesman." *New England Quarterly* 46 (December 1973): 591–613. African American Boston clothier who led rescues of the Crafts and Shadrach, and participated in the Sims and Burns rescue attempts.

839. Schwartz, Harold. "Fugitive Slaves in Boston." *New England Quarterly* 57 (June 1954): 191–212. After the sensational rescue of Fred Wilkins, or Shadrach as he liked to be known, Fillmore ordered the prosecution of his rescuers.

840. Von Frank, Albert J. *The Trials of Anthony Burns: Freedom and Slavery in Emerson's Boston.* Cambridge: Harvard University Press, 1998. Political antislavery increased due to the Boston fugitive slave cases. Fillmore's appointee to the Supreme Court Benjamin R. Curtis, and his family, were prominent defenders of the Fugitive Slave Laws.

2. Syracuse

841. Finkelman, Paul. *Slavery in the Courtroom: An Annotated Bibliography of American Cases.* Washington, DC: Library of Congress, 1985. 103–7. Two pamphlets on the Jerry escape.

842. Finkelman, Paul, ed. *Slavery, Race and the American Legal System, 1700–1872. 16 vols. Fugitive Slaves and American Courts: The Pamphlet Literature, Series 2.* New York: Garland Publishing, Inc., 1988. 4 vols. 2: 205–326, 327–42. Trial against the Marshall who attempted to arrest Jerry, and the anti Fugitive Slave Law arguments of Gerrit Smith at the trial.

843. Galpin, W. Freeman. "The Jerry Rescue." *New York History* 26 (January 1945): 19–34. Uses local Syracuse newspapers to follow the 1851 trial and rescue of the fugitive.

843a. Hunter, Carol. " 'The Rev. Jermain Loguen: As a Slave and as a Freeman; A Narrative of Real Life.' " *Afro-Americans in New York Life and History* 13 (July 1989): 33–46. Reviews Loguen's published narrative and describes his participation in the Jerry rescue.

844. May, Samuel J. *Some Recollections of Our Antislavery Conflict.* New York: Arno Press and the New York Times, 1968 [1869]. Central New York abolitionist and Unitarian minister recalls his participation in the Jerry escape and his bitterness toward fellow Unitarian Millard Fillmore.

845. Roseboom, William F., and Henry W. Schram. *They Built a City: Stories and Legends of Syracuse and Onondaga County.* Fayetteville, NY: Marpro Co., 1976. 99–101.

846. Sokolow, Jayne A. "The Jerry McHenry Rescue and the Growth of Northern Antislavery Sentiment during the 1850s." *Journal of American Studies* 16 (December 1982): 427–45. Reviews the Syracuse demonstrations against the Fugitive Slave Law, with profiles of 52 demonstrators.

846a. Wellman, Judith. "Larry Gara's *Liberty Line* in Oswego County, New York 1838–1854: A New Look at the Legend." *Afro-Americans in New York Life and*

History 25 (January 2001): 33–55. Many believed the Jerry arrest was planned by the federal government to provoke and suppress abolitionists.

3. Christiana

847. Ampere, J. J. "Ampere in Philadelphia." *Eclectic Review* 30 (September 1853): 52–68. Translation of an article from the *Revue des Deux Mondes*. French traveler judged the Fugitive Slave Law constitutional but believed its local judicial methods scandalous. He heard those accused of treason for participating in the resistance at Christiana would not be convicted.

848. Asante, Molifi Kete. *African American History: A Journey of Liberation.* Maywood, NJ: People's Publishing Group, 1995. Reviews the Fugitive Slave Law and uses the Christiana episode as an example of African American resistance. Reprints a section from Fillmore's 1851 Annual Message citing that resistance.

849. Eggert, Gerald G. "The Impact of the Fugitive Slave Law on Harrisburg: A Case Study." *Pennsylvania Magazine of History and Biography* 109 (October 1985): 537–69. The study chronicles a change toward the fugitive law from indifference in 1850 to resistance by 1853.

850. Finkelman, Paul. *Slavery in the Courtroom: An Annotated Bibliography of American Cases.* Washington, DC: Library of Congress, 1985. 95–102. Four pamphlets on the Christiana violence and escape.

851. Finkelman, Paul. ed. *Slavery, Race and the American Legal System, 1700–1872. 16 vols. Fugitive Slaves and American Courts: The Pamphlet Literature, Series 2.* New York: Garland Publishing, Inc., 1988. 4 vols. 2: 51–203. Contemporary report on the Castner Hanway treason trial for allegedly helping the Christiana fugitives escape.

852. ———. "The Treason Trial of Castner Hanway." In *American Political Trials,* ed. Michal R. Belknap. Westport, CT: Greenwood Press, 1994. Examines the political motivations behind Fillmore's charge of treason against participants.

853. Finkenbine, Roy E. "Christiana Revolt of 1851." In *Encyclopedia of African-American Culture and History,* ed. Jack Salzman, Davis Lionel Smith, and Cornel West. New York: Simon & Schuster Macmillan, 1996. 5 vols. 1: 541.

854. ———. "Christiana Riot." In *Dictionary of Afro-American Slavery,* ed. Randall M. Miller and John David Smith. Westport, CT: Greenwood Press, 1988. 103.

854a. Forbes, Ella. " 'By My Own Right Arm': Redemptive Violence and the 1851 Christiana, Pennsylvania Resistance." *Journal of Negro History* 83 (Summer 1998):

159–67. Uses William Parker's recollections to describe the background of the area's African American mutual protection league's defense of fugitive slaves.

855. Hensel, W. U. *The Christiana Riot and the Treason Trials of 1851, An Historical Sketch.* 2d ed. Lancaster: New Era Printing Company, 1911. Important episode of African American resistance to the fugitive law and abolitionist resistance to the administration's allegations of treason against those helping the fugitives. Includes pictures of participants.

856. Hurst, J. W. "Treason in the United States, III: Under the Constitution." *Harvard Law Review* 58 (July 1945): 806–57. In U.S. vs. Hanaway, Mr. Justice Robert C. Grier annulled the treason indictment against the Christiana participants.

857. Katz, Jonathan. *Resistance at Christiana: The Fugitive Slave Rebellion, Christiana, Pennsylvania, September 11, 1851.* New York: Thomas Y. Cromwell, 1974. Narrative of resistance and treason trials.

858. Nash, Roderick W. "William Parker and the Christiana Riot." *Journal of Negro History* 46 (January 1961): 24–31. Parker's African American mutual protection association was hiding fugitives when a violent episode of resistance left one white slave owner dead. Parker left for Canada by way of Frederick Douglass's home in Rochester.

859. Nichols, Charles H., ed. *Black Men in Chains: Narratives by Escaped Slaves.* New York: Lawrence Hill & Co., 1972. Reprints William Parker's recollection of the Christiana affair from the *Atlantic Monthly* of February and March 1866.

860. Slaughter, Thomas P. *Bloody Dawn: The Christiana Riot and Racial Violence in the Antebellum North.* New York: Oxford University Press, 1991. Uses local documents to narrate African American community resistance.

861. Still, William. *The Underground Railroad.* New York: Arno Press and the New York Times, 1968 [1872]. Contains a lengthy narrative on the Christiana affair, including the federal indictments for aiding the fugitives.

4. South Carolina Secession

862. Ames, Herman V. *John C. Calhoun and the Secession Movement of 1850.* Freeport: Books for Libraries Press, 1971 [1918]. Calhoun incited the Southern states to call conventions promoting secession and press the North to accept the extension of slavery. Calhoun died before the conventions met.

863. Barney, William. *The Road to Secession: A New Perspective on the Old South.* New York: Praeger Publishers, 1972. Secessionist forces were undermined by the

Compromise of 1850, the cotton boom, and Southern moderates who resented radicals charging them with disloyalty to the South.

864. Barnwell, John, ed. " 'In the Hands of the Compromisers': Letters of Robert W. Barnwell to James H. Hammond." *Civil War History* 29 (June 1983): 154–68. Barnwell replaced Calhoun in the Senate. The letters articulate the secessionist's hope that the Compromise would motivate the Nashville Conventions into a Southern unification movement for secession.

865. ———— . *Love of Order: South Carolina's First Secession Crisis.* Chapel Hill: University of North Carolina Press, 1982. Fillmore was very concerned about the state's call for secession.

866. Boucher, Chauncey S. "*In Re* That Aggressive Slavocracy." *Mississippi Valley Historical Review* 8 (June–September, 1921): 13–79. Argues against the claims for a unified antebellum South. Describes southern debates about the Compromise of 1850 and the South's confusion over South Carolina's secession movement.

867. Calhoun, Richard J. *Witness to Sorrow: The Antebellum Autobiography of William J. Grayson.* Columbia: University of South Carolina Press. 1990. Prominent Southern literary figure opposed secession and feared for his state's future as a small, weak nation surrounded by U.S. arms.

868. Cashin, Joan E. " 'Decidedly Opposed to *the Union*': Women's Culture, Marriage, and Politics in Ante-bellum South Carolina." *Georgia Historical Quarterly* 78 (Winter 1994): 735–59. This study mentions two upper-class, educated white women advocating secession and publicly encouraging allegations of Northern wrongdoing.

869. Cole, Arthur C. "The South and the Right of Secession in the Early Fifties." *Mississippi Valley Historical Review* 1 (December 1914): 376–99. Pioneering study on the secession conventions and their relation to the Compromise of 1850.

870. Degler, Carl N. *The Other South: Southern Dissenters in the Nineteenth Century.* New York: Harper & Row, Publishers, 1974. The vast majority of Southerners still held to their Unionist sentiment and prevented the breakup of the Union in 1850–51.

871. ———— . "There Was Another South." *American Heritage* 11 (August 1960): 52–55; 100–103. Southern Unionists stopped the incipient secessionist movement of 1851.

872. Ford, Lacy K., Jr. *Origins of Southern Radicalism: The South Carolina Upcountry, 1800–1860.* New York: Oxford University Press, 1988. Analysis of

secession movements highlighting the different circumstances of the 1851 and 1860–61 movements.

873. Halsey, Ashley, Jr. "South Carolina Began Preparing for War in 1851." *Civil War Times Illustrated* 1 (April 1962): 8–13. In 1850 and 1852 South Carolina appropriated money for ordinance.

874. Heidler, David S. *Pulling the Temple Down: The Fire-Eaters and the Destruction of the Union.* Mechanicsburg, PA: Stackpole Books, 1994. Fillmore acted decisively to quell violence along the Texas-New Mexico border giving time for the passage of the Compromise of 1850. Both actions deflated the excitement for secession.

874a. Huston, James L. "Southerners Against Secession: The Arguments of the Constitutional Unionists in 1850–51." *Civil War History* 46 (December 2000): 281–99. They should receive more recognition for successfully quieting the secession movement by their arguments and at the polls.

875. Jennings, Thelma. *The Nashville Convention: Southern Movement for Unity, 1848–1851.* Memphis: Memphis State University Press, 1980. Describes the interaction between the Southern conventions debating secession and the Compromise of 1850.

876. Johnson, Ludwell H. *Division and Reunion: America, 1848–1877.* New York: John Wiley & Sons, 1978. Contends Southern secession would have followed the defeat of the Compromise of 1850.

876a. Mayer, Henry, " 'A Leaven of Disunion'. The Growth of the Secessionist Faction in Alabama, 1847–1851." *Alabama Review* 22 (April 1969): 83–116. William Lowndes Yancy led state secessionists opposed to the Compromise of 1850. They lost the 1851 state referendum to secede.

876b. McCardell, John. "John A Quitman and the Compromise of 1850 in Mississippi." *Journal of Mississippi History* 37 (August 1975): 239–66. Governor Quitman led state forces opposed to the Compromise and was defeated by a Union party coalition in 1851.

877. Moltke-Hansen, David. "The Expansion of Intellectual Life: A Prospectus." In *Intellectual Life in Antebellum Charleston,* ed. Michael O'Brien and David Moltke-Hansen. Knoxville: University of Tennessee Press, 1986. Charleston developed into a closed center of regional culture as it became geographically isolated from the economic dynamism of the West, the lower South, and even the state's interior.

878. Osterweis, Rollin G. *Romanticism and Nationalism in the Old South.* Gloucester, MA: Peter Smith, 1964 [1949]. South Carolina's secession is characterized as a defensive society longing to promote its culture into a separate nation superior to the Union.

879. Perkins, Howard C. "A Neglected Phase of the Movement for Southern Unity, 1847–1852." *Journal of Southern History* 12 (May 1946): 153–203. History of the Washington, DC pro-Southern newspaper *Southern Press.* It was anti-compromise and defended Southern rights.

880. Russel, Robert R. "Southern Secessionists *Per Se* and the Crisis of 1850." In Russel, *Critical Studies in Antebellum Sectionalism: Essays in American Political and Economic History.* Westport, CT: Greenwood Press, 1972. Finds continuity in the economic secessionists of 1833 persisting in the slavery secessionists of 1850–1851.

881. "Separate Secession." *Southern Quarterly Review* 4 (October 1851): 298–317. Report on the meeting of the Southern Rights Association of South Carolina. Argues against a single state secession and for the patience to persuade other slave states to join a cooperative Southern union of secession.

881a. Sinta, Manisha. "Revolution or Counterrevolution? The Political Ideology of Secession in Antebellum South Carolina." *Civil War History* 46 (September 2000): 205–26. The growth of a distinct anti-democratic ideology inspired the planter class on its road to disunion.

882. Siorissat, St. George L. "Tennessee, the Compromise of 1850, and the Nashville Convention." *Mississippi Valley Historical Review* 2 (December 1915): 313–47. Groundbreaking scholarship on the two Southern conventions discussing secession.

883. "South Carolina: Her Present Attitude and Future Action. *"Southern Quarterly Review* 4 (October 1851): 273–98. Reviews proposals for secession and the possibility of federal coercion to prevent it.

884. Stegmaier, Mark J. "Treachery or Hoax? The Rumored Southern Conspiracy to Confederate with Mexico." *Civil War History* 35 (March 1989): 28–38. Fillmore did not believe newspaper stories that the South would secede and join Mexico.

885. Stephenson, N. W. "Southern Nationalism in South Carolina in 1851." *American Historical Review* 36 (January 1931): 314–35. Follows immediate secessionists through their defeat by cooperationist secessionists who wanted to wait for other Southern states to join them.

886. Takaki, Ronald. "The Movement to Reopen the African Slave Trade in South Carolina." In *Slave Trade and Migration: Domestic and Foreign,* ed. Paul Finkelman. New York: Garland Publishing Inc., 1989. 364–80. After nonslaveholders refused to support secession in 1851, some slaveholders advocated opening the African Slave Trade to lower slave prices and increase the number of new slaveholders who would support a future secession.

887. Thornton, J. Mills, III. "The Ethic of Subsistence and the Origins of Southern Secession." *Tennessee Historical Quarterly* 48 (Summer 1989): 67–85. Summary of Southern Democrat and Whig policies and their anxiety about constituent sympathy for secession.

888. Tucker, Nathaniel Beverly. "South Carolina: Her Present Attitude and Future Action." *Southern Quarterly Review* 4 (October 1851): 273–98. Virginia secessionist supported South Carolina's secession movement.

889. Wakelyn, Jon L. "Party Issues and Political Strategy of the Charleston Taylor Democrats of 1848.*"South Carolina Historical Magazine* 73 (April 1972): 72–86. Without a two-party system in the state, radical Democrats challenged the national Democrats. Subsequently, these men were in the vanguard of the secessionist cooperation movement of 1851–52.

890. Walther, Eric H. *The Fire-Eaters.* Baton Rouge: Louisiana State University Press, 1992. Well-known secessionists throughout the South believed the Compromise of 1850 was reason enough to dissolve the Union.

5. Filibustering

890a. Ball, Durwood. "Filibusters and Regular Troops in San Francisco, 1851–1855." *Military History of the West* 28 (1998): 161–83. Fillmore ordered army commanders in the Pacific Division to intervene against filibusters.

891. Chaffin, Tom. *Fatal Glory: Narcisco Lopez and the First Clandestine U.S. War Against Cuba.* Charlottesville: University Press of Virginia, 1996. Narrative of Lopez's expeditions, his American and Cuban supporters, and the administration's efforts to thwart them.

892. ———. " 'Sons of Washington': Narcisco Lopez, Filibustering, and U.S. Nationalism, 1848–1851."*Journal of the Early Republic* 15 (Spring 1995): 79–108. Northern urban merchants and maritime interests supported the Lopez expeditions. Claims the desire for capital expansion superseded slavery expansion.

893. Claiborne, J. F. H. *Life and Correspondence of John A. Quitman: Major-General, U.S.A. and Governor of the State of Mississippi.* New York: Harper & Brothers,

Publishers, 1860. 2 vols. Volume Two contains Quitman's indictment against Fillmore's anti-filibustering policy. Quitman supported the Lopez expeditions.

894. Curtis, Ray Emerson. "The Law of Hostile Military Expeditions as Applied by the United States." *American Journal of International Law* 8 (January 1914): 1–37. Uses Fillmore as authority to explain why filibusters can be punished by their home country for jeopardizing its peace with another country.

895. De la Cova, Antonio Rafael. "Filibusters and Freemasons: The Sworn Obligation." *Journal of the Early Republic* 17 (Spring 1997): 95–120. Freemasonry served as a support system for Lopez's expeditions. Fillmore snubbed a suggestion that the government retrieve a mason's son held prisoner in Cuba.

896. Fornell, Earl W. "Texans and Filibusters in the 1850's." *Southwestern Historical Quarterly* 59 (April 1956): 411–28. Texans gave significant support to Lopez's expeditions.

897. "General Lopez, the Cuban Patriot." *United States Magazine and Democratic Review* 26 (February 1850): 97–112. Favorable sketch of Lopez.

898. *Gleason's Pictorial Drawing-Room Companion,* May 31, 1851. Illustration of volunteers ready to invade Cuba. Despite abandonment of the invasion, Southern cities resolved to obtain Cuba.

899. *Gleason's Pictorial Drawing-Room Companion,* September 20, 1851. Illustration of the massacre of American captives in Havana after the failed Lopez expedition.

900. *Gleason's Pictorial Drawing-Room Companion,* September 27, 1851. Illustration of General Narcisco Lopez. If his invasion of Cuba had been successful he would be another Washington.

901. *Gleason's Pictorial Drawing-Room Companion,* October 25, 1851. Illustration of the sad departure from Cuba to Spain of the remaining U.S. captives from the Lopez expedition. Hopefully the Queen of Spain will show mercy and release them.

902. Langley Lester D. "The Whigs and the Lopez Expeditions to Cuba, 1849–1851: A Chapter in Frustrating Diplomacy." *Revista de Historia de América* 71 (Enero-Junio, 1971): 9–22. The Whigs are not credited for their efforts to prevent the expeditions. Contains extracts from Fillmore's circular to stop filibusters.

903. May, Robert E. *John A. Quitman: Old South Crusader.* Baton Rouge: Louisiana State University Press, 1985. Biography of Mississippi secessionist who supported the annexation of Cuba. He believed Fillmore would not help the South.

903a. ———— . "Manifest Destiny's Filibusters." In *Manifest Destiny and Empire: American Antebellum Expansion,* ed. Sam W. Haynes and Christopher Morris. College Station: Texas A&M University Press, 1997. Review of 1850s filibustering with an examination of participants and consequences for foreign policy.

904. ———— . "The Slave Power Conspiracy Revisited: United States Presidents and Filibustering, 1848–1861." In *Union & Emancipation: Essays on Politics and Race in the Civil War Era,* ed., David W. Blight and Brooks D. Simpson. Kent: Kent State University Press, 1997. Fillmore consistently opposed Southern filibustering

905. Morrison, Michael A. *Slavery and the American West: The Eclipse of Manifest Destiny and the Coming of the Civil War.* Chapel Hill: University of North Carolina Press, 1997. Expansionists were critical of Fillmore's anti-filibustering policies.

906. "Narcisco Lopez and His Companions." *United States Magazine and Democratic Review* 29 (October 1851): 291–301. Recounts the unsuccessful Lopez expedition and blames Fillmore for allowing the execution of American filibusters.

907. Shearer, Ernest C. "The Carvajal Disturbances." *Southwestern Historical Quarterly* 55 (October 1951): 201–30. Fillmore used the same anti-filibustering policies on expeditions into Mexico that he did against the Lopez expeditions into Cuba.

908. "The Spaniards at Havana and the Whigs at Washington." *United States Magazine and Democratic Review* 31 (October 1852): 326–36. Scolds Fillmore for his humiliating inactivity during Spain's fatal revenge against American participants in the failed Lopez expedition.

909. Stout, Joe A. "Joseph C. Morehead and Manifest Destiny: A Filibuster in Sonora, 1851." *Pacific Historian* 15 (Spring 1971): 62–71. Stories of filibustering into Mexico and their pursuit by U.S. federal agents.

910. Tansey, Richard. "Southern Expansionism: Urban Interests in the Cuban Filibusters." *Plantation Society in the Americas* 1 (June 1979): 227–51. Newspapers provide the major source for this study of economic inducements persuading businessmen to support filibustering in Cuba.

911. Urban, Chester Stanley. "The Ideology of Southern Imperialism: New Orleans and the Caribbean, 1845–1860." *Louisiana Historical Quarterly* 39 (January 1956): 48–73. Analyzes reasons for annexing Cuba.

912. ———— . "New Orleans and the Cuban Question During the Lopez Expedition of 1849–51: A Local Study of 'Manifest Destiny'." *Louisiana Historical Quarterly*

22 (October 1939): 1095–167. Studies the New Orleans connection to the Lopez expedition and opposition to Fillmore's neutrality policy.

6. Beaver Island Kingdom

913. Titus, W. A. "Historic Spots in Wisconsin." *Wisconsin Magazine of History* 4 (1925–1926): 435–41. Fillmore used federal powers to help arrest the Mormon James Strang for treason. Strang established a renegade Mormon kingdom on Beaver Island in Lake Michigan.

914. Van Noord, Roger. *King of Beaver Island: The Life and Assassination of James Jesse Strang.* Urbana: University of Illinois Press, 1988. Fillmore allowed the use of the only U.S. warship on the Great Lakes to help arrest the schismatic Mormon leader. All federal charges were later dropped, and Strang continued to lead his island stronghold.

915. Weeks, Robert P. "A Utopian Kingdom in the American Grain." *Wisconsin Magazine of History* 61 (Autumn 1977): 3–20. It was thought that Fillmore's decision to arrest Strang for treason might hinder Whig efforts in the 1852 election.

E. GOVERNANCE

1. Finance

916. Cohen, Henry. *Business and Politics in America from the Age of Jackson to the Civil War: The Career Biography of W. W. Corcoran.* Westport, CT: Greenwood Publishing Corporation, 1971. Like former Presidents, Fillmore used Corcoran's bank as an informal fiscal agent and advisor on government funds.

917. "Expenditures of the Government During the Fiscal Year Ending 30th June, 1852." *Whig Almanac, 1853.* New York: New York Tribune, 1853. 29–30. List of Executive Department payments, including the outlay for the Fugitive Slave Law.

918. Kammen, Michael. *A Machine That Would Go of Itself: The Constitution in American Culture.* New York: Alfred A. Knopf, Inc., 1986. Fillmore's Third Message to Congress expressed the popular perception that the Constitution gave happiness and prosperity to the nation so care should be taken when calling to change it.

919. Savage, James D. *Balanced Budgets & American Politics.* Ithaca: Cornell University Press, 1988. Whigs could not implement national policies because of party disruption following the deaths of their elected Presidents, Harrison and Taylor.

919a. Socwell, Clarence P. "Peter Skene Ogden: Fur Trader Extraordinaire: Trapping, Exploration, and Adventure on the Canadian and American Frontiers." *American West* 10 (May 1973): 42–47, 61. Fillmore refused to give the Hudson's Bay Company compensation for its loss of property to the United States.

920. Stabile, Donald R., and Jeffrey A. Cantor. *The Public Debt of the United States: An Historical Perspective, 1775–1990.* New York: Praeger, 1991. From 1850 to 1858, the federal revenues exceeded expenditures. However, because of previous legislation, Fillmore's administration could not apply the surplus to reduce the public debt.

921. Taus, Esther Rogoff. *Central Banking Functions of the United States Treasury, 1789–1941.* Appendixes provide data on Treasury balances, customs receipts, public debt, and total receipts and expenditures.

922. Williamson, Jeffrey G. *American Growth and the Balance of Payments, 1820–1913: A Study of the Long Swing.* Chapel Hill: University of North Carolina Press, 1964. The early 1850s were a period of rapid growth according to indicators on railroads, foreign capital investment, exports of cotton, gold, and grain.

2. Tariff

923. Curtis, George B. *Protection and Prosperity.* New York: Garland Publishing, Inc., 1974 [1896]. 2 vols. Volume Two uses Fillmore's 1851 message to describe the recent failure of low tariffs to increase foreign demand for farm produce.

924. Eckes, Alfred E., Jr. *Opening America's Market: U.S. Foreign Trade Policy Since 1776.* Chapel Hill: University of North Carolina Press, 1995. Fillmore endorsed the protective tariff of the American System. He believed it went beyond protecting a segment of manufacturers by providing fiscal stability to the country and generating revenues to operate the government.

925. Goss, John Dean. "The History of Tariff Administration in the United States from Colonial Times to the McKinley Administrative Bill." In *Studies in History, Economics and Public Law, Vol. 1.* New York: Columbia University Press, 1891. Mentions changes in appraising goods and commissions during Fillmore's administration.

926. Stanwood, Edward. *American Tariff Controversies in the Nineteenth Century.* Boston: Houghton Mifflin Company, 1903. 2 vols. Volume Two summarizes Fillmore's tariff comments from his three messages. Describes his moderate tariff principles, and the country's weak manufacturing sector under low tariffs.

3. Internal Improvements

927. Ampere, J. J. "First Impressions of America." *Eclectic Review* 29 (May 1853): 84–97. Translation of an article from the *Revue des Deux Mondes*. His observations of Fillmore, Webster, and Canada's Governor General, Lord Elgin, at the Boston Railroad Jubilee.

928. "Atlantic and Pacific Central Railway; Ship-Canal at Panama." *Whig Almanac, 1850.* New York: New York Tribune, 1850. 17–19. Explains why the government should build a continental railroad.

929. Boutwell, George S. *Reminiscences of Sixty Years in Public Office.* New York: McClure, Phillips & Co., 1902. Recalls Webster's public performance and speeches throughout the Boston Railroad Jubilee.

930. Condit, Carl W. *The Port of New York: A History of the Rail and Terminal System from the Beginnings to Pennsylvania Station.* Chicago: University of Chicago Press, 1980. Mentions Fillmore at the opening of the New York and Erie Railroad celebrations and includes an extract from the Elmira *Republican* on the railroad's benefits to southern New York.

931. Dodge, Phyllis B. *Tales of the Phelps-Dodge Family.* New York: New-York Historical Society, 1987. Railroad financier William E. Dodge invited Fillmore and Webster to the 1851 opening of the New York and Erie Railroad.

932. Everett, Edward. "Beneficial Influence of Railroads." In *Orations and Speeches on Various Occasions.* Boston: Little, Brown, and Company, 1897. 4 vols. 3: 82–87. At the Boston Railroad Jubilee he mentioned that Fillmore took only 24 hours to arrive in Boston from Washington, while Canada's Governor General had breakfast in Montreal and dinner in Boston.

933. Fishlow, Albert. *American Railroads and the Transformation of the Anti-Bellum Economy.* Cambridge: Harvard University Press, 1965. Quantitative analysis stresses the mid-century benefit to agricultural development and social mobility.

934. Galloway, John Debo. *The First Transcontinental Railroad: Central Pacific, Union Pacific.* New York: Simmons-Boardman, 1950. On March 1, 1853, Fillmore approved an amendment to an Army appropriation bill to find a railroad passage from the Mississippi to the Pacific Ocean.

935. Gates, Paul W. *The Illinois Central Railroad and Its Colonization Work.* Cambridge: Harvard University Press, 1934. Fillmore approved the initial congressional land grant to the railroad on September 20, 1850. The landmark grant opened the way for further lavish land grants to railroads.

936. *Gleason's Pictorial Drawing-Room Companion,* October 11, 1851. Fillmore and Lord Elgin gave the Boston Railroad Jubilee an international character as they celebrated the opening of the first Canada-U.S. railroad line.

937. *Gleason's Pictorial Drawing-Room Companion.* June 7, 1851. Illustrations and comments on Fillmore's receptions at Philadelphia and New York City as he traveled to the opening of the New York and Erie Railroad.

938. Harlow, Alvin F. *Steelways of New England.* New York: Creative Age Press, Inc., 1946. In September 1851, Fillmore attended Boston's three-day celebration opening the Boston-to-Montreal railroad.

939. Hungerford, Edward. *Men of Erie: A Story of Human Effort.* New York: Random House, 1946. Descriptive account of Fillmore on the first cross-state run of the New York and Erie Railroad.

939a. Inventor's True Advocate. "To Millard Fillmore, President of the United States." *Scientific American* 6 (July 5, 1851): 331. Asks Fillmore to fill vacancies in the Patent Office with practical mechanics and manufacturers who can understand mechanical inventions.

940. Jackson, W. Turrentine. *Wagon Roads West: A Study of Federal Road Surveys and Construction in the Trans-Mississippi West, 1846–1869.* New Haven: Yale University Press, 1952. In January 1853, Fillmore signed two bills for road construction in the Minnesota and Oregon territories. Bibliography on internal improvements.

941. Kimmel, Lewis H. *Federal Budget and Fiscal Policy, 1789–1958.* Washington, DC: Brookings Institute, 1959. Fillmore advanced the cause of internal improvements while using unemotional and reasoned arguments to guard against criticism from state's rights advocates.

942. Kohlmeier, A. L. *The Old Northwest as the Keystone of the Arch of American Federal Union: A Study in Commerce and Finance.* Bloomington, IN: Principia Press, Inc., 1938. In 1850 the federal government gave land grants to a number of railroads headed by the Illinois Central. Politicians failed to use the favorable inclination of Congress to adopt a Central Pacific Railroad bill in the Compromise of 1850.

943. Laut, Agnes C. *The Romance of the Rails: The Story of the American Railroads.* New York: Tudor Publishing Company, 1936. Humorous description of the President's railroad tour of southern New York.

944. "Literature, Science, Art, Personal Movements etc. "*Harper's Monthly* 3 (June 1851) 134. Fillmore tours southern New York by rail.

945. Malin, James C. *The Nebraska Question, 1852–1854.* Ann Arbor: Edwards Brothers Inc., 1953. Describes congressional concern for national railroads during Fillmore's last months in office.

946. Massachusetts Historical Society, *Proceedings* 47 (1914): 475–76. In November 1851, Fillmore claimed his remarks at the Boston Railroad Jubilee were all impromptu.

947. Mott, Edward Harold. *Between the Ocean and the Lakes: The Story of Erie.* New York: John S. Collins, 1901. Colorful account of Fillmore's tour during the opening of the New York and Erie Railroad.

948. Nelson, E. C. "Presidential Influence on the Policy of Internal Improvements. " *Iowa Journal of History and Politics* 4 (January 1904): 3–69. Fillmore is given high marks for articulating the Whig policy of promoting federal aid to local improvements that will have national economic utility and improve national unity.

949. Neu, Irene D. "The Building of the Sault Canal: 1852–55." *Mississippi Valley Historical Review* 40 (June 1953): 25–46. Fillmore signed the bill that gave federal aid to the construction of the canal.

950. Osborne, Brian S., and Donald Swainson. *The Sault Ste. Marie Canal: A Chapter in the History of Great Lakes Transport.* Ottawa: Parks Canada, 1986. The successful American Sault Canal, aided by Fillmore, inspired a Canadian drive for their own Sault Canal.

951. Pabis, George S. "Delaying the Deluge: The Engineering Debate over Flood Control on the Lower Mississippi River, 1846–1861." *Journal of Southern History.* 64 (August 1998): 421–54. In 1851, Secretary of War Conrad authorized the Mississippi Delta Survey to prevent flooding. The ten-year study set a federal precedent for later western water surveys and water management.

951a. Stark. "Railroad Jubilee." *Scientific American* 7 (September 27, 1851): 10. Describes Boston's celebration, Fillmore's reception, Webster's speech, and the placing of "mere politicians" at the front while the engineers and mechanics were in the "low seats" at the end of the table.

952. Stover, John F. *Iron Road to the West: American Railroads in the 1850s.* New York: Columbia University Press, 1978. Fillmore attended railroad openings, supported congressional railroad legislation, and signed land grants to railroads amounting to over seven million acres. Maps.

953. Taylor, George Rogers. *The Transportation Revolution, 1815–1860.* New York: Holt, Rinehart and Winston, 1951. Significant federal land subsidies to railroads began during the maneuvers to pass the Compromise of 1850.

954. White, Ruth. *Yankee From Sweden: The Dream and the Reality in the Days of John Ericsson.* New York: Henry Holt and Company, 1960. Describes the administration's support for the experimental oceangoing steam paddlewheeler *Ericsson.*

955. Wilgus, William J. *The Railway Interrelations of the United States and Canada.* New York: Russell & Russell, 1970 [1937]. Contains a foldout map of railroads operating in 1851.

956. Williams, Mentor L. "The Chicago River and Harbor Convention, 1847." *Mississippi Valley Historical Review* 35 (March 1949): 607–26. Fillmore was an absent delegate to this convention, which organized Whig opposition to Democratic vetoes on internal improvements. In 1852 he sanctioned over two million dollars for a rivers and harbors appropriation.

957. Woodruff, Robert E. *Erie Railroad—Its Beginnings, 1851.* New York: Newcomen Society of England, American Branch, 1945. Pamphlet describes Fillmore's speeches promoting internal improvements.

4. Appraising the Colonization of African Americans

958. *African Repository* 29 (March 1853): 72–73. Fillmore was made a life director of the American Colonization Society at the end of his presidency. Includes Fillmore's letter of acceptance and approval of the society's goals. He wrote that African Americans could attain equality only in Africa.

959. Everett, Edward. "Address of the Hon. Edward Everett." In *Annual Reports of the American Society for Colonizing the Free People of Color of the United States. Volumes 34–43, 1851–60.* New York: Negro Universities Press, 1969. 36: 20–31. At the 1853 meeting, the Secretary of State reported that America's prejudice conditioned the life of African Americans to unredeemed hardship. African Americans were not naturally inferior but they needed to colonize Africa to gain the freedom that would improve their race.

960. Fredrickson, George M. *The Black Image in the White Mind: The Debate on Afro-American Character and Destiny, 1817–1914.* New York: Harper & Row, Publishers, 1971. Describes mid-century attitude that African Americans were inferior, a social danger to the nation, and the revival of plans to emigrate African Americans out of America.

961. Fuller, Rev. Dr. "Speech of the Rev. Dr. Fuller." In *Annual Reports of the American Society for Colonizing the Free People of Color of the United States. Volumes 34–43, 1851–60.* New York: Negro Universities Press, 1969. 43–55. At the 1851 meeting, Fuller recognized Fillmore in the audience and mentioned that the President's rise from poverty to greatness was not, and would not be, available to free men of color in America.

962. Knobel, Dale T. " 'Native Soil': Nativists, Colonizationists, and the Rhetoric of Nationality." *Civil War History* 27 (December 1981): 314–37. Fillmore's sympathy for African American colonization fit his policy of suppressing sectional excitement. He hoped to see free African Americans emigrate to allay profound racial animosity in the North and West while slowly ending slavery in the South. He intended to say so in his final address but he suppressed it at the urging of his cabinet.

963. "Monthly Report of Current Events—United States." *Harper's Monthly* 6 (April 1853): 695. Friends contributed $1,000 to make Fillmore a lifetime member in the American Colonization Society, whose goals he approved.

964. O'Reilly, Kenneth. *Nixon's Piano: Presidents and Racial Politics from Washington to Clinton.* New York: Free Press, 1995. Though he considered the Fugitive Slave Law repugnant, Fillmore followed his Whig principles and executed the law of the land. Privately he worried that a race war would ensue if slaves were freed and not colonized.

965. Severance, Frank H., ed. "Mr. Fillmore's Views Relating to Slavery." *Millard Fillmore Papers, 2 Volumes. Publications of the Buffalo Historical Society, Volume 10.* Buffalo: Buffalo Historical Society, 1907. 1: 311–24. Reprints the self-suppressed portion of his 1852 presidential message where he promotes the policies of the American Colonization Society. He further writes that the manumission of slaves and subsequent emigration of free African Americans should be a national work supported by public revenues. Fillmore believed in protecting African American's by directing them back to Africa and away from a probable violent battle with white America in which African Americans would lose to superior forces.

966. Staudenraus, P. J. *The African Colonization Movement, 1816–1865.* New York: Columbia University Press, 1961. At mid-century there was a growing sentiment for removal of slaves and free African Americans. The American Colonization Society found approval from prominent politicians like Fillmore, Webster, and Everett.

967. Webster, Daniel. "Address of the Hon. Daniel Webster." In *Annual Reports of the American Society for Colonizing the Free People of Color of the United States. Volumes 34–43, 1851–60.* New York: Negro Universities Press, 1969. 35: 26–29.

At the 1852 meeting, the Secretary of State announced that it was not possible to amalgamate the races in America. African Americans should emigrate to Africa were they would not be subject to prejudice but could work for their own improvement.

5. Veto

968. Spitzer, Robert J. *The Presidential Veto: Touchstone of the American Presidency.* Albany: State University of New York Press, 1988. Presidents Taylor and Fillmore followed Whig principles and refrained from using the veto.

969. Watson, Richard A. "Origins and Early Development of the Veto Power." *Presidential Studies Quarterly* 17 (Spring 1987): 401–12. Fillmore vetoed no legislation.

6. Pardon, Drayton Affair

970. Drayton, Daniel. *Personal Memoir of Daniel Drayton.* New York: American and Foreign Anti-Slavery Society, 1855. Account of the Captain who was imprisoned for transporting escaped slaves on his ship and was later pardoned by Fillmore.

971. Finkelman, Paul, ed. *Slavery, Race and the American Legal System, 1700–1872. 16 vols. Slave Rebels, Abolitionists, and Southern Courts: The Pamphlet Literature, Series 4.* New York: Garland Publishing, Inc., 1988. 2 vols. 2: 445–68, 471–592. Contains a narrative of the *Pearl* episode by S. G. Howe and the *Memoirs* of convicted Captain Daniel Drayton.

972. Lewis, David L. *District of Columbia: A Bicentennial History.* New York: W. W. Norton & Company, Inc., 1976. The capture of the fugitive slaves on the *Pearl,* and the incarceration of Drayton influenced the bill to abolish slavetrading in the District.

973. Mann, Horace. "Sketch of the Opening Arguments in the Case of the United States *vs.* Daniel Drayton." In *Slavery Letters and Speeches.* New York: Burt Franklin, 1969. 84–118. Original defense of Drayton for stealing slaves to freedom.

974. Paynter, John H. *Fugitives of the Pearl.* New York: A M S Press, 1971 [1930]. Imaginative narrative.

975. ———. "Fugitives of the *Pearl.*" *Journal of Negro History* 1 (July 1916): 243–60. The ordeal of the Edmondson family's return to slavery and later ransom.

976. Rohrs, Richard C. "Antislavery Politics and the *Pearl Incident of 1848.*" *Historian* 56 (Summer 1994): 711–24. Fillmore pardoned Drayton after failing to receive the nomination for President.

977. Sumner, Charles. "Pardoning Power of the President." In *Charles Sumner: His Complete Works*. New York: Negro Universities Press, 1969 [1900]. 20 vols. 3: 219–33. At Fillmore's request Sumner wrote a legal brief based on local Washington law and the President's pardoning powers. Attorney General Crittenden agreed with the brief, and Fillmore signed Drayton's pardon on August 4, 1852.

7. Patronage and Civil Service

978. Fish, Carl Russell. *The Civil Service and the Patronage*. Cambridge: Harvard University Press, 1920. Fillmore made 88 removals to reward friends. He also suggested to his political enemy, Thurlow Weed, that he accept the ministry in Austria.

979. ———— . "Removal of Officials by the President of the United States." In *Annual Report of the American Historical Association Volume 1, for the Year 1899*. Washington, DC: Government Printing Office, 1900. 2 vols. 1: 65–86. The tables and graphs covering removals show Fillmore's restrained policy.

980. Fritz, Christian G. *Federal Justice in California: The Court of Ogden Hoffman, 1851–1891*. Lincoln: University of Nebraska Press, 1991. Influential friends helped Fillmore decide appointments.

981. Hall, Kermit L. "Mere Party and the Magic Mirror: California's First Lower Federal Judicial Appointments." *Hastings Law Journal* 32 (March 1981): 819–37. A primer on patronage. Analyses the many factors that went into Fillmore's California patronage appointments.

982. ———— . *The Politics of Justice, Lower Federal Judicial Selection and the Second Party System, 1829–61*. Lincoln: University of Nebraska Press, 1979. Revealing study of Fillmore's judicial and territorial appointments and their relation to the Compromise of 1850.

983. Tabachnik, Leonard. "Political Patronage and Ethnic Groups: Foreign-born in the United States Customhouse Service, 1821–1861." *Civil War History* 17 (September 1971): 222–31. There was a slight decline in Irish patronage at the New York Custom House during Fillmore's administration.

984. Titlow, Richard E. *Americans Import Merit: Origins of the United States Civil Service and the Influence of British Models*. Washington, DC: University Press of America, Inc., 1979. Congress requested Fillmore's Cabinet to make recommendations to professionalize the Civil Service. Fillmore signed a reform law in 1853, but it had little effect.

985. United States Civil Service Commission. *History of the Civil Service, 1789 to the Present.* Washington, DC: United States Printing Office, 1941. One of Fillmore's last presidential acts was signing the first Civil Service Law.

8. The Press

986. Ames, William E. *A History of the* National Intelligencer. Chapel Hill: University of North Carolina Press, 1972. Official organ of the administration. Supported Webster's nomination in 1852 and gave Fillmore lukewarm support in 1856 because he was too much of an antislavery man to suit the editors.

987. Laracey, Mel. "The Presidential Newspaper: The Forgotten Way of Going Public." In *Speaking to the People: The Rhetorical Presidents in Historical Perspective,* ed. Richard J. Ellis. Amherst: University of Massachusetts Press, 1998. Fillmore made the old Whig *National Intelligencer* his administration paper. It carried no administration rhetoric.

988. Marbut, F. B., *News from the Capital: The Story of Washington Reporting.* Carbondale: Southern Illinois University Press, 1971. Fillmore was the first to send out advanced copies of his annual messages so newspapers could have them as they were being read to Congress.

989. Pollard, James E. *The Presidents and the Press.* New York: Macmillan Company, 1947. Fillmore used the partisan press throughout his early career, but he did not use it for his own advantage while in the White House and rarely in retirement.

990. Rogers, David A. "The Buffalo *Commercial Advertiser:* Its Editorial Attitude Toward National Issues, 1835–1896." Master's Thesis, Archives, State University of New York at Buffalo, 1950. Whig and pro-Fillmore paper throughout the 1850s but criticized his disapproval of Lincoln's conduct of the Civil War.

991. Smith, Culver. *The Press, Politics and Patronage: The American Government's Use of Newspapers, 1789–1875.* Athens: University of Georgia Press, 1977. Fillmore and Webster distributed federal payments to Whig papers for publishing federal notices. Fillmore looked for papers supporting the Compromise while Webster looked for papers that would support his presidential nomination in 1852.

992. Tebbel, John, and Sarah Miles Watts. *The Press and the Presidency from George Washington to Ronald Reagan.* New York: Oxford University Press, 1985. Fillmore shunned the press in order to subdue partisan and sectional conflict.

9. Washington, DC

993. Brown, Glenn. *History of the Capital.* Washington, DC: Government Printing Office, 1902. 2 vols. Volume Two contains designs for the Capital extension approved by Fillmore. He disregarded pleas from Congress to consult with them.

994. Cole, John Y. *For Congress and the Nation: A Chronological History of the Library of Congress.* Washington, DC: Library of Congress, 1979. After the Library fire in December 1851, Fillmore approved emergency funds to pay for the fire-fighting bills and the temporary quarters for the Library.

995. Federal Writers' Project. *Washington, City and Capital: Federal Writers' Project, Works Progress Administration for the District of Columbia, Washington, D.C.: A Guide to the National Capital.* New York: Hastings House, 1937. Mentions Fillmore's work on the Capitol, the White House, and his association with area churches.

996. Gillette, Howard, Jr. *Between Justice and Beauty: Race, Planning, and the Failure of Urban Policy in Washington, D.C.* Baltimore: Johns Hopkins University Press, 1995. Fillmore wanted to improve the look and sanitation of the Washington Mall. Andrew Jackson Downing prepared designs but died in 1852 and little more was done.

997. *Gleason's Pictorial Drawing-Room Companion,* August 2, 1851. Two engravings of Fillmore laying the cornerstone of the extension to the Capitol on July 4th.

998. *Gleason's Pictorial Drawing-Room Companion,* March 13, 1852. Illustrations and comments on the extension of the Capitol. Fillmore chose the architect and design, which drew admiration as construction progressed.

998a. Goode, James M. "Thomas U. Walter and the Search for Property." In *The United States Capital: Designing a National Icon.* ed. Donald R. Kennon. Athens: Ohio University Press, 2000. Congress authorized Fillmore to select an architect and decide on a new Capitol or expand the old one. He chose Walter, who added wings on the old building for the Senate and House of Representatives.

999. Liscombe, Rhodri Winsor. *Altogether American: Robert Mills, Architect and Engineer, 1771–1855.* New York: Oxford University Press, 1994. Fillmore appointed Thomas U. Walter the architect for the Capitol extension. Contains many architectural drawings and reproductions of Washington buildings and monuments. Extensive bibliography on Washington and its architecture.

1000. McLaughlin, Charles Capen, and Charles E. Beveridge, eds. *The Papers of Frederick Law Olmstead.* Baltimore: Johns Hopkins University Press, 1977. 5 vols.

In volume 1. Olmstead thought the Mall Park, commissioned by Fillmore, was the first great public landscaping by the government.

1001. O'Malley, Therese. " 'A Public Museum of Trees': Mid-Nineteenth Century Plans for the Mall." In *The Mall in Washington, 1791–1991,* ed. Richard Longsteth. Hanover: University Press of New England, 1991. Fillmore began improving the Washington Mall before asking Andrew Jackson Downing to develop plans for a formal park. Includes letter from Downing to Fillmore explaining his plans.

1002. Patterson, Richard S., and Richardson Dougall. *The Eagle and the Shield: A History of the Great Seal of the United States.* Washington, DC: Department of State, 1978. Fillmore reintroduced the use of the Presidential Seal.

1003. *We, the People: The Story of the United States Capital, Its Past and Its Promise.* Washington, DC: National Geographic Society, 1967. After congressional approval, Fillmore authorized the expansion of the Capitol.

10. Territories

1004. Avery, Mary W. *Washington, A History of the Evergreen State.* Seattle: University of Washington Press, 1965. Fillmore signed the bill creating Washington Territory two days before he left office.

1005. Brown, Robert M. "A Territorial Delegate in Action." *Minnesota History* 31 (September 1950): 172–78. Political sketch of Henry H. Sibley, Minnesota delegate to Congress during Fillmore's presidency.

1006. Carey, Charles H. *General History of Oregon, Through Early Statehood.* Portland: Binfords & Mort, Publishers, 1971.

1007. Carter, Clarence Edwin, ed. *Territorial Papers of the United States.* Washington, DC: Government Printing office, 1934. 28 vols. Volume One lists the territorial officers from 1789 to 1872.

1008. Eblen, Jack Ericson. *The First and Second United States Empires: Governors and Territorial Government, 1784–1912.* Pittsburgh: University of Pittsburgh Press, 1968. After signing the Washington Territory Bill, Fillmore let Pierce appoint the first set of federal officials.

1009. Fuller, George W. *A History of the Pacific Northwest.* New York: Alfred A. Knopf, 1931. Describes efforts to organize the Territory of Washington.

1010. *Gleason's Pictorial Drawing-Room Companion,* May 29, 1852. Description of the Oregon Territory.

1011. Gluek, Alvin C., Jr. *Minnesota and the Manifest Destiny of the Canadian Northwest: A Study in Canadian-American Relations.* Toronto: University of Toronto Press, 1965. Reviews Minnesota's territorial years, 1849–1857, and mentions the Indian treaties submitted by Fillmore to the Senate.

1012. Johannsen, Robert W. *The Frontier, The Union and Stephen A. Douglas.* Urbana: University of Illinois Press, 1989. Describes the Oregon Territory movement for self government.

1013. Johansen, Dorothy O., and Charles M. Gates. *Empire of the Columbia: A History of the Pacific Northwest.* New York: Harper & Brothers, Publishers, 1957. Mentions Fillmore's signing the bill creating Washington Territory and attempting new Indian policies.

1014. McMullin, Thomas A., and David Walker. *Biographical Directory of American Territorial Governors.* Westport, CT: Meckler Publishing, 1984.

1015. Onuf, Peter S. "Territories and Statehood." In *Encyclopedia of American Political History: Studies of the Principal Movements and Ideas,* ed. Jack P. Greene. New York: Charles Scribner's Sons, 1984. 3 vols. 3: 1283–304. Different political times and diplomatic circumstances worked against a standard criteria for territorial development and applications for statehood. Bibliography.

1016. Parker, David W. *Calendar of Papers in Washington Archives Relating to the Territories of the United States (to 1873).* New York: Kraus Reprint Corporation, 1965 [1911]. Identifies Fillmore letters regarding Minnesota, New Mexico, Utah, and Oregon.

1017. Roderick, Janna. "Indian-White Relations in the Washington Territory: The Question of Treaties and Indian Fishing Rights." *Journal of the West* 16 (July 1977): 23–34. In 1850, Fillmore signed the Oregon Donation Land Act to encourage rapid American settlement in Oregon Territory.

1018. Thorpe, Francis Newton, comp. *The Federal and State Constitutions, Colonial Charters, and Other Organic Laws of the States, Territories, and Colonies.* Buffalo: William S. Hein & Co., Inc., 1993 [1909]. 7 vols. 7: 3963–71. An Act to establish the Territorial Government of Washington, 1853.

F. INDIAN AFFAIRS

1. Office of Indian Affairs

1019. Berthrong, Donald J. "Nineteenth-Century United States Government Agencies." In *Handbook of North American Indians, Volume 4: History of Indian-White*

Relations, ed. Wilcomb E. Washburn and William C. Sturtevant. Washington, DC: Smithsonian Institution, 1988. 4: 255–63. In 1849, the Bureau of Indian Affairs was transferred from the War Department to the Interior Department. The new territories brought new regional departments: Oregon, 1848; New Mexico and Utah, 1850; California, 1852; and Washington, 1853.

1020. Hill, Edward E. *The Office of Indian Affairs, 1824–1880: Historical Sketches.* New York: Clearwater Publishing Company, Inc., 1973. Brief histories of Indian Affairs field offices, including an index to archival material.

1021. Lea, Luke. "Report of Commissioner Luke Lea (1851)." In *The American Indian and the United States: A Documentary History,* ed. Wilcomb E. Washburn. New York: Random House, 1973. 4 vols. 1: 50–61. Reviews continental distribution of Indians, their treaties, and white encroachment. Lea believed Indians capable of elevation to white civilization.

1022. Neil, William M. "The Territorial Governor as Indian Superintendent in the Trans-Mississippi West." *Mississippi Valley Historical Review* 43 (September 1956): 213–38. Duties of the men appointed by the president to oversee Indian relations.

1023. Schmeckebier, Laurence F. *The Office of Indian Affairs: Its History, Activities and Organization.* Baltimore: Johns Hopkins University Press, 1927. The executive and legislative branches contributed little to the progress of Indian culture or their assimilation during the mid decades of the nineteenth century.

1024. Tennert, Robert A. "Luke Lea." In *The Commissioners of Indian Affairs, 1824–1977,* ed. Robert M. Kvasnicka and Herman J. Viola. Lincoln: University of Nebraska Press, 1979. During Fillmore's administration, Lea reorganized the office and successfully negotiated with the Plains Indians.

2. Indian-U.S. Relations

1025. Abel Annie H. "Proposals for an Indian State, 1778–1878." In *Annual Report of the American Historical Association, for the Year 1907.* Washington, DC: Government Printing Office, 1908. 2 vols. 1: 89–104. Includes a letter to Fillmore from Wisconsin Congressman James Duane Doty recommending a territorial organization run by Indians with more individual property and civic rights. The administration ignored the letter.

1026. Champagne, Duane, ed. *Chronology of Native North American History: From Pre-Columbian Times to the Present.* Detroit: Gale Research Inc., 1994. Includes Fillmore's refusal to finance the California militia's harassment of natives.

1027. Heard, J. Norman. *Handbook of the American Frontier: Four Centuries of Indian-White Relations.* Lanham, MD: Scarecrow Press, Inc., 1987–1998. 5 vols. Volumes arranged by geographic area. Volume Five has chronology, bibliography and index.

1028. Hill, Edward E. *Guide to Records in the National Archives of the United States Relating to American Indians.* Washington, DC: National Archives and Records Service, 1981. Guide to federal records and correspondence.

1029. Institute for the Development of Indian Law. *A Chronological List of Treaties and Agreements Made by Indian Tribes with the United States.* Washington, DC: Institute for the Development of Indian Law, 1973. Includes Fillmore's administration.

1030. Jackson, Helen Hunt. *A Century of Dishonor: The Early Crusade for Indian Reform.* New York: Harper & Row, Publishers, 1965 [1881]. Critical assessment of the United States' veracity in making and fulfilling Indian treaties. Describes the Fort Laramie Treaty of 1851 with the Plains Indians, and the 1851 treaties with the Eastern Sioux at Traverse de Sioux and Mendota. Contains large extracts from the treaties.

1031. Kappler, Charles J. *Indian Affairs: Laws and Treaties.* Washington, DC: Government Printing Office, 1904. 7 vols. Volumes 2 and 4 contain material from Fillmore's administration.

1032. Martin, John H. *List of Documents Concerning the Negotiation of Ratified Indian Treaties, 1801–1869.* Milwood, NY: Kraus Reprint Co., 1975 [1949]. Select list of treaties from Fillmore's administration with list of administrators.

1033. Nichols, Roger L. *American Frontier and Western Issues: A Historiographical Review.* Westport, CT: Greenwood Press, 1986. Bibliographic essays.

1034. Prucha, Francis Paul. *A Bibliographic Guide to the History of Indian-White Relations in the United States.* Chicago: University of Chicago Press, 1977. Exhaustive bibliography.

1035. ——— , ed. *Documents of United States Indian Policy.* Lincoln: University of Nebraska Press, 1975. Contains edited documents pertaining to Indian policy during the Fillmore administration.

1036. ——— . *The Great Father: The United States Government and the American Indians.* Lincoln: University of Nebraska Press, 1984. 2 vols. Volume One reviews the government's sensitivity to white settlers during the 1850s and the move toward a national system of reservations for Indians.

1037. ——— . "Indian Relations." In *Encyclopedia of American Political History: Studies of the Principal Movements and Ideas,* ed. Jack P. Greene. New York: Charles Scribner's Sons, 1984. 3 vols. 2: 609–22. The massive western migration in the late 1840s and 1850s demolished the barrier separating Indian and whites. A movement began to concentrate the Plains Indians North and South of an open path to the West.

1038. ——— . *Indian-White Relations in the United States: A Bibliography of Works Published 1975–1980.* Lincoln: University of Nebraska Press, 1982. Supplement to the 1977 guide.

1039. Spicer, Edward H. "American Indians, Federal Policy Toward." In *Harvard Encyclopedia of American Ethnic Groups,* ed. Stephan Thernstrom. Cambridge: Harvard University Press, 1980. Overview of U.S. policy.

1040. Sturtevant, William C., ed. *Handbook of North American Indians.* Washington, DC: Smithsonian Institution, 1978–1986. 20 vols. Encyclopedic summary of the prehistory, history, and cultures of the aboriginal peoples living north of central Mexico. Volumes 5 through 15 are devoted to major geographic cultural areas in North America. Extensive bibliography plus maps, paintings, and photographs.

1041. Tennert, Robert A., Jr. *Alternative to Extinction: Federal Indian Policy and the Beginnings of the Reservation System, 1846–1851.* Philadelphia: Temple University Press, 1975. Under Taylor and Fillmore, a policy of restricting western tribes to designated areas was introduced to protect Indians and defend settlers.

1042. Viola, Herman J. *Diplomats in Buckskins: A History of Indian Delegations in Washington City.* Washington, DC: Smithsonian Institution Press, 1981. Entertaining illustrated history including accounts of Fillmore as the Great White Father.

1043. Weeks, Philip Charles. "The United States and the Search for the Solution to the 'Indian Question' in the Nineteenth Century." Ph.D. diss., Case Western Reserve University, 1989. The administration participated in a "policy of concentration" for Native Americans to facilitate the migration of white settlers.

3. Eastern Plains Indians

1044. Babcock, Willoughby M. "With Ramsey to Pembina: A Treaty-Making Trip in 1851." *Minnesota History* 38 (March 1962): 1–10. Treaty with the Chippewa for Red River Valley land in Minnesota.

1045. Current, Richard N. *The History of Wisconsin, Vol. 2: The Civil War Era, 1848–1873.* Madison: State Historical Society of Wisconsin, 1976. Fillmore delayed removal of the Chippewa and Menominee after learning their new western lands were not ready.

1046. Folwell, William Wates. *A History of Minnesota.* St. Paul: Minnesota Historical Society, 1956. 4 vols. Volume One contains reports on the 1851 Treaty of Traverse des Sioux.

1047. Haygood, William Converse. "Red Child, White Child: The Strange Disappearance of Casper Partridge.*" Wisconsin Magazine of History* 58 (Summer 1975): 259–312. Fillmore was sympathetic to the Menominees' reasoned protest against their proposed removal.

1048. Heilbron, Bertha L. "Frank B. Mayer and the Treaties of 1851." *Minnesota History* 22 (June 1941): 133–56. Describes the Northern Plains treaty at Traverse des Sioux and Mendota.

1049. ———— , ed. *With Pen and Pencil on the Frontier in 1851: The Diary and Sketches of Frank Blockwell Mayer.* St. Paul: Minnesota Historical Society Press, 1986. Mayer attended the Treaty of Traverse de Sioux in July 1851.

1050. Ourada, Patricia K. *The Menominee Indians, A History.* Norman: University of Oklahoma Press, 1979. Fillmore delayed the tribe's removal to ensure its safety on new land reserves.

1051. Turner Katherine C. *Red Men Calling on the Great White Father.* Norman: University of Oklahoma Press, 1951. Recalls Fillmore's meeting with Menominee spokesperson Oshkosh, which resulted in the tribe remaining on their old land until new reserve land was obtained.

1052. Wrone, David R. "Indian Treaties and the Democratic Idea." *Wisconsin Magazine of History* 70 (Winter 1986–1987): 83–106. Credits Fillmore for interrupting the removal of the Chippewa and Menominee before proper new reserves were available.

4. Great Plains and Mountain Indians

1053. Hafen, Leroy R., and W. J. Ghent. *Broken Hand: The Life Story of Thomas Fitzpatric, Chief of the Mountain Men.* Denver: Old West Publishing Company, 1931. Sketch of Fillmore meeting with Plains Indians after the 1851 Great Indian Council at Fort Laramie.

1054. Hafen, Leroy R. *Fort Laramie and the Pageant of the West, 1834–1890.* Glendale: Arthur H. Clark Company, 1938. Description of the historic 1851 Plains Indian Council, with a sketch of the Indian delegation to Fillmore.

1055. Hill, Burton S. "The Great Indian Treaty Council of 1851." *Nebraska History* 47 (March 1966): 85–110. Describes the unique tribal gathering at Fort Laramie leading to agreements between tribes and a treaty with the United States.

1056. Institute for the Development of Indian Law. *Treaties & Agreements of the Northern Plains.* Washington, DC: Institute of the Development of Indian Law, 1973. Reprints September 1851 Treaty of Ft. Laramie with the Sioux, Cheyenne, Arapaho, Crow, Assinaoine, Gros-Ventre, Mandans, and Arickara.

1057. Malouf, Carling I., and John Findlay. "Euro-American Impact Before 1870." In *Handbook of North American Indians, Volume 11: Great Basin,* ed. William C. Sturtevant and Warren D'Azevedo. Washington, DC: Smithsonian Institution, 1986. 499–516. Reviews Mormon and non-Mormon incursions into the Indian cultural regions of Utah territory.

1058. Price, Catherine. *The Ogalala People, 1841–1879: A Political History.* Lincoln: University of Nebraska Press, 1996. Indian and government representatives differed about the functions of the 1851 treaty.

1059. Russel, Robert R. "Removing an Obstacle from Northern Routes: The Kansas-Nebraska Bill." In Russel, *Critical Studies in Antebellum Sectionalism: Essays in American Political and Economic History.* Westport, CT: Greenwood Press, 1972. Indian removal treaties, such as the Fort Laramie Treaty in 1851, were the first step to open territory for railroads and settlers.

1060. "Treaty of Fort Laramie." In *The American Indian and the United States: A Documentary History,* ed. Wilcomb E Washburn. New York: Random House, 1973. 4 vols. 4: 2477–80.

1061. White, Richard. "The Winning of the West: The Expansion of the Western Sioux in the Eighteenth and Nineteenth Centuries." *Journal of American History* 65 (September 1978): 319–43. The Fort Laramie Treaty confirmed Sioux dominance in the region while the details proved irrelevant as boundary incursions and intertribal war continued.

5. Southwest Indians

1062. Bender, A. B. "Frontier Defense in the Territory of New Mexico, 1846–1853." *New Mexico Historical Society* 9 (July 1934): 249–72. Inadequate military strength frustrated the administration's policy to locate Indians away from white settlements.

1063. Clemmer, Richard O. *Roads in the Sky: The Hopi Indians in a Century of Change.* Boulder, CO: Westview Press, 1995. In 1852 a delegation presented

Fillmore a pair of feathers symbolizing the relationship of the Hopi and the President. Twentieth-century traditionalist leaders would send a similar set of prayer feathers to President Jimmy Carter.

1064. Faulk, Odie B. *Crimson Desert: Indian Wars of the American Southwest.* New York: Oxford University Press, 1974. Fillmore and Conrad used troops to protect travelers and prevent Indian incursions into Mexico.

1065. ———. *Land of Many Frontiers: A History of the American Southwest.* New York: Oxford University Press, 1968. Chapter Four reviews the hostility between settlers and Indians, and Fillmore's attempts to use the military for separating the belligerents.

1066. Harmon, George D. "The United States Indian Policy in Texas, 1845–1860." *Mississippi Valley Historical Review* 17 (December 1930): 377–403. Fillmore's policy to set aside reserve lands for Indians became Texas policy after years of federal-state confusion.

1067. Institute for the Development of Indian Law. *Treaties & Agreements of the Indian Tribes of the Southwest including Western Oklahoma.* Washington, DC: Institute for the Development of Indian Law, 1973. Contains the Santa Fe Treaty with the Apache and the unratified California treaties.

1068. Park, Joseph E. "The Apaches in Mexican-American Relations, 1848–1861." In *U.S.-Mexico Borderlands: Historical and Contemporary Perspectives,* ed. Oscar J. Martinez. Wilmington, DE: Scholarly Resources Inc., 1996. To stop Indian border hostilities, the United States and Apaches signed the Santa Fe Treaty in 1852. Hostilities continued because the United States did not enforce the treaty and the informality of Apache government allowed non-compliance.

1069. Smith, F. Todd. *The Caddos, the Wichitas, and the United States, 1846–1901.* College Station: Texas A&M University Press, 1996. Fillmore failed to convince the Texas legislature to establish a reserve for Indians.

1070. Sunseri, Alvin R. *Seeds of Discord: New Mexico in the Aftermath of American Conquest, 1846–1861.* Chicago: Nelson-Hall, 1979. Fillmore received a delegation of Pueblo Indians and pledged to look into their land and water problems with white settlers.

1071. Timmons, W. H. "American El Paso: The Formative Years, 1848–1854." *Southwestern Historical Quarterly* 87 (July 1983): 1–36. El Paso was the center for Fillmore's response to Indian hostilities and for border diplomacy with Mexico.

6. Pacific Coast Indians

1072. Beckman, Stephan Dow. "History of Western Oregon Since 1846." In *Handbook of North American Indians, Volume 7: Northwest Coast,* ed. William C. Sturtevant and Wayne Suttles. Washington, DC: Smithsonian Institution, 1990. 180–88. Reviews consequences of the 1850 Oregon Donation Act on Indians. Lists the ratified and unratified treaties from 1850 to 1855.

1073. Coan, C. F. "The First Stage of the Federal Indian Relations in the Pacific Northwest, 1849–52." *Oregon Historical Quarterly* 22 (March 1921): 46–88. Treaty negotiations with Indian Affairs Commissioner Luke Lea.

1074. Ellison, William H. "The Federal Indian Policy in California, 1846–1860." *Mississippi Valley Historical Review* 9 (June 1922): 37–67. Describes the trips of federal Indian commissioners to count, assess, and treaty with tribes coming under U.S. jurisdiction for the first time. Their treaties were not ratified because of settler opposition to the proposed large land reserves.

1075. Ghent, W. J. "Beale, Edward Fitzgerald." *DAB* (1964), 1, pt. 2: 88–89. Adventurous Naval officer who served in California during the Mexican War and later explored the new state. Fillmore appointed him superintendent of Indian Affairs for California in late 1852.

1076. Heizer, Robert F. "Treaties." In *Handbook of North American Indians, Volume 8: California,* ed. Robert F. Heizer and William C. Sturtevant. Washington, DC: Smithsonian Institution, 1978. 15 vols. 8: 701–4. Volume Eight describes Fillmore's treaty commissioners and the Senate's refusal to ratify 18 treaties on objections from California.

1077. Howard, Helen Addison. "Unique History of Fort Tejon." *Journal of the West* 18 (January 1979): 41–51. Fillmore appointed Edward F. Beale, former Naval officer and California explorer, as superintendent of Indian Affairs for California in 1852.

1078. Kibby, Leo P. "California, The Civil War, and the Indian Problem: An Account of California's Participation in the Great Conflict." *Journal of the West* 4 (July 1965): 377–410. To Fillmore's disappointment, eighteen 1851 treaties with California Indians were rejected by the Senate in 1852.

1079. Kopp, April. "Camel Corps U S A." *American History Illustrated* 16 (December 1981): 8–17. Fillmore appointed Edward F. Beale the superintendent of Indian Affairs in California. He later tested the viability of camels in the Southwest.

1080. Marino, Cesare. "History of Western Washington Since 1846." In *Handbook of North American Indians, Volume 7: Northwest Coast,* ed. William C. Sturtevant and Wayne Suttles. Washington, DC: Smithsonian Institution, 1990. 169–79. Brief mention of the Indian impediment to white expansion after the 1853 Washington Organization Act.

7. Southeastern Indians

1081. Bittle, George C. "Florida Frontier Incidents During the 1850s." *Florida Historical Quarterly* 49 (October 1970): 153–60. Florida was relatively safe but Seminoles would live off their reservation, steal livestock, and frustrate the state militias.

1082. Covington, James W. *The Seminoles of Florida.* Gainesville: University Press of Florida, 1993. Fillmore supported Seminole removal.

1083. Sefton, James E. "Black Slaves, Red Masters, White Middlemen: A Congressional Debate of 1852." *Florida State Historical Quarterly* 51 (October 1972): 113–28. Fillmore signed a bill reimbursing slaveowners for slaves living with Indians.

8. Iroquois Indians

1084. Abber, Thomas S., and Elisabeth Tooker. "Seneca." In *Handbook of North American Indians, Volume 15: Northeast,* ed. William C. Sturtevant and Bruce G Trigger. Washington, DC: Smithsonian Institution, 1978. 505–17. History of the Seneca nation, including its sale of the Buffalo Creek Reservation, which allowed expansion of the eastern boundaries of the City of Buffalo.

1085. Armstrong, William H. *Warrior in Two Camps: Ely S. Parker, Union General and Seneca Chief.* Syracuse: Syracuse University Press, 1978. The Seneca Indians felt bitter toward Fillmore for condoning their removal from western New York reserves.

1086. Hass, Marilyn L. *The Seneca and Tuscarora Indians: An Annotated Bibliography.* Metuchen, NJ: Scarecrow Press, 1994. Excellent comprehensive resource on history and culture.

1087. Tooker, Elisabeth. "Iroquois Since 1820." In *Handbook of North American Indians, Volume 15: Northeast,* ed. William C. Sturtevant and Bruce G Trigger. Washington, DC: Smithsonian Institution, 1978. 449–65. Historical and cultural review. Maps and bibliography.

1088. ——— . "The League of the Iroquois: Its History, Politics, and Ritual." In *Handbook of North American Indians, Volume 15: Northeast,* ed. William C. Sturtevant and Bruce G Trigger. Washington, DC: Smithsonian Institution, 1978. 418–41. History of the Iroquois governing assembly.

G. THE ARMED SERVICES

1. The U.S. Army

1089. Bender, Averam B. *The March of Empire: Frontier Defense in the Southwest, 1848–1860.* Lawrence: University of Kansas Press, 1952. Secretary of War Conrad established military posts for the security of settlers and to show strength to Indians.

1090. Coffman, Edward M. *The Old Army: A Portrait of the American Army in Peacetime, 1784–1898.* New York: Oxford University Press, 1986. Reviews problems supplying western military posts.

1091. Frazer, Robert W. *Forts and Supplies: The Role of the Army in the Economy of the Southwest, 1846–1861.* Albuquerque: University of New Mexico Press, 1983. Fillmore and Conrad were criticized for reducing expenditures to the Army while creating western forts.

1092. Frazer, Robert W., ed. *Mansfield on the Condition of the Western Forts, 1853–54.* Norman: University of Oklahoma Press, 1963. Includes an October 1853 report by Col. Joseph Mansfield on new forts, including Fort Fillmore.

1093. Higham, Robin. *A Guide to the Sources of the United States Military History.* Hamden: Archon Books, 1975. Bibliographic essays on the domestic and international activities of the services.

1094. Ingersoll, L[urton]. D[unham]. *History of the War Department of the United States with Biographical Sketches of the Secretaries.* Washington, DC: Francis B. Mohun, 1880. Little on the early 1850s but contains biographies of Winfield Scott and Secretary Conrad.

1095. Kellstrom, Carl Wykoff. "Administration and Policy Formation in the U.S. War Department, 1849–1861." Ph.D. diss., University of California-Los Angeles, 1974. Describes the department's control of the Army while inadequately funded by Congress.

1096. May, Robert E. "Young American Males and Filibustering in the Age of Manifest Destiny: The United States Army as a Cultural Mirror." *Journal of American History* 78 (December 1991): 857–86. The Army lacked resources to suppress filibusters. Even some of its own young officers were tempted by the romance of battle in foreign lands, higher rank, riches, and public adulation.

1097. "Military Posts of the United States." *Whig Almanac, 1853.* New York: New York Tribune, 1853. 31–32. List of posts, commanders, and number of troops, including Fort Fillmore in New Mexico.

1098. Prucha, Francis Paul. *A Guide to the Military Posts of the United States, 1789–1895.* Madison: State Historical Society of Wisconsin, 1964. Includes maps, descriptions, and bibliographies.

1099. Skelton, William B. *An American Profession of Arms: The Army Officer Corps, 1784–1861.* Lawrence: University Press of Kansas, 1992. Fillmore used the Army as an instrument of government while able to continue its separation from sectional controversies.

1100. ———. "Officers and Politicians: The Origins of Army Politics in the United States Before the Civil War." *Armed Forces and Society* 6 (Fall 1979): 22–48. The military played a peripheral role in American politics and were subordinate to national and foreign policy. However, the sectional crisis in the later 1850s did disrupt the professional commitment to the national army.

1101. Totten, J. G. *Report of General J. G. Totten, Chief Engineer, on the Subject of National Defense.* 1851. New York: Arno Press, 1979 [1851]. Report on U.S. coastal defenses.

1102. Utley, Robert M. *Frontiersmen in Blue: The United States Army and the Indian, 1848–1865.* New York: Macmillan Company, 1967. The administration tried to defend the new western territories with reduced Army expenditures.

1103. Wade, Arthur P. "Forts and Mounted Rifles Along the Oregon Trail, 1846–1853." *Kansas Quarterly* 10 (Summer 1978): 3–15. Troops were pulled out of California and Oregon in the early 1850s to reduce the expense of transportation and supply. There were also reduced escorts on the Oregon trail.

1104. Williams, T. Harry. *The History of American Wars, from 1745 to 1918.* New York: Alfred A. Knopf, 1981. Despite limited funds and men, the Army tried to protect settlers and pacify Indians during the 1850s.

2. The U.S. Navy

1105. Coletta, Paolo E. *A Bibliography of American Naval History.* Annapolis: Naval Institute Press, 1981. Chapter Four contains sources on Naval operations between 1820 to 1860.

1106. Crawford, Michael J. "*White-Jacket* and the Navy in which Melville Served." *Melville Society Extracts* 94 (September 1993): 1–5. Herman Melville's novel remains the most comprehensive description of the antebellum Navy at sea.

1107. Feipel, Louis N. "The Navy and Filibustering in the Fifties." *United States Naval Institute Proceedings* 44 (1918): 767–80, 1009–29. The Navy's antifilibustering actions in the Caribbean.

1108. Long, David F. *Gold Braid and Foreign Relations: Diplomatic Activities of U.S. Naval Officers, 1798–1883.* Annapolis: Naval Institute Press, 1988. Valuable reference work on Naval activities and diplomacy in foreign lands. Includes portraits and maps.

1109. Love, Robert W., Jr. *History of the U.S. Navy.* Harrisburg, PA: Stackpole Books, 1992. 2 vols. Volume One describes Fillmore's use of the Navy in the opening of Japan. He also used the Navy in a show of force off Cuba, while Webster spoke with Spain to retrieve captured American filibusters from the failed Lopez expedition.

1110. Miller, Nathan. *The U.S. Navy: An Illustrated History.* New York: American Heritage Publishing Co., Inc., 1977. An oversized book containing extraordinary Japanese paintings of Perry in Japan.

1111. Paullin, Charles Oscar. *Paullin's History of Naval Administration, 1775–1911.* Annapolis: U.S. Naval Institute Press, 1968 [1911–1914]. Chapter Six describes duties and personnel from 1840 to 1860, including a sketch of Secretary of the Navy John Pendleton Kennedy.

1112. Schroeder, John H. *Shaping a Maritime Empire: The Commercial and Diplomatic Role of the American Navy, 1829–1861.* Westport, CT: Greenwood Press, 1985. Fillmore used the Navy to enhance commerce and exploration.

1113. Smith, Geoffrey S. "An Uncertain Passage: The Bureau Runs the Navy, 1842–1861." In *In Peace and War, Interpretations of American Naval History, 1775–1978,* ed. Kenneth J. Hagan. Westport, CT: Greenwood Press, 1978. Fillmore promoted the Navy's scientific and diplomatic duties to support commercial expansion.

1114. Sprout, Harold, and Margaret Sprout. *The Rise of American Naval Power, 1776–1918.* Princeton: Princeton University Press, 1939. Taylor and Fillmore gave only timid support to fleet expansion.

3. Naval Explorations

1115. *African Repository* 27 (September 1851): 279, 281. Report on plans presented to the Secretary of the Navy to explore Africa.

1116. Bennett, Frank M. *The Steam Navy of the United States: A History of the Growth of the Steam Vessel of War in the U.S. Navy and of the Naval Engineering Corps.* Pittsburgh: Warren & Co., Publishers, 1896. The new vessels contributed to Naval exploration and engineering science.

1117. Blessing, Arthur R. "William Lewis Herndon." *DAB* (1960), 4, pt. 2: 579–80. U.S. Naval explorer who surveyed the main branch of the Amazon River system in 1851 and 1852.

1118. Bradford, James C., ed. *Captains of the Old Steam Navy: Makers of the American Naval Tradition, 1840–1880.* Annapolis: Naval Institute Press, 1986. Chapters on Matthew Perry and Matthew Fontaign Maury and their contributions to mid-century exploration.

1119. Bruce, Robert V. *The Launching of Modern American Science, 1846–1876.* New York: Alfred A. Knopf, 1987. Scientists were members of Naval expeditions and Army boundary surveys.

1120. Cole, Allan B. "The Ringgold-Rogers-Brooke Expedition to Japan and the North Pacific, 1853–1859." *Pacific Historical Review* 16 (May 1947): 152–62. In 1852, Secretaries Graham and Kennedy prepared a survey expedition to the Pacific. It embarked during the Pierce administration.

1121. ———, ed. *Yankee Surveyors in the Shogun's Sea: Records of the United States Surveying Expedition to the North Pacific Ocean, 1853–1856.* Princeton: Princeton University Press, 1947. The administration proposed the expedition to test the new treaty with Japan, survey the north Pacific, and chart Pacific steamship routes.

1122. Dow, Margaret Elden. "Elisha Kent Kane." *DAB* (1961), 5, pt. 2: 256–57. Commanded the second Grinnel Arctic Expedition to look for missing explorer Sir John Franklin.

1123. Dupree, A. Hunter. *Science in the Federal Government: A History of Politics and Activities to 1940.* Cambridge: Belknap Press of Harvard University Press, 1957. Naval officers and Army engineers were capable recorders of scientific data.

1124. ———. "Science vs. the Military: Dr. James Morrow and the Perry Expedition." *Pacific Historical Review* 22 (February 1953): 29–37. Scientists argued about their subordination to Perry and the final disposition of their valuable Japanese plant collection.

1125. Elliott, Clark A. *History of Science in the United States: A Chronological and Research Guide.* New York: Garland Publishing, Inc., 1996. Mentions Naval explorations. Useful bibliography on science in the mid-nineteenth century.

1126. "Exploration of the Interior of Liberia." *African Repository* 29 (January 1853): 1–3. Encouraging report on the possible exploration of Africa east of Liberia. Mentions Fillmore's favorable reference to it in his third annual message.

1127. Gill, Harold B., Jr., and Joanne Young. *Searching for the Franklin Expedition: Arctic Journal of Robert Randolph Carter.* Annapolis: Naval Institute Press, 1998. Describes the exploration goals of the expedition.

1128. *Gleason's Pictorial Drawing-Room Companion,* May 15, 1852. Illustrations of the ships composing the Japanese squadron and the flagship *Mississippi.*

1129. Harrison, Frederick G. "Elisha Kent Kane." In *Biographical Sketches of Preëminent Americans.* Boston: Consolidated Book Company, 189–?. Surgeon on the first Arctic Expedition to find the lost British explorer John Franklin. He commanded the second expedition. No pagination, documentation or index.

1130. Harrison, John P. "Science and Politics: Origins and Objectives of Mid-Nineteenth-Century Government Expeditions to Latin America." *Hispanic American Historical Review* 35 (May 1955): 175–202. Describes the policies and support for Naval expeditions to Chile, the Amazon, and the Rio de la Plata.

1131. Hawks, Francis L. *Narration of the Expedition of an American Squadron to the China Seas and Japan Performed in the Years 1852, 1853 and 1854, Under the Command of Commodore M. C. Perry, United States Navy.* Washington, DC: A.O.P. Nicholson, Printer, 1856. 3 vols. Official publication of Perry's expedition. Volume One is the narrative of the mission. Volumes Two and Three contain scientific data.

1132. Hoogenboom, Olive. "Ringgold, Cadwalader." In *American National Biography,* ed. John A. Garraty and Mark C. Carnes. New York: Oxford University Press, 1999. 24 vols. 18: 525–26. Asked to explore commercial routes from California to the Far East.

1133. Kane, Elisha Kent. *Arctic Exploration: The Second Grinnell Expedition in Search of Sir John Franklin during the Years 1853,' 54' 55.* Philadelphia: Childs & Peterson, 1856. 2 vols. The expedition was organized with help from Fillmore's administration.

1134. ———. *The United States Grinnell Expedition in Search of Sir James Franklin: A Personal Narrative.* New York: Harper, 1853. Account of the first Grinnell arctic expedition in 1852.

1135. Kazar, John Dryden, Jr. "The United States Navy and Scientific Exploration, 1837–1860." Ph.D. diss., University of Massachusetts, 1973. Reviews fifteen expeditions to chart oceans, advance science, and promote national glory.

1136. MacMaster, Richard K. "United States Navy and African Exploration, 1851–1860." *Mid-America* 46 (July 1964): 187–203. Fillmore approved a proposal to explore the interior of Africa east of Liberia. The expedition never took place.

1137. Paullin, Charles Oscar. *American Voyages to the Orient, 1690–1865: An Account of Merchant and Naval Activities in China, Japan, and the Various Pacific Islands.* Annapolis: United States Naval Institute, 1971 [1910–1911]. Describes the selection of Perry to command the expedition to Japan. Includes summary of Perry's meeting with the Japanese.

1138. ———. *Diplomatic Negotiations of American Naval Officers, 1778–1883.* Baltimore: Johns Hopkins University Press, 1912. Same as *American Voyages to the Orient, 1690–1865.*

1139. Ponko, Vincent, Jr. *Ships, Seas, and Scientists, U.S. Naval Exploration and Discovery in the Nineteenth Century.* Annapolis: Naval Institute Press, 1974. Reviews the explorations during Fillmore's administration.

1140. Poore, Ben: Perly. "Japan and the Japanese." *Gleason's Pictorial Drawing-Room Companion,* April 9, 1853. Reports the American excitement about the opening of Japan with extracts from the Secretary of the Navy's report on its commercial benefits.

1141. Rasmussen, Wayne D. "The United States Astronomical Expedition to Chile, 1849–1852." *Hispanic American Historical Review* 34 (February 1954): 103–13. Examines reports of the expedition.

1142. Reddick, James P., Jr. "Herndon, Maury, and the Amazon Basin." *U.S. Naval Institute Proceedings* 97 (1971): 56–63. Reviews highlights of the Amazon expedition. Includes 7 undocumented photographs.

1143. Slotten, Hugh Richard. *Patronage, Practice and the Culture of American Science: Alexander Bache and the U.S. Coast Survey.* New York: Cambridge University Press, 1994. The civilian Coast Survey rivaled the Naval Observatory for geographic and oceanographic science.

1144. Smith, Geoffrey Sutton. "The Navy Before Darwinism: Science, Exploration, and Diplomacy in Antebellum America." *American Quarterly* 28 (Spring 1976): 41–55. Reviews the diplomatic significance of explorations for science and commerce.

1145. Wallach, Sidney. *Narrative of the Expedition of an American Squadron to the China Seas and Japan Performed in the Years 1852, 1853 and 1854, Under the Command of Commodore M. C. Perry United States Navy.* London: Macdonald, 1952. This is an edited version of the official narrative.

1146. Wermuth, Paul C. *Bayard Taylor.* New York: Twayne Publishers, Inc., 1973. Popular travel writer was assigned to Perry's expedition.

1147. Wescott, Alan. "Cadwalader Ringgold." *DAB* (1963). 8, pt. 1: 617–18. Commanded the North Pacific surveying expedition planned during Fillmore's administration.

1148. ———. "Thomas Jefferson Page." *DAB* (1963), 7, pt. 2: 140–41. Commander of the exploration of the Rio de la Plata River.

4. The African Squadron

1149. *African Repository* 27 (April 1851): 105–14. Fillmore attended the annual meeting of the American Colonization Society in Washington on January 21, 1851. Henry Clay acknowledged Fillmore and urged diverting funds from the African Squadron to establish more colonies in West Africa.

1150. Berstein, Barton J. "Southern Politics and Attempts to Reopen the African Slave Trade." In *Slave Trade and Migration: Domestic and Foreign,* ed. Paul Finkelman. New York: Garland Publishing Inc., 1989. 22–35. Occasional secret African slave running was tolerated in the South but not the renewal of a legal African slave trade. Legitimacy would disrupt slave prices and endanger the association of the deep South with the upper South's intrastate slavetrading.

1151. Booth, Alan R. "The United States African Squadron, 1843–1861." In *Boston University Papers in African History. Vol. 1,* ed. Jeffrey Butler. Boston: Boston University Press, 1964. The squadron failed to suppress slave cargoes because its primary purpose was to encourage commerce and protect American vessels. Squadron ships were in poor condition and stayed in ports with inadequate facilities.

1152. DuBois, W. E. B. "The Enforcement of the Slave Trade Laws." In *Slave Trade and Migration: Domestic and Foreign,* ed. Paul Finkelman. New York: Garland Publishing Inc., 1989. 109–20. Classic paper describing the inadequate Naval enforcement against the trade, inappropriate treaty articles with Britain hindering ocean searches, and the lax punishment of slavetraders.

1153. Foote, Andrew H. *Africa and the American Flag.* New York: D. Appleton and Company, 1854. Narrative of the African Squadron in the early 1850s by its Commander. Reviews U.S. policy and activities to protect commerce and suppress slavery in partnership with Britain.

1154. ———. "Letter from Capt. Andrew H. Foote, of the U.S. Navy." *African Repository* 27 (July 1851): 216–20. Reviews the problems of capturing slave ships at sea.

1155. ———. "Letter from Captain A. H. Foote." *African Repository* 28 (November 1852): 345–47. Defends the operation of the African Squadron against congressional proposals to transfer its funding to colonization societies.

1156. Harmon, J. Scott. "The United States Navy and the Suppression of the Illegal Slave Trade, 1830–1850." In *New Aspects of Naval History: Selected Papers Presented at the Fourth Naval History Symposium, United States Naval Academy, 25–26 October 1979,* ed. Craig L. Symonds. Annapolis: Naval Institute Press, 1981. The Navy attempted to suppress the slave trade but was unable to stop it.

1157. Howard, Warren S. *American Slavers and the Federal Law, 1837–1862.* Berkeley: University of California Press, 1963. Naval Secretary Graham was mistakenly optimistic on the reduction of the slave trade. He favored shifting the African Squadron to the Brazilian and American coasts to continue its antislavery patrols. Bibliography.

1158. Littlefield, Daniel C., Greg Robinson, and Petra E. Lewis. "Slave Trade." In *Encyclopedia of African-American Culture and History,* ed. Jack Salzman, Davis Lionel Smith, and Cornel West. New York: Simon & Schuster Macmillan, 1996. 5 vols. 5: 2471–86. Overview of Atlantic Slave Trade. In the antebellum years, American policy and Naval tactics hindered the apprehension of slavetrading vessels. Bibliography.

1158a. McNeilly, Earl E. "The United States Navy and the Suppression of the West African Slave Trade, 1819–1862." Ph.D. diss., Case Western Reserve University, 1973. Examines the Navy's ineffectiveness at suppression in the early 1850s.

1159. "Proceedings at the Annual Meeting of the American Colonization Society." *African Repository* 28 (March 1852): 70–91. Fillmore attended the meeting on January 20, 1852, with Daniel Webster. Webster urged that funds for the ineffective African Squadron be diverted to subsidize steamships for the emigration of African Americans to Liberia.

1160. Shavit, David. *The United States in Africa: A Historical Dictionary.* Westport, CT: Greenwood Press, 1989. Includes Naval personnel in the African Squadron and members of the American Colonization Society interested in Africa.

1161. Thomas, Hugh. *The Slave Trade: The Story of the Atlantic Slave Trade: 1440–1870.* New York: Simon & Schuster, 1997. Chapters 33 through 35 narrate Britain's efforts to stop the mid-century slave trade despite inadequate support from the United States Navy, and ineffective criminal proceedings against American slavers.

1162. Westcott, Allan. "Foote, Andrew Hull." *DAB* (1959), 3, pt. 2: 499–500. Commanded the African Squadron. His publication about the Atlantic slave trade aroused sentiment against it. He ended a distinguished career conducting Union Naval campaigns in the Civil War.

5. Naval Reform

1163. Chapel, Robert B. "The Word Against the Cat: Melville's Influence on Seaman's Rights." *American Neptune* 42 (January 1982): 57–65. Herman Melville's novel *White-Jacket* reinforced the efforts of proponents to abolish cruel punishments on Navy and commercial vessels.

1164. Glenn, Myra C. *Campaigns Against Corporal Punishment: Prisoners, Sailors, Women, and Children in Ante-bellum America.* Albany: State University of New York Press, 1984. The reform of Naval punishments and the abolition of flogging were associated with the sectional debates in Congress about slave labor and their punishments.

1165. ———. "The Naval Reform Campaign Against Flogging: A Case in Changing Attitudes Toward Capital Punishment, 1830–1850." *American Quarterly* 35 (Fall 1983): 408–25. The plantation punishment of slaves was important to the congressional debate on naval flogging of free men.

1166. Langley, Harold D. *Social Reform in the United States Navy, 1798–1862.* Urbana: University of Illinois Press, 1967. Fillmore signed the bill to abolish flogging in the Navy. His administration later issued a new code of discipline.

1167. Miller, Marion Mills. *Great Debates in American History: From the Debates in the British Parliament on the Colonial Stamp Act (1764–1765) to the Debates in Congress at the Close of the Taft Administration (1912–1913).* New York: Current Literature Publishing Company, 1913. 14 vols. 9: 225–39. Contains administration arguments against a petition to reinstate flogging.

H. WHIG INTERNAL POLITICS

1168. Aldrich, John H. *Why Parties: The Origins and Transformation of Political Parties in America.* Chicago: University of Chicago Press, 1995. Follows the decline of the Whig party in the 1850s.

1169. Auchampaugh, Philip Gerald. "Politics and Slavery, 1850–60." In *History of the State of New York, Volume 7: Modern Party Battles,* ed. Alexander C. Flick. New York: Columbia University Press, 1935. 10 vols. 7: 61–97. Quotes moderate New York politicians from both parties who supported the Compromise and Fillmore's Union-first policy.

1170. Brady, David W. *Critical Elections and Congressional Policy Making.* Stanford: Stanford University Press, 1988. An analysis of congressional voting describes the breakup of the Whig party in the early 1850s and the demise of the party after 1854.

1171. Carman, Harry J., and Reinhard H. Luthin. "The Seward-Fillmore Feud and the Disruption of the Whig Party." *New York History* 24 (July 1943): 335–57. The Seward Whigs' successful opposition to Fillmore's Silver Greys helped unravel the national Whig party.

1172. Davis, Sherman J. "Millard Fillmore and the Whig Decline, 1848–1852." M.A. Thesis, University of Buffalo, 1947. Excellent use of Buffalo and Albany newspapers to highlight the Fillmore-Seward feud over state patronage.

1173. Donald, Aida DiPace. "Prelude to Civil War: The Decline of the Whig Party in New York, 1848–1852." Ph.D. diss., University of Rochester, 1961. Examines Fillmore's inability to unite factions of the New York and national Whig party.

1174. Forness, Norman O. "The Seward-Fillmore Feud and the U.S. Patent Office." *Historian* 54 (Winter 1992): 255–68. The Patent commissioner, a Seward supporter, politicized the bureau, victimized Fillmore men, and withdrew reports favorable to the slave system.

1175. Gienapp, William E. "The Crisis of American Democracy: The Political System and the Coming of the Civil War." In *Why the Civil War Came,* ed. Gabor S. Boritt. New York: Oxford University Press, 1996. Fillmore was a competent if undistinguished President whose vendetta against antislavery Whigs deepened the division in the Whig party.

1176. Hammond, Jabez D. *Political History of the State of New York.* Syracuse: L. W. Hall, 1852. 3 vols. In Volume Three, Hammond takes Seward's side in the feud with Fillmore. States Fillmore ended his friendship with Seward to further his dream of being President.

1176a. Huston, Reeve. "The Parties and 'The People: ' The New York Anti-Rent Wars and the Contours of Jacksonian Politics." *Journal of the Early Republic* 20 (Summer 2000): 241–71. By 1850 conservative New York Whigs opposed Seward's siding with the Anti-Rent farmers. It further divided and weakened the state party.

1177. Johnson, Willis Fletcher. *History of the State of New York: Political and Governmental.* Syracuse: Syracuse Press, Inc., 1922. 6 vols. Volume Two describes the decline of the Whig party and Fillmore's unsuccessful national leadership.

1178. "The Late Election-New York Politics." *U. S. Magazine and Democratic Review* 27 (December 1850): 529–33. Democrats failed to win the governorship because of the tenuous truce between the Fillmore and Seward factions.

1179. Rayback, Robert J. "The Silver Grey Revolt." *New York History* 30 (April 1949): 151–64. The demise of the national Whig party began with the rivalry between Fillmore and Seward for leadership of the New York Whigs.

1180. "State of Parties." *U. S. Magazine and Democratic Review* 27 (November 1850): 387–98. Hopeful Democrats believed they could win elections while the Fillmore and Seward factions continued their estrangement.

1181. Warner, Lee H. "The Perpetual Crisis of Conservative Whigs: New York's Silver Greys." *New-York Historical Society Quarterly* 57 (July 1973): 213–36. History and policies of Fillmore's faction.

I. WHIG PRESIDENTIAL CONVENTION, 1852

1182. Bain, Richard C., and Judith H. Parris. *Conventions and Voting Records.* Washington, DC: Brookings Institute, 1973. 2d ed.

1183. Bigelow, John. *Retrospective of an Active Life.* New York: Baker & Taylor Co., 1909–1913. 5 vols. 1: 119–20. In July 1851, Charles Sumner wrote that Fillmore would be the Whig candidate in 1852. He would enter the convention with Southern support while Webster's friends would go to Fillmore.

1184. Brownson, Orestes. "Politics and Political Parties, Resolutions Unanimously Adopted by the Democratic National Convention which Assembled at Baltimore, June 1, 1852." *Brownson's Quarterly Review* 14 (October 1852): 493–523. Analysis of the Whig, Democratic, and Free Soil parties by the independent Catholic editor.

1185. Clingman, Thomas L. *Selections from the Speeches and Writings of Hon. Thomas L. Clingman of North Carolina.* Raleigh: John Nichols, 1877. Recalls cabinet pressure on Fillmore not to run in 1852. However, threats from Southern Whigs, fearful of Seward Whigs, pressed him to stand for the nomination.

1186. Haas, Garland A. *The Politics of Disintegration: Political Party Decay in the United States, 1840 to 1900.* Jefferson, NC: McFarland & Company, Inc., 1994. Fillmore failed to win the 1852 nomination because he was never in the high councils of the Whig party, his patron Henry Clay was dead, and he was unable to develop his own organization.

1187. Menna, Larry K. "Embattled Conservatism: The Ideology of the Southern Whigs." Ph.D. diss., Columbia University, 1991. The South appreciated Fillmore's statesmanship for placing the Union above party. His lost nomination confirmed for them the extent of the Northern Whigs' Free Soil sentiment.

1188. Mering, John Vollmer. *The Whig Party in Missouri.* Columbia: University of Missouri Press, 1967. Missouri Whigs supported Fillmore.

1189. "Monthly Report of Current Events." *Harper's Monthly* 4 (May 1852): 834–35. List of state Whig conventions for Fillmore, including Henry Clay's support.

1190. "Monthly Report of Current Events." *Harper's Monthly* 5 (August 1852): 402. Reports Winfield Scott's nomination and Fillmore's letter to withdraw.

1191. Moore, John Bassett, ed. *The Works of James Buchanan: Comprising His Speeches, State Papers and Private Correspondence.* New York: Antiquarian Press Ltd., 1960 [1908–1911]. 12 vols. 8: 463. In an 1852 anti-Whig campaign speech, Buchanan said that Scott was not as good or as safe a candidate as Fillmore.

1192. "National Platforms." *Whig Almanac, 1853.* New York: New York Tribune, 1853. 12–13. Results of the Democratic and Whig conventions with their platforms.

1193. Nichols, Roy, and Jeannette Nichols. "Elections of 1852." In *History of American Presidential Elections, 1789–1968,* ed. Arthur M. Schlesinger, Jr. New York: Chelsea House Publications, 1971. 4 vols. 2: 921–1003. Describes the Whig and Democratic party internal factions, Fillmore's nomination defeat by Scott, the importance of the Compromise of 1850 for all the nominees, and the election results.

1194. Putnam, James O. "George R. Babcock." In *Addresses, Speeches and Miscellanies.* Buffalo: Peter Paul & Brother, 1880. Brief biography of the man

Fillmore allowed to submit his letter of withdrawal at the Whig nominating convention.

1195. Schouler, James. "The Whig Party in Massachusetts." Massachusetts Historical Society, *Proceedings* 50 (1917): 39–53. Describes Webster's obsession for the 1852 Whig presidential nomination. After losing, he made his disappointment known and said he could no longer serve under Fillmore.

1196. Schultz, Charles R. "The Last Great Conclave of the Whigs." *Maryland Historical Magazine* 63 (December 1968): 379–400. Describes the 53 ballots required to defeat Fillmore and nominate Winfield Scott.

1197. Silbey, Joel H. "1852." In *Running for President: The Candidates and Their Images,* ed. Arthur M. Schlesinger, Jr. New York: Simon and Shuster, 1994. 2 vols. 1: 204–19. Scott was chosen because his military background would gain a broader segment of voters. Extraordinary reproductions of campaign materials.

1198. Thompson, Arthur W. "Political Nativism in Florida, 1848–1860: A Phase of Anti-Secessionism." *Journal of Southern History* 15 (February 1949): 39–65. Florida Whigs supported Fillmore for President at the 1852 Whig convention. In 1856, Whig strongholds supported Fillmore and the American party.

J. PIERCE INAUGURAL

1199. Mrs. Kirkland. "Society in Washington." *Eclectic Review* 33 (November 1854): 421–30. Article reprinted from *Bentley's Review* covering the inauguration of Pierce. Reports that no one at the inaugural excelled Fillmore's smiling grace. At a Willard Hotel party Fillmore received congratulations from his cabinet and friends. Includes extract from Fillmore's letter thanking his cabinet.

K. FOREIGN AFFAIRS

1. General Works

1200. Adler, David Gray. "The Constitution and Presidential Warmaking: The Enduring Debate." *Political Science Quarterly* 103 (Spring 1988): 1–36. Secretary of State Webster spoke for the Fillmore administration when he stated that the warmaking power rests with Congress and not the President.

1201. Bevins, Charles I., ed. *Treaties and Other International Agreements of the United States of America, 1776–1949.* Washington, DC: Government Printing Office, 1968–1976. 13 vols. Supersedes the 1937 edition of Hunter Miller. Volumes 5 through 12 are alphabetical bilateral agreements. Volume 13 is the index.

1202. Brauer, Kinley J. "1821–1860, Economics and the Diplomacy of American Expansion." In *Economics and World Power, An Assessment of American Diplomacy Since 1789,* ed. William H. Becker and Samuel F. Wells, Jr. New York: Columbia University Press, 1984. Economic relations with other nations provided the framework for American diplomacy.

1203. Brune, Lester H. *Chronological History of United States Foreign Relations, 1776 to January 20, 1981.* New York: Garland Publishing, Inc., 1985. 2 vols. Chronology of world events and American foreign policy. Bibliography.

1204. Burns, Gerald Edward. "A Collective Biography of Consular Officers, 1828–1861." Ph.D. diss., University of Pittsburgh, 1973. Studies the composition and dispatches of middle-level consular appointees who tended to be merchants interested in the economic expansion of the United States.

1205. Burns, Richard Dean, ed. *Guide to American Foreign Relations Since 1700.* Santa Barbara: ABC-CLIO, Inc., 1983. Valuable annotated guide to American and foreign sources.

1206. Congressional Quarterly, Inc. *Powers of the Presidency.* Washington, DC: Congressional Quarterly Inc., 1989. Fillmore's use of the military to lead the Japan Expedition was an early example of martial display in aid of foreign policy.

1207. Curti, Merle E. "Young America." *American Historical Review* 32 (October 1926): 34–55. Analysis of the Democratic party's interventionist foreign policy.

1208. "Department of State." *Whig Almanac 1849.* New York: New York Tribune, 1849. 21–22. A register of positions and salaries during Polk's last year.

1209. Dougall, Richardson, Mary Patricia Chapman, and Evan M Duncan. *United States Chiefs of Mission, 1778–1982.* Washington, DC: United States Department of State, 1982. Alphabetical list of countries with a chronological list of U.S. ministers.

1210. Ferrell, Robert H. *American Diplomacy: A History.* New York: W. W. Norton & Company Inc., 1959. Reviews the Japan expedition, diplomatic interest in China, filibustering in Cuba and its diplomatic consequences with Spain.

1211. Findling, John E. *Dictionary of American Diplomatic History.* Westport, CT: Greenwood Press, 1980. Useful one-volume listing of American diplomats.

1212. "Governments of Europe and America." *Whig Almanac 1851.* New York: New York Tribune, 1851. 9. List of governments and sovereigns.

1213. Graber, D. A. *Crisis Diplomacy, A History of U.S. Intervention Policies and Practices.* Washington, DC: Public Affairs Press, 1959. Fillmore's presidential messages articulated a noninterventionist foreign policy.

1214. Graebner, Norman A., ed. *Ideas and Diplomacy: Readings in the Intellectual Tradition of American Foreign Policy.* New York: Oxford University Press, 1964. Uses Fillmore's 1851 presidential message to explain American noninterventionist diplomacy.

1215. Hasse, Adelaide R. *Index to United States Documents Relating to Foreign Affairs, 1828–1861.* New York: Kraus Reprint Co., 1971 [1914]. 3 vols. This valuable index includes a chronological list of Fillmore's remarks and messages on foreign policy.

1216. Hietala, Thomas R. *Manifest Design: Anxious Aggrandizement in Late Jacksonian America.* Ithaca: Cornell University Press, 1985. Lack of strong executive leadership in the 1850s undermined expansion policies.

1217. Holt, W. Stull. *Treaties Defeated by the Senate, A Study of the Struggle between President and Senate over the Conduct of Foreign Relations.* Baltimore: Johns Hopkins University Press, 1933. Reports two minor unsigned treaties during Fillmore's administration: one with Belgium, another on copyright privileges with Great Britain.

1218. Kavass, Igor I., and Mark A. Michael, comps. *United States Treaties and Other International Agreements: Cumulative Index 1776–1946: . . . As Published in Statutes at Large, Molloy, Miller, Bevans and Other Related Sources.* Buffalo: Wm. S. Hein & Co., Inc., 1975. 4 vols. 2: 46–49. Chronological list during Fillmore administration.

1219. LaFeber, Walter. *The American Age: United States Foreign Policy at Home and Abroad since 1750.* New York: W. W. Norton & Company, 1989. Despite Fillmore's nonintervention policy the administration participated in the expansionist sentiment of the era through its bombastic declarations for republicanism in Europe, its welcome of Louis Kossuth, and the opening of Japan.

1220. Lanman, Charles. "Diplomatic Agents in the United States from Foreign Countries." In *Biographical Annals of the Civil Government of the United States, during Its First Century.* Detroit: Gale Research Company, 1976 [1876]. 612–24. Chronological lists of foreign diplomats by country.

1221. ———. "Diplomatic Agents of the United States." In *Biographical Annals of the Civil Government of the United States, during Its First Century.* Detroit: Gale

Research Company, 1976 [1876]. 587–612. Chronological lists of diplomats by country.

1222. Manning, William R., ed. *Diplomatic Correspondence of the United States: Inter-American Affairs, 1831–1860.* Washington, DC: Carnegie Endowment for International Peace, 1932–39. 12 vols. Correspondence to and from countries in the Caribbean, and those south of the United States, including correspondence with Britain on Latin America.

1223. May, Arthur J. "The United States and the Mid-Century Revolutions." In *The Opening of an Era, 1848: An Historical Symposium,* ed. Francois Fejtö. New York: Howard Fertig, 1966 [1948]. 204–22. Fillmore refused to intervene in European revolutions despite sympathizing with their new republican governments. He hoped America would be their model for self government and enterprise.

1224. McGrane, Reginald C. *Foreign Bondholders and American State Debts.* New York: Macmillan Company, 1935. Europeans returned to the U.S. bond and railroad stock markets because of the 1848 revolutions, a new confidence in American finance, and high investment returns.

1225. Miller, Hunter, ed. *Treaties and Other International Acts of the United States of America, 1776–1863.* Washington, DC: Government Printing Office, 1931–1948. 8 vols. Volumes 5 and 6 analyze the agreements entered into by the Fillmore Administration.

1226. Plischka, Elmer. *Diplomat in Chief: The President at the Summit.* New York: Praeger, 1986. Fillmore's use of Perry in Japan set a precedent for presidential special emissaries.

1227. ———. *United States Diplomats and Their Missions, A Profile of American Diplomatic Emissaries Since 1778.* Washington, DC: American Enterprise Institute for Public Policy Research, 1975. Useful material on the expansion of the diplomatic establishment during the 1840s and 1850s.

1228. "Position of Parties: Fogyism, 'Fuss,' and Foreign Policy." *U.S. Magazine and Democratic Review* 31 (July 1852): 88–96. Urges Pierce to correct the noninterventionist foreign policy of Fillmore and Webster.

1229. Pudelka, Leonard William. "American Whig Party's Far Eastern Foreign Policy: A Prelude to Imperialism." Ph.D. diss., Syracuse University, 1972. Fillmore executed Whig commercial policy when he opened Japan, supported inter-ocean transportation, and sought security for an independent Hawaii.

1230. Reynolds, Larry J. *European Revolutions and the American Literary Renaissance.* New Haven: Yale University Press, 1988. Enlightening study on the reaction of major writers to Europe's republican and restoration movements.

1231. Smith, Harold F. *American Travelers Abroad: A Bibliography of Accounts Published before 1900.* Lanham, MD: Scarecrow Press, Inc., 1999. Annotated sources include well-known authors, travel writers, and naval accounts.

1232. Smith, Louis R., Jr. "Fillmore, Millard." In *Encyclopedia of United States Foreign Relations,* ed. Bruce W. Jentleson and Thomas G. Paterson. New York: Oxford University Press, 1999. 4 vols. 2: 136. Surveys administration and directs readers to other foreign policy positions.

1233. Varg, Paul A. *United States Foreign Relations, 1820–1860.* East Lansing: Michigan State University Press, 1979. Fillmore made judicious foreign policy statements while other leaders of both parties seized on foreign affairs to strengthen their own political positions.

1234. Winchester, Simon. *Pacific Rising: The Emergence of a New World Culture.* New York: Prentice-Hall, 1991. Fillmore should be remembered for opening Japan. It was America's true beginning as a global power.

2. Africa and the Middle East

1235. *African Repository* 27 (June 1851). The back of this issue contains contemporary maps of the African continent and Liberia.

1236. "Appendix, Acknowledgment of the Independence of Liberia." In *Annual Reports of the American Society for Colonizing the Free People of Color of the United States. Volumes 34–43, 1851–60.* New York: Negro Universities Press, 1969. 34: 69–71. At the 1851 meeting Webster and Fillmore showed interest in recognizing the new republic, but no action was taken.

1237. Bryson, Thomas A. *American Diplomatic Relations with the Middle East, 1784–1975: A Survey.* Metuchen, NJ: Scarecrow Press, Inc., 1977. With the exception of the Ottoman Empire's help in the Kossuth affair, America maintained a non-interventionist policy. However, businessmen and missionaries were active in the area.

1238. Chester, Edward W. *Clash of Titans.* Maryknoll, NY: Orbis Books, 1974. Reviews Atlantic slave trade, the U.S. Navy's African Squadron, and colonizers in West Africa. Bibliography.

1239. Clendenen, Clarence C., and Peter Duignan. *Americans in Black Africa up to 1865.* Stanford: Stanford University Press, 1964. Lists important traders, Naval officers, colonizers, and missionaries. Includes an account of gunboat diplomacy near Zanzibar in 1851 to compel respect for American shipping and commercial agreements.

1240. Duignan, Peter, and L. H. Gann. *The United States and Africa: A History.* Cambridge: Cambridge University Press, 1984. Reviews the ineffectiveness of the U.S. African Squadron in apprehending slave ships. Describes Liberian colonization and gunboat diplomacy off East Africa.

1241. Everett, Edward. "The Colonization of Africa." In *Orations and Speeches on Various Occasions.* Boston: Little, Brown, and Company, 1897. 4 vols. 3: 167–85. The Secretary of State declared the civilizing of Africa would be conducted by free African Americans colonizing the continent.

1242. Foote, A. H. "Address of Capt. Foote." *African Repository* 29 (March 1853): 237–41. Foote informed Fillmore about President J. J. Roberts of Liberia. Roberts welcomed the African Squadron as a deterrent against encroachments by local slavetraders.

1243. Howard, Lawrence. *American Involvement in Africa South of the Sahara, 1800–1860.* New York: Garland Publishing, Inc., 1988. Valuable study using little-known sources on trading, political relations, and the suppression of the slave trade. These concerns produced a limited imperial relationship with Africa. Bibliography.

1244. McPherson, J. H. T. *History of Liberia.* Baltimore: Johns Hopkins University Press, 1891. Liberia sought an alliance with the United States after its independence in 1847. However the sectional debates during the 1850s delayed recognition until 1862.

1245. "Mr. Webster's Views in Reference to the Recognition of the Independence of the Republic of Liberia by the U.S. Government." *African Repository* 28 (May 1852): 150–51. At an informal gathering Webster said there was no good reason for withholding recognition. He said the United States already recognized the Sandwich Islands, which had a less intelligent population than Liberia.

1246. Roberts, J. J. "Annual Message of the President of Liberia." *African Repository* 27 (April 1851): 114–25. President Roberts reviews problems in West Africa and Liberia's relationship with American colonization societies.

1247. Shick, Tom W. *Behold the Promised Land: A History of Afro-American Settler Society in Nineteenth-Century Liberia.* Baltimore: Johns Hopkins University Press,

1977. Generally, African American leaders withheld endorsement for the colonization of Liberia. Maps, photographs, and bibliography.

1248. ———. "Liberia." In *Dictionary of Afro-American Slavery,* ed. Randall M. Miller and John David Smith. Westport, CT: Greenwood Press, 1988. 400–402. Large emigration never occurred, and Liberia remained a symbol of colonization's futility.

1248a. Skinner, Elliott P. *African Americans and U.S. Policy Toward Africa, 1850–1924.* Washington, DC: Howard University Press, 1992. Chapter One reviews African American ambitions for their own settlements in Africa.

1249. Stevens, Kenneth R. "Of Whaling Ships and Kings: The Johanna Bombardment of 1851." *Prologue* 18 (Winter 1986): 241–49. Gunboat diplomacy used to humiliate the Sultan of Johanna in the Comoro Islands in the Mozambique Channel.

1250. Taylor, Bayard. *A Journey to Central Africa.* New York: G. P. Putnam, 1862 [1854]. Describes traveling in Egypt and Ethiopia in 1851.

1251. Wickstrom, Werner Theodore. "The American Colonization Society and Liberia (An Historical Study in Religious Motivation and Achievement), 1817–1867." Ph.D. diss., Hartford Seminary Foundation, 1958. Reviews the establishment of Liberia as a nation state in the late 1840s and 1850s.

3. Australia

1252. Bartlett, Norman. *1776–1976, Australia and America Through 200 Years.* Sydney: Fine Arts Press, 1976. Gold rushes in both countries at mid-century produced an exchange of miners. The British colonial administration worried about an invasion of American republicanism.

1253. *Gleason's Pictorial Drawing-Room Companion,* April 9, 1853. Illustrations of Australia with a report that "go ahead Yankees" are part of the new self-governing colonies.

1254. "The Gold Discoveries in Australia." *Eclectic Review* 27 (December 1852): 506–16. Article from the *Quarterly Review* reported the gold strikes, their value to Great Britain, and comparisons to the California gold rush.

1255. "Gold Fields of Australia." *Gleason's Pictorial Drawing-Room Companion,* October 9, 1852. Illustrations and commentary on strikes by miners. It reports the convict population is becoming an orderly society under the influence of the discoveries.

1256. Gratten, C. Hartley. *The United States and the Southeast Pacific.* Cambridge: Harvard University Press, 1961. Australians were familiar with Tocqueville's work on America. They used it to assess the pros and cons of self government.

1257. Guernsey, A. H. "Australia and Its Gold." *Harper's New Monthly Magazine* 6 (December 1852): 16–32. Reports 5,000 Yankees in the gold fields.

1258. Kociumbas, Jan. *The Oxford History of Australia.* Oxford: Oxford University Press, 1986–1992. 5 vols. 2: 294–319. Australia's gold rush, like California's, caused social turmoil. Americans in Australia and at home predicted it would become an independent republic and then the United States would annex it.

1259. Monaghan, Jay. *Australians and the Gold Rush: California and Down Under, 1849–1854.* Berkeley: University of California Press, 1966. Britain heard rumors that American gold miners were planning a revolution in Australia. British consuls in America were unable to discover any such plot. However, they reported an independent Australia would be acceptable to most Americans.

1260. Potts, E. Daniel, and Annette Potts. *Young America and Australian Gold: America and the Gold Rush of the 1850s.* St. Lucia, Queensland: University of Queensland Press, 1974. The integration of California miners in Australian gold-fields brought no direct American influence on colonial self government. However, Australians were attentive to American democracy in their own discussions of self government.

4. Austria

1261. Bled, Jean-Paul. *Franz Joseph.* Oxford: Blackwell Publishers, 1992. Emperor Joseph was too concerned with the suppression of the Hungarian Revolution and his status as a monarch to be concerned with American policies.

1262. Brownson, Orestes. "Webster's Answer to Hulseman [sic]." *Brownson's Quarterly Review* 13 (April 1851): 198–230. Critical of Webster's letter to Austrian chargé d'affaires Hülsemann in which he zealously defended America's interest in European revolutions.

1263. "Foreign Policy of the United States, the Webster and Hulseman [*sic*] Correspondence." *The Whig Almanac 1852.* New York: New York Tribune, 1852. 28–33. Reprints Hülsemann's accusation of American interference in Austrian affairs and Webster's reply.

1264. *Gleason's Pictorial Drawing-Room Companion,* November 15, 1851. Illustration of the Hungarian rebel Louis Kossuth. From November 1851 to July 1852, the magazine illustrated and commented on Kossuth's tour of America.

1264a. Grant, Philip A., Jr. "The United States and the Hungarian Revolt, 1848–1850." *Consortium on Revolutionary Europe 1750–1850: Proceedings* (1979): 318–24. Fillmore was sympathetic to the revolt but did not involve the nation.

1265. Huck, Ronald K. "Patriotism Verses Philanthropy: A Letter from Gerrit Smith to Frederick Douglass." *New York History* 49 (July 1968): 327–35. Smith commented on the hypocrisy of the government holding millions in bondage while saving one Hungarian rebel, Louis Kossuth.

1266. "Hungary and the Hungarians." *Eclectic Review* 22 (January 1851): 43–49. Reprint of an article from the *English Review* summarizing the recent revolution, the leadership of Kossuth, and its repression by Russian troops and the Austrian monarchy.

1267. Klay, Andor. *Daring Diplomacy: The Case of the First American Ultimatum.* Minneapolis: University of Minnesota Press, 1957. At the White House, Austrian chargé d'affaires Chevalier Hülsemann threatened to resign if Webster continued his republican broadsides against the Austrian Empire. Fillmore refused Hülsemann's request to suppress Webster.

1268. "Kossuth and Intervention." *Southern Quarterly Review* 6 (July 1852): 221–34. Argues against following Kossuth into a military intervention in Europe. The country should not follow a man who wants to be a dictator himself.

1269. May, Arthur J. "Seward and Kossuth." *New York History* 34 (July 1953): 267–83. Fillmore brought Kossuth to America, but Senator Seward gladly became Kossuth's enthusiastic patron.

1270. Potter, Clifton W., Jr. "Francis Joseph I." In *Great Lives From History: Renaissance to 1900 Series,* ed. Frank N. Magill. Pasadena: Salem Press, 1989. 5 vols. 2: 785–89. Crowned Emperor in 1848, he methodically revoked reforms and sought a centralized absolutism. Annotated bibliography.

1271. "Presidential Courtesies." *U.S. Magazine and Democratic Review* 30 (January 1852): 38–41. Partisan critique of Fillmore's unenthusiastic behavior toward Louis Kossuth.

1272. Pulsky, Francis, and Theresa Pulsky. *White, Red, Black: Sketches of Society in the United States During the Visit of Their Guest.* New York: Negro Universities Press, 1968 [1853]. 3 vols. Volume One describes traveling with Kossuth, and their astute diagram of American political parties.

1273. Spencer, Donald S. *Louis Kossuth and Young America: A Study of Sectionalism and Foreign Policy, 1848–1852.* Columbia: University of Missouri Press,

1977. Narration of Fillmore's successful efforts to save Kossuth from Austrian reprisals. Describes Kossuth's American journey, his meeting with Fillmore, and his effect on foreign policy and antislavery debates.

1274. Strout, Cushing. *The American Image of the Old World.* New York: Harper & Row, Publishers, 1963. Fillmore informed Kossuth that he had no intention of abandoning his nonintervention policy to aid a Hungarian revolution.

5. Britain

1275. Allen, H. C. *Great Britain and the United States: A History of Anglo-American Relations (1783–1952).* New York: St. Martin's Press, Inc., 1960. Contains the diplomatic concerns over a Central American interocean canal in the early 1850s.

1276. Bach, John. "The Imperial Defense of the Pacific Ocean in the Mid-Nineteenth Century: Ships and Bases." *American Neptune* 32 (October 1972): 233–46. The British Navy was overextended during the 1850s, so it had a plan to vacate the eastern Pacific if there was a war with the United States.

1277. Barnes, James J. *Authors, Publishers and Politicians: The Quest for an Anglo-American Copyright Agreement, 1815–1854.* London: Routledge & Kegan Paul, 1974. A reluctant Fillmore signed a copyright treaty weeks before he left office. It never went into effect.

1278. Barnes, James J., and Patience P. Barnes. *Private and Confidential: Letters from British Ministers in Washington to the Foreign Secretaries in London, 1844–67.* Toronto: Associated University Presses, 1993. The letters report that Webster guided Fillmore and that favorable legislation could be bought in Congress. Good description of sources.

1279. Blumberg, Arnold. "Queen Victoria." In *Great Lives From History: British and Commonwealth Series,* ed. Frank N. Magill. Pasadena: Salem Press, 1987. 5 vols. 5: 2505–10. Queen Victoria read important diplomatic dispatches, causing her Foreign Ministers to send controversial orders under cover of their personal stationery.

1280. Bourne, Kenneth. *Britain and the Balance of Power in North America, 1815–1908.* Berkeley: University of California Press, 1967. Unique study of British military contingency plans for war with the United States.

1281. ———. *The Foreign Policy of Victorian England, 1830–1902.* Oxford: Clarendon Press, 1970. The United States was a minor concern for Britain at mid-century.

1282. Brauer, Kinley J. "The United States and British Imperial Expansion, 1815–60." *Diplomatic History* 12 (Winter 1988): 19–37. The United States was unable to compete against British economic imperialism.

1283. Brightfield, Myron F. "America and the Americans, 1840–1860, as depicted in English Novels of the Period." *American Literature* 31 (November 1959): 309–24. Americans are boorish caricatures when compared with British social manners.

1284. Cecil, Algernon. *Queen Victoria and Her Prime Ministers*. London: Eyre & Spottiswoode, 1953. Contains individual essays on the Prime Ministers during Fillmore's administration.

1285. Chambers, William. *Things As They Are in America*. New York: Negro Universities Press, 1968 [1854]. Reported that white Americans would never associate with African Americans equally. White repugnance toward persons of color amounted to "an absolute monomania."

1286. Crawford, Martin. *The Anglo-American Crisis of the Mid-Nineteenth Century:* The Times *and America, 1850–1862*. Athens: University of Georgia Press, 1987. The *London Times* reported a diplomatic frustration with America owing to its presidency always filled by unknowns like Fillmore.

1287. ———. *"The Times* and American Slavery in the 1850s." *Slavery & Abolition* 3 (December 1982): 228–42. The paper found the Fugitive Slave Law morally offensive but also thought the baiting language of the abolitionists potentially disruptive to transatlantic harmony.

1288. Cunliffe, Marcus. "America at the Great Exhibition of 1851." In *In Search of America: Transatlantic Essays, 1951–1990*. Britain acknowledged a new respect for American manufacturing while praising its own superior industrial position.

1289. "Diplomacy and Diplomatists." *Eclectic Review* 20 (July 1850): 425–32. Reprint of an article from *Fraser's Magazine* critical of the "mob of peers" in the British Foreign Office. Lists British ministers around the world, their salaries, and rent allowances.

1290. Drake, Thomas E. *Quakers and Slavery in America*. Gloucester, MA: Peter Smith, 1965 [1950]. English Quakers personally delivered an antislavery appeal to Fillmore.

1291. Fladeland, Betty. *Men and Brothers: Anglo-American Antislavery Cooperation*. Urbana: University of Illinois Press, 1972. British and American abolitionists successfully petitioned Britain to prevent the return of fugitive slaves from Canada.

1292. Gibson, Florence E. *The Attitudes of the New York Irish Toward State and National Affairs, 1848–1892.* New York: Columbia University Press, 1951. Though sympathetic with Irish-American petitioners, Fillmore refused to intercede with Britain for the release of Ireland's political prisoners.

1293. Griffin, Grace Gordon. *A Guide to Manuscripts Relating to American History in British Depositories Reproduced for the Division of Manuscripts of the Library of Congress.* Washington, DC: Library of Congress, 1946. Guide to British Foreign Office Records, Legation Archives, and Mission Correspondence with a catalogue of copies at the Library of Congress.

1294. Hamer, Philip M. "British Consuls and the Negro Seaman Acts, 1850–1860." *Journal of Southern History* 1 (May 1935): 138–68. Fillmore supported Britain's attempt to have South Carolina pass laws admitting Britain's free Negro seamen on terms of equality with whites. Critics accused Fillmore of allowing the secession-minded state to negotiate for recognition with Britain.

1295. Hidy, Ralph W. *The House of Barings in American Trade and Finance: English Merchant Bankers at Work, 1763–1861.* Cambridge: Harvard University Press, 1949. In 1852, Barings' new confidence in American securities led to increased sales of federal, state, and railroad bonds.

1296. Home, William Douglas, ed. *The Prime Ministers.* London: W. H. Allen, 1987. Includes essays on Prime Ministers during Fillmore's administration.

1297. Humphreys, R. A. "Anglo-American Rivalries in Central America." *Transactions of the Royal Historical Society* 18 (1968): 174–208. 5th series. Reviews Britain's assessment of American expansion.

1298. Hyam, Ronald. *Britain's Imperial Century, 1815–1914: A Study of Empire and Expansion.* 2d ed. Lanham: Barnes & Noble Books, 1993. Concludes the United States presented a challenge to the British Empire though India was its major problem.

1299. "The Industrial Exhibition." *Eclectic Review* 23 (August 1851): 513–31. Reprinted article from the *Westminster and Foreign Quarterly Review* congratulating "Brother Jonathan" on the many useful inventions at the 1851 London exhibit. Then it warns America to abandon tariffs and proclaim free trade.

1300. "The Irish Census." *Eclectic Review* 23 (August 1851): 569–70. Reprint of an article from the *Athenaeum* expressing surprise at the great number of Irish in America who are demonstrating an improveable character not expressed in their native land.

1301. "Japan." *Eclectic Review* 28 (January 1853): 21–40. Article from the *Edinburgh Review* looks forward to the opening of Japan but speculates on the possibility that Perry will meet armed resistance.

1302. "Japanese Expeditions." *Eclectic Review* 26 (July 1852): 420–25. Article from *Sharpe's Magazine* reviews Britain's failure to open trade with Japan and hopes the Americans will succeed.

1303. Jones, Wilbur Devereux. *The American Problem in British Diplomacy, 1841–1861.* Athens: University of Georgia Press, 1974. During Fillmore's administration the United States was a low priority in Britain's diplomatic affairs.

1304. Judd, Denis. *Empire: The British Imperial Experience, from 1765 to the Present.* London: HarperCollins *Publishers,* 1996. Chapter Five describes Canada's strained relations with Britain and its possible accession by America. To quiet discontent Britain allowed more self government and negotiated a free trade agreement between the United States and Canada.

1305. MacDonagh, Oliver. "Irish Emigration to the United States of America and the British Colonies During the Famine." In *The Great Famine: Studies in Irish History, 1845–52,* ed. R. Dudley Edwards and T. Desmond Williams. New York: New York University Press, 1957. 319–88. Describes the internal problems that released the tremendous emigration to America with its consequent social and political disturbances.

1306. Manning, William R., ed. *Diplomatic Correspondence of the United States: Inter-American Affairs, 1831–1860.* Washington, DC: Carnegie Endowment for International Peace, 1932–39. 12 vols. Volume Seven covers Great Britain.

1307. Mowat, R. B. *The Diplomatic Relations of Great Britain and the United States.* New York: Longmans, Gree & Co., 1925. A dated survey containing a useful chronology of American diplomats.

1308. O'Connor, Luke Symth, Major. "On the Links Connecting the Atlantic and the Pacific." *Eclectic Review* 20 (May 1850): 40–43. Describes three potential routes through Central America that would ease the way to California's gold and allow Britain to increase its two-ocean commerce.

1309. Perkins, Bradford. *The Cambridge History of American Foreign Relations, vol. 1, Creation of a Republican Empire, 1776–1865.* New York: Cambridge University Press, 1993.

1310. Potter, George. *To the Golden Door: The Story of the Irish in Ireland and America.* Westport, CT: Greenwood Press, 1973 [1960]. Despite receiving the first

Irish-American delegation to the White House, Fillmore would not intervene with Britain for the release of Irish political prisoners.

1311. Prest, John. *Lord John Russell.* London: Macmillan, 1972. Britain's Prime Minister when Fillmore took office.

1312. "The Recent Growth of the United States of America." *Eclectic Review* 32 (August 1854): 468–82. Reviews the success of internal improvements to suppress secession.

1313. Ridley, James. *Lord Palmerston.* London: Constable, 1970. British Foreign Secretary when Fillmore took office.

1314. Smith, Edward. *England and America After Independence: A Short Examination of Their International Intercourse, 1783–1872.* Westminster: Archibald Constable & Co., 1900. Contains Fillmore's protest against Britain's Ruatan island colony off British Honduras.

1315. Soulsby, Hugh G. *The Right of Search and the Slave Trade in Anglo-American Relations, 1814–1862.* Baltimore: Johns Hopkins University Press, 1933. Britain was never satisfied with American strategy to apprehend slave ships off Africa.

1316. "The United States." *Eclectic Review* 22 (January 1851): 62–79. Reprint of an article from the *Edinburgh Review* surveying books on America. States the United States is not in moral decline as Europe thinks but only suffering from the evils of growth. Supports the recent Compromise of 1850 and the new administration.

1317. "The Valedictory of the Whig Administration." *United States Magazine and Democratic Review* 32 (May 1853): 458–78. Argues against Whig policies allowing England to intervene in Central America.

1318. Van Alstyne, Richard W. "Anglo-American Relations, 1853–57: British Statesmen on the Clayton-Bulwer Treaty and American Expansion." *American Historical Review* 42 (April 1837): 491–500. British minister to America assesses Everett's rejection of a tripartite convention to protect Cuba. He reasons on America's probable self restraint toward Britain: all arguments degenerate into sectionalism, and too much love for materialism to waste it on war.

1319. ———— . "British Diplomacy and the Clayton-Bulwer Treaty, 1850–1860." *Journal of Modern History* 11 (June 1939): 149–83. Treaty conferred equal rights to United States and Britain in Central America. Problems arose over rival shipping interests, U.S. adventurers, and British claims to unilateral oversight of certain regions.

1320. Van Thal, Herbert, ed. *The Prime Ministers.* London: George Allen & Unwin Ltd., 1975. 2 vols. Volume Two contains biographies of Prime Ministers during Fillmore's administration.

1321. Ward, A. W., and G. P. Gooch, eds. *The Cambridge History of British Foreign Policy 1783–1919.* New York: Macmillan Press, 1923. Reviews Britain's Central American policies.

1322. Weigall, David. *Britain and the World, 1815–1986: A Dictionary of International Relations.* London: B. T. Batsford Ltd., 1987. Useful introduction to British diplomacy.

1323. "Wellington, Webster, Gioberti." *Eclectic Review* 28 (February 1853): 180–85. Article from *Bentley's Miscellany* mourns Webster's death and the Americans reluctance to make their great men president. Americans accept the Fillmores and then ask the Websters to guide their administration.

1324. White, Laura A. "The South in the 1850's as Seen by British Consuls." *Journal of Southern History* 1 (February 1935): 29–48. Reports on Consuls' protests against Southern states allowing British Negro seamen to be kidnapped into slavery. Also describes the South Carolina secession debates.

1325. ———. "The Unites States in the 1850's as Seen by British Consuls." *Mississippi Valley Historical Review* 19 (March 1933): 509–36. Depicts a lawless American democracy and a corrupt Congress. Warns of American adventurers immigrating to Australia and the possible secession of the American West Coast from the United States.

1325a. Wilkins, Joe Bassette, Jr. "Window on Freedom: The South's response to the Emancipation of the Slaves in the British West Indies, 1833–1861." Ph.D. diss., University of South Carolina, 1977. The South saw only economic and social ruin where Britain freed slaves. The experiment discredited the idea of compensated emancipation.

1326. Willson, Beckles. *Friendly Relations: A Narrative of Britain's Ministers and Ambassadors to America (1791–1930).* Boston: Little, Brown, and Company, 1934. Minister Bulwer believed the Fillmore administration was honorable, just, and prudent. Minister Crampton submitted a Canadian reciprocity treaty and a fisheries treaty which were not finalized until 1854.

1327. Zorn, Romon J. "Criminal Extradition Menaces the Canadian Haven for Fugitive Slaves, 1841–1861." *Canadian Historical Review* 38 (December 1957): 284–94. British abolitionists lobbied to exclude the extradition of fugitive slaves from the Webster-Ashburton treaty. They made a point of reasserting its exclusion after the passage of the 1850 Fugitive Slave Law.

6. Canada, British North America

1328. Allin, Cephas D., and George M. Jones. *Annexation, Preferential Trade and Reciprocity.* Toronto: Musson Book Co., Limited, 1912. Chapter Ten sets forth the sympathy in America for the annexation of Canada. Fillmore did not act on these sentiments. His policy also appeased Southern fears of acquiring more territory free of slavery.

1329. Baglier, Janet Dorothy. "The Niagara Frontier: Society and Economy in Western New York and Upper Canada, 1794–1854." Ph.D. diss., State University of New York at Buffalo, 1993. Fillmore wanted a reciprocity treaty with Canada to expand commerce along the Niagara Frontier and in his hometown, Buffalo.

1330. Callahan, James Morton. *The Neutrality of the American Lakes and Anglo American Relations.* Baltimore: Johns Hopkins University Press, 1898. Based on reports of friendly Canadian-American relations, Secretary of the Navy Graham turned down a request for a navy yard on Lake Erie.

1331. Careless, J. M. S. "1850s." In *Colonists & Canadiens, 1760–1867.* Toronto: Macmillan of Canada, 1971. The decade proved to be one of commercial expansion, more self government, and economic integration with the United States.

1332. Craig, Gerald M. *The United States and Canada.* Cambridge: Harvard University Press, 1968. The early 1850s saw increased proposals for cross border trade, which led to the Reciprocity Treaty of 1854.

1333. *Gleason's Pictorial Drawing-Room Companion,* October 4, 1851. Illustration of the Earl of Elgin, Governor General of Canada. He and Fillmore met in Boston where he displayed an agreeable and pleasant character.

1334. Landon, Fred. "The Anti-Slavery Society of Canada." *Journal of Negro History* 4 (January 1919): 33–40. Organized in February 1851 to aid the influx of fugitive African Americans, it was allied with similar societies in the United States and Great Britain.

1335. LeDuc, T. H. "I. D. Andrews and the Reciprocity Treaty of 1854." *Canadian Historical Review* 15 (December 1934): 437–38. Suggests America's special agent in Canada received compensation from Britain in the early 1850s. Britain wanted the treaty.

1336. MacDonald, Helen G. *Canadian Public Opinion on the American Civil War.* New York: Octogon Books, 1974 [1926]. Substantial background on Canada's small but influential movement for annexation by the United States, Canadians greater desire for a reciprocity treaty, and its universal condemnation of the Fugitive Slave Law.

1337. Manning, William R., ed. *Diplomatic Correspondence of the United States-Canadian Relations, 1784–1860.* Washington, DC: Carnegie Endowment for International Peace, 1940–45. 4 vols.

1338. Masters, Donald C. "A Further Word on I. D. Andrews and the Reciprocity Treaty of 1854." *Canadian Historical Review* 17 (June 1936): 159–67. Andrews wanted compensation for his work promoting the treaty in Canada during Fillmore's administration.

1339. ———. "Reciprocity." In *The Canadian Encyclopedia,* ed. James H. Marsh. Edmonton: Hurtig Publishers, 1985. 3 vols. 3: 1551. During Fillmore's administration, British and U.S. officials sought free trade for North America. At the same time Britain began restricting its fishing territories to American fleets off the Canadian Maritimes to register the importance of reciprocity.

1340. Monet, Jacques, "Elgin, James Bruce, 8th Earl of." In *The Canadian Encyclopedia,* ed. James H. Marsh. Edmonton: Hurtig Publishers, 1985. 3 vols. 1: 562. Governor General of British North America from 1846 to 1854. He is credited with promoting more self government for Canadians.

1341. Morison, J. L. *The Eighth Earl of Elgin: A Chapter in Nineteenth-Century Imperial History.* Westport, CT: Greenwood Press, 1970 [1928]. Governor General of Canada in the early 1850s. He supported increased self government and a free trade treaty with the U.S. His correspondence reveals his keen analysis of Fillmore's administration.

1342. Murray, Alexander L. "Canada and the Anglo-American Anti-Slavery Movement: A Study in International Philanthropy." Ph.D. diss., University of Pennsylvania, 1960. After passage of the Fugitive Slave Law, British and American abolitionists recognized Canada's unique role as a haven for fugitives.

1343. ———. "The Extradition of Fugitive Slaves from Canada, A Re-evaluation." *Canadian Historical Review* 43 (December 1962): 298–314. The British government recognized that the Webster-Ashburton Treaty prohibited the extradition of U.S. fugitive slaves from Canada.

1344. Overman, Wm. D. "I. D. Andrews and Reciprocity in 1854: An Episode in Dollar Diplomacy." *Canadian Historical Review* 15 (September 1934): 248–63.

The Canadian-American Treaty relied on data gathered by Andrews in the early 1850s.

1345. Parker, David W. *Guide to the Materials for United States History in Canadian Archives.* New York: Kraus Reprint Corporation, 1965 [1913]. Limited material on Fillmore.

1346. Porritt, Edward. *Sixty Years of Protection in Canada, 1846–1907: Where Industry Leans on the Politicians.* London: Macmillan and Co., Limited, 1907. Congress did not act on Fillmore's recommendation for a Canadian-U.S. reciprocity treaty. In response, Britain enforced restrictions on U.S. fishing in Canadian waters to force a reconsideration.

1347. "Recent Travelers in North America." *Eclectic Review* 24 (September 1851): 98–112. Reprint of an article from the *Quarterly Review.* It comments on the increased Canadian animosity toward Americans advocating the accession of British North America, particularly after the immoral passage of the Fugitive Slave Law. Instead of eyeing Canada, America should be aware of the possible secession of California and Oregon.

1348. Steward, Gordon T. *The American Response to Canada Since 1776.* East Lansing: Michigan State University Press, 1992. Fillmore believed Britain's recent aggressive actions over the perennial fisheries dispute was an unfair ploy to negotiate a free trade treaty. There was also a concern that Britain would avoid U.S. tariffs by shipping items over a free trade United States-Canadian border. Bibliography and historiography.

1349. Stuart, Reginald C. *United States Expansionism and British North America, 1775–1871.* Chapel Hill: University of North Carolina Press, 1988. Fillmore supported increased commerce with Canada while suppressing arguments to annex it. Bibliography.

1350. ———. "United States Expansionism and the British North American Provinces, 1783–1871." In *Arms at Rest: Peacemaking and Peacekeeping in American History,* ed. Joan R. Challinor and Robert L. Beisner. Westport, CT: Greenwood Press, 1987. Reviews the integration of Canada into the U.S. economy.

1351. Thompson, John Herd, and Stephen J. Randall. *Canada and the United States: Ambivalent Allies.* Athens: University of Georgia Press, 1994. Prospects for the American annexation of Canada were subdued by increased trade and prosperity for both countries in the 1850s.

1352. Turner, A. J. "Annexation of Canada." *De Bow's Southern and Western Review* 9 (October 1850): 397–412. Despite commercial advantages the South would resist annexing Canada if abolitionists inflicted their principles on that land.

1353. Weigley, Russell F. "The Anglo-American Armies and Peace, 1783–1868." In *Arms At Rest: Peacemaking and Peacekeeping in American History,* ed. Joan R. Challinor and Robert L. Beisner. New York: Greenwood Press, 1987. Summary of U.S., British, and Canadian military and diplomatic experience along the borders.

1354. Winks, Robin W. *The Blacks in Canada: A History.* New Haven: Yale University Press, 1971. There was a mixed response to the influx of African Americans escaping the Fugitive Slave Law but Canada remained antislavery and supported no extradition.

1355. Wise, S. F. "The Annexation Movement and Its Effect on Canadian Opinion, 1837–67." In *Canada Views the United States, Nineteenth Century Political Attitudes,* ed. S. F. Wise and Robert Craig Brown. Seattle: University of Washington Press, 1967. Canadian political groups used their caricature or misunderstanding of U.S. democracy to support their own political goals.

7. Caribbean

1356. Bushnell, David, and Neil Macaulay. *The Emergence of Latin America in the Nineteenth Century.* New York: Oxford University Press, 1988. Good introduction to the Caribbean, Central America, Mexico, and South America. Annotated bibliography.

1357. Durden, Robert F. "J. D. B. De Bow: Convolutions of a Slavery Expansionist." *Journal of Southern History* 17 (November 1951): 441–61. *De Bow's Review* was the foremost Southern journal of commerce. It advocated expansion of plantation slavery into the Caribbean.

1358. Fifer, J. Valerie. *United States Perception of Latin America, 1850–1930, A 'New West' South of Capricorn?* New York: Manchester University Press, 1991. Surveys American interest in Latin America during the early 1850s. Includes bibliography and land surveys.

1358a. Hunt, Alfred N. *Haiti's Influence on Antebellum America: Slumbering Volcano in the Caribbean.* Baton Rouge: Louisiana State University Press, 1988. Haiti's violent slave rebellion and existence as an independent black nation had a profound effect on both proslavery and antislavery advocates. Though not mentioned by the author, Fillmore referred to Haiti's violent beginning in his self-suppressed portion on slavery in his last presidential address.

1359. Langley, Lester D. *Struggle for the American Mediterranean: United States-European Rivalry in the Gulf-Caribbean, 1776–1904.* Athens: University of Georgia Press, 1976. Despite his passive appearance, Fillmore was committed to a European-free Western Hemisphere.

1360. Manning, William R. *Diplomatic Correspondence of the United States Inter-American Affairs, 1831–1860.* Washington, DC: Carnegie Endowment for International Peace, 1932–39. 12 vols. Volume Six covers the Dominican Republic.

1361. Martinez-Fernandez, Luis. *Torn Between Empires: Economy, Society and Patterns of Political Thought in the Hispanic Caribbean, 1840–1878.* Athens: University of Georgia Press, 1994. The Caribbean at mid-century was shifting commercial relations to the United States.

1362. May, Robert E. "Epilogue to the Missouri Compromise: The South, the Balance of Power, and the Tropics in the 1850s." *Plantation Society in the Americas* 1 (February 1979): 201–25. The South's Caribbean expansion movement was an alternative way to expand southern congressional representation and halt secession.

1363. ———. *The Southern Dream of a Caribbean Empire, 1854–1865.* Baton Rouge: Louisiana State University Press, 1973. Like conservative Southern Whigs, Fillmore opposed the annexation of non-English-speaking and racially mixed tropical islands.

1364. Nauman, Ann K. *A Handbook of Latin American and Caribbean National Archives.* Detroit: Elaine Ethridge-Books, 1983. Brief comments on English and Spanish archival materials.

1365. Perkins, Dexter. *The Monroe Doctrine, 1826–1867.* Baltimore: Johns Hopkins University Press, 1933. A French-British blockade of Haiti to stop its aggression against the Dominican Republic brought Democratic complaints against Fillmore for allowing Europeans in the hemisphere.

1366. Tansill, Charles Callan. *The United States and Santo Domingo, 1789–1873: A Chapter in Caribbean Diplomacy.* Baltimore: Johns Hopkins University Press, 1938. Fillmore hoped to mediate a stop to Haitian aggression against the Dominican Republic.

1367. Wallace, Edwards. *Destiny and Glory.* New York: Coward-McCann Inc., 1957. Describes filibustering in Latin America and the Caribbean.

1368. Wilgus, A. Curtis. "Official Expression of Manifest Destiny Sentiment Concerning Hispanic America, 1848–1871." *Louisiana Historical Quarterly* 15

(July 1932): 486–506. Fillmore opposed the Democratic party's expansionist policies.

8. Central America

1369. Bartlett, Ruhl J., ed. *The Record of American Diplomacy: Documents and Readings in the History of American Foreign Relations.* New York: Alfred A. Knopf, 1964. Chapter 15 reprints Secretary of State Clayton's letter to Fillmore explaining the negotiations with England.

1370. Bevins, Charles I., ed. *Treaties and Other International Agreements of the United States of America, 1776–1949.* Washington, DC: Government Printing Office, 1968–1976. 13 vols. 6: 1013–1018. Commercial agreement with Costa Rica.

1371. "British Encroachments and Aggressions in Central America, The Moscito Question." *American Whig Review* 27 (February 1850): 188–203; (March 1850): 235–68. Description of Nicaragua's Mosquito Coast, Britain's historical claim, and their intention to secure Central America.

1372. Burns, E. Bradford. *Patriarch and Folk: The Emergence of Nicaragua, 1798–1858.* Cambridge: Harvard University Press, 1991. U.S. entrepreneurs wanted to build an interocean passage despite Nicaraguan and British obstacles.

1373. "Central America, Nicaragua, and the Ocean Ship-Canal." *Whig Almanac, 1851.* New York: New York Tribune, 1851. 36–38. Sketch of Nicaragua, British interests, and the intention of U.S. businessmen to build an interocean canal.

1374. Folkman, David I., Jr. *The Nicaragua Route.* Salt Lake City: University of Utah Press, 1972. In 1852, Fillmore submitted Commodore Vanderbilt's canal plans to the U.S. Topographical Engineers, who approved the proposal. Includes the plan's map.

1375. Karnes, Thomas L. *The Failure of Union: Central America, 1824–1975.* Tempe: Arizona State University, 1976. Fillmore and Britain refused to recognize an 1851 confederation of Nicaragua, Honduras, and El Salvador because it lacked local popular support.

1376. Manning, William R., ed. *Diplomatic Correspondence of the United States: Inter-American Affairs, 1831–1860.* Washington, DC: Carnegie Endowment for International Peace, 1932–39. 12 vols. Volumes Three and Four cover Fillmore's administration.

1377. Olien, Michael D. "E. G. Squires and the Miskito: Anthropological Scholarship and Political Propaganda." *Ethnohistory* 32 (1985): 111–33. Former chargé d'affaires worked for American commercial interests and against Britain's presence in Nicaragua.

1378. "Our Foreign Relations, Central America—the Crampton and Webster Project." *United States Magazine and Democratic Review* 31 (October 1852): 337–51. Partisan opposition to the familiarity between the United States and Britain in Central America.

1379. Russel, Robert R. *Improvement of Communication with the Pacific Coast as an Issue in American Politics, 1783–1864*. Cedar Rapids: Torch Press, 1948. Survey of U.S. activities to open canals and railroads across North and Central America.

1380. Schott, Joseph L. *Rails Across Panama: The Story of the Building of the Panama Railroad, 1849–1855*. New York: Bobbs-Merrill Company, Inc., 1967. Stories of building the interocean railroad and the travelers who rode it. Includes bibliography.

1381. "Treaties." *Whig Almanac, 1853*. New York: New York Tribune, 1853. 28–29. Summarizes commercial agreements with Guatemala, Costa Rica, and Peru.

9. China

1382. Arkusk, R. David, and Leo O. Lee, eds. *Land Without Ghosts: Chinese Impressions of America from the Mid-Nineteenth Century to the Twentieth Century*. Berkeley: University of California Press, 1989. Contains two unique short reports on the United States from 1848 and 1868. Excellent bibliography.

1383. Baron, Deborah G., and Susan B. Gall. *Asian American Chronology*. New York: U X L, 1996. Includes American relations with China and Chinese immigrants in the early 1850s.

1384. Davids, Jules, ed. *American Diplomatic and Public Papers: The United States and China, Series 1: The Treaty System and the Taiping Rebellion, 1842–1860*. Wilmington: Scholarly Resources Inc., 1973. 21 vols. Reproductions of correspondence. Each volume begins with a historical introduction and ends with biographies of important participants. Volumes 4, 12, 17, and 18 are of particular concern to the Fillmore administration and its Minister to China, Humphry Marshall.

1385. Dennett, Tyler. *Americans in Eastern Asia: A Critical Study of United States' Policy in the Far East in the Nineteenth Century*. New York: Barnes & Noble, Inc., 1963 [1922]. U.S. Minister Humphrey Marshall reported on China's weak Manchu government but favored American support.

1386. Huebner, Jon W. "The Unequal Treaties and United States Policy in China, 1842–1868." *Asian Profile* 14 (August 1986): 409–17. Summary of U.S. treaties that followed British inroads into China.

1387. Hunt, Michael H. *The Making of a Special Relationship: The United States and China to 1914.* New York: Columbia University Press, 1983. Narrates the build-up of trade and minor diplomatic relations in the first half of the nineteenth century. Annotated bibliography.

1388. Swisher, Earl. *China's Management of the American Barbarians: A Study of Sino American Relations, 1841–1861, with Documents.* New Haven: Far Eastern Association, 1953. The Chinese had little contact with Americans but were still contemptuous of their behavior.

1389. Teng, S. Y. *The Taiping Rebellion and the Western Powers: A Comprehensive Survey.* Oxford: Clarenden Press, 1971. U.S. Minister Humphrey Marshall favored the Manchu rulers and forbade missionaries any contact with the Taiping agrarian rebels. He took advantage of the rebellion to gain concessions for the United States.

1390. Yu-wen, Jen. *The Taiping Revolutionary Movement.* New Haven: Yale University Press, 1973. Humphrey Marshall was unable to establish relations with the Taiping rebels but found favor with the Manchu rulers. He advocated U.S. intervention to protect Chinese territory from Russia and Britain. Maps and chronology of rebellion.

10. Cuba and Spain

1391. Bartlett, Ruhl J., ed. *The Record of American Diplomacy: Documents and Readings in the History of American Foreign Relations.* New York: Alfred A. Knopf, 1964. Chapter 14 reprints Secretary of State Everett's objection to the British-French declaration to protect Cuba.

1392. Brownson, Orestes. "The Piratical Expeditions of American Citizens Against the Island of Cuba and the Relations of the United States with Spain Resulting from Them." *Brownson's Quarterly Review* 14 (January 1852): 66–95. Critical of Fillmore's inability to prevent filibustering into Cuba.

1393. Caldwell, Robert G. *The Lopez Expeditions to Cuba, 1848–1851.* Princeton: Princeton University Press, 1915. Narrative of the expeditions using Havana archives.

1394. Callahan, James Morton. *Cuba and International Relations: A Historical Study in American Diplomacy.* New York: A M S Press, 1972 [1899]. Cuba's influence on U.S. sectional debates and Spanish-American relations.

.

1395. "Cuba and the United States, the Proposed Tripartite Treaty." *Whig Almanac, 1854.* New York: New York Tribune, 1854. 18–25. Contains the French-British correspondence proposing a three-nation agreement never to acquire Cuba. Everett declined to participate.

1396. Ettinger, Amos Aschback. *The Mission to Spain of Pierre Soule, 1853–1855: A Study in the Cuban Diplomacy of the United States.* New Haven: Yale University Press, 1932. Begins with an assessment of Fillmore's noninterventionist Cuban policy.

1397. Foner, Philip S. *A History of Cuba and Its Relations with the United States.* New York: International Publishers, 1963. 2 vols. In Volume Two, Fillmore is faulted for not suppressing the Lopez expedition. He is credited for opposing the annexation of Cuba.

1398. Foner, Philip S., and Richard C. Winchester. *The Anti-Imperialist Reader: From the Mexican War to the Election of 1900.* New York: Holman & Meier Publishers, Inc., 1984. Reprints an article from Frederick Douglass's paper suggesting that Fillmore's Cuban neutrality cannot be trusted while the slaveocracy runs America.

1399. Horsman, Reginald. *Race and Manifest Destiny: The Origins of American Racial Anglo-Saxonism.* Cambridge: Harvard University Press, 1981. Fillmore resisted Cuban annexation because he believed the United States was unable to amalgamate a large non-English-speaking race.

1400. "The Invasion of Cuba." *Southern Quarterly Review* 5 (January 1852): 1–47. Review of books on Cuba and the Lopez invasion. Credits the defeat of the invasion to the U.S. government which prevented more filibusters reinforcing Lopez.

1401. Jones, Howard. *Mutiny on the* Amistad: *The Saga of a Slave Revolt and Its Impact on American Abolition, Law, and Diplomacy.* New York: Oxford University Press, 1987. Fillmore asked the Senate to decide the old issue of a U.S. reparation to Spain for freeing Cuban slave mutineers. Bibliography.

1402. Kiernan, V. G. *The Revolution of 1854 in Spanish History.* Oxford: Clarendon Press, 1966. Isabella II wanted a return to monarchy, but the different desires of her Court, the Church, the Parliament, and foreign powers only made for an unstable government.

1403. Langley, Lester D. "Slavery, Reform and American Policy in Cuba, 1823–1878." *Revista de Historia de America* 65–66 (1968): 71–84. Fillmore was attacked by Southern expansionists for his neutral policy toward Cuba and Spain.

1404. Logan, John A., Jr. *No Transfer: An American Security Principle.* New Haven: Yale University Press, 1961. Chapter Eight is a review of Fillmore's policy toward filibusters and Cuba.

1405. Manning, William R., ed. *Diplomatic Correspondence of the United States: Inter-American Affairs, 1831–1860.* Washington, DC: Carnegie Endowment for International Peace, 1932–39. 12 vols. Volume Eleven covers Spain.

1406. Martin, Christopher. *The* Amistad *Affair.* London: Abelard-Schuman, 1970. The unresolved payment over the *Amistad* affair rankled Spain. Its ministers continually raised the question of compensation. Fillmore tried to achieve a settlement in 1853, but nothing was resolved. Spain finally dropped the matter in the 1880s.

1407. McClendon, R. Earl. "The *Amistad* Claims: Inconsistencies of Policy." *Political Science Quarterly* 48 (September 1933): 386–412. Reviews congressional arguments over paying Spain reparations for freeing Cuban mutineer slaves. In 1853, Fillmore sent a noncommittal request for a decision. None was made.

1407a. Oberholzter, Ellis Paxson. *A History of the United States Since the Civil War.* New York: Macmillan Company, 1928. 5 vols. 2: 246. In 1869, Spain asked the United States to issue a proclamation, as Fillmore did in 1851, warning Americans to desist from helping Cuban revolutionaries.

1408. Opatrný, Josef. *U.S. Expansionism and Cuban Annexation in the 1850s.* Lewistown, NY: Edwin Miller Press, 1993. Chapter Seven describes the several Lopez expeditions, Fillmore's attempt to prevent them, and his desire to maintain good relations with Spain.

1409. Poyo, Gerald E. "Evolution of Cuban Separatist Thought in the Émigré Communities of the United States, 1848–1895." *Hispanic American Historical Review* 66 (August 1986): 485–507. Describes the range of Cuban émigré thought about separation from Spain and the U.S. timidity to acquire Cuba.

1410. ———. *"With All, and for the Good of All": The Emergence of Popular Nationalism in the Cuban Communities of the United States, 1848–1898.* Durham: Duke University Press, 1989. Cuban émigrés looked for diplomatic means to separate Cuba from Spain and did not support Lopez's second and third expeditions. Uses Spanish and English sources.

1411. Rauch, Basil. *American Interest in Cuba: 1848–1855.* New York: Columbia University Press, 1948. Fillmore sustained an honorable and just noninterventionist policy toward Cuba despite the difficult problems of American filibusters.

1412. Van Alstyne, Richard W. "Empire in Midpassage, 1845–1867." In *From Colony to Empire: Essays in the History of American Foreign Relations,* ed. William Appleman Williams. New York: John Wiley & Sons Inc., 1972. Summary of Fillmore's policy toward Cuba.

11. Europe, General Works

1413. Bruun, Geoffrey. *Revolution and Reaction, 1848–1852: A Mid-Century Watershed.* Princeton: D. Van Nostrand Company, Inc., 1958. Survey and analysis of European republican revolutions and their conservative restorations.

1414. Cook, Chris, and John Paxton. *European Political Facts, 1848–1918.* New York: Facts on File, 1978. Chronology of events, Heads of State, Prime Ministers, and Foreign Ministers. Bibliography on European internal relations.

1415. Cunliffe, Marcus. *The Age of Expansion, 1848–1917.* London: Weidenfeld and Nicholson, 1974. Illustrated world history with European impressions of the United States.

1416. "Europe in 1848." *Whig Almanac, 1849.* New York: New York Tribune, 1849. 10–16. Describes the republican revolutions of 1848 and warns of the struggle to maintain them.

1417. "Europe in 1849." *Whig Almanac, 1850.* New York: New York Tribune, 1850. 6–15. Describes conservative efforts to overturn the revolutions of 1848.

1418. "Europe in 1850." *Whig Almanac 1851.* New York: New York Tribune, 1851. 30–33. A country-by-country analysis.

1419. "Europe in 1851." *Whig Almanac, 1852.* New York: New York Tribune, 1852. 34–35. Reviews the restored authoritarian hold on Europe and the American hope that France will soon overthrow President Louis Napoleon.

1420. Field, James A., Jr. *America and the Mediterranean World, 1776–1882.* Princeton: Princeton University Press, 1969. Uses State Department archives to survey the U.S. Naval, diplomatic, and missionary presence.

1421. Fisher, Marvin. "The 'Garden' and the 'Workshop': Some European Conceptions and Preconceptions of America, 1830–1860." *New England Quarterly* 34 (September 1961): 311–27. British, French, and German observers describe the natural farming potential of America and note the rural settings for manufacturing. Some anticipate a unique blend of husbandry and industry inviting a future of progress and paradise.

1422. Gildea, Robert. *Barricades and Borders: Europe, 1800–1914.* 2d ed. Oxford: Oxford University Press, 1996. Part Two is a synthesis of mid-century political, economic, and social history. The United States was seen as an exporter of grain and an importer of immigrants. Helpful biographical dictionary of major figures. Bibliography.

1423. Grenville, J. A. S. *Europe Reshaped, 1848–1878.* Ithaca: Cornell University Press, 1976. Parts One and Two are introductions to the European revolutions of 1848 and their authoritarian restorations. These events superseded any reason to make the United States a foreign policy priority.

1424. Palmer, Alan. *The Chancelleries of Europe.* London: George Allen & Union, 1983. Introduction to the foreign ministries of Europe and the men who made foreign policy.

1425. Whitridge, Arnold. *Men in Crisis: The Revolutions of 1848.* New York: Charles Scribner's Sons, 1949. Summary of major European revolutions and restorations. Chapter Five discusses the importance of immigrants to America.

12. France

1426. Aguihon, Maurice. *The Republican Experiment, 1848–1852.* Cambridge: Cambridge University Press, 1983. Interprets the failure of the French revolution and the return to a monarchy under Napoleon III. Helpful chronology.

1427. Blumenthal, Henry. *American and French Culture, 1800–1900: Interchanges in Art, Science, Literature, and Society.* Baton Rouge: Louisiana State University Press, 1975. Napoleon III disliked U.S. republicanism, but France adopted many U.S. inventions.

1428. ———— . *A Reappraisal of Franco-American Relations, 1830–1871.* Chapel Hill: University of North Carolina Press, 1959. Fillmore preferred the 2d Republic but recognized Napoleon III.

1429. Casper, Henry W. *American Attitudes Toward the Rise of Napoleon III: A Cross Section of Public Opinion.* Washington, DC: Catholic University of America Press, 1947. Fillmore resented Napoleon III and waited before recognizing the new Emperor. Contains an extract of Fillmore's letter to Napoleon expressing his preference for republicanism.

1430. Echard, William E. *Napoleon III and the Concert of Europe.* Baton Rouge: Louisiana State University Press, 1938. From 1849 to 1853, Napoleon III's foreign policy focused on Europe.

1431. Larson, Eugene S. "Napoleon III." In *Great Lives From History: Renaissance to 1900 Series,* ed. Frank N. Magill. Pasadena: Salem Press, 1989. 5 vols. 5: 1691–95. Louis Napoleon abolished the Second Republic for a Second Empire proclaiming himself Emperor Napoleon III. Annotated bibliography.

1432. Manning, William R., ed. *Diplomatic Correspondence of the United States: Inter-American Affairs, 1831–1860.* Washington, DC: Carnegie Endowment for International Peace, 1932–39. 12 vols. 6: 437–706.

1433. Marx, Karl. *The 18th Brumaire of Louis Bonaparte.* New York: International Publishers, 1963 [1852]. Scathing analysis of the revolution, the second republic, and Louis Bonaparte.

1434. Rorhs, Richard. "American Critics of the French Revolution of 1848." *Journal of the Early Republic* 14 (Fall 1994): 359–77. Americans were disappointed that France did not imitate their republican system. Later they were confused by France's intervention against the Roman Republic. Finally, French acceptance of Louis Napoleon as Emperor made France appear hopelessly corrupt.

1435. Tombs, Robert. *France: 1814–1914.* London: Longman, 1996. Chapters 19 and 20 narrate the 1848 revolution and reaction. Bibliography.

1436. Willson, Beckles. *America's Ambassadors to France (1777–1927): A Narrative of Franco-American Diplomatic Relations.* London: John Murray, 1928. Fillmore's administration recognized the Second Empire but was disappointed at Napoleon III's accession.

13. Germany

1437. Adams, Willi Paul. "German Translations of the American Declaration of Independence." *Journal of American History* 85 (March 1999): 1325–49. The activists of 1848 used their rough knowledge of American government to propose its freedoms into their new constitution. Includes references to German-language histories covering the mid-century.

1438. Gatzke, Hans W. *Germany and the United States.* Cambridge: Harvard University Press, 1980. At mid-century, Germany was forming its loose association of sovereign states. During the revolution of 1848, Andrew J. Donelson, Fillmore's future running-mate in 1856, was Minister to Berlin. He later represented the United States at the revolutionary provisional government. Annotates the few sources.

1439. Gazley, John Gerow. *American Opinion of German Unification, 1848–1871.* New York: Columbia University, 1926. There was overwhelming American sympathy for the revolutionary movement but concern about the reaction of the despotic Austrian and Prussian regimes.

1440. Grabbe, Hans-Jürgen. "Weary of Germany-Weary of America: Perceptions of the United States in Nineteenth Century Germany." In *Transatlantic Images and Perceptions: Germany and America Since 1776,* ed. David E. Barclay and Elisabeth Glaser-Schmidt. Cambridge: Cambridge University Press, 1997. Published opinion in Germany admired the American federal union but demeaned its lack of culture and feared its democratic "mobs."

1441. Hargest, George E. *History of Letter Post Communication Between the United States and Europe, 1845–1875.* The United States signed a closed-mail convention with Prussia in August 1852.

1442. Jonas, Manfred. *The United States and Germany: A Diplomatic History.* Ithaca: Cornell University Press, 1984. After the failure of the German revolution in 1849, a half million Germans emigrated to the United States. Few sources on pre-1860s German-U.S. relations.

1443. Pflange, Otto, ed. *The Unification of Germany, 1848–1871.* New York: Holt, Rinehart and Winston, 1968. Collection of excerpts from articles on the 1848 revolution, the reaction, and the movement for unification.

1444. Taylor, Bayard. *A School History of Germany: From the Earliest Period to the Establishment of the German Empire in 1871.* New York: D. Appleton and Company, 1891 [1874]. Reviews the 1848 revolution and its consequences.

1445. Thompson, Wayne C., Susan L. Thompson, and Juliet S. Thompson. *Historical Dictionary of Germany.* Metuchen: Scarecrow Press, Inc., 1994. Broad chronological work includes the internal development of Germany in the 1850s.

1446. Zu Stolberg-Werngerode, Otto. *Germany and the United States of America During the Era of Bismarck.* Reading, PA: Henry James Foundation, 1937. Prior to the American Civil War there was little concern about the United States.

14. Hawaii and the Pacific

1447. Brooks, Jean Ingram. *International Rivalry in the Pacific Islands.* Berkeley: University of California Press, 1941. The administration worked to keep Hawaii neutral despite France's efforts to accession the islands and a local movement for U.S. acquisition. Includes summaries of the opening of Japan and naval explorations.

1448. Dudden, Arthur Power. *The American Pacific: From the Old China Trade to the Present.* New York: Oxford University Press, 1992. Mentions the Japan expedition, the North Pacific explorations, and the policy to protect Hawaiian neutrality.

1449. Dulles, Foster Rhea. *America in the Pacific: A Century of Expansion.* Boston: Houghton Mifflin Company, 1932. Describes Fillmore as the noninterventionist exception between Democratic party annexationists.

1450. Griffin, Eldon. *Clippers and Consuls: American Consular and Commercial Relations with Eastern Asia, 1845–1860.* Ann Arbor: Edward Brothers, Inc., 1938. Description of consular duties and involvement in commercial relations.

1451. Kittelson, David. "Hawaii." In *Pacific Island Studies: A Survey of the Literature,* ed. Miles M. Jackson. New York: Greenwood Press, 1986. Useful bibliographic essay.

1452. McDougall, Walter A. *Let the Sea Make a Noise...: A History of the North Pacific from Magellan to MacArthur.* New York: Basic Books, 1993. The opening of Japan was part of a Pacific strategy to create coaling stations for commercial and naval steamships.

1453. Perry, John Curtis. *Facing West: Americans and the Opening of the Pacific.* Westport, CT: Praeger, 1994. Mentions Perry's goal for naval domination in the Pacific and Fillmore's desire to expand commercial shipping. Describes the Ringgold-Rogers scientific expedition in the Pacific, which surveyed parts of Japan before Perry negotiated the treaty.

1454. Van Alstyne, Richard W. "Great Britain, The United States, and Hawaiian Independence, 1850–1855." *Pacific Historical Review* 4 (March 1935): 15–24. Confidential British Foreign Office documents report Fillmore's willingness to agree to a tripartite agreement to protect Hawaii.

15. India

1455. Bhagat, G. *Americans in India, 1784–1860.* New York: New York University Press, 1970. Describes minor commercial relations.

16. Italy and the Papal States

1456. Beales, Derek. *The Risorgemento and the Unification of Italy.* New York: Barnes and Noble Inc., 1971. Introduction to the unification of Italy.

1457. Brownson, Orestes. "Pius the Ninth, and the Political Regeneration of Italy." *Brownson's Quarterly Review* 10 (January 1848): 117–34. Catholic editor looks forward to the secular rule of the new Pope.

1458. ———. "Where is Italy?" *Brownson's Quarterly Review* 16 (April 1854): 219–52. Catholic journalist reviews books on the recent Italian political upheavals and reports on Protestant perceptions of them.

1459. Feiertag, Sister Loretta Clare. *American Public Opinion on the Diplomatic Relations Between the United States and the Papal States (1848–1867).* Washington, DC: Catholic University of America Press, 1933. Good summary of diplomatic activities under Taylor but no mention of Fillmore.

1460. *Gleason's Pictorial Drawing-Room Companion,* February 21 1852. Illustration of Pius IX. Mentions his growing secular weakness just like the other monarchs of Europe.

1461. Hales, E. E. Y. *Pio Nono: A Study in European Politics and Religion in the Nineteenth Century.* Garden City: Image Books, 1962. Studies the reign of Pius IX.

1462. Hibbert, Christopher. *Garibaldi and His Enemies.* New York: Penguin Books, 1987 [1965]. The military hero of the unification of Italy spent a year of his exile in the early 1850s working in a factory on Staten Island.

1463. Marraro, Howard R. *American Opinion on the Unification of Italy, 1846–1861.* New York: A M S Press, 1969 [1932]. Americans witnessing the fall of the Roman Republic urged Fillmore to intervene and stop the brutality of the restoration. He replied that he would not interfere in the domestic affairs of other nations.

1464. Rush, Alfred C. "Diplomatic Relations: The United States and the Papal States." *American Ecclesiastical Review* 126 (January 1952): 12–27. Review of Papal consuls in America and U.S. representatives to the Papal States.

1465. Stock, Leo Francis. *United States Ministers to the Papal States: Instructions and Dispatches, 1848–1868.* Washington, DC: Catholic University Press, 1933. Correspondence highlights the continuing unrest over the Pope's misuse of his secular powers.

17. Japan

1466. Barr, Pat. *The Coming of the Barbarians: The Opening of Japan to the West, 1853–1870.* New York: E. P. Dutton & Co., Inc., 1967. Perry's expedition occurred during Japan's reassessment of its foreign relations.

1467. Beasley, W. G. *The Modern History of Japan.* London: Weidenfeld and Nicolson, 1981 [1963]. Places Perry's expedition within Japan's rise to a world power.

1468. ———, ed. *Selected Documents on Japanese Foreign Policy, 1853–1868.* London: Oxford University Press, 1955. Contains Japanese and U.S. documents pertinent to Perry's expedition and Japan's changing foreign relations.

1469. Bevins, Charles I., ed. *Treaties and Other International Agreements of the United States of America, 1776–1949.* Washington, DC: Government Printing Office, 1968–1976. 13 vols. 9: 351–358. The peace and amity agreements of the Perry expedition were signed in 1854.

1470. Cameron, Meribeth E., Thomas H. D. Mahoney, and George E. McReynolds. *China, Japan and the Powers: A History of the Modern Far East.* New York: Ronald Press Company, 1960. Reviews the impact of the Occident upon the Far East, including Perry's expedition to Japan.

1471. "Commodore Perry's Expedition to Japan." *Harper's Monthly* 12 (1856): 441–66, 733–56. Lengthy, illustrated report.

1472. Davis, W. Watson. "The Monroe Doctrine and Perry's Expedition to Japan." *Cosmopolitan* 37 (June 1904): 219–25. Fillmore's opening of Japan is almost as significant as Monroe's Doctrine to protect America.

1473. Dennett, Tyler. *Americans in Eastern Asia: A Critical Study of United States' Policy in the Far East in the Nineteenth Century.* New York: Barnes & Noble, Inc., 1963 [1922]. Must credit Fillmore and not Pierce for the successful Japanese initiative.

1474. "The Expedition to Japan." *The Whig Almanac,* 1854. New York: New York Tribune, 1854. 7. Concise account of Perry's expedition.

1475. Falk, Edwin A. *From Perry to Pearl Harbor: The Struggle for Supremacy in the Pacific.* Gardin City, NJ: Doubleday, Dorn and Company, Inc., 1943. Informal review of Perry's expedition in light of Japan's 1941 attack on Hawaii.

1476. Fredman, Lionel E. *The United States Enters the Pacific.* Sydney, Australia: Angus and Robertson LTD., 1969. Summary of Perry's expedition, with extracts from Fillmore's letter to the Emperor.

1477. Goldsborough, John. "Commodore Perry's Landing in Japan—1853, From the Journal of Commodore John Rodgers Goldsborough, U.S.N." *American Neptune* 7 (January 1947): 9–20. Perry's first days in Yeddo Bay.

1478. Griffis, William Elliot. "Millard Fillmore and His Part in the Opening of Japan." *Publications of the Buffalo Historical Society Volume 9*. Buffalo: Buffalo Historical Society, 1906. 53–79. Fillmore receives equal honors with Perry.

1479. Head, Timothy E., and Govan Daws. "The Bonins—Isles of Contention." *American Heritage* 19 (February 1968): 58–64, 69–74. Perry believed the United States should claim the Bonin Islands south of Japan. Photographs and map.

1480. Hildreth, Richard. *Japan as It Was and Is*. Boston: Phillip, Sampson and Company, 1855. Extraordinary review of literature available on Japan prior to the publication of Perry's expedition. Contains Fillmore's letter to the Emperor and Webster's shorter first draft, which Hildreth says the Emperor would have preferred.

1481. "The Japan Expedition and Its Results." *United States Magazine and Democratic Review* 32 (January 1853): 64–79. Criticizes Fillmore for delaying the expedition and for his weak message to the Emperor.

1482. LaFeber, Walter. *The Clash: A History of US-Japan Relations*. New York: W. W. Norton & Company, 1997. Begins with Fillmore's letter to the Emperor asking to open trade between the two nations.

1483. Livermore, Seward W. "American Naval Base Policy in the Far East, 1850–1914." *Pacific Historical Society* 13 (June 1944): 113–35. Perry wanted to occupy Pacific islands to compete with Britain's naval power and commerce.

1484. Montgomery, Michael. *Imperial Japan: The Yen to Dominate*. London: Christopher Helm, 1987. Presents Perry's expedition from a Japanese perspective. Includes maps, illustrations, and bibliography.

1485. Neuman, William L. "Religion, Morality and Freedom: The Ideological Background of the Perry Expedition." *Pacific Historical Review* 23 (August 1954): 247–57. Americans believed Japan would gain culturally and morally from its commercial contact with the West.

1486. "Religion, Civilization and Social State of the Japanese." *Christian Examiner* 55 (July 1853): 22–42. Fillmore's administration sparked interest and publications about Japan.

1487. Sakamaki, Shunzo. "Western Concepts of Japan and the Japanese." *Pacific Historical Review* 6 (1937): 1–14. Little was known about Japan at the time of the Perry expedition. Only the Dutch were allowed a yearly commercial visit.

1488. Taylor, Bayard. *India, China and Japan in the Year 1853.* New York: G. P. Putnam & Co., 1864 [1855]. Travel writer describes his association with Commodore Perry and his eye-witness account of the opening of Japan.

1489. Vernon, Manfred C. "The Dutch and the Opening of Japan by the United States." *Pacific Historical Review* 28 (February 1959): 39–48. The State Department negotiated with the Dutch for information and charts to help Perry.

1490. Weisberger, Bernard A. "First Encounter." *American Heritage* 42 (December 1991): 20–22. Reviews the consequences of Perry's expedition in light of the anniversary of the Japanese attack on Pearl Harbor.

1491. Wiley, Peter Booth. *Yankees in the Land of the Gods: Commodore Perry and the Opening of Japan.* New York: Viking, 1990. Fillmore is credited with setting the diplomatic and commercial tone of the expedition. Good use of visual arts to dramatize both ethnocentric perspectives on first meeting. Maps and bibliography.

1492. Wilson, George M. *Patriots and Redeemers in Japan: Motives in the Meije Restoration.* Chicago: University of Chicago Press, 1992. Perry's arrival intensified Japan's internal problems.

18. Mexico

1493. "Arista, Mariano." In *Historical Dictionary of Mexico*, ed. Donald C. Briggs and Marvin Alisky. Metuchen, NJ: Scarecrow Press, Inc., 1981. 13. President from 1851 to January 1853. Honest executive who tried to bring reforms to the government despite military unrest.

1494. Bazant, Jan. "From Independence to the Liberal Republic, 1821–1867." In *Mexico Since Independence,* ed. Leslie Bethell. Cambridge: Cambridge University Press, 1991. Reviews the politics and problems of Presidents José Joaquín Herrera and Mariano Arista in the early 1850s. Bibliography.

1495. Callahan, James Morton. *American Foreign Policy in Mexican Relations.* New York: Macmillan Company, 1932. Surveys the complex negotiations for an American-owned interocean railroad across Mexico.

1496. Cotner, Thomas Ewing. *The Military and Political Career of José Joaquín De Herrera, 1792–1854.* Austin: University of Texas Press, 1949. President Herrera was burdened by a great national debt incurred during the U.S. war. Includes photograph, speeches, and correspondence.

1497. Faulk, Odie B. *Destiny Road: The Gila Trail and the Opening of the Southwest.* New York: Oxford University Press, 1973. Reviews the controversy over the Mexican-U.S. border survey during Fillmore's administration.

1498. Goetzman, William H. *Army Explorations in the American West, 1803–1863.* New Haven: Yale University Press, 1959. Explains the controversy of Fillmore's negotiations over the Mexican-American border.

1499. Griswald del Castillo, Richard. *The Treaty of Guadalupe Hidalgo: A Legacy of Conflict.* Norman: University of Oklahoma Press, 1990. Fillmore sent troops and spent millions of dollars to protect settlers from border-crossing nomadic Indian raids. Bibliography and maps.

1500. "Herrera, José Joaquín." In *Historical Dictionary of Mexico,* ed. Donald C. Briggs and Marvin Alisky. Metuchen, NJ: Scarecrow Press, Inc., 1981. 109–10.

1501. Hine, Robert V. "An Artist Draws the Line." *American Heritage* 19 (February 1968): 28–35, 102–3. Reviews the Mexican-U.S. boundary expedition of John Russel Bartlett. Contains map and Bartlett's drawings.

1502. Kajencki, Francis C. "Charles Radziminski and the United States-Mexican Boundary Survey." *New Mexico Historical Review* 63 (July 1988): 211–40. Describes the problems of the Boundary Commission from the perspective of the assistant surveyor.

1503. Manning, William R., ed. *Diplomatic Correspondence of the United States: Inter-American Affairs, 1831–1860.* Washington, DC: Carnegie Endowment for International Peace, 1932–39. 12 vols. Volume Eight covers 1848–60.

1504. Martinez, Oscar J., ed. *U.S.-Mexico Borderlands: Historical and Contemporary Perspectives.* Wilmington, DE: Scholarly Resources Inc., 1996. Highlights the Treaty of Guadalupe Hidalgo's sections on border control and describes Mexican difficulties protecting its new border against U.S. filibusters and nomadic Indians.

1505. Rippy, J. Fred. "Border Troubles Along the Rio Grand, 1848–1860." *Southwestern Historical Quarterly* 23 (October 1919): 91–111. Examines the smuggling, Indian raids, and filibustering along the 550 miles of river boundary with Mexico.

1506. ———. "Diplomacy of the United States and Mexico Regarding the Isthmus of Tehuantepec, 1848–1860." *Mississippi Valley Historical Review* 6 (March 1920): 503–31. Covers the diplomatic problems, business prospects, and failure to build an interocean railroad.

1507. ———— . "The Indians of the Southwest in the Diplomacy of the United States and Mexico, 1848–1853." *Hispanic American Historical Review* 2 (August 1919): 363–96. Borderland raiding by nomadic tribes caused regional and diplomatic problems for Fillmore.

1508. Russel, Robert R. "The Pacific Railroad Issue in Politics Prior to the Civil War." *Mississippi Valley Historical Review* 12 (September 1925): 187–201. Describes the rivalry for a railroad across Mexico.

1509. Stout, Joe A., Jr. "Idealism or Manifest Destiny? Filibustering in Northern Mexico 1850–1865." *Journal of the West* 11 (April 1972): 348–60. Summary of American filibusters trying to annex northwestern Mexico.

1510. Taylor, Bayard. *Eldorado, or, Adventures in the Path of Empire.* New York: George P. Putman, 1850. 2 vols. Volume Two describes his journey through Mexico with descriptions of the Mexican Congress and President Herrera's meeting with U.S. Envoy Robert Letcher.

1511. Vazquez, Josefina Zoraida, and Lorenzo Meyer. *The United States and Mexico.* Chicago: University of Chicago Press, 1985. Mexicans were upset that their more powerful northern conqueror did not fulfill its obligation to control the border as stated in the Treaty of Guadalupe Hidalgo. The United States could not control Indian raids, filibusters, cattle rustling, smuggling, or the controversies of mapping the border. Bibliography of Spanish and English sources.

1512. Werne, Joseph Richard. "Partisan Politics and the Mexican Boundary Survey, 1848–1853." *Southwestern Historical Quarterly* 90 (April 1987): 329–46. Politics hindered the efficiency of the boundary survey, prompting Fillmore to suspend it.

19. Netherlands

1513. Bevins, Charles I., ed. *Treaties and Other International Agreements of the United States of America, 1776–1949.* Washington, DC: Government Printing Office, 1968–1976. 13 vols. 10: 27. Commercial agreement.

1514. Manning, William R., ed. *Diplomatic Correspondence of the United States: Inter-American Affairs, 1831–1860.* 12 vols. Washington, DC: Carnegie Endowment for International Peace, 1932–39. Volume 10.

20. Russia

1515. Berlin, Isaiah. "Russia and 1848." In *Russian Thinkers,* ed. Henry Hardy and Aileen Kelly. New York: Viking Press, 1978. Russia helped to suppress the European revolutions while enforcing isolation on its own population.

1516. Kushner, Howard I. *Conflict on the Northwest Coast: American-Russian Rivalry in the Pacific Northwest, 1790–1867.* Westport, CT: Greenwood Press, 1975. Fillmore supported the U.S. commercial and whaling interests in the Northwest, including trade with Russia.

1517. Lincoln, W. Bruce. *Nicholas I, Emperor and Autocrat of All the Russias.* Bloomington: Indiana University Press, 1978.

1518. Reinhartz, Dennis. "Nicholas I: Nikolay Pavlovich." In *Great Lives From History: Renaissance to 1900 Series,* ed. Frank N. Magill. Pasadena: Salem Press, 1989. 5 vols. 5: 1711–15.

1519. Saul, Norman E. *Distant Friends: The United States and Russia, 1763–1867.* Lawrence: University Press of Kansas, 1991. Both countries saw each other as progressive governments conducting similar economic expansions. Contains descriptions by U.S. travelers in Russia and correspondence from the Russian Ambassador to the U.S., Alexander Bodiska. Bibliography.

1520. Shavit, David. *United States Relations with Russia and the Soviet Union: A Historical Dictionary.* Westport, CT: Greenwood Press, 1993.

1521. Thomas, Benjamin Platt. *Russo-American Relations, 1815–1867.* Baltimore: Johns Hopkins University Press, 1930. Brief mention of good relations in the early 1850s.

21. South America

1522. Barman, Roderick. *Brazil: The Forging of a Nation, 1798–1852.* Stanford: Stanford University Press, 1988. Fillmore's administration coincided with Brazil's revitalized nationalism.

1523. Bevins, Charles I., ed. *Treaties and Other International Agreements of the United States of America, 1776–1949.* Washington, DC: Government Printing Office, 1968–1976. 13 vols. 10: 1002–1016. Friendship agreement with Peru ratified July 16, 1852.

1524. Clayton, Lawrence. *Peru and the United States: The Condor and the Eagle.* Athens: University of Georgia Press, 1999. Mentions Fillmore's recognition of Peru's claim to the Lobos Islands.

1525. Manning, William R., ed. *Diplomatic Correspondence of the United States: Inter-American Affairs, 1831–1860.* Washington, DC: Carnegie Endowment for International Peace, 1932–39. 12 vols. Volume One: Argentina; Volume Two:

Bolivia; Volume Five: Chile and Colombia; Volume Six: Ecuador; Volume Ten: Paraguay and Peru; Volume 12: Venezuela.

1526. Manthorne, Katherine Emma. *Tropical Renaissance: North American Artists Exploring Latin America, 1839–1879.* Washington, DC: Smithsonian Institutional Press, 1989. The early 1850s found George Catlin, Frederic Church, and others painting Central and South America.

1527. Martin, Percy Alvin. "The Influence of the United States on the Opening of the Amazon to the World's Commerce." *Hispanic American Historical Review* 1 (May 1918): 146–62. Southern enthusiasm for the commercial potential of the Amazon led to a Brazilian anti-U.S. reaction.

1528. Miller, Hunter, ed. *Treaties and Other International Acts of the United States of America, 1776–1863.* Washington, DC: Government Printing Office, 1931–1948. 8 vols. 5: 1005–1053. Treaty of friendship, commerce, and navigation with Peru ratified July 16, 1852.

1529. Nichols, Roy F. *Advance Agents of American Destiny.* Philadelphia: University of Pennsylvania Press, 1956. Fillmore was dissatisfied with Webster's challenge to Peru's claim of the Lobos Islands. Fillmore settled the claim in Peru's favor.

1530. Robertson, William Spence. "The Recognition of the Hispanic American Nations by the United States." *Hispanic American Historical Review* 1 (August 1918): 239–69. Fillmore recognized Paraguay in April 1852.

1531. Sherman, William Roderick. *The Diplomatic and Commercial Relations of the United States and Chile, 1820–1914.* New York: Russell & Russell, 1973 [1926]. There were strained relations in the early 1850s.

1532. Skaggs, Jimmy M. *The Great Guano Rush: Enterprise and American Overseas Expansion.* New York: St. Martins Press, 1994. Fillmore appears to have initialed Webster's approval for U.S. businessmen to mine guano on the Lobos islands off Peru. Later he stopped military protection of U.S. shipping after recognizing Peru's right to the Lobos. Bibliography.

22. Switzerland

1533. Bevins, Charles I., ed. *Treaties and Other International Agreements of the United States of America, 1776–1949.* Washington, DC: Government Printing Office, 1968–1976. 13 vols. 11: 894–900. Negotiation for a commercial and extradition agreement began in 1850 but was not ratified until 1855.

1534. Meier, Heinz. *The United States and Switzerland.* The Hague: Moutan & Co., 1963. Fillmore had reservations about entering into the first treaty with Switzerland.

1535. Stokes, Anson Phelps. *Church and State in the United States: Historical Development and Contemporary Problems of Religious Freedom Under the Constitution.* New York: Harper & Brothers, 1950. 3 vols. 2: 438–39. In 1851 Fillmore objected to a clause in the Swiss-American treaty allowing only Christians to partake of the treaty.

Chapter 9

Administration Personalities

A. MEMBERS OF THE CABINET

1. General Works

1536. Burch, Philip H., Jr. *Elites in American History: The Federalist Years to the Civil War.* New York: Holmes & Meier Publishers, Inc., 1981. Fillmore was a non-elite whose Cabinet consisted of regional economic elites.

1537. Hoxie, R. Gordon. "The Cabinet in the American Presidency, 1789–1984." *Presidential Studies Quarterly* 14 (Spring 1984) 209–30. From 1829 to 1861, Cabinets were manned for the political management of administration policies. The Whig Cabinets of Tyler and Fillmore were notable for their more-than-usual changes.

1538. Poore, Ben: Perly. "Waifs from Washington, No. V." *Gleason's Pictorial Drawing-Room Companion,* February 5, 1853. Description of secretaries and their department buildings.

1539. Smith, William Henry. *History of the Cabinet of the United States of America.* Baltimore: Industrial Printing Company, 1925. Brief histories of the departments with biographies of Secretaries and Attorneys General.

1540. Vexler, Robert I. *The Vice-Presidents and Cabinet Members: Biographies Arranged Chronologically by Administration.* Dobbs Ferry: Oceana Publications, Inc., 1975. 2 vols. Volume One is a useful reference.

2. Biographies

Charles Magill Conrad, Secretary of War, 8/15/1850–3/3/1853

1541. Bell, William Gardiner. *Secretaries of War and Secretaries of the Army: Portraits and Biographical Sketches.* Washington, DC: Center of Military History, U.S. Army, 1981. Good introduction to Conrad.

1542. "Conrad, Charles Magill." In *Biographical Dictionary of the Confederacy,* ed. Jon L. Wakelyn. Westport, CT: Greenwood Press, 1977. 146–47. After trying to prevent war in 1860–61, he ultimately supported secession and represented Louisiana in the Confederate Congress.

1543. Violette, Eugene M. "Conrad, Charles Magill." *DAB* (1958), 2, pt. 2: 354. He campaigned for the Constitutional Union party in 1860.

1544. Wooster, Robert. "Expansion and the Plains Indian Wars." In *Encyclopedia of the American Military: Studies of the History, Tradition, Policies, Institution, and Roles of the Armed Forces in War and Peace,* ed. John E. Jessup and Louise B. Kety. New York: Charles Scribner's Sons, 1994. 3 vols. 2: 709–42. To reduce expenditures, Conrad proposed the government buy all non-Indian land in New Mexico and restrict settlement to curtail funding a territorial army. He also suggested each garrison grow food.

Thomas Corwin, Secretary of the Treasury 7/23/1850–3/6/1853

1545. Auer, J. Jeffrey. "Cooper Institute: Tom Corwin and Abraham Lincoln." *New York History* 32 (October 1951): 399–413. As a Republican lecturer, Corwin exonerated Fillmore's administration and admitted advising him to sign the Fugitive Slave Law.

1546. ———. "A Northern Whig and the Southern Cause." *Southern Speech Journal* 16 (September 1950): 15–39. Reviews Whig career and his later efforts to bring Fillmore men into the Republican party.

1547. Carothers, Neil. *Fractional Money: A History of the Small Coins and Fractional Paper Currency of the United States.* New York: John Wiley & Sons, Inc., 1930. A scarcity of coinage in the early 1850s prompted Congress and Corwin to recommend a reduction in the weight of silver coins. This and other measures created an adequate supply.

1548. Carroll, Stephen Graham. "Thomas Corwin and the Agonies of the Whig Party." Ph.D. diss., University of Colorado, 1970. Examines political career but contains little on his tenure as Secretary.

1549. Graebner, Norman A. "Thomas Corwin and the Election of 1848: A Study in Conservative Politics." *Journal of Southern History* 17 (May 1951): 162–79. Corwin campaigned for Taylor and Fillmore while opposing Ohio Free Soilers.

1550. Hepburn, A. Barton. *A History of Currency in the United States.* New York: Macmillan Company, 1924. Corwin and Congress worked to increase silver coinage to rectify a shortage in daily usage.

1551. Hockett, Homer Carey, "Corwin, Tom." *DAB* (1958), 2, pt. 2: 457–58.

1552. Mitchell, Jack. *Executive Privilege: Two Centuries of White House Scandals.* New York: Hippocrene Books, 1992. Corwin was accused of violating the Treasury Act when he used private bankers to back government bonds.

1552a. Schwarz, Ted. *A History of United States Coinage.* San Diego: A. S. Barnes & Company, Inc., 1980. Mentions requests to Corwin for smaller denominations of gold coinage and introduction of silver coinage.

1553. Shanks, W. F. G. "Tom Corwin of Ohio." *Harper's New Monthly Magazine* 35 (June 1867): 80–84. Reminiscences and anecdotes.

1554. Timberlake, Richard H. *Monetary Policy in the United States: An Intellectual and Institutional History.* Chicago: University of Chicago Press, 1993. California gold and tariff surpluses allowed Corwin to ask for authorization to purchase outstanding public debt. Congress passed the legislation in 1853.

John J. Crittenden, Attorney General, 7/22/1850–3/7/1853

1555. Coulter, E. Merton. "Crittenden, John Jordan." DAB (1958), 2, pt. 2: 546–49. Little on Cabinet position but good summary of political career.

1556. Dept. of Justice. *Attorneys General of the United States, 1789–1985.* Washington, DC: Government Printing Office, 1985. A chronology of Crittenden's political career and his 1856 official portrait by John Mix Stanley.

1557. Faust, Patricia L. "Crittenden, John Jordan." In *Historical Times Illustrated Encyclopedia of the Civil War,* ed. Patricia L. Faust. New York: Harper & Row, Publishers, 1986. Highlights his efforts to avert civil war. Includes photograph.

1558. Kelly, Jack. "John J. Crittenden and the Constitutional Union Party." *Filson Club History Quarterly* 48 (1974): 265–76. Crittenden, like many of Fillmore's former supporters, helped to establish the Constitutional Union party in 1860.

1559. Kirwin, Albert D. *John J. Crittenden, The Struggle for the Union.* Lexington: University of Kentucky Press, 1962. Standard political biography containing his advice that the Fugitive Slave Law was constitutional.

1560. Ledbetter, Patsy S. "John J. Crittenden and the Compromise Debacle.*" Filson Club History Quarterly* 51 (April 1977): 125–42. Unlike the Compromise of 1850, Crittenden was unable to work a sectional compromise during the winter of 1860–1861.

1561. Stephens, Thomas E. "Crittenden, John Jordan." In *American National Biography,* ed. John A. Garraty and Mark C. Carnes. New York: Oxford University Press, 1999. 24 vols. 5: 740–42. Political biography.

1562. Zacharias, Donald W. "Crittenden, John Jordan." In *The Encyclopedia of Southern History,* ed. David C. Roller and Robert W. Twyman. Baton Rouge: Louisiana State University Press, 1979. 313. Brief section on the Crittenden Compromise.

Edward Everett, Secretary of State, 11/6/1852–3/6/1853

1563. Brown, Thomas. "Edward Everett and the Constitutional Union Party of 1860." *Historical Journal of Massachusetts* 11 (June 1983): 69–81. In 1859 and 1860, Everett corresponded with former Cabinet colleagues Crittenden and Kennedy about a Union party. In 1860 he ran as Vice President on the party ticket.

1564. "Edward Everett." In *American Foreign Service Authors: A Bibliography,* ed. Richard Fyfe Boyce and Katherine Randall Boyce. Metuchen, NJ: Scarecrow Press, Inc., 1973. 105–6.

1565. "Everett, Edward." In *Dictionary of American Foreign Affairs,* ed. Stephen A. Flanders and Carl N. Flanders. New York: Macmillan Publishing Company, 1993. Highlights Everett's warning to France and Britain not to meddle in Cuban affairs.

1566. "Everett's Orations and Speeches." *Christian Examiner* 49 (November 1850): 396–417. Favorable review of Everett's patriotism and scholarship.

1567. Frothingham, Paul Revere. *Edward Everett, Orator and Statesman.* Boston: Houghton Mifflin Company, 1925. Dated biography.

1568. Howe, Daniel Walker. "Everett, Edward." In *American National Biography,* ed. John A. Garraty and Mark C. Carnes. New York: Oxford University Press, 1999. 24 vols. 7: 629–30.

1569. Pearson, Henry G. "Everett, Edward." DAB (1959), 3, pt. 2: 223–26. Good brief biography.

1570. Reid, Ronald. "Edward Everett: Rhetorician of Nationalism, 1824–1855." *Quarterly Journal of Speech* 42 (October 1956): 273–82. Examines the nationalist themes in Everett's ceremonial oratory.

1571. ———. *Edward Everett, Unionist Orator*. Westport, CT: Greenwood Press, 1990. Substantial biographical essay emphasizing Everett's oratorical style, Unionist sentiment, and compromising manner. A comprehensive bibliography and an introduction to the manuscript collection.

1572. Stearns, Foster. "Edward Everett." In *The American Secretaries of State and Their Diplomacy,* ed. Samuel Flagg Bemis. New York: Pageant Book Company, 1958 [1928]. 18 vols. 6: 117–41. Describes his four months as Secretary at the end of Fillmore's administration.

William A. Graham, Secretary of the Navy, 7/22/1850–7/25/1852

1573. Faust, Patricia L. "Graham, William Alexander." In *Historical Times Illustrated Encyclopedia of the Civil War,* ed. Patricia L. Faust. New York: Harper & Row, Publishers, 1986. Before and during the Civil War, Graham worked to promote peace and negate sectionalism.

1574. "Graham, William Alexander." In *Biographical Dictionary of the Confederacy,* ed. Jon L. Wakelyn. Westport, CT: Greenwood Press, 1977. 208–9. He served in Confederate Senate where he opposed Jefferson Davis' executive powers.

1575. Langley, Harold D. "William Alexander Graham, 2 August 1850–3 June 1852." In *American Secretaries of the Navy,* ed. Poalo E. Coletta. Annapolis: Naval Institute Press, 1980. 2 vols. 1: 257–67. Depicts Graham's tenure as a "go slow" Secretary.

1576. Nash, Frank. "Graham, William A." DAB (1960), 4, pt. 1: 480–81. Refused Taylor's offer of a foreign mission but accepted Fillmore's offer of Naval Secretary.

1577. Powell, William S. *Dictionary of North Carolina Biography*. Chapel Hill: University of North Carolina Press, 1986. 6 vols. Volume Two contains biography.

1578. Walton, Brian G. "Elections to the United States Senate in North Carolina, 1835–1861." *North Carolina Historical Review* 53 (April 1976): 168–92. Includes a portrait and political biography.

1579. Williams, Max R. "The Education of William A. Graham." *North Carolina Historical Review* 40 (Winter 1963): 1–14. Reviews Graham's education through his years at the University of North Carolina.

1580. ——— . "Graham, William Alexander." In *American National Biography,* ed. John A. Garraty and Mark C. Carnes. New York: Oxford University Press, 1999. 24 vols. 9: 392–93.

1581. ——— . "Graham, William Alexander." In *The Encyclopedia of Southern History,* ed. David C. Roller and Robert W. Twyman. Baton Rouge: Louisiana State University Press, 1979. 551–52.

1582. ——— . "Secretary William A. Graham, Naval Administrator, 1850–1852." *North Carolina Historical Review* 48 (Winter 1971): 53–72. Finds Graham an able administrator during a period of technical innovation and Naval disciplinary reform.

1583. ——— . "William A. Graham, North Carolina Whig Party Leader, 1804–1849." Ph.D. diss., University of North Carolina at Chapel Hill, 1965. Political career prior to Fillmore's administration.

Nathan K. Hall, Postmaster General, 7/23/1850–8/31/1852

1584. Blossom, Thomas. "The Postal Service of the United States in Connection with the Local History of Buffalo." *Publications of the Buffalo Historical Society. Volume. 4.* Buffalo: Buffalo Historical Society, 1896. 299–316. Information on international, U.S., and Buffalo mail service.

1585. Chester, Alden. *Courts and Lawyers of New York: A History, 1609–1925.* New York: American Historical Society, Inc., 1925. 3 vols. 3: 1259, 1274.

1586. ——— . *Legal and Judicial History of New York.* New York: National Americana Society, 1911. 3 vols. 3: 379. Mentions Hall's political, judicial, and public offices.

1587. Cullinan, Gerald. *The United States Postal Service.* New York: Praeger Publishers, 1973 [1968]. In 1851, Fillmore signed a law, initiated by Congress, to lower pre-paid postal rates. It also promoted postal service for all Americans despite deficit postal revenues.

1588. Fowler, Dorothy Ganfield. *The Cabinet Politician: The Postmaster General, 1829–1909.* New York: Columbia University Press, 1943. Describes the use of patronage to counter the Seward Whigs and promote Fillmore's nomination in 1852. Appendix contains the number of postmasters and their removals.

1589. "Hall, Nathan K." *The National Cyclopedia of American Biography.* New York: James T. White & Company, 1929. 63 vols. 4: 183. Left office when Fillmore made him a federal judge. Includes portrait.

1590. Hargest, George E. *History of Letter Post Communication Between the United States and Europe, 1845–1875.* Hall worked with Britain to lower European postal rates for Americans.

1591. "The Last Session of Congress." *Whig Almanac, 1850.* New York: New York Tribune, 1850. 24. Congressman Hall moved for an inquiry into the Treasury's annual waste.

1592. McAdam, David, et al., eds. *History of the Bench and Bar of New York.* New York: New York History Company, 1897. 2 vols. 1: 341. Hall was a student of Fillmore's and then his law partner in Buffalo. Active judicial career before and after becoming Postmaster General.

1593. "Postal Reform—Cheap Postage." *Harper's Monthly* 3 (November 1851): 837–39. Proposal for postal rate reductions and hopeful reforms in the department's patronage.

1594. Putnam, James O. "Nathan K. Hall." *Addresses, Speeches And Miscellanies.* Buffalo: Peter Paul & Brothers, 1880. Memorial honoring his public service. He died in Buffalo one week before Fillmore.

1595. ———. "Nathan K. Hall." *Publications of the Buffalo Historical Society Volume 4.* Buffalo: Buffalo Historical Society, 1896. 285–98. A memorial tribute with extracts from a brief autobiography of Hall's early years. Includes a description of the public benefits from the 1851 Postal Reform Act.

1596. Smith, H. Perry. *History of the City of Buffalo and Erie County.* Syracuse: D. Mason & Co. Publishers, 1884. 2 vols. 2: 470. Reviews Hall's legal, political, and charitable work.

1597. Thompson, Holland. "Hall, Nathan Kelsey." *DAB* (1960), 4, pt. 2: 140. Reviews legal and political career.

1598. Wilson, James Grand, and John Fiske, eds. *Appleton's Cyclopedia of American Biography.* New York: D. Appleton and Company, 1887. 6 vols. 3: 42–43. Brief item on his public service.

Samuel Dickinson Hubbard, Postmaster General, 8/31/1852–3/7/1853

1599. "Hubbard, Samuel Dickinson." *The National Cyclopedia of American Biography.* New York: James T. White & Company, 1929. 63 vols. 6: 183.

John Pendleton Kennedy, Secretary of the Navy, 7/26/1852–3/3/1853

1600. Baker, Jean H. "Kennedy, John Pendleton." In *American National Biography,* ed. John A Garraty and Mark C. Carnes. New York: Oxford University Press, 1999. 24 vols. 12: 573–74.

1601. Bohner, Charles H. *John Pendleton Kennedy, Gentleman from Baltimore.* Baltimore: Johns Hopkins University Press, 1961. Describes his political career, his writings on the Whig party, and his short but active term as Secretary. Bibliography and review of Kennedy Papers.

1602. Langley, Harold D. "John Pendleton Kennedy, 26 July 1852–3 March 1853." *American Secretaries of the Navy,* ed. Paolo E. Coletta. Annapolis: Naval Institute Press, 1980. 2 vols. 1: 269–77. Kennedy was a vigorous advocate for Naval exploration and thorough reports.

1603. Massachusetts Historical Society, Boston. *Tributes to the Memory of Hon. John Pendleton Kennedy.* Cambridge: J. Wilson and Son, 1870. 16-page pamphlet with memorials from Robert C. Winthrop, James Russell Lowell, George S. Hibbard, and Oliver Wendell Holmes.

1604. Parrington, Vernon Louis. "John Pendleton Kennedy: A Southern Whig," In *Main Currents in American Thought.* New York: Harcourt, Brace and Company, 1930. 3 vols. 2: 46–56. Reviews Kennedy's Whig principles and compliments his fictional works.

1605. Ridgely, J. V. *John Pendleton Kennedy.* New York: Twayne Publishers, Inc., 1966. Reviews his literary work. Includes chronology and selected bibliography.

1606. ———. "Kennedy, John Pendleton." In *The Encyclopedia of Southern History,* ed. David C. Roller and Robert W. Twyman. Baton Rouge: Louisiana State University Press, 1976. 668.

1607. Simms, L. Moody, Jr. "Kennedy, John Pendleton." In *Encyclopedia of Southern Culture,* ed. Charles Reagan Wilson and William Ferris. Chapel Hill: University of North Carolina Press, 1989. 887–88.

1608. Spellman, Georgia Peterman. "The Whig Rhetoric of John Pendleton Kennedy, Spokesman for Industry." Ph.D. diss., Indiana University, 1974. Kennedy romanticized Whig political history into a consistent doctrine promoting Congress and opposing presidential aggrandizement.

1609. Tomlinson, David O. "John Pendleton Kennedy (1795–1870)." In *Fifty Southern Writers Before 1900: A Bio-Bibliographical Sourcebook,* ed. Robert Bain and Joseph M. Flora. Westport, CT: Greenwood Press, 1987. Biographical essay and literary criticism.

1610. Tuckerman, Henry T. *The Life of John Pendleton Kennedy.* New York: G. P. Putnam & Sons, 1871. Excerpts from letters and diary describe his cabinet term and friendly association with Fillmore.

1611. Williams, Mary Wilhelmine. "Kennedy, John Pendleton." *DAB* (1961), 5, pt. 2: 333–34.

1612. Winthrop, Robert C. "Tributes to Hon. John P. Kennedy, by the President." *Proceedings of the Massachusetts Historical Society* 11 (1871): 354–69. Credits Kennedy for encouraging Naval scientific expeditions.

Thomas McKean Thompson McKennan, Secretary of the Interior, 8/15/1850–8/26/1850

1613. Bowden, Witt. "McKennan, Thomas McKean Thompson." DAB (1961), 6, pt. 2: 88–89. Secretary for only a few days in August, 1850. He left office for a position in railroads.

Alexander H. H. Stuart, Secretary of the Interior, 9/1850–3/1853

1614. Abernathy, Thomas P. "Stuart, Alexander H. H." *DAB* (1964), 9, pt. 2: 160–61. Includes his support for Fillmore in 1856.

1615. Bearss, Sara B. "Stuart, Alexander High Holmes." In *American National Biography,* ed. John A. Garraty and Mark C. Carnes. New York: Oxford University Press, 1999. 24 vols. 21: 62–64.

1616. Robertson, Alexander F. *Alexander Hugh Holmes Stuart, 1807–1891.* Richmond: William Byrd Press, Inc., 1925. Little on Stuart's cabinet role but does include eleven 1856 essays supporting Fillmore and the American party.

1617. Shade, William G. *Democratizing the Old Dominion: Virginia and the Second party System, 1824–1861.* Charlottesville: University Press of Virginia, 1996. Stuart was a western Virginia Whig unionist.

1618. Shields, Johanna Nicol. "Stuart, Alexander Hugh Holmes." In *The Encyclopedia of Southern History,* ed. David C. Roller and Robert W. Twyman. Baton

Rouge: Louisiana State University Press, 1976. Continually opposed secession and was an unenthusiastic Confederate.

Daniel Webster, Secretary of State, 7/22/1850–10/24/1852

1619. Arnston, Paul, and Craig R. Smith. "The Seventh of March Address: A Mediating Influence." *Southern Speech Communication Journal* 40 (Spring 1975): 288–301. Webster impressed the North's pragmatic majority with his favorable views on the Compromise.

1620. Bartlett, Irving H. *Daniel Webster.* New York: W. W. Norton & Company, Inc., 1978. Biography and study of his public image.

1621. Baxter, Maurice G. "Webster, Daniel." In *American National Biography,* ed. John A. Garraty and Mark C. Carnes. New York: Oxford University Press, 1999. 24 vols. 22: 865–68.

1622. Birkner, Michael. "Daniel Webster and the Crisis of Union, 1850." *Historical New Hampshire* 37 (Summer–Fall 1982): 150–73. Examines his preparation for the March 7th speech and his goal to inspire passion for moderation, the Compromise, and the Union.

1623. Cole, Arthur C. "Webster, Daniel." *DAB* (1964), 10, pt. 1: 585–92. Substantial review of Webster's life.

1624. Dalzell, Robert F., Jr. *Daniel Webster and the Trial of American Nationalism, 1843–1852.* Boston: Houghton Mifflin, 1973. Examines his commitment to the Compromise, the Union, and his desire to be President.

1625. "Daniel Webster." In *Dictionary of American Foreign Affairs,* ed. Stephen A. Flanders and Carl N. Flanders. New York: Macmillan Publishing Company, 1993. 640–42.

1626. "Daniel Webster." *Whig Almanac, 1853.* New York: New York Tribune, 1853. 11. Reviews career, his service under Fillmore, and his "zealous advocacy" for the Fugitive Slave Law.

1627. Duniway, Clyde Augustus. "Daniel Webster (Second Term)." In *The American Secretaries of State and Their Diplomacy,* ed. Samuel Flagg Bemis. New York: Pageant Book Company, 1958 [1928]. 18 vols. 6: 77–113. Review of Webster's diplomatic policies.

1628. Everett, Edward. "The Death of Daniel Webster." In *Orations and Speeches on Various Occasions.* Boston: Little, Brown, and Company, 1897. 4 vols. 3: 158–66. Public eulogy by Webster's replacement as Secretary of State.

1629. Foreman, Edward R. "Daniel Webster in Rochester." *Rochester Historical Society Publications, Volume 3* (1924): 243–52. In May 1851, Webster defended the Compromise and opposed western New York's resistance to the Fugitive Slave Law.

1630. Foster, Herbert Darling. "Webster's Seventh of March Speech and the Secession Movement, 1850." *American Historical Review* 27 (January 1922): 245–70. Webster's speech and the Compromise pacified secessionist activities.

1631. *Gleason's Pictorial Drawing-Room Companion,* May 3, 1851. Illustrations of Webster and his new carriage presented by the citizens of New York City for his statesmanship and defense of the Union.

1632. *Gleason's Pictorial Drawing-Room Companion,* July 31, 1852. Report and illustration of the Boston reception for Webster after his defeat at the Whig presidential convention.

1633. *Gleason's Pictorial Drawing-Room Companion,* November 13, 1852. Illustrations and memorial on the death of Webster.

1634. Harvey, Peter. *Reminiscences and Anecdotes of Daniel Webster.* Boston: Little, Brown, and Company, 1877. After losing the 1852 Whig presidential nomination Webster admitted that Fillmore's administration was fair, impartial, able, and a credit to the Whig party. However, he was deeply hurt that Clay informed delegates to vote for Fillmore.

1635. Hawthorne, Nathaniel. "The Great Stone Face." *National Era,* January 24, 1850. Hawthorne's fictional statesman is marred by character flaws. The story acquired a prophetic character six weeks later when Webster supported the Fugitive Slave Law which helped promote his presidential ambitions with the South.

1636. Johnson, Gerald W. "Great Man Eloquent." *American Heritage,* December 1957: 74–79, 121–22. Reviews Webster's career.

1637. Jones, Howard. "Daniel Webster: The Diplomatist." In *Daniel Webster, "The Completest Man,"* ed. Kenneth E. Shewmacker. Hanover, NH: University Press of New England, 1990. Fillmore overrode Webster's aggressive decision to support American guano mining on Peru's Lobos Islands because Peru's claim to the islands was correct.

1637a. Meade, Catherine Mary. "Daniel Webster and the Decline of the Whig Party in Massachusetts, 1848–1852." Ph.D. diss., Boston College, 1972. Webster's vindictive and coercive actions for the presidential nomination in 1852 stifled the party and its leadership.

1638. Parker, Theodore, Rev. *The Life of Webster: A Sermon, Preached at the Melodeon in Boston, On Sunday Morning, October 31, 1852.* Rochester: Book & Job Office, 1852. Webster threw away any chance for greatness when his presidential ambition spurred him to support the Compromise of 1850.

1639. Poore, Ben: Perly. "Daniel Webster at Home." *Gleason's Pictorial Drawing-Room Companion,* November 20, 1852. Describes Webster's homes: the State Department, his childhood home, and his Marshfield estate. Includes illustrations of his funeral, tomb, and lying in state at Marshfield.

1640. Remini, Robert. *Daniel Webster: The Man and His Time.* New York: W. W. Norton and Company, 1997. Credits Fillmore for taking Webster into his cabinet. Reviews the administration's foreign policy including Webster's blunders.

1641. Shewmacker, Kenneth E. " 'Congress only can declare war' and 'the President is Commander in Chief': Daniel Webster and the War Power." *Diplomatic History* 12 (Fall 1988): 383–409. Webster stated that only Congress could declare war, yet he made warlike declarations in Fillmore's name.

1642. ———— . "Daniel Webster and the Politics of Foreign Policy, 1850–1852." *Journal of American History* 63 (September 1976): 303–15. Webster used aggressive diplomacy to promote national unity.

1643. ———— . "Forging the 'Great Chain': Daniel Webster and the Origins of American Foreign Policy Toward East Asia and the Pacific, 1841–1852." *Proceedings of the American Philosophical Society* 129 (September 1985): 225–59. Webster is credited as the pivotal statesman in opening new foreign relations with East Asia.

1644. ———— . " 'Hook and Line, and bob and sinker': Daniel Webster and the Fisheries Dispute of 1852." *Diplomatic History* 9 (Spring 1985): 113–29. Webster's declining health and absence from Washington confounded and delayed Fillmore's response to British fishing restrictions off the Canadian Maritimes.

1645. ———— . " 'Untaught Diplomacy': Daniel Webster and the Lobos Island Controversy." *Diplomatic History* 1 (Fall 1977): 321–40. Webster's rash claims and his department's inadequacies led to an embarrassing confrontation with Peru. Fillmore resolved the issue in Peru's favor.

1646. Stuart, Graham H. *The Department of State: A History of Its Organization, Procedure, and Personnel*. New York: Macmillan Company, 1949. Brief reviews of Webster's and Everett's tenure at State. Includes an informative section on the department's personnel and patronage problems.

1647. Van Tassel, Daniel D. "Gentlemen of Property and Standing: Compromise Sentiment in Boston in 1850." *New England Quarterly* 23 (September 1950): 307–19. Prominent Boston citizens endorsed the Compromise after Webster's speech on March 7, 1850.

1648. Whittier, John Greenleaf. "Ichabod." In *The Poetical Works of Whittier,* ed. Hyatt H. Waggoner. Boston: Houghton Mifflin Company, 1975. A poem lamenting Webster's support for the Fugitive Slave Law.

1649. Wilson, Major L. "Of Time and the Union: Webster and His Critics in the Crisis of 1850." *Civil War History* 14 (December 1968): 293–306. Webster urged compromise as a progressive technique in a republic; otherwise, the evolution of disparate interests would breakup the Union.

1650. Wiltse, Charles M. "Daniel Webster and the British Experience." *Proceedings of the Massachusetts Historical Society* 85 (1973): 58–77. Webster's personal acquaintance with British ministers helped Fillmore interpret the recently ratified Clayton-Bulwer Treaty and engage Britain in further diplomatic discussions about Central America.

B. UNITED STATES ARMED FORCES

Matthew Fontaine Maury, Director of the Naval Observatory

1651. Bell, Whitfield J. "The Relations of Herndon and Gibbon's Exploration of the Amazon to North American Slavery, 1850–1855." *Hispanic American Historical Review* 19 (November 1939): 494–503. Describes Maury's dream of opening the Amazon to U.S. plantation slavery.

1652. Burstyn, Harold L. "Maury, Matthew Fontaine." In *Dictionary of Scientific Biography,* ed. Charles Coulston Gillispie. New York: Charles Scribner's Sons, 1970. 18 vols. 9: 195–97.

1653. Dozer, Donald Marquand. "Matthew Fontaine Maury's Letter of Instruction to William Lewis Herndon." *Hispanic American Historical Review* 28 (May 1948): 212–28. Reprints Maury's April 1850 letter initiating the exploration of the Amazon for American commerce and possible plantation slavery.

1654. Lewis, Charles L. *Matthew Fontaine Maury, The Pathfinder of the Seas.* Annapolis: United States Naval Institute, 1927. Emphasizes the technical achievements of the Superintendent of the Naval Observatory.

1655. "Maury, Matthew Fontaine." In *Biographical Dictionary of the Confederacy,* ed. Jon L. Wakelyn. Westport, CT: Greenwood Press, 1977. 315–16. Appointed Commander of Confederate Navy.

1656. Maury, M. F., U. S. N. "Commercial Prospects of the South." *Southern Literary Messenger* 17 (October–November 1851): 686–98. Proposes the Amazon valley for commercial exploitation by the South.

1657. Poore, Ben: Perly, "Waifs from Washington, No. IX." *Gleason's Pictorial Drawing-Room Companion,* March 12, 1853. Describes the Naval Observatory and its brilliant director.

1658. Williams, Francis Leigh. *Matthew Fontaine Maury, Scientist of the Sea.* New Brunswick: Rutgers University Press, 1963. Stresses the scientific activities of Maury, who helped Fillmore's cabinet plan Naval explorations.

Matthew C. Perry, Commander of the Japan Expedition

1659. Griffis, William Elliot. *Matthew Calbraith Perry, A Typical American Naval Officer.* Boston: Houghton, Mifflin and Company, 1890. Biography by a specialist on Japan, who was also one of Fillmore's biographers.

1660. Morrison, Samuel Eliot. *'Old Bruin': Commodore Matthew C. Perry, 1794–1856.* Boston: Little, Brown and Company, 1967. Standard biography of Perry, with illustrations and bibliographic essay.

1661. Swisher, Earl. "Commodore Perry's Imperialism in Relation to America's Present-Day Position in the Pacific." *Pacific Historical Review* 16 (February 1947): 30–40. Outlines Perry's scheme for control and development of the Pacific.

1662. Zabriskie, George A. "Commodore Matthew Calbraith Perry." *New-York Historical Society Quarterly* 30 (October 1946): 197–207. Brief account of Perry's expedition with photos of silver set presented by the New York Chamber of Commerce.

Winfield Scott, General in Chief of the Army

1663. Castel, Albert. "Winfield Scott, The Commander." *American History Illustrated,* July 1981, 20–29. Reviews Scott's military career from the Mexican War to the Civil War.

1664. Eisenhower, John S. D. *Agent of Destiny: The Life and Times of General Winfield Scott.* New York: Free Press: 1997. Fillmore and Scott were old friends. Fillmore appears not to have resented Scott's nomination in 1852 and worked for his election.

1665. Elliott, Charles Winslow. *Winfield Scott, The Soldier and the Man.* New York: Arno Press, 1979 [1937]. Scott was Fillmore's Acting Secretary of War until Conrad entered the Cabinet.

1666. Johnson, Timothy D. *Winfield Scott: The Quest for Military Glory.* Lawrence: University Press of Kansas, 1998. A conservative and elitist personality, he naturally adhered to the Whig party.

C. DIPLOMATS

Daniel Dewey Barnard

1667. "Barnard, Daniel Dewey." In *American Foreign Service Authors: A Bibliography,* ed. Richard Fyfe Boyce and Katherine Randall Boyce. Metuchen, NJ: Scarecrow Press, Inc., 1973. 23.

1668. Ekirch, Arthur A., Jr. "Daniel Dewey Barnard: Conservative Whig." *New York History* 28 (October 1947): 420–39. The political career and conservative principles of Fillmore's Minister to Berlin.

1669. Everett, Edward. "Daniel Dewey Barnard." *Orations and Speeches.* Boston: Little, Brown, and Company, 1892. 4 vols. 4: 339–44. Memorial on the death of Barnard in 1861. Barnard elevated the Berlin Ministry from a discreditable condition.

1670. Penny, Sherry H. "Barnard, Daniel Dewey." In *American National Biography,* ed. John A. Garraty and Mark C. Carnes. New York: Oxford University Press, 1999. 24 vols. 2: 170–72.

1671. ———. *Patrician in Politics: Daniel Dewey Barnard of New York.* Port Washington: Kennikat Press, 1974. The Albany Whig and ally of Fillmore was Minister to Berlin from 1850 to 1853.

Daniel Moreau Barringer

1672. Findling, John E. "Barringer, Daniel Moreau (1806–1873)." In *Dictionary of American Diplomatic History.* 2d ed. Westport, CT: Greenwood Press, 1989. Established cordial relations with Spain despite setbacks from filibusters invading Cuba and unwanted proposals to acquire the island.

1673. Hamilton, J. G. de Roulhac. "Barringer, Daniel Moreau." *DAB* (1964), 1, pt. 1: 648–49. Barringer subsumed his desire to acquire Cuba to Fillmore's nonintervention policy. Barringer left the ministry with excellent U.S.-Spanish relations.

1674. Jeffrey, Thomas E. "Barringer, Daniel Moreau." In *American National Biography*, ed. John A. Garraty and Mark C. Carnes. New York: Oxford University Press, 1999. 24 vols. 2: 236–37.

Neill Smith Brown

1675. Baylen, Joseph O. "A Tennessee Politician in Imperial Russia, 1850–1853." *Tennessee Historical Quarterly* 14 (September 1955): 227–52. Conservative Whig who interpreted American republicanism to Russian diplomats while relaying their fears of European radicals and Napoleon III. Informed the State Department that letters from immigrants to their European families were better propaganda than Congressional speeches.

1676. "Brown, Neill S." *The National Cyclopaedia of American Biography*. New York: James T. White & Company, 1893. 63 vols. 7: 209. Nothing on his Ministry but mentions his support for Fillmore in 1856.

1677. Frierson, William Little. "Brown, Neill Smith." *DAB* (1958), 2, pt. 1: 147–48. Reviews his political career but nothing on his Ministry.

1678. Shavit, David. "Brown, Neill Smith (1810–1886)." *United States Relations with Russia and the Soviet Union: A Historical Dictionary*. Westport, CT: Greenwood Press, 1993. Minister to Russia from 1850 to 1853. Short political biography.

Lewis Cass, Jr.

1679. "Cass, Lewis, Jr." *The National Cyclopedia of American Biography*. New York: James T. White & Company, 1897. 63 vols. 7: 528. Chargé d'affairs to the Papal States and son of the Democratic senator.

John Randolph Clay

1680. Oeste, George Irim. *John Randolph Clay, America's First Career Diplomat.* Philadelphia: University of Pennsylvania Press, 1966. The diplomat in Peru who mediated the Lobos Island crisis and helped prevent a war.

Alfred Conklin

1681. "Conklin, Alfred." In *American Foreign Service Authors: A Bibliography*, ed. Richard Fyfe Boyce and Katherine Randall Boyce. Metuchen, NJ: Scarecrow Press, Inc., 1973. 67–68.

1682. "Conklin, Alfred." In *Encyclopedia of Biography of New York,* ed. Charles Elliott Fitch. Boston: American Historical Society, Inc., 1916. 3 vols. 3: 378. Fillmore appointed him Minister to Mexico.

1683. Jordan, David M. *Roscoe Conklin of New York, Voice in the Senate.* Ithaca: Cornell University Press, 1971. Son's biography.

William Duer

1684. Snyder, Charles M. *Oswego, From Buckskin to Bustles.* Port Washington: Ira J. Franklin, Inc., 1968. Fillmore rewarded his support for the Compromise with the Ministry to Chile.

Thomas M. Foote

1685. Bryan, George J. "Journalism." In *Biographies and Journalism.* Buffalo: Courier Company, Printers, 1886. 185–217. Appointed consul to Bogota and then Minister to Austria after editing the Buffalo *Commercial Advertiser* for Fillmore.

1686. Severance, Frank H., comp. "The Periodical Press of Buffalo, 1811–1915." *Publications of the Buffalo Historical Society. Volume 19.* Buffalo Historical Society, 1915. 177–312. Informative sketch of Foote. Includes photograph.

Joseph Reed Ingersoll

1687. Findling, John E. "Ingersoll, Joseph Reed (1786–1868)." In *Dictionary of American Diplomatic History.* 2d ed. Westport, CT: Greenwood Press, 1989. Replaced Abbott Lawrence as Minister to Great Britain from late 1852 to April 1853.

1688. Willson, Beckles. *America's Ambassadors to England, 1785–1929: A Narrative of Anglo-American Diplomatic Relations.* New York: Frederick A. Stokes Company, 1929. Reported on Britain's increasing respect for America's power and material progress.

Abbott Lawrence

1689. Everett, Edward. "Abbott Lawrence." In *Orations and Speeches on Various Occasions.* Boston: Little, Brown, and Company, 1897. 4 vols. 3: 367–73. Eulogy.

1690. Findling, John E. "Lawrence, Abbott (1792–1855)." In *Dictionary of American Diplomatic History.* 2d ed. Westport, CT: Greenwood Press, 1989. Taylor appointed him Minister to Great Britain. He helped finalize the Clayton-Bulwer Treaty, reported on Irish emigration, and international postage issues.

1691. *Gleason's Pictorial Drawing-Room Companion,* August 23, 1851. Illustration of Lawrence and the Duke of Wellington being entertained by American merchants in London.

1692. *Gleason's Pictorial Drawing-Room Companion,* November 13, 1852. Illustration and brief biography of Lawrence after his return from England.

1693. Hill, Hamilton Andrews. *Memoir of Abbott Lawrence.* Cambridge: J. Wilson and Son, 1883. He was Minister to Great Britain from 1849 to October 1852. Endeavored to secure a canal across Nicaragua and keep England a noninterventionist in Central America. He also reviewed Irish emigration, international postage, and helped U.S. exhibitors at the 1851 international exhibition in London.

1694. Holcomb, Arther N. "Lawrence, Abbott." *DAB* (1933), 6, pt. 1: 44–46. Business and political biography, little on Ministry.

1695. Josephson, Hannah. *The Golden Threads: New England's Mill Girls and Magnates.* New York: Duell, Sloan and Pearce, 1949. Critical study of Lawrence's financial empire and political career before he assumed the Ministry to Great Britain.

1696. "Lawrence, Abbott." In *American Foreign Service Authors: A Bibliography,* ed. Richard Fyfe Boyce and Katherine Randall Boyce. Metuchen, NJ: Scarecrow Press, Inc., 1973. 185.

1697. "Lawrence, Abbott." *The National Cyclopaedia of American Biography.* New York: James T. White & Company, 1893. 63 vols. 7: 62–63.

1698. Willson, Beckles. *America's Ambassadors to England, 1785–1929: A Narrative of Anglo-American Diplomatic Relations.* New York: Frederick A. Stokes Company, 1929. Describes his contributions to the Clayton-Bulwer Treaty and his reports on British-U.S. shipping disputes off Canada and Central America.

1699. Zanderman, David A. "Lawrence, Abbott." In *American National Biography,* ed. John A. Garraty and Mark C. Carnes. New York: Oxford University Press, 1999. 24 vols. 13: 275–77.

Ambrose Dudley Mann

1700. Ferris, Norman B. "Mann, Ambrose." In *American National Biography,* ed. John A Garraty and Mark C. Carnes. New York: Oxford University Press, 1999. 24 vols. 14: 420–21.

1701. "Mann, Ambrose Dudley." In *American Foreign Service Authors: A Bibliography*, ed. Richard Fyfe Boyce and Katherine Randall Boyce. Metuchen, NJ: Scarecrow Press, Inc., 1973. 197.

1702. "Mann, Ambrose Dudley." In *Biographical Dictionary of the Confederacy*, ed. Jon L. Wakelyn. Westport, CT: Greenwood Press, 1977. 309–10. Mann was a Confederate diplomat in Europe during the war.

1703. "Mann, Ambrose Dudley." In *The National Cyclopedia of American Biography*, 62 vols. New York: James T. White & Company, 1936. 63 vols. 25: 371–72.

1704. Owsley, Frank Lawrence. "Mann, Ambrose Dudley." *DAB* (1961), 6, pt. 2: 239–40. In 1849 he was appointed U.S. special agent to Kossuth's revolutionary government in Hungary. After its collapse he was special agent to Switzerland where he negotiated a general convention of friendship and reciprocal trade.

George Perkins Marsh

1705. Everett, Edward. "The Ottoman Empire." In *Orations and Speeches on Various Occasions*. Boston: Little, Brown, and Company, 1897. 4 vols. 3: 51–57. At a toast to the U.S. legation to Constantinople, Everett complimented Minister George Marsh.

1706. Larson, Sylvia B. "Marsh, George Perkins." In *American National Biography*, ed. John A. Garraty and Mark C. Carnes. New York: Oxford University Press, 1999. 24 vols. 14: 535–37.

1707. Lowenthal, David. *George Perkins Marsh: Prophet of Conservation*. Seattle: University of Washington Press, 2000. Supersedes the 1958 biography. Marsh was a constant critic of Fillmore after the Vice President opposed his appointment to Turkey.

1707a. Lowenthal, David. *George Perkins Marsh, Versatile Vermonter.* New York: Columbia University Press, 1958. Includes Marsh's three years as Minister to Turkey and his intervention to release Kossuth from Turkish detention.

1708. "Marsh, George Perkins." In *American Foreign Service Authors: A Bibliography*, ed. Richard Fyfe Boyce and Katherine Randall Boyce. Metuchen, NJ: Scarecrow Press, Inc., 1973. 198.

Humphrey Marshall

1709. Bain, Chester A. "Commodore Matthew Perry, Humphrey Marshall and the Taiping Rebellion." *Far Eastern Quarterly* 10 (May 1951): 258–70. Marshall was sent to China to deal with the ruling Manchu dynasty and/or the Taiping rebels. He

exploited the turmoil to gain U.S. diplomatic advantage with the Manchu government over Commodore Perry's objections.

1710. Coulter, E. Merton. "Marshall, Humphrey." *DAB* (1961). 6, pt. 2: 310–11.
Prominent Kentucky Whig Congressman in the early 1850s. Accepted Fillmore's
appointment as Minister to China arriving in January 1853. Dealt with American
shipping problems, Chinese emigration, and foreign intervention in China.

1711. "Marshall, Humphrey." In *Biographical Dictionary of the Confederacy,* ed.
Jon L. Wakelyn. Westport, CT: Greenwood Press, 1977. 311–12. Joined Confederate Army to protect Kentucky.

John Howard Payne

1712. "Documents of Early Days.*" Publications of the Buffalo Historical Society.
Volume* 25. Buffalo: Buffalo Historical Society, 1921. 369–80. Letter from Payne
requesting a consular position at Tunis. His application was supported by Thomas
Corwin and Washington Irving. Fillmore approved the appointment. Payne later
died in Tunis.

1713. Grant, E. Allison, and Stanley T. Williams, "Payne, John Howard." *DAB*
(1962), 7, pt. 2: 327–29. Highlights early career as actor and playwright. He was
the author of the sentimental poem "Home Sweet Home."

1714. Harrison, Frederick G. "John Howard Payne." In *Biographical Sketches of
Preëminent Americans.* Boston: Consolidated Book Company, 189–[sic]. Good
biography but no pagination, documentation, or index.

1715. "Payne, John Howard." In *American Foreign Service Authors: A Bibliography,* ed. Richard Fyfe Boyce and Katherine Randall Boyce. Metuchen, NJ:
Scarecrow Press, Inc., 1973. 229–31.

1716. "Payne, John Howard." *The National Cyclopaedia of American Biography.*
New York: James T. White & Company, 1921. 3 vols. 2: 347–48. In the early 19th
century, Payne was a highly regarded actor. Full-page portrait.

William Cabel Rives

1717. Abernathy, Thomas. "Rives, William Cabel." *DAB* (1963), 8, pt. 1: 635–37.
Minister to France, 1849–1853. Little on Ministry, however his horror of European
civil wars made him an American peace convention member in 1861.

1718. Liston, Ann Elizabeth. "W. C. Rives: Diplomat and Politician, 1829–53."
Ph.D. diss., Ohio State University, 1972. Rives was appointed Minister to Paris by
Taylor and continued to serve under Fillmore.

1719. "Rives, William Cabel." In *Biographical Dictionary of the Confederacy,* ed. Jon L. Wakelyn. Westport, CT: Greenwood Press, 1977. 369. As a confederate Senator he looked for opportunities to end secession.

1720. Snay, Mitchell. "William Cabel Rives." In *American National Biography,* ed. John A Garraty and Mark C. Carnes. New York: Oxford University Press, 1999. 24 vols. 18: 574–75.

1721. Sowle, Patrick. "The Trials of a Virginia Unionist: William Cabel Rives and the Secession Crisis, 1860–1861." *Virginia Magazine of History and Biography* 80 (January 1972): 3–22.

1722. Willson, Beckles. *American Ambassadors to France (1777–1927): A Narrative of Franco-American Diplomatic Relations.* London: John Murry, 1928. Reported the rise of Napoleon III, their discussions about mutual protection for Hawaii and Cuba, and the emperor's satisfaction with Fillmore's belated letter congratulating his plebiscite to the monarchy.

Henry Sanford

1723. Fry, Joseph A. *Henry Sanford: Diplomacy and Business in Nineteenth-Century America.* Reno: University of Nevada Press, 1982. Begins with Sanford's appointment as secretary to the Minister of France.

1724. Giffen, M. B. "Sanford, Henry Shelton." *DAB* (1963), 8, pt. 2: 348–49.

1725. "Sanford, Henry." In *American Foreign Service Authors: A Bibliography,* ed. Richard Fyfe Boyce and Katherine Randall Boyce. Metuchen, NJ: Scarecrow Press, Inc., 1973. 250.

D. CONGRESS

1. General Works

1726. Congressional Quarterly. *Members of Congress Since 1789.* Washington, DC: Congressional Quarterly Inc., 1985. 3d ed.

1727. Jacobs, Kathryn Allamond. *Guide to Research Collections of Former United States Senators, 1789–1982.* Washington, DC: U.S. Senate, 1983. Description and location of correspondence and papers.

1728. Miller, Cynthia Pease. *Guide to Research Collections of Former Members of the United States House of Representatives, 1789–1989.* Washington, DC: House of Representatives, 1988. Description and location of correspondence and papers.

1729. Poore, Ben: Perly. *The Political Register and Congressional Directory: A Statistical Record of the Federal Officials, Legislative, Executive and Judicial, of the United States of America, 1776–1878.* Boston: Houghton, Osgood and Company, 1878. Brief biographies of members in the 31st and 32nd Congress.

1730. United States. National Archives and Records Administration. *Guide to the Records of the United States House of Representatives at the National Archives, 1789–1989.* Washington, DC: U.S. House of Representatives, 1989.

1731. United States. National Archives and Records Administration. *Guide to the Records of the United States Senate at the National Archives, 1789–1989, Bicentennial Edition.* Washington, DC: Government Printing Office, 1989.

1732. United States Congress. *A Biographical Congressional Directory, 1774–1903.* Washington, DC: Government Printing Office, 1903. Superseded by the 1961 *Biographical Directory,* but still useful for Fillmore's era.

1733. United States Congress. *Biographical Directory of the American Congress, 1774–1961.* Washington, DC: Government Printing Office, 1961.

2. Senators

John Bell

1734. Parks, Joseph Howard. *John Bell of Tennessee.* Baton Rouge: Louisiana State University Press, 1950. Moderate who supported the Compromise and campaigned for Fillmore in 1856.

Thomas Hart Benton

1735. Benton, Thomas Hart. *Thirty Years' View; or, A History of the Working of the American Government for Thirty Years, From 1820 to 1850.* New York: D. Appleton and Company, 1856. 2 vols. 2: 767–88. Describes Fillmore's inauguration and reviews the sectional crisis that prompted the compromise measures.

1735a. Morton, John D. " 'A High Wall and a Deep Ditch': Thomas Hart Benton and the Compromise of 1850." *Missouri Historical Review* 94 (October 1999): 1–24. Benton argued for separate votes on the Compromise issues in order to reject items favorable to the north and remain acceptable to his Democratic party.

John C. Calhoun

1736. Ford, Lacy K. "Republican Ideology in a Slave Society: The Political Economy of John C. Calhoun." *Journal of Southern History* 54 (August 1988):

405–24. Calhoun believed the Whig system of political economy promoted government corruption.

1737. Niven, John. *John C. Calhoun and the Price of Union.* Baton Rouge: Louisiana State University Press, 1988. Calhoun opposed the Compromise but died before its passage.

1738. Silbey, Joel H. "John C. Calhoun and the Limits of Southern Congressional Unity, 1841–1850." *Historian* 30 (November 1967): 58–71. Despite Calhoun's opposition to the Compromise, most Southern congressmen voted for it.

Lewis Cass

1739. Klunder, William Carl. "Lewis Cass and Slavery Expansion: 'The Father of Popular Sovereignty and Ideological Infanticide.' " *Civil War History* 32 (December 1986): 293–317. Examines "popular sovereignty" through its triumph in the Compromise of 1850 and its demise in the Kansas constitutional confusion.

1740. Sears, Louis Martin. "Cass, Lewis. *"DAB* (1958), 2, pt. 1: 562–64. Approved Compromise and Fugitive Slave Law.

1741. Spencer, Donald S. "Lewis Cass and Symbolic Intervention: 1848–1852." *Michigan History* 63 (Spring 1969): 1–17. Advocated a moral diplomacy by promoting republicanism in Europe rather than Kossuth's request for armed intervention or Fillmore's nonintervention.

Salmon P. Chase

1742. Blue, Frederick J. *Salmon P. Chase, A Life in Politics.* Kent: Kent State University Press, 1987. The Ohio Free Soil Senator opposed the Compromise and believed Fillmore surrendered to the Slave Power.

1743. "Diary and Correspondence of Salmon P. Chase." In *Annual Report of the American Historical Association for the Year 1902.* Washington, DC: Government Printing Office, 1903. 2 vols. 1: 11–527. Contains letters assessing antislavery's opposition to the Compromise, and Fillmore's improbable nomination in 1852.

1744. Niven, John. *Salmon P. Chase: A Biography.* New York: Oxford University Press, 1995. Chase despised Fillmore's administration and voted against the compromise measures.

1745. Schuckers, J. H. *The Life and Public Services of Salmon Portland Chase.* New York: D. Appleton and Company, 1874. Vehemently opposed the Compromise. Despite Fillmore's enforcement of the Fugitive Slave Law, he could raise little discussion about slavery in the 32nd Congress.

Henry Clay

1745a. Bearss, Sara B. "Henry Clay and the American Claims Against Portugal, 1850." *Journal of the Early Republic* 7 (Summer 1987): 167–80. Henry's son James, a Taylor appointee, refused a reparations settlement with Portugal. When Taylor refused to support James, Henry Clay ended his support for Taylor's compromise plans.

1746. Eaton, Clement. "Everybody Liked Henry Clay." *American Heritage,* October 1956, 26–29, 108–9. Sketch of Clay's personal life including a portrait by John Neagle.

1747. "Henry Clay." *Whig Almanac, 1853.* New York: New York Tribune, 1853. 8–10. Reviews career and his recent efforts for the Compromise of 1850.

1748. Peterson, Merrill D. *The Great Triumvirate: Webster, Clay and Calhoun.* New York: Oxford University Press, 1987. Mentions a Clay-Webster-Fillmore collusion to pass the Compromise and Clay's support for Fillmore's presidential nomination in 1852.

1749. Remini, Robert V. *Henry Clay, Statesman for the Union.* New York: W. W. Norton & Company, 1991. Clay was elated by Fillmore's succession. He helped Fillmore select the Cabinet and was a spokesman for the White House in Congress.

Jefferson Davis

1750. Collins, Bruce. "The Making of Jefferson Davis." *Journal of American Studies* 18 (December 1984): 437–46. Davis opposed the Compromise.

1751. Crist, Lynda Lasswell, ed. *The Papers of Jefferson Davis.* Baton Rouge: Louisiana State University Press, 1971–95. 8 vols. Volumes Four and Five cover Fillmore's administration. During speeches in 1851 and 1852, Davis berated Fillmore for threatening military force against Texas, South Carolina, and Cuban filibusters.

1752. Davis, William C. *Jefferson Davis, The Man and His Hour.* New York: HarperCollins Publishers, 1991. While out of office in 1852, Davis spoke against Fillmore's imbecile administration.

1753. Eaton, Clement. *Jefferson Davis.* New York: Free Press, 1977. Davis opposed every provision of the Compromise except the Fugitive Slave Law.

1754. Mapp, Alf J., Jr., *Frock Coats and Epaulets.* New York: Thomas Yoseloff, 1963. In 1852, Davis revived his political career with a speech against Fillmore's administration.

1754a. Taylor, John M. "Compassion is Always Due to an Enraged Imbecile." *American History Illustrated* 10 (February 1976): 14–20. Senator Davis unsuccessfully opposed Winfield Scott's promotion to Lieutenant-General during Fillmore's administration.

Stephen A. Douglas

1755. Denault, Patricia. " 'The Little Giant': Stephen Douglas." *American History Illustrated* October, 1970, 22–33. Biographical essay on this enigmatic man who played a major role in the passage of the Compromise.

1756. Harmon, George D. "Douglas and the Compromise of 1850." *Journal of the Illinois State Historical Society* 21 (January 1929): 453–99. Pioneering study on Douglas and the Compromise.

1757. Hodder, F. H. "The Authorship of the Compromise of 1850." *Mississippi Valley Historical Review* 22 (March 1936): 525–36. Explains the importance of Douglas and other congressional Democrats to the final passage of the Compromise.

1758. Johannsen, Robert W., ed. *The Letters of Stephen A. Douglas.* Urbana: University of Illinois Press, 1961. Little on Fillmore but numerous letters covering the Compromise of 1850. Douglas continued to refer to the Compromise throughout the 1850s and during his presidential campaign in 1860.

1759. ———. *Stephen A. Douglas.* New York: Oxford University Press, 1973. Fillmore approved of Douglas's solution for the passage of the Compromise. He later helped Douglas set aside federal lands for railroads. Excellent study of Democratic policies and pursuits in the early 1850s.

1760. ———. "Stephen A. Douglas and the Territories in the Senate." In *The American Territorial System,* ed. John Porter Bloom. Athens: Ohio University Press, 1973. Douglas chaired the powerful Senate Committee on Territories from 1847 to 1858.

1761. Milton, George Fort. *The Eve of Conflict: Stephen A. Douglas and the Needless War.* Boston: Houghton Mifflin Co., 1934. Early work showing Douglas's importance to the Compromise.

Thomas Ewing

1762. McGrane, Reginald C. "Ewing, Thomas." *DAB* (1931), 6, pt. 2: 237–38. Taylor's Secretary of the Interior replaced Tom Corwin in the Senate. He opposed the Fugitive Slave Law.

Henry Stuart Foote

1763. Coleman, James P. "Two Irascible Antebellum Senators: George Poindexter and Henry Foote." *Journal of Mississippi History* 46 (February 1984): 17–27. President Taylor sat in the hot sun during Foote's July 4th speech. He later consumed quantities of cold milk and fruit that were said to have contributed to his death.

1764. "Foote, Henry Stuart." In *Biographical Dictionary of the Confederacy,* ed. Jon L. Wakelyn. Westport, CT: Greenwood Press, 1977. 187–88. Represented Tennessee in Confederate Congress.

1765. Gonzales, John Edmond. "Henry Stuart Foote: A Forgotten Unionist of the Fifties. *The Southern Quarterly* 1 (January 1963): 129–39. Ardent supporter of the Compromise in Washington and Mississippi. A Unionist in 1856, he declared Fillmore the only man who could save the Union.

William McKendree Gwin

1766. Ellison, William H. "Memoirs of Hon. William M. Gwin." *California Historical Society Quarterly* 19 (1940): 1–26, 157–84, 256–77, 344–67. As a California senator, he and Fillmore found a harmony of purpose selecting Whigs to fill federal offices in the state.

1767. May, Robert E. "Gwin, William McKendree." In *American National Biography,* ed. John A Garraty and Mark C. Carnes. New York: Oxford University Press, 1999. 24 vols. 9: 755–57.

1768. Stanley, Gerald. "Senator William Gwin: Moderate or Racist?" *California Historical Quarterly* 50 (September 1971): 243–55. Reviews Gwin's career in light of his defense of slavery and support for the Fugitive Slave Law.

1769. Thomas, Lately. *Between Two Empires: The Life Story of California's First Senator, William McKendree Gwin.* Boston: Houghton Mifflin Company, 1969. Lobbyist for California statehood and Democratic senator when Fillmore signed the Compromise.

John P. Hale

1770. Sewell, Richard H. *John P. Hale and the Politics of Abolition.* Cambridge: Harvard University Press, 1965. New Hampshire senator who opposed the Compromise.

Hannibal Hamlin

1771. Hamlin, Charles Eugene. *The Life and Times of Hannibal Hamlin.* Cambridge: Riverside Press, 1899. Maine antislavery senator who said Fillmore led a good administration with the exception of the Compromise laws.

Sam Houston

1772. Friend, Llerena. *Sam Houston, The Great Designer.* Austin: University of Texas Press, 1954. Helped Fillmore settle the Texas-New Mexico boundary dispute.

Robert Mercer Taliaferro Hunter

1773. Ambler, Charles Henry, ed. "Correspondence of Robert M. T. Hunter, 1826–1876." In *Annual Report of the American Historical Association, 1916.* Washington, DC: Government Printing Office, 1918. 2 vols. 2: 3–383. Contains letters about the Compromise, the increasing sectional tension, and Fillmore's presidential possibilities in 1856.

1774. "Hunter, Robert Mercer Taliaferro." In *Biographical Dictionary of the Confederacy,* ed. Jon L. Wakelyn. Westport, CT: Greenwood Press, 1977. 244. Served in Confederate Senate.

1775. Simms, Henry H. *Life of Robert M. T. Hunter: A Study in Sectionalism and Secession.* Richmond: William Byrd Press, 1935. The Virginian opposed the Compromise while chairman of the Senate Finance Committee.

William Rufus King

1776. Martin, John M. "William R. King and the Compromise of 1850." *North Carolina Historical Review* 39 (Autumn 1962): 500–18. As President *Pro Tem* of the Senate after Fillmore's succession, he presided over the final debates of the Compromise. He supported all except the abolition of slave trading in the District of Columbia.

1777. Nichols, Roy F. "King, William Rufus Devane." *DAB* (1961), 5, pt. 2: 406–7. Alabama Democrat supported the Compromise and was elected to preside over the Senate after Fillmore's succession. He was Pierce's Vice President but died just weeks after assuming office.

1778. Thornton, J. Mills, III. "King, William Rufus." In *American National Biography,* ed. John A Garraty and Mark C. Carnes. New York: Oxford University Press, 1999. 24 vols. 12: 720–21.

James Murray Mason

1779. "Mason, James Murray." In *Biographical Dictionary of the Confederacy,* ed. Jon L. Wakelyn. Westport, CT: Greenwood Press, 1977. 314. Appointed Confederate Commissioner to Great Britain and France.

1780. Mason, Virginia. *The Public Life and Diplomatic Correspondence of James M. Mason, with Some Personal History by His Daughter.* Roanoke: Stone Printing and Manufacturing Co., 1903. Virginia Democrat and chairman of the Foreign Relations Committee who opposed the admission of California. He authored the Fugitive Slave Law's stringent enforcement procedures and deleted its former due process provisions.

1781. Owsley, Frank Lawrence. "Mason, James Murray." *DAB* (1961), 6, pt. 2: 364–65.

1782. Young, Robert W. *Senator James Murray Mason: Defender of the Old South.* Knoxville: University of Tennessee Press, 1998. He was displeased with the Compromise though he voted for the organizing of New Mexico and Utah and his version of the Fugitive Slave Law. In foreign affairs, he supported the President's wishes and opposed filibustering.

Robert Rantoul

1783. *Gleason's Pictorial Drawing-Room Companion,* August 28, 1852. Illustration and memorial biography.

1784. Hamilton, Luther, ed. *Memoirs, Speeches and Writings of Robert Rantoul, Jr.* Boston: John P. Jewett and Company, 1854. Massachusetts Democrat argued against increasing the federal powers in the Fugitive Slave Law.

William H. Seward

1785. Bancroft, Frederick. *The Life of William Seward.* New York: Harper & Brothers Publishers, 1900. 2 vols. Volume One explains the national consequences of the Fillmore-Seward feud.

1786. Crofts, Daniel W. "Seward, William Henry." In *American National Biography,* ed. John A. Garraty and Mark C. Carnes. New York: Oxford University Press, 1999. 24 vols. 19: 676–81.

1787. "The Doctrine of the 'Higher Law:' Mr. Seward's Speech." *Southern Literary Messenger* 17 (March 1851): 130–42. Criticizes Seward's speech and scolds him for his impudence.

1788. Finkelman, Paul. "The Protection of Black Rights in Seward's New York." *Civil War History* 34 (September 1988): 211–34. As New York governor from 1839 to 1843, Seward broadened civil liberties for African Americans, stood up to Southern politicians, and was an example for political abolitionists.

1789. Pease, Jane H. "The Road to the Higher Law." *New York History* 40 (April 1959): 117–36. Seward's 1850 "Higher Law" speech was an honest articulation of his public, personal, and legal antislavery activities.

1790. Phillips, Wendell. "Disunion." In *Speeches, Lectures, and Letters.* New York: Negro University Press, 1968 [1884]. In 1861 Phillips criticized Seward, as he had Fillmore, for his readiness to compromise with the South. He believed Lincoln could save the Union as Washington and Fillmore had done: by giving patronage to Union men.

1791. Seward, Frederick W. *Reminiscences of a War-Time Statesman and Diplomat, 1830–1915.* New York: G. P. Putnam's Sons, 1916. Seward's son reviews the Thurlow Weed-Seward partnership and their rivalry with Fillmore.

1792. ———. *Seward at Washington as Senator and Secretary of State: A Memoir of His Life, with Selections from His Letters.* New York: Derby and Miller, 1891. 2 vols. Copious selections from Seward's letters in the 1850s with many unflattering comments about Fillmore. Seward believed the Fugitive Slave Law was unnecessary to the Compromise of 1850.

1793. Taylor, John M. *William Henry Seward, Lincoln's Right Hand.* New York: HarperCollins Publishers, 1991. Comments on his rivalry with Fillmore. After 1861 Seward is described as a Union man first and reformer second.

1794. Van Deusen, Glyndon G. *William Henry Seward.* New York: Oxford University Press, 1967. Describes Seward's initial friendly relations with Fillmore and their later rivalry.

1795. "William H. Seward." *American Whig Review* 30 (June 1850): 622–39. Political biography includes his election to the Senate.

Charles Sumner

1796. Blue, Frederick J. *Charles Sumner and the Conscience of the North.* Arlington Heights, IL: Harlan Davidson, Inc., 1994. Sumner attempted to repeal the Fugitive Slave Law in 1852. He succeeded in April 1864.

1797. Donald, David. *Charles Sumner and the Coming of the Civil War.* New York: Alfred A. Knopf, 1961. Ridiculing Fillmore and the Fugitive Slave Law helped elect Sumner to the Senate in 1851.

1798. Haynes, George H. *Charles Sumner.* Philadelphia: George W. Jacobs & Company, 1909. Sumner's extravagant criticism of Fillmore did not prevent him from accepting Fillmore's cordiality at the White House.

1799. Lester, C. Edwards. *Life and Public Service of Charles Sumner.* New York: United States Publishing Company, 1874. Sumner died a week after Fillmore. His death and funeral displaced the public mourning for the ex-President.

1800. Pierce, Edward L. *Memoir and Letters of Charles Sumner.* Boston: Roberts Brothers, 1893. 4 vols. Volume Three covers Fillmore's administration and reviews Sumner's resistance to the Fugitive Slave Law.

1801. Richards, Laura E., ed. *Letters and Journals of Samual Gridley Howe.* New York: A M S, 1973 [1909]. 2 vols. 2: 374. Fillmore believed Sumner liked him despite Sumner's disparaging remarks against him.

1802. Sumner, Charles. *Charles Sumner, His Complete Works.* New York: Negro Universities Press, 1969. 20 vols. Volumes Three and Four cover to the late 1840s and early 1850s.

1803. ———— . "Speech on Our Present Anti-Slavery Duties, at the Free Soil State Convention in Boston, October 3, 1850." In *Orations And Speeches.* Boston: Tickner, Reed and Fields, 1850. 2 vols. 2: 396–420. Claimed the Fugitive Slave Law placed the United States with the reactionary regimes of Europe. He condemned Fillmore and said it was better he was never born, and better for his memory and for the good name of his children that he was never President.

John Wentworth

1804. Fehrenbacher, Don E. *Chicago Giant: A Biography of "Long John" Wentworth.* Madison: American History Research Center, Inc., 1957. Illinois Democrat favored admitting California but opposed the Compromise.

Robert C. Winthrop

1805. Bolton, Charles K. "Winthrop, Robert Charles." *DAB* (1964), 10, pt. 2: 416–17. Massachusetts Whig appointed to replace Webster in the Senate. He reluctantly opposed the Fugitive Slave Law. He was defeated for the Senate by Charles Sumner in 1851.

1806. Mooney, Booth. *Mr. Speaker: Four Men Who Shaped the United States House of Representatives.* Chicago: Follett Publishing, 1964. 196–97. Winthrop was Speaker of the House for one term in the 1840s.

3. Representatives

Judah P. Benjamin

1807. Evans, Eli N. *Judah P. Benjamin, The Jewish Confederate.* New York: The Free Press, 1988. Fillmore almost nominated the Louisiana Democrat to the Supreme Court.

Linn Boyd

1808. Coulter, Ellis Merton. "Boyd, Linn." *DAB* (1964), 1, pt. 2: 527–28. Democratic supporter of the Compromise and Speaker of the House from 1851 to 1855.

1809. Kennon, Donald R. *The Speakers of the House of Representatives: A Bibliography, 1789–1984.* Baltimore: Johns Hopkins University Press, 1986. 120–21. A guide to sources on Boyd.

1810. Mooney, Booth. *Mr. Speaker: Four Men Who Shaped the United States House of Representatives.* Chicago: Follett Publishing, 1964. 198.

Thomas Lanier Clingman

1811. Boyd, William K. "Clingman, Thomas Lanier." *DAB* (1958), 2, pt. 2: 220–21. North Carolina Whig supported the Fugitive Slave Law but later joined the Democratic party fearing the increasing influence of antislavery Whigs.

1812. Clingman, Thomas L. *Selections from the Speeches and Writings of Hon. Thomas L. Clingman of North Carolina.* Raleigh: John Nichols, 1877. His progressive fear of Seward Whigs was confirmed by the nomination of Winfield Scott instead of Fillmore in 1852.

1813. Insloe, John C. "Thomas Clingman, Mountain Whiggery, and the Southern Cause." *Civil War History* 33 (March 1987): 42–62. He opposed the Compromise during his conversion from Whig to Democratic defender of the South.

1814. Jeffrey, Thomas E. " 'Thunder from the Mountains' ": Thomas Lanier Clingman and the End of Whig Supremacy in North Carolina." *North Carolina Historical Review* 56 (October 1979): 366–95. The antislavery Whig assault on the South allowed him to vote against the Compromise and support the Democratic party.

Howell Cobb

1815. Brooks, R. P. "Howell Cobb and the Crisis of 1850." *Mississippi Valley Historical Review* 4 (December 1917): 279–98. Georgia Democrat, Speaker of the House, and supporter of the Compromise.

1816. "Cobb, Howell." In *Biographical Dictionary of the Confederacy,* ed. Jon L. Wakelyn. Westport, CT: Greenwood Press, 1977. 141–42. Presided as president of the provisional Confederate Congress.

1817. Kennon, Donald R. *The Speakers of the House of Representatives, A Bibliography, 1789–1984.* Baltimore: Johns Hopkins University Press, 1986. 113–19. A guide to sources on Cobb, who was Speaker from 1849 to 1851.

1818. Mooney, Booth. *Mr. Speaker: Four Men Who Shaped the United States House of Representatives.* Chicago: Follett Publishing, 1964. 197–98.

1819. Simpson, Brooks D. "Cobb, Howell." In *American National Biography,* ed. John A. Garraty and Mark C. Carnes. New York: Oxford University Press, 1999. 24 vols. 5: 99–100. Georgia Democrat received patronage from Fillmore for supporting the Compromise.

1820. Simpson, John Eddins. *Howell Cobb, The Politics of Ambition.* Chicago: Adams Press, 1973. His rulings as Speaker helped pass the Compromise.

Joshua R. Giddings

1821. Stewart, James Brewer. *Joshua R. Giddings and the Tactics of Radical Politics.* Cleveland: Press of Case Western Reserve University, 1970. The Ohio Free Soiler opposed the Compromise, especially the Fugitive Slave Law.

Solomon G. Haven

1822. Chester, Alden. *Courts and Lawyers of New York: A History, 1609–1925.* New York: American Historical Society, Inc., 1925. 3 vols. 3: 1272. Haven was the prince of jury lawyers in Buffalo and Fillmore's law partner.

1823. ———. *Legal and Judicial History of New York.* New York: National Americana Society, 1911. 3 vols. 3: 378–79. Haven was dexterous in court and a die-hard Fillmore man.

1824. "Haven, Solomon George." *The National Cyclopaedia of American Biography.* New York: James T. White & Company, 1909. 63 vols. 11: 371. A law partner and longtime friend of Fillmore. He continued his support when elected to Congress in 1850.

1825. Karin, Daniel B. "Haven, Solomon G. (1810–61)." *Biographical Dictionary of American Mayors, 1820–1980: Big City Mayors,* ed. Melvin G. Holli and Peter A. Jones. Westport, CT: Greenwood Press, 1981. 154–55.

1826. McAdam, David, et al., eds. *History of the Bench and Bar of New York.* New York: New York History Company, 1897. 2 vols. 1: 356, 2: 177.

1827. Proctor, L. B. *The Bench and Bar of New York.* New York: Diossy & Company, 1870. 692–713. Like Fillmore he grew up poor, practiced law and entered public service.

1828. Smith, H. Perry. *History of the City of Buffalo and Erie County.* Syracuse: D. Mason & Co. Publishers, 1884. 2 vols. 1: 670–74. Congressman Haven worked best in the committee room. Includes memorial tributes.

1829. ———— . *History of the City of Buffalo and Erie County.* Syracuse: D. Mason & Co. Publishers, 1884. 2 vols. 2: 468–69. Sketch of legal career.

1830. Wilson, James Grand, and John Fiske, eds. *Appleton's Cyclopedia of American Biography.* New York: D. Appleton and Company, 1887. 6 vols. 3: 118. Brief notice of legal partnership with Fillmore and his public offices.

George W. Julian

1831. Haworth, Paul L. "Julian, George Washington." *DAB* (1961), 5, pt. 2: 245–46. Indiana Free Soiler voted against the Compromise of 1850. Free-Soil Vice Presidential candidate in 1852.

1832. Julian, George W. *Political Recollections, 1840 to 1872.* Miami, OH: Mnemosyne Publishing Co., Inc., 1969 [1884]. He claimed Fillmore deserted to slaveholders when he signed the Compromise.

1833. ———— . "Some Ante-Bellum Politics." *North American Review* 163 (August 1896): 195–206. Recalls the mortification of Free Soil congressmen when Fillmore repudiated his liberal principles and signed the compromise bills.

Horace Mann

1834. Gara, Larry. "Horace Mann: Antislavery Congressman." *Historian* 32 (November 1969): 19–33. The educational reformer was outspoken against the Fugitive Slave Law.

1835. Lock, Edward L., Jr. "Mann, Horace." In *American National Biography,* ed. John A. Garraty and Mark C. Carnes. New York: Oxford University Press, 1999.

24 vols. 14: 424–27. After the Compromise he became a Free-Soiler and unsuccessfully moved to repeal the Fugitive Slave Law.

1836. Mann, George C. *Life and Work of Horace Mann.* Boston: Lee and Shepard, 1891. 5 vols. 1: 362, 395. In early 1852, Mann mentions a great Northern hostility to Fillmore, especially in western New York. Mann said he would not shake the hand that signed the Fugitive Slave Law.

1837. Mann, Horace. "Speech, Delivered at Worchester September 16, 1851, on taking the Chair as President of the Free-Soil State Convention." In *Slavery Letters and Speeches.* New York: Burt Franklin, 1969. 536–64. Fillmore's administration and the Compromise did more for slavery than Free-Soilers predicted President Taylor would do.

1838. Swift, Fletcher Harper. "Mann, Horace." *DAB* (1961), 6, pt. 2: 240–43. Antislavery Whig congressman in the late 1840s. He took over John Quincy Adams's seat.

Alexander H. Stephens

1839. Avary, Myrta Lockett, ed. *Recollections of Alexander H. Stephens: His Diary.* New York: Doubleday, Page & Company, 1910. In 1871, the former Georgia Whig and Confederate Vice President recalled his support for Fillmore's administration.

1840. Schott, Thomas E. *Alexander H. Stephens of Georgia, A Biography.* Baton Rouge: Louisiana State University Press, 1988. Describes his influence during the passage of the Compromise.

1841. "Stephens, Alexander Hamilton." In *Biographical Dictionary of the Confederacy,* ed. Jon L. Wakelyn. Westport, CT: Greenwood Press, 1977. 398–99. As Vice President of the Confederacy he opposed Jefferson Davis's executive powers.

1842. Van Abele, Rudolph. *Alexander H. Stephens, A Biography.* New York: Alfred A. Knopf, 1946. Dated but worthwhile biography.

Thaddeus Stevens

1843. Current, Richard Nelson. *Old Thad Stevens, A Story of Ambition.* Madison: University of Wisconsin Press, 1942. New to Congress, the Pennsylvania Whig played down his opposition to the Compromise.

1844. Trefousse, Hans L. *Thaddeus Stevens: Nineteenth-Century Egalitarian.* Chapel Hill: University of North Carolina Press, 1997. He approved Fillmore's opposition to the Texas incursion into New Mexico but opposed the compromise.

Robert Augustus Toombs

1845. Thompson, William Y. *Robert Toombs of Georgia.* Baton Rouge: Louisiana State University Press, 1966. The Georgia Whig and Unionist praised Fillmore and supported the Compromise.

1846. "Toombs, Robert Augustus." In *Biographical Dictionary of the Confederacy,* ed. Jon L. Wakelyn. Westport, CT: Greenwood Press, 1977. 413–14. Supported Crittenden's compromise in 1861 but joined the Confederacy and Georgia militia.

David Wilmot

1847. Going, Charles Buxton. *David Wilmot, Free Soiler: A Biography of the Great Advocate of the Wilmot Proviso.* New York: D. Appleton and Company, 1924. His Proviso during the Mexican War crystallized sentiment against the extension of slavery into the new territories.

E. UNITED STATES SUPREME COURT

1. General Works

1848. Carson, Hampton L. *The History of the Supreme Court of the United States, With Biographies of All the Chief and Associate Justices.* Philadelphia: P. W. Ziegler Company, 1904. 2 vols. Contains biographies and portraits of justices during Fillmore's administration.

1849. Congressional Quarterly. *Guide to the U.S. Supreme Court.* 2d ed. Washington, DC: Congressional Quarterly Inc., 1990. Comprehensive resource. Benjamin R. Curtis was Fillmore's only Court appointee. Later the Senate refused to confirm three other Fillmore nominations for one opening.

1850. Elliot, Stephen P. *A Reference Guide to the United States Supreme Court.* New York: Facts on File Publications, 1986. An illustrated chronological guide.

1851. Hall, Kermit L. *The Oxford Companion to the Supreme Court of the United States.* New York: Oxford University Press, 1992. Includes biographies of Benjamin R. Curtis and the three Fillmore nominees who were not confirmed. Contains a chronological list of sitting justices and nominees, bibliographies, and cross-references.

1852. Halper, Thomas. "Senate Rejection of Supreme Court Nominees." In *The First Branch of American Government, The United States Congress and Its Relations to the Executive and Judiciary. The Congress of the United States, 1789–1989,* ed. Joel H. Silbey. Brooklyn: Carlson Publishing, Inc., 1991. 4 vols. 2: 569–80.

Fillmore falls into the category of "lame duck" Presidents whose nominees were rejected twice as much as other Presidents.

1853. Russel, Robert R. "Constitutional Doctrines with Regard to Slavery in the Territories." *Journal of Southern History* 32 (November 1966): 446–86. Reviews congressional power over slavery in the territories and the Taney Court decision to establish nonintervention by Congress.

1854. Stephenson, D. Grier, Jr. *The Supreme Court and the American Republic: An Annotated Bibliography*. New York: Garland Publishing, Inc., 1981. Resource for Court decisions, constitutional interpretations, and biographies.

1855. Wigdor, Alexander K. *The Personal Papers of Supreme Court Justices: A Descriptive Guide*. New York: Garland Publishing Inc., 1986. Annotated guide to manuscripts.

2. Benjamin Robbins Curtis

1856. Abraham, Henry J. *Justices and Presidents, A Political History of Appointments to the Supreme Court*. New York: Oxford University Press, 1974. Reviews Fillmore's 1851 appointment of Curtis along with Fillmore's three rejected nominees.

1857. Blaustein, Albert P., and Roy M. Mersky. *The First One Hundred Justices: Statistical Studies on the Supreme Court of the United States*. Hamden: Archon Books, 1978. Curtis rates "near great" for his brilliance in commercial law and his courageous dissenting opinion on the Dred Scott decision.

1858. Curtis, Benjamin R. *A Memoir of Benjamin Robbins Curtis, LL.D., with Some of His Professional and Miscellaneous Writings*. Boston: Little, Brown and Company, 1879. 2 vols. Contains letters concerning his appointment and a later exchange with Fillmore giving his reasons for resigning in 1857. Fillmore took pride in his appointment and pleaded with Curtis to stay on the bench.

1859. Dickinson, John. "Curtis, Benjamin Robbins." *DAB* (1958), 2, pt. 2: 609–11. Congratulated Webster on his 7th of March speech and opposed Free Soil candidates. It was through Webster that he was appointed to the Supreme Court at age 41.

1860. Dudley, William, ed. *Slavery, Opposing Viewpoints*. San Diego: Greenhaven Press, Inc., 1992. Contains Curtis's dissent to the Dred Scott decision. Incorrectly places him on the Supreme Court from 1840 to 1857.

1861. Gillette, William. "Benjamin R. Curtis." In *The Justices of the United States Supreme Court, 1789–1969: Their Lives and Major Opinions,* ed. Leon Friedman and Fred I. Israel. New York: R. R. Bowker Company, 1969. A biography and examination of his decisions.

1862. Leach, Richard N. "Benjamin Robbins Curtis: Judicial Misfit." *New England Quarterly* 25 (December 1952): 507–23. Fillmore appreciated his defense of the Fugitive Slave Law but was disappointed when Curtis retired early.

1863. Morris, Robert C. "Curtis, Benjamin Robbins." In *American National Biography,* ed. John A. Garraty and Mark C. Carnes. New York: Oxford University Press, 1999. 24 vols. 5: 884–87. Called a slave catching judge for supporting fugitive slave laws.

1864. Robbins, Chandler, Rev. "Memoirs of the Hon. Benjamin Robbins Curtis, LL.D." *Proceedings of the Massachusetts Historical Society* 16 (1878): 16–35. Describes Fillmore's nomination of Curtis and reprints the 1857 letter to Curtis expressing his disappointment at his resignation from the Court.

1865. Warren, Charles. *The Supreme Court in United States History.* Boston: Little, Brown and Company, 1922–1926. 2 vols. Volume Two includes Fillmore's Court nominations and describes Curtis's tenure and decisions.

3. Robert Cooper Grier

1866. Goble, George W. "Grier, Robert Cooper." *DAB* (1958), 4, pt. 1: 612–13.

1867. Streichler, Stuart A. "Grier, Robert Cooper." In *American National Biography,* ed. John A. Garraty and Mark C. Carnes. New York: Oxford University Press, 1999. 24 vols. 9: 583–84. He believed in the constitutionality of the fugitive laws. However, his instructions to the jury in the Christiana, PA., treason trials left no doubt that the original fugitive resistance was not treason nor was it a war against the federal government.

4. John McLean

1868. Haines, Charles Grove, and Foster H. Sherwood. *The Role of the Supreme Court in American Government and Politics, 1835–1865.* Berkeley: University of California Press, 1957. Reviews the constitutional history and court cases establishing the Fugitive Slave Law. Reviews McLean's defense of Court decisions on slavery.

1869. Weisenburger, Francis P. *The Life of John McLean, A Politician on the United States Supreme Court*. New York: DaCapo Press, 1971 [1937]. McLean was a longtime acquaintance of Fillmore.

5. Roger B. Taney, Chief Justice

1870. "The Case of Dred Scott." *Tribune Almanac, 1858*. New York: New York Tribune, 1858. 37–44. Contemporary analysis of the decision with the dissenting opinions of Curtis and McLean.

1871. Fehrenbacher, Don E. *The Dred Scott Case: Its Significance in American Law and Politics*. New York: Oxford University Press, 1978. Informative background on the Fugitive Slave Laws, the extension of slavery, and their relation to the Taney Court.

1872. ———. "Roger B. Taney and the Sectional Crisis." *Journal of Southern History* 43 (November 1977): 555–66. His hostility to abolitionists influenced his defense of slavery and Southern society.

1873. Newmeyer, R. Kent. *The Supreme Court Under Marshall and Taney*. Arlington Heights, VA: Harlan Davidson, Inc., 1968. Surveys commerce, slavery, and sectionalism.

1874. Schwartz, Bernard. *From Confederation to Nation: The American Constitution, 1835–1877*. Baltimore: Johns Hopkins University Press, 1973. Critical survey of Taney's decisions on slavery.

1875. Wiecek, William W. "Slavery and Abolition Before the United States Supreme Court, 1820–1860." *Journal of American History* 65 (June 1978): 34–59. The Taney Court embraced slavery questions and made gratuitous arguments supporting slavery. The Court's decisions contributed to sectional antagonism and hastened the Civil War.

F. PROMINENT CITIZENS, JOURNALISTS, AND WRITERS

Gamaliel Bailey

1876. Harrold, Stanley. *Gamaliel Bailey and Antislavery Union*. Kent: Kent State University Press, 1986. Antislavery editor of the Washington, DC, *National Era*, which serialized *Uncle Tom's Cabin*.

Edward Bates

1877. Cain, Marvin R. *Lincoln's Attorney General, Edward Bates of Missouri.* Columbia: University of Missouri Press, 1965. Bates turned down a post in Fillmore's Cabinet but was a consistent supporter.

Henry Bibb

1878. Landon, Fred. "Henry Bibb, A Colonizer." *Journal of Negro History* 5 (October 1920): 437–47. In 1851 he established the Canadian *Voice of the Fugitive,* a newspaper that extolled the slaves' desire for freedom.

Mary Bibb

1878a. Cooper, Afua. "The Search for Mary Bibb, Black Woman Teacher in Nineteenth-Century Canada." *Ontario History* 83 (March 1991): 39–54. After Henry and Mary fled to Canada she opened schools for fugitive children, helped run Henry's paper, and organized aid for other fugitives.

Orestes Brownson

1879. Bates, Ernest Sutherland. "Brownson, Orestes Augustus." *DAB* (1958) 2, pt. 1: 178–79. Reviews his early political journalism and later religious conversion to Catholicism but nothing on his political concerns in the 1850s.

1880. Brownson, Orestes. "Fugitive Slave Law." *Brownson's Quarterly Review* 13 (July 1851): 383–411. Supports the constitutionality of the Fugitive Slave Law and condemns the Free Soil criticism of the Compromise.

1881. ———. "The Higher Law." *Brownson's Quarterly Review* 13 (January 1851): 80–97. This independent Catholic editor believed Catholics supported the Fugitive Slave Law despite a suspicion that Fillmore's administration was anti-Catholic.

William Cullen Bryant

1882. Brown, Charles H. *William Cullen Bryant.* New York: Charles Scribner's Sons, 1971. Prominent independent Democratic editor of the New York *Evening Post.* He denounced Fillmore's order for military enforcement of the Fugitive Slave Law.

Rufus Choate

1883. Choate, Rufus. "Speech Delivered at the Constitutional Meeting in Faneuil Hall, November 26, 1850." In *Addresses and Orations of Rufus Choate.* Boston: Little, Brown and Company, 1878. 396–418. The North and South should accept the Compromise and abolitionists must accept the constitutionality of the Fugitive Slave Law.

1884. Matthews, Jean V. *Rufus Choate: The Law and Civic Virtue.* Philadelphia: Temple University Press, 1980. The legal Brahmin of Massachusetts supported the Compromise and worked for Webster's presidential nomination in 1852.

James Fenimore Cooper

1885. Cooper, James Fenimore. *New York.* New York: William Farquhar Payson, 1930. Essay from Cooper's introduction to an 1850–1851 unpublished manuscript entitled *The Towns of Manhattan.* He believed the North would accept the Fugitive Slave Law because he saw no significant public disposition to repeal it.

Richard Henry Dana, Jr.

1886. Lucid, Robert F. *The Journal of Richard Henry Dana, Jr.* Cambridge: Belknap Press of Harvard University Press, 1968. 3 vols. 2: 407–78, 493. Author and lawyer who defended fugitive slaves in Boston.

1887. Shapiro, Samuel. *Richard Henry Dana, Jr., 1815–1882.* East Lansing: Michigan State University Press, 1961. Well-known author and lawyer for Boston fugitive slaves.

J. D. B. De Bow

1888. "De Bow, James Dunwoody Brownson." In *Biographical Dictionary of the Confederacy,* ed. Jon L. Wakelyn. Westport, CT: Greenwood Press, 1977. 166–67. A secessionist in the 1850s, he supported the Confederacy.

1889. Mitchell, Broadus. "De Bow, James Dunwoody Brownson." *DAB* (1959), 3, pt. 1: 180–82. *De Bow's Review* was the largest circulation periodical in the South. It promoted sectional economic independence and slavery expansion.

Dorothea Dix

1890. Brown, Thomas J. *Dorothea Dix: New England Reformer.* Cambridge: Harvard University Press, 1998. Reviews the friendship between Dix and Fillmore.

1891. Gollaher, David. *Voice for the Mad: The Life of Dorothea Dix.* New York: Free Press, 1995. Whig principles and mutual appreciation helped Dix and Fillmore work together for the first Government Hospital for the Insane.

1892. Marshall, Helen E. "Dix, Dorothea Lynde." In *Notable American Women, 1607–1950: A Biographical Dictionary,* ed. Edward T. James, Janet Wilson James, and Paul S. Boyer. Cambridge: Belknap Press, 1971. 3 vols. 1: 486–89. Prominent lobbyist for federal support of insane asylums.

1893. Snyder, Charles M., ed. *The Lady and the President: Letters of Dorothea Dix and Millard Fillmore.* Lexington: University of Kentucky Press, 1975. Intimate friend of Fillmore and his family.

Frederick Douglass

1894. Douglass, Frederick. *Narrative of the Life of Frederick Douglass, An American Slave.* New York: New American Library, Inc., 1968 [1845]. Classic slave narrative by the self-liberating fugitive and radical abolitionist.

1895. "Douglass, Frederick." In *The African American Encyclopedia,* ed. Michael W. Williams. New York: Marshall Cavendish, 1993. 5 vols. 2: 472–74.

1896. Foner, Phillip S., ed. *The Life and Writings of Frederick Douglass: Pre-Civil War Decades 1850–1860.* New York: International Publishers, 1950. 4 vols. Volume Two contains his scorn for the Fugitive Slave Law and his appeals to resist it. He despised Fillmore for pretending the Union was in danger over sectionalism.

1897. Martin, Waldo E., Jr. "Douglass, Frederick." In *Encyclopedia of African American Culture and History,* ed. Jack Salzman, Davis Lionel Smith, and Cornel West. New York: Simon & Schuster Macmillan, 1996. 5 vols. 2: 783–85.

1898. McFeeley, William S. *Frederick Douglass.* New York: W. W. Norton & Company, 1991. Douglass believed that resistance to the Fugitive Slave Law helped to increased opposition to slavery.

1899. Quarles, Benjamin. *Frederick Douglass.* New York: Atheneum, 1976 [1948]. Vehemently opposed the Fugitive Slave Law and actively supported the underground railway.

Andrew Jackson Downing

1900. Schuyler, David. *Apostle of Taste: Andrew Jackson Downing, 1815–1852.* Baltimore: Johns Hopkins University Press, 1996. Fillmore approved his appointment to develop the Washington Mall into a National Park. It was noted that the improvements would render the neighborhood a healthier place for Presidents' families.

1901. ———. "The Washington Park and Downing's Legacy to Public Landscape Design." In *Prophet without Honor: The Career of Andrew Jackson Downing, 1815–1852,* ed. George B. Tatum and Elisabeth Blair MacDougall. Washington, DC: Dumbarton Oaks Research Library and Collection, 1987. Downing began improvements on the Mall in the spring of 1851 and through Fillmore's intervention was given personal supervision of the project.

Ralph Waldo Emerson

1902. Carter, George E. "Democrat in Heaven—Whig on Earth—The Politics of Ralph Waldo Emerson." *Historical New Hampshire* 27 (Fall 1972): 123–40. Emerson held Whig sentiments until disillusioned by the Fugitive Slave Law.

1903. Emerson, Ralph Waldo. "The Fugitive Slave Law." In *Works of Emerson.* Boston: Houghton, Mifflin and Company, 1904. 12 vols. *Miscellanies.* Vol. 11. In 1851 Emerson equated the law with arson and murder. He condemned Webster and the merchants of Boston for supporting it.

1904. ———— . "The Fugitive Slave Law." In *Works of Emerson.* Boston: Houghton Mifflin and Company, 1904. 12 vols. *Miscellanies.* Vol. 11. In a second lecture on the law, Emerson blamed Webster for its passage and said Fillmore was without self-respect for signing and enforcing it.

1905. Gougeon, Len. *Virtue's Hero: Emerson, Antislavery, and Reform.* Athens: University of Georgia Press, 1990. Describes his arousal against the fugitive laws and the Harvard students who heckled him and cheered for Webster and Fillmore.

1906. Gougeon, Leonard G. "Emerson and the Campaign of 1851." *Historical Journal of Massachusetts* 16 (January 1988): 20–33. After the Fugitive Slave Law passed, Emerson consented to campaign for Free Soil candidates.

1907. Plumstead, A. W., et al., ed. *The Journal and Miscellaneous Notebooks of Ralph Waldo Emerson.* Cambridge: The Belknap Press, 1960–1982. 16 vols. In Volume Eleven he wrote that Fillmore should not take Boston's abolitionists lightly.

William Maxwell Evarts

1908. Barrows, Chester L. *William M. Evarts: Lawyer, Diplomat, Statesman.* Chapel Hill: University of North Carolina Press, 1941. New York City Assistant District Attorney and conservative Whig who defended the Fugitive Slave Law and endorsed the Compromise.

1909. Dyer, Brainerd. *The Public Career of William M. Evarts.* Berkeley: University of California Press, 1933. Detained the filibustering ship *Cleopatra* from joining Lopez's Cuban expedition.

1910. Evarts, William Maxwell. "Speech at the Union Meeting in Castle Garden, New York, October 30, 1850—Fugitive Slave Law." In *Arguments and Speeches of William Maxwell Evarts,* ed. Sherman Evarts. New York: Macmillan Company,

1919. 3 vols. 2: 420–34. Argued for the constitutionality of the law and against those resisting its execution.

William Lloyd Garrison

1911. Mayer, Henry. *All on Fire: William Lloyd Garrison and the Abolition of Slavery.* New York: St. Martin's Press, 1998. Biography and scholarship on a heroic scale.

1912. Ruchames, Louis, ed. *The Letters of William Lloyd Garrison.* Volume Four, *From Disunionism to the Brink of War, 1850–1860.* Cambridge: Belknap Press of Harvard University Press, 1975. 5 vols. To Garrison, Fillmore was only a prop for the slave system.

1913. Stewart, James B. "The Aims and Impact of Garrisonian Abolitionism, 1840–1860." *Civil War History* 15 (September 1969): 197–209. The Fugitive Slave Law revitalized Garrison's radical disunionist campaign while his rhetoric can be heard in the speeches of political abolitionists throughout the 1850s.

Francis Granger

1914. "Granger, Francis." In *Encyclopedia of Biography of New York,* ed. Charles Elliott Fitch. Boston: American Historical Society, Inc., 1916. 3 vols. 3: 203–5. He split with Seward at the 1850 New York State Whig Convention over a resolution critical of the Compromise. Granger and other Fillmore delegates formed a conservative Whig faction called the Silver Grays, named for Granger's gray hair.

1915. Perkins, Dexter. "Granger, Francis." *DAB* (1960), 4, pt. 1: 482–83. Review of his support for conservative Whigs and Fillmore.

Horace Greeley

1916. Greeley, Horace. *Reflections of a Busy Life.* New York: J. B. Ford & Company, 1869. Greeley's interpretation of history includes a critical assessment of Fillmore.

1917. ———. "Why I Am a Whig." *Whig Almanac, 1852.* New York: New York Tribune, 1852. 6–13. Whig principles include the necessity to improve home industry, suppress the lust for new territory, and combat the political corruption of the Democratic party.

1918. Van Deusen, Glyndon G. *Horace Greeley, Nineteenth-Century Crusader.* Philadelphia: University of Pennsylvania Press, 1953. Biography of the Whig and Republican editor of the New York *Tribune.*

Nathaniel Hawthorne

1919. Flint, Allan. "Hawthorne and the Slavery Crisis." *New England Quarterly* 41 (September 1968): 393–408. The Fugitive Slave Law changed his thinking from an indifferent presumption of African American inferiority to a new sympathy for slaves though he never supported abolitionists. He followed the Democratic party's policy of supporting the Compromise of 1850.

1920. Hawthorne, Nathaniel. "The Life of Franklin Pierce." In *The Complete Writings of Nathaniel Hawthorne.* Boston: Houghton, Mifflin and Company, 1900. 22 vols. 17: 75–193. Finished in August 1852, Hawthorne reports that Pierce approved all the acts in the Compromise of 1850.

1921. "Hawthorne's Life of Pierce-Perspective." *U. S. Magazine and Democratic Review* 31 (September 1852): 276–88. Partisan review of Hawthorne's campaign biography with proposals to correct the errors of Fillmore.

1922. Mellow, James R. *Nathaniel Hawthorne in His Times.* Boston: Houghton Mifflin Company, 1980. His distaste for the Fugitive Slave Law was grounded in his regional patriotism against Southern intervention and not in any sympathy for the abolitionist movement or for slaves.

1923. Warner, Lee H. "Nathaniel Hawthorne and the Making of the President— 1852." *Historical New Hampshire* 28 (Spring 1973): 21–36. Demonstrates how Hawthorn fictionalized Pierce's unspectacular career into an attractive campaign biography.

George W. Hosmer

1924. Cutter, G. W., Rev. *Memorial Discourse in Honor of Rev. George W. Hosmer, D. D., Preached at the Church of Our Father, Buffalo, N.Y. July 10 1881.* Buffalo: Courier Company Printers, 1881. It was remembered that Hosmer tried to dissuade Fillmore, his friend and parishioner, from signing the Fugitive Slave Law. They remained friends, and Fillmore participated in Hosmer's 25th anniversary as a Unitarian minister in Buffalo in 1861.

1925. Horton, John T. "Millard Fillmore and the Things of God and Caesar, I." *Niagara Frontier* 2 (Spring 1955): 1–7. Hosmer and some of Fillmore's Unitarian friends criticized him for signing the Fugitive Slave Law.

1926. Hosmer, James Kendall. *The Last Leaf: Observations During Seventy-Five Years of Men and Events in America and Europe.* New York: G. P. Putnam's Sons, 1912. Son recalls his father's friendship with Fillmore despite rebuking him for signing the Fugitive Slave Law. He recalled Fillmore saying he chose between two evils: temporary suffering or bloodshed.

Washington Hunt

1927. Carmen, Henry J. "Hunt, Washington." *DAB* (1961), 5, pt. 1: 395–96. He was the Whig Governor of New York from 1850 to 1852, and later supported Fillmore's 1856 campaign.

1928. "Hunt, Washington." In *Directory of the Governors of the United States, 1789–1978,* ed. Robert Sobel and John Raimo. Westport, CT: Meckler Books, 1978. 4 vols. 3: 1081.

1929. "Hunt, Washington." In *Encyclopedia of Biography of New York,* ed. Charles Elliott Fitch. Boston: American Historical Society, Inc., 1916. 3 vols. 3: 344–45. New York governor who supported the Fillmore administration and followed him into the American party.

1930. Lincoln, Charles Z., ed. *State of New York Messages of the Governors.* Albany: J. B. Lyon Company, State Printers, 1909. 11 vols. 4: 538–639. In January 1851, Governor Hunt advised following the duties of the Fugitive Slave Law while representatives reviewed and modified clauses that might be defective. In January 1852, he advocated the proposals of the American Colonization Society. It reads very much like Fillmore's suppressed portion of his message to Congress later in the year.

Washington Irving

1931. Hellman, George S. W*ashington Irving, Esquire: Ambassador at Large from the New World to the Old.* New York: A. A. Knopf, 1925. Through John P. Kennedy, Fillmore and his family became friends with Irving.

1932. Irving, Pierre M. *The Life and Letters of Washington Irving.* Detroit: Gale Research Company, 1967 [1867]. 4 vols. Volume Four reveals the friendship that developed between Fillmore's family and Irving. Irving was shocked at Abigail's death following their attendance at Pierce's inauguration. He attributed it to their standing outside in the wet and cold during the ceremony.

1933. Williams, Stanley T. T*he Life of Washington Irving.* New York: Octagon Books, 1971 [1935]. 2 vols. Volume Two reveals that Irving became a great favorite with Fillmore's family and at the President's levees during the final months of the administration.

Abraham Lincoln

1934. Beveridge, Albert J. *Abraham Lincoln, 1809–1858.* Boston: Houghton Mifflin Company, 1928. 2 vols. 2. Lincoln preferred Fillmore in 1852. Beveridge surmises Lincoln would have followed the course Fillmore did in the early 1850s.

1935. Donald, David Herbert. *Lincoln.* New York: Simon & Schuster, 1995. Lincoln always accepted the constitutionality of the Fugitive Slave Law.

1936. Thomas, Benjamin P. *Abraham Lincoln: A Biography.* New York: Alfred A. Knopf, 1952. While in political retirement, he endorsed the Compromise of 1850 while assailing the abolitionists and southern secessionists.

John C. Lord

1937. Brooks, Charles E. "John C. Lord and the Old School Presbyterian Thought in Buffalo, 1837–1864." Unpublished MS. State University of New York at Buffalo Archives, n.d. Examines Lord's defense of the Fugitive Slave Law and support for Fillmore in the context of religious doctrine. Lord's defense received national attention.

1938. Bryan, George J. "Biography of John C. Lord, D. D." In *Biographies and Journalism.* Buffalo: Courier Company, Printers, 1886. 133–46. Lord became a national figure after publishing his defense of the Fugitive Slave Law.

1939. Horton, John T. "Millard Fillmore and the Things of God and Caesar, II." *Niagara Frontier* 3 (Summer 1955): 39–48. Lord's religious reasons for obeying government laws started as a local sermon and became a national appeal.

1940. Lord, John C. *'The Higher Law' in Its Applications to the Fugitive Slave Bill: A Sermon on the Duties Men Owe to God and to Government, Delivered at the Central Presbyterian Church on Thanksgiving Day.* Buffalo: George H. Derby and Co., 1851. Lord's theological discourse against the "Higher Law" arguments of antislavery men.

1941. Putnam, James O. "John C. Lord, D. D." In *Addresses, Speeches and Miscellanies.* Buffalo: Peter Paul & Brothers, 1880. Lord believed that Christianity compelled citizens to support the government's Fugitive Slave Law.

1942. ———. "Memorial Paper." In *Memoir of John C. Lord, D. D.: Pastor of the Central Presbyterian Church for Thirty-Eight Years.* Buffalo: Courier Company, Printers, 1878. 87–126. Reviews the background and consequences of Lord's defense of the Fugitive Slave Law. After 1861 Lord supported the Union and emancipation.

1943. Wood, Chas. "Biographical Sketch." In *Memoir of John C. Lord, D. D.: Pastor of the Central Presbyterian Church for Thirty-Eight Years.* Buffalo: Courier Company, Printers, 1878. 5–43. Reprints Fillmore's letter of gratitude to Lord for defending the Fugitive Slave Law. He reports that thousands of reprints of Lord's defense are being distributed under the congressional franking privilege.

Samuel J. May

1944. May, Samuel. *Fugitive Slave Law and Its Victims.* New York: American Anti-Slavery Society, 1861. Syracuse Unitarian minister accused Fillmore of introducing plantation discipline into the North by enforcing the Fugitive Slave Law.

1945. Mood, Fulmer. "May, Samuel Joseph." *DAB* (1961), 6, pt. 2: 447–48. More humanitarian than theologian, he was a radical activist against the Fugitive Slave Law and Fillmore.

1946. Pease, Jane H., and William H Pease. *Bound with Them in Chains: A Biographical History of the Antislavery Movement.* Westport, CT: Greenwood Press, Inc., 1972. Chapter Twelve surveys May's antislavery career, reviews his participation in the Jerry escape at Syracuse, and mentions his annual Jerry rescue celebration.

1947. Yacovone, Donald. *Samuel Joseph May and the Dilemmas of the Liberal Persuasion, 1797–1871.* Philadelphia: Temple University Press, 1991. Led an unsuccessful campaign among Unitarians to condemn Fillmore and oust him from the church.

Herman Melville

1947a. Buell, Lawrence. "Melville and the Question of American Decolonization." *American Literature*: 64 (June 1992): 215–37. Follows themes in Melville's work derived from issues in the Compromise of 1850.

1948. Foster, Charles H. "Something In Emblems: A Reinterpretation of *Moby Dick.*" *New England Quarterly* 34 (March 1961): 3–35. While writing in the winter of 1850–51, antislavery themes erupted in the novel in consequence of his Boston relative, Judge Lemuel Shaw, remanding Thomas Sims into slavery.

1949. Heimert, Alan. "*Moby Dick* and American Political Symbolism." *American Quarterly* 15 (Winter 1963): 498–534. Exegesis of political themes and symbols belonging to the Compromise of 1850.

1950. Karcher, Carolyn L. *Shadow Over the Promised Land: Slavery, Race and Violence in Melville's America.* Baton Rouge: Louisiana State University Press, 1980. Review of race and slavery in Melville's fiction. Informative bibliography on literature and racial attitudes in the 1850s.

1951. Melville, Herman. *Moby-Dick, or the Whale.* New York: Bobbs-Merrill Company, Inc., 1964 [1851]. The author dives deep beneath surface appearances to hunt for meaning in his mid-century world.

1952. ———— . *White Jacket, or the World in a Man-of-War.* New York: Rinehart and Winston, 1967 [1850]. The best available description of Navy ship life. Describes sailors prison-like routine and plantation punishments. The work reinforced arguments against flogging in the Navy.

1953. Stessel, H. Edward. "Melville's *White Jacket*: A Case Against the 'Cat.' " *Clio* 13 (Fall 1988): 37–55. Highlights Melville's call to amend the Articles of War which allowed officers to treat sailors like convicts and discipline them like slaves.

Theodore Parker

1954. Commager, Henry Steele. *Theodore Parker: Yankee Crusader.* Boston: Boston Press, 1960 [1936]. Parker thought the rescue of Shadrack by local Boston African Americans the noblest deed since the destruction of tea in 1773. He opposed Fillmore's prosecution of the rescuers.

1955. Fellman, Michael. "Theodore Parker and the Abolitionist Role in the 1850s." *Journal of American History* 61 (December 1974): 666–84. His abolitionism had nothing to do with raising African Americans to equality but with correcting the dependency of whites on slaves and freeing their Anglo-Saxon instinct for progress.

1956. Frothingham, Octavius Brooks. *Theodore Parker: A Biography.* Boston: James R. Osgood and Company, 1876. Reprints Parker's letter to Fillmore informing the President he will resist the Fugitive Slave Law.

1957. Parker, Theodore. "The Boston Kidnapping." In Parker, *The Slave Power.* Boston: American Unitarian Association, 1916. At the first anniversary of the rendering of Thomas Sims into slavery, Parker accused Webster and Fillmore of lowering themselves to that of kidnappers.

1958. ———— . *The Trial of Theodore Parker.* Boston: Published by the Author, 1855. His defense against the federal indictment for obstructing the Fugitive Slave Law. The charges were dropped before trial. He is critical of Associate Justice Benjamin P. Curtis and his family for their history of upholding the fugitive laws.

1959. Weiss, John. *Life and Correspondence of Theodore Parker.* New York: D. Appleton and Company, 1864. 2 vols. 2: 101–2. In an 1850 letter to Fillmore, Parker admitted that he had fugitive slaves in his congregation and that Christianity compelled that he protect them.

James Louis Petigru

1960. Carson, James Petigru. *Life, Letters and Speeches of James Louis Petigru: The Union Man of South Carolina.* Washington, DC: H. L. & J. B. McQueen Inc., 1920. Reprints Petigru's 1851 letters to Fillmore accepting the U.S. District

Attorney's office in South Carolina. Fillmore referred to him as a moral hero for accepting the federal position while secession was openly advocated in his state.

1961. Ford, Lacy. "James Louis Petigru: The Last South Carolina Federalist." In *Intellectual Life in Antebellum Charleston,* ed. Michael O'Brien and David Moltke-Hanson. Knoxville: University of Tennessee Press, 1986. Describes his Federalist background and engaging personality to explain the singularity of a slaveholder and Unionist in secessionist Charleston.

1962. Hamilton, J. G. De R. "James Louis Petigru." *DAB* (1962) 7, pt. 2: 514–15.

1963. Pease, Jane E., and William H. Pease. "Law, Slavery, and Petigru: A Study in Paradox." In *The Moment of Decision: Biographical Essays on American Character and Regional Identity,* ed. Randall M. Miller and John R. McKivigan. Westport, CT: Greenwood Press, 1994. While federal attorney he defended Britain's position to secure the freedom of their black sailors from seizure by South Carolina.

1964. ———. "Petigru, James Louis." In *American National Biography,* ed. John A. Garraty and Mark C. Carnes. New York: Oxford University Press, 1999. 24 vols. 19: 399–401.

Wendell Phillips

1965. Phillips, Wendell. "Surrender of Sims." In *Speeches, Lectures, and Letters.* New York: Negro Universities Press, 1968 [1884]. This 1852 speech describes his indignation at the rendition of Thomas Sims back to slavery.

1966. Stewart, James Brewer. *Wendell Phillips, Liberty's Hero.* Baton Rouge: Louisiana State University Press, 1986. Boston abolitionist and orator defended fugitive slaves.

James Osbourne Putnam

1967. Sanders, Neill F. " 'Fairness, and Fairness Only':' Lincoln's Appointment of James O. Putnam as Consul at Le Harve." *Lincoln Herald* 87 (Fall 1985): 76–82. Reviews friendship with Fillmore, and his association with the Whig and the American party.

1968. Viets, Henry R. "Putnam, James Osbourne." *DAB* (1963), 8, pt. 1: 283–84. Fillmore appointed his friend Postmaster of Buffalo after removing the pro-Seward appointee.

Thomas Richie

1969. Osthaus, Carl R., *Partisans of the Southern Press: Editorial Spokesmen of the Nineteenth Century.* Lexington: University of Kentucky, 1994. At the end of his career, Thomas Richie, the Democratic editor of the Washington *Union,* aligned with the Compromise of 1850 and was attacked by extremists of the North and South.

Lemuel Shaw

1970. Chafee, Zechariah, Jr. "Shaw, Lemuel." *DAB* (1961), 9, pt. 1: 42–43. Massachusetts Chief Justice who opposed slavery but felt bound by the federal constitution to uphold the Fugitive Slave Law.

1971. Chase, Frederic Hathaway. *Lemuel Shaw: Chief Justice of the Supreme Court of Massachusetts, 1830–1860.* Boston: Houghton Mifflin Company, 1918. To quell the antislavery agitation in Boston, Shaw argued for the constitutionality of the Fugitive Slave Law while hoping to subdue Webster's tirade to convict and punish agitators.

1972. Finkelman, Paul. "Shaw, Lemuel." In *American National Biography,* ed. John A. Garraty and Mark C. Carnes. New York: Oxford University Press, 1999. 24 vols. 19: 745–48. Reviews important cases.

1973. *Gleason's Pictorial Drawing-Room Companion,* September 13, 1851. Illustration and favorable comments on Chief Justice Shaw.

1974. Levy, Leonard W. *The Law of the Commonwealth and Chief Justice Shaw: The Evolution of American Law, 1830–1860.* New York: Harper Torchbooks, 1967 [1957]. The Massachusetts Chief Justice gave the first formal judicial opinion sustaining the constitutionality of the Fugitive Slave Law.

William Gilmore Simms

1975. Parks, Edd Winfield. *Ante-Bellum Southern Literary Critics.* Athens: University of Georgia Press, 1962. Chapter Six has an analysis of Simms's review of Harriet Beecher Stowe's portrayal of slavery.

1976. Ridgely, Joseph V. *Nineteenth-Century Southern Literature.* Lexington: University Press of Kentucky, 1980. Chapter Five reviews Simms's defense of the South.

1977. ———— . " '*Woodcraft*': Simms's First Answer to *Uncle Tom's Cabin.*" *American Literature* 31 (January 1960): 421–33. The leading champion of Southern institutions used his novel to show the mutual affection between master and slave.

1978. Simms, W. Gilmore. "The Morals of Slavery." In *The Pro-Slavery Argument; as Maintained by the Most Distinguished Writers of the Southern States*. New York: Negro Universities Press, 1968 [1852]. Defended slavery, secession, and southern culture.

1979. Wakelyn, Jon L. *The Politics of a Literary Man: William Gilmore Simms.* Westport, CT: Greenwood Press, Inc., 1973. Simms supported the early 1850s secession movement.

1980. Watson, Charles S. *From Nationalism to Secessionism: The Changing Fiction of William Gilmore Simms.* Westport, CT: Greenwood Press, Inc., 1993. From a proud writer on South Carolina's contribution to American independence, he became a militant sectionalist whose fiction and essays promoted secession.

1981. Wimsatt, Mary Ann. "Simms, William Gilmore." In *Encyclopedia of Southern Culture*, ed. Charles Reagan Wilson and William Ferris. Chapel Hill: University of North Carolina Press, 1989. 895. Simms was the embodiment of the antebellum Southern man of letters.

Harriet Beecher Stowe

1982. Cross, Barbara M. "Stowe, Harriet Beecher." In *Notable American Women, 1607–1950: A Biographical Dictionary*, ed. Edward T. James, Janet Wilson James, and Paul S. Boyer. Cambridge: Belknap Press, 1971. 3 vols. 3: 393–402. Summary and analysis of *Uncle Tom's Cabin.*

1983. Crozier, Olive C. "Uncle Tom's Cabin." In *Encyclopedia of Southern Culture*, ed. Charles Reagan Wilson and William Ferris. Chapel Hill: University of North Carolina Press, 1989. 1141–42. Novel portrays an innocent South threatened by the cruelty of slavery.

1984. Gossett, Thomas F. *Uncle Tom's Cabin and American Culture.* Dallas: Southern Methodist University Press, 1985. Examines the impact of the novel and the adapted stage plays on antebellum audiences.

1984a. Levine, Robert S. "*Uncle Tom's Cabin* in *Frederick Douglass' Paper*: An Analysis of Reception." *American Literature* 64 (March 1992): 71–93. Douglass favored the novel because he believed its power and popularity could overcome the acceptance of the Fugitive Slave Law.

1985. Loveland, Anne C. "Harriet Beecher Stowe Publishes *Uncle Tom's Cabin.*" In *Great Events from History: American Series*, ed. Frank N. Magill. Englewood Cliffs: Salem Press, Inc., 1975. 3 vols. 2: 859–64. Published in March 1852, the book sold 50,000 copies in two months and 300,000 copies in one year.

1986. Reynolds, Moira Davidson. Uncle Tom's Cabin *and Mid-Nineteenth Century United States.* Jefferson, NC: McFarland & Company, Inc., Publishers, 1985. On May 8, 1851, the *National Era* announced a new serial entitled *Uncle Tom's Cabin, or The Man That was a Thing.*

1986a. Ryan, Susan M. "Charity Begins at Home: Stowe's Antislavery Novels and the Forms of Benevolent Citizenship." *American Literature* 72 (December 2000): 751–82. Reviews her sympathy for the colonization of Africa by former slaves in *Uncle Tom's Cabin* and her change of mind in the later novel *Dred.*

1987. Stowe, Harriet Beecher. *Uncle Tom's Cabin; Or, Life Among the Lowly.* New York: Viking Penguin, 1981 [1852]. The book that aroused America to the brutality of slavery and the humanity of slaves. Published as a serial and a book during Fillmore's term.

Henry David Thoreau

1988. Neufeldt, Leonard N. "Thoreau's Enterprise of Self Culture in a Culture of Enterprise." *American Quarterly* 39 (Summer 1987): 231–51. Contrasts Thoreau's critical assessment of American enterprise with Fillmore's public exuberance for its virtues.

1989. Thoreau, Henry David. "Slavery in Massachusetts." In *The Writings of Henry David Thoreau.* Boston: Houghton Mifflin and Company, 1906. 6 vols. 4: 388–408. First delivered at an antislavery convention in 1854 then published in the *Liberator.* He condemns lawyers and judges for arguing the expediency of the Fugitive Slave Law and not judging whether it is right.

1990. Torrey, Bradford, and Francis H. Allen. *The Journal of Henry D. Thoreau.* Boston: Houghton Mifflin Company, 1949 [1906]. 14 vols. Volume Two contains comments on the Sims case and local resistance to the Fugitive Slave Law.

Sojourner Truth

1991. Painter, Nell Irvin. "Representing Truth: Sojourner Truth's Knowing and Becoming Known." *Journal of American History* 81 (September 1994): 461–92. Her name meant itinerant preacher. She joined the antislavery/feminist lecture circuit in the late 1840s.

1992. ———. *Sojourner Truth: A Life, A Symbol.* New York: W. W. Norton, 1996. Her lectures profoundly affected the antislavery and women's rights movements at the time of Fillmore's administration.

1993. ———. "Sojourner Truth (1797–1883): Abolitionist, Women's Rights Activist, Lecturer, Religious Leader." In *Notable Black American Women,* ed. Jessie

Carney Smith. Detroit: Gale Research Inc., 1992. 2 vols. 1: 1147–51. She made her famous "Arn't I a Woman?" speech at Akron, Ohio, in 1851.

1994. Redding, Saunders. "Truth, Sojourner." In *Notable American Women, 1607–1950: A Biographical Dictionary,* ed. Edward T. James, Janet Wilson James, and Paul S. Boyer. Cambridge: Belknap Press, 1971. 3 vols. 3: 479–81.

1995. "Sojourner Truth [Isabella Van Wagener] (1797–1883)." In *The Pen Is Ours: A Listing of Writings by and about African American Women Before 1910, With Secondary Bibliography to the Present,* comp. Jean Fagin Yellin and Cynthia D. Bond. New York: Oxford University Press, 1991. 226–33.

Harriet Tubman

1996. Davidson, Nancy A. "Harriet Tubman 'Moses' (c. 1820–1913): Underground Railroad Conductor, Union Scout and Spy, Nurse, Feminist." In *Notable Black American Women,* ed. Jessie Carney Smith. Detroit: Gale Research Inc., 1992. 2 vols. 1: 1151–55. Includes photo and bibliography.

1997. Franklin, John Hope. "Tubman, Harriet." In *Notable American Women, 1607–1950: A Biographical Dictionary,* ed. Edward T. James, Janet Wilson James, and Paul S. Boyer. Cambridge: Belknap Press, 1971. 3 vols. 3: 481–83.

1998. "Harriet Tubman [Davis] (182?–1913)." In *The Pen Is Ours: A Listing of Writings by and about African American Women Before 1910, With Secondary Bibliography to the Present,* comp. Jean Fagin Yellin and Cynthia D. Bond. New York: Oxford University Press, 1991. 234–40.

1999. Petry, Ann. *Harriet Tubman: Conductor on the Underground Railroad.* New York: Archway Paperback, 1971 [1955]. Fearing legal rendition of fugitives in the North she decided her escape route needed to go into Canada.

2000. Thompson, Priscilla. "Harriet Tubman, Thomas Garrett, and the Underground Railway." *Delaware History* 22 (Spring–Summer 1986): 1–21. The Fugitive Slave Law convinced Tubman that slaves needed to go to Canada for total protection.

2001. Williams, Lorraine A. "Tubman, Harriet." In *Dictionary of American Negro Biography,* ed. Rayford W. Logan and Michael R. Winston. New York: W. W. Norton, 1982. 606–7. Escaping slavery in 1849, she returned approximately nineteen times to rescue her family and 300 other fugitive slaves.

John Tyler

2002. Seager, Robert. *And Tyler Too: A Biography of John & Julia Gardiner Tyler.* New York: McGraw-Hill Book Company, Inc., 1963. Ex-President Tyler feared that Fillmore was not bold enough to enforce the Fugitive Slave Law and satisfy the South.

Samuel Ringgold Ward

2003. Burke, Ronald K. "The Anti-Slavery Activities of Samuel Ringgold Ward in New York State." *Afro-Americans in New York Life and History* 2 (January 1978): 17–28. African American abolitionist leader whose faith in Christ led him to participate in the Jerry rescue. He followed Jerry into Canada fleeing prosecution.

2004. ———. *Samuel Ringgold Ward: Christian Abolitionist.* New York: Garland Publishing, Inc., 1995. Substantial review of Ward's career and his oratorical style. Includes his speech against the Fugitive Slave Law in April 1850.

2005. Filler, Louis. "Ward, Samuel Ringgold." In *Dictionary of American Negro Biography,* ed. Rayford W. Logan and Michael R. Winston. New York: W. W. Norton, 1982. 631–32. Ward was an African American Congregational pastor who aided Jerry's escape from Syracuse in 1851.

2006. Prettyman, Quandra. "Ward, Samuel Ringgold." In *Encyclopedia of African American Culture and History,* ed. Jack Salzman, Davis Lionel Smith, and Cornel West. New York: Simon & Schuster Macmillan, 1996. 5 vols. 5: 2775. Well-known African American abolitionist and clergyman in western New York. Photograph.

2007. Sorin, Gerald. *The New York Abolitionists: A Case Study of Political Radicalism.* Westport, CT: Greenwood Press, 1971. Reviews early career.

2008. Ward, Samuel Ringgold. *Autobiography of a Fugitive Negro.* New York: Arno Press and the *New York Times,* 1968 [1855]. He considered Fillmore a "convenient, subservient instrument of slavery."

2009. Winks, Robin W. "Ward, Samuel Ringgold." In *Dictionary of Canadian Biography,* ed. Frances G. Halpenny. Toronto: University of Toronto Press, 1976. 13 vols. 9: 820–21. The abolitionist fled to Canada and worked for the Anti-Slavery Society of Canada.

Thurlow Weed

2010. Barnes, Thurlow Weed. *The Life of Thurlow Weed, Volume 2, Memoir of Thurlow Weed.* Boston: Houghton, Mifflin and Company, 1883. 2 vols. States that Fillmore sold out to the slave South and that he was rejected by his own party.

2011. Boatfield, Helen C. "Weed, Thurlow." *DAB* (1964), 10, pt. 1: 598–600. Powerful Whig leader and editor of the Albany *Evening Journal.* Claims Weed was a humanitarian "but never to the point of endangering the serious business of elections."

2012. Field, Phyllis F. "Weed, Thurlow." In *American National Biography,* ed. John A. Garraty and Mark C. Carnes. New York: Oxford University Press, 1999. 24 vols. 22: 882–83.

2013. Van Deusen, Glyndon G. *Thurlow Weed, Wizard of the Lobby.* Boston: Little, Brown and Company, 1947. Political biography describes his close association with Seward and their evolving rivalry with Fillmore.

2014. Weed, Harriet A., ed. *The Life of Thurlow Weed, Volume 1, Autobiography of Thurlow Weed.* Boston: Houghton, Mifflin and Company, 1883. 2 vols. Claims Weed and Seward broke with Fillmore over the Vice President's patronage policy and his later signing of the Fugitive Slave Law.

James Monroe Whitfield

2014a. Brawley, Benjamin. *The Negro Genius: A New Appraisal of the Achievement of the American Negro in Literature and the Fine Arts.* New York: Biblo and Tannen, 1966 [1937]. Short section on Whitfield with passages from antislavery poem "How Long?"

2015. Davis, Arthur P., et al., ed. *The New Cavalcade: African American Writing from 1760 to the Present.* Washington, DC: Howard University Press, 1991. 2 vols. 1: 130–41. Contains long antislavery poems "America" and "How Long."

2016. Laryea, Doris Lucas. "James Monroe Whitfield." In *Afro-American Writers Before the Harlem Renaissance.*, ed. Trudier Harris and Thadious M. Davis. Detroit: Gale Research Company, 1986. African American Buffalo antislavery poet who published in Frederick Douglass's newspapers.

2017. Sherman, Joan R. *African American Poetry of the Nineteenth Century: An Anthology.* Urbana: University of Illinois Press, 1992. Contains selections from Whitfield's poetry.

2018. ———— . *Invisible Poets: Afro-Americans of the Nineteenth Century.* Urbana: University of Illinois Press, 1974. Contains a biography of the African American Buffalo barber and analysis of his poetry.

2019. Whitfield, James Monroe. *America and Other Poems.* Buffalo: James S. Leavitt, 1853. Integrating the American revolution and the European revolutions of 1848 these antislavery poems mourned America's hypocrisy of freedom.

Walt Whitman

2020. Kaplan, Justin. *Walt Whitman: A Life.* New York: Simon and Schuster, 1980. In 1848, Whitman was dismissed as Democratic editor of the Brooklyn *Eagle* for turning it into a Free-Soil paper. Later in September he published the Brooklyn *Freeman*, dedicated to opposing slavery in the new territories.

2021. Klammer, Martin. *Whitman, Slavery, And the Emergence of* Leaves of Grass. University Park: Pennsylvania State University Press, 1995. In 1856, Whitman wrote but did not publish *"The Eighteenth Presidency!,"* a vehement attack against the weak Presidents of the 1850s. He opposed the Fugitive Slave Law because it jeopardized the rights of Northern communities. Bibliography on slavery and the literature of the period.

2022. Reynolds, David S. *Walt Whitman's America: A Cultural Biography.* New York: Alfred A. Knopf, 1995. Whitman's Free Soil activism was crushed by the accession of Fillmore and the passage of the Compromise. He always regarded Fillmore as a weak and wicked leader.

2023. Sewell, Richard H. "Walt Whitman, John P. Hale, and the Free Democracy: An Unpublished Letter." *New England Quarterly* 34 (June 1961): 239–42. In 1852, Whitman urged Hale to run for President on his Free-Soil principles, which surpassed those of the "drag-parties" supporting the Compromise.

2024. Whitman, Walt. *The Eighteenth Presidency!,* ed. Edward F. Grier. Lawrence: University of Kansas Press, 1956. Whitman's unpublished diatribe against weak Northern politicians who compromised with slavery. Whitman sought a redeemer President from the ranks of young working men in the free states.

Chapter 10

Post-Presidential Career

A. GENERAL WORKS

2025. Boorstin, Daniel J. "Saving a National Resource: An Address on the Role of Former Presidents in American Public Life." In *Farewell to the Chief: Former Presidents in American Public Life,* ed. Richard Norton Smith and Timothy Walsh. Worland, NY: High Plains Publishing Co., Inc., 1990. Refers to the unique period at the beginning of the Civil War when there were five living former Presidents including Fillmore.

2026. Clark, James C. *Faded Glory, Presidents Out of Power.* New York: Praeger Publishers, 1985. Political biography with special reference to the election of 1856.

2027. Cunningham, Homer F. *The Presidents' Last Years: George Washington to Lyndon Johnson.* Jefferson, NC: McFarland & Company, Inc., Publishers, 1989. A fair account of Fillmore's busy life.

2028. Martin, Asa E. *After the White House.* State College, PA: Penns Valley Publishers, Inc., 1951. Good summary of Fillmore's post-presidential years.

2029. McCoy, Donald J. "Be Yourself: Harry S. Truman as a Former President." In *Farewell to the Chief: Former Presidents in American Public Life,* ed. Richard Norton Smith and Timothy Walsh. Worland, NY: High Plains Publishing Co., Inc., 1990. Fillmore was one of the longest living former Presidents.

B. TRAVELS

2030. Coulter, E. Merton. "Presidential Visits to Georgia During Antebellum Times." *Georgia Historical Quarterly* 5 (Fall 1971): 329–61. Fillmore was enthusiastically received during his 1854 Southern tour.

2031. Crews, Clyde F. "The Political Gateway to the South: Presidents in Louisville." *Filson Club History Quarterly* 56 (April 1982): 181–200. An account of Fillmore's arrival in 1854.

2032. Everett, Edward. "Mr. Everett's Oration on Washington." *Proceedings of the Massachusetts Historical Society* 4 (1860): 86–106. Reports Fillmore heard the famous lecture in Albany in March 1857.

2033. Garrett, Franklin M. *Atlanta and Environs: A Chronicle of Its People and Events.* Athens: University of Georgia Press, 1969 [1954]. 3 vols. Volume One reprints a newspaper account of Fillmore's enthusiastic reception in 1854.

2034. Oliphant, Mary C. Simms, et al., eds. *The Letters of William Gilmore Simms.* Columbia: University of South Carolina Press, 1954. 5 vols. 3. In 1854 the writer invited Fillmore to his South Carolina plantation.

2035. Peterson, William J. "The Rock Island Railroad Excursion of 1854." *Minnesota History* 15 (December 1934): 405–20. Local sources describe Fillmore and his daughter enjoying a northern tour where he praised internal improvements.

2036. Poore, Ben: Perly. "Waifs from Washington, No. VIII." *Gleason's Pictorial Drawing-Room Companion,* March 5, 1853. Fillmore intended to tour the South soon after leaving office.

2037. Powell, C. Perry. *Lincoln Day by Day: A Chronology, 1809–1865.* Washington, DC: Lincoln Sesquicentennial Commission, 1960. 3 vols. 2. In June 1854, Fillmore made a brief speech in Lincoln's hometown of Springfield.

2038. "Rails West, The Rock Island Excursion of 1854 as Reported by Charles F. Babcock." *Minnesota History* 34 (Winter 1954): 133–43. Reprints a letter mentioning Fillmore's internal improvement speech at St. Paul.

2039. Severance, Frank H., ed. *Millard Fillmore Papers, Publications of the Buffalo Historical Society, Vol. 10.* Buffalo: Buffalo Historical Society, 1907. 429–445. Addresses made on the 1854 American tours and the European tour in 1855–56.

2040. ———, ed. *Millard Fillmore Papers, Publications of the Buffalo Historical Society, Vol. 11.* Buffalo: Buffalo Historical Society, 1907. 351–60. Letters during European trip.

C. THE ELECTION OF 1856, GENERAL WORKS

2041. Burnham, W. Dean. *Presidential Ballots, 1836–1892.* Baltimore: Johns Hopkins University Press, 1955. The distribution of the presidential vote by counties.

2042. Congressional Quarterly. *Guide to U.S. Elections.* Washington, DC: Congressional Quarterly Inc., 1975. Contains voting data on the presidential, gubernatorial, and congressional elections.

2043. Davis, Kenneth C. *Don't Know Much About the Civil War?* New York: William Morrow and Company, Inc., 1996. Chronological reference for context of the 1856 election and Fillmore's former administration.

2044. Dinkin, Robert J. *Campaigning in America: A History of Election Practices.* Westport, CT: Greenwood Press, 1989. Surveys campaign techniques in 1856.

2045. "Election Returns . . . New York." *Tribune Almanac, 1857.* New York: New York Tribune, 1857. 46, 64. New York State's 1856 county election returns plus the returns from the "free" and "slave" states.

2046. Ellis, John Tracy. *American Catholicism.* Chicago: University of Chicago Press, 1956. Contains descriptions of mid-century prejudice and summarizes the First Plenary Council of American Catholic Bishops in 1852 which counseled patriotism but not partisan politics.

2047. Gienapp, William E. " 'Politics Seem to Enter into Everything': Political Culture in the North, 1840–1860." In *Essays on American Antebellum Politics, 1840–1860,* ed. Stephen E. Maizlish and John J. Kushma. College Station: Texas A&M Press, 1982. Concludes that sectionalism and nativism revitalized politics. Both the Republicans and Know-Nothings recruited younger men with weak ties to the older parties.

2048. Havel, James T. *U.S. Presidential Candidates and the Elections: A Biographical and Historical Guide.* New York: Simon & Schuster Macmillan, 1996. 2 vols. Volume One contains biographies of Fillmore and Donelson. Volume Two includes facts on the 1856 elections.

2049. Holt, Michael F. "1856." In *Running for President: The Candidates and Their Images,* ed. Arthur M. Schlesinger, Jr. New York: Simon and Shuster, 1994. 2 vols.

1: 221–39. Despite Know-Nothing pressure to promote nativism Fillmore emphasized his Unionist goals. Includes campaign materials using Fillmore's image.

2050. Johnson, Willis Fletcher. *History of the State of New York: Political and Governmental.* Syracuse: Syracuse Press, Inc., 1922. 6 vols. Volume Six contains the Know-Nothing and Whig party platforms supporting Fillmore.

2051. McClure, A. K. *Our Presidents and How We Make Them.* New York: Harper & Brothers Publishers, 1900. First-hand observations on the nominations, party platforms, and election of 1856.

2052. Miles, William. *The Image Makers: A Bibliography of American Presidential Campaign Biographies.* Metuchen, NJ: Scarecrow Press, 1979. Unique reference for partisan biographies including those of Fillmore and Donelson.

2053. ———, comp. *The People's Voice: An Annotated Bibliography of American Presidential Campaign Newspapers, 1828–1984.* Westport, CT: Greenwood Press, 1987. List of 1856 partisan papers including 15 from the American party and Know-Nothing movement.

2054. Minnigerode, Meade. "Presidential Campaigns: The Buchaneers, 1856." *Saturday Evening Post,* March 17, 1929, 39–40, 42, 157, 158. Popular history of the 1856 election.

2055. "National Platforms." *Tribune Almanac, 1858.* New York: New York Tribune, 1858. 33–37. Reprints the 1856 party platforms.

2056. Nevins, Allen. *Ordeal of the Union, Volume 2: A House Dividing, 1852–1857.* New York: Charles Scribner's Sons, 1947. Covers Fillmore's presidential defeat in 1856.

2057. *New York Times. Great Presidential Campaigns as Reported in the New York Times.* New York: Microfilming Corporation of America, 1980. This guide highlights 42 New York *Times* references to election reports between January 24, 1854, and March 5, 1857.

2058. Nichols, Roy F., and Philip S. Klein. "Election of 1856: Emergence of the Republican Party." In *History of American Presidential Elections 1789–1968,* ed. Arthur M. Schlesinger, Jr. New York: Chelsea House Publishers, 1971. 4 vols. 2: 1007–94. Examines the effect of Fillmore's nomination on the campaign. Includes contemporary readings and voting statistics.

2059. Roseboom, Eugene H. *A History of Presidential Elections.* New York: Macmillan Company, 1969.

2060. Schlesinger, Arthur M., Jr., ed. *The Coming to Power: Critical Elections in American History.* New York: Chelsea House Publications, 1971. A one-volume selection of essays from *History of American Presidential Elections 1789–1968,* containing the Nichols and Klein chapter, "Election of 1856."

2061. Silbey, Joel H. " 'The Surge of Republican Power': Partisan Antipathy, American Social Conflict, and the Coming of the Civil War." In Silbey, *The Partisan Imperative: The Dynamics of American Politics Before the Civil War.* New York: Oxford University Press, 1985. Southern fear of New England's reformism increased as Republicans and nativists established a powerful Northern antislavery/anti-Catholic coalition.

2062. Thomas, G. Scott. *The Pursuit of the White House: A Handbook of Presidential Election Statistics and History.* Westport, CT: Greenwood Press, 1987.

D. THE AMERICAN AND WHIG PARTIES

2063. Abernathy, Thomas P. "Donelson, Andrew Jackson." *DAB* (1959), 3, pt. 1: 363–64. Fillmore's Vice Presidential candidate.

2064. Adams, Bluford. *E Pluribus Barnum: The Great Showman and the Making of U.S. Popular Culture.* Minneapolis: University of Minneapolis Press, 1997. Barnum's test vote in September 1856 had Fillmore in the lead.

2065. Albion, Robert G. "George Law." *DAB* (1961), 6, pt. 1: 39–40. Law lost the Know-Nothing nomination to Fillmore. He later wrote anti-Fillmore material for Frémont.

2066. [American Party]. *Is Millard Fillmore an Abolitionist?* Boston: American Patriot Office, 1856. Party pamphlet used in New England to attract the antislavery vote. It used excerpts from the Democrats' anti-Fillmore pamphlet *The Agitation of Slavery,* which described him as opposed to slavery.

2067. Anbinder, Tyler. *Nativism and Slavery: The Northern Know-Nothings and the Politics of the 1850s.* New York: Oxford University Press, 1992. Fillmore did not promote the nativist anti-immigrant agenda. He emphasized Unionism as an alternative to sectional politics.

2068. Baker, Jean H. *Ambivalent Americans, The Know-Nothing Party in Maryland.* Baltimore: Johns Hopkins University Press, 1977. Analysis of Fillmore's only statewide victory.

2069. Barre, W. L. *The Life and Public Services of Millard Fillmore.* Buffalo: Wagner, McKim & Co., 1856. American Party biography promoting his Unionism.

2069a. Basso, Ralph. "Nationalism, Nativism, and the Black Soldier: Daniel Ullman, A Biography of a Man Living in a Period of Transition, 1810–1892." Ph.D. diss., St. John's University, 1986. A New York state associate of Fillmore in the Whig and American parties.

2070. Baum, Dale, and Dale T. Knobel. "Anatomy of a Realignment: New York Presidential Politics, 1848–1860." *New York History* 65 (January 1984): 61–81. Statistical analysis concludes that a large percentage of 1852 Whigs voted Know-Nothing in 1856 but did not necessarily vote Republican in 1860.

2071. Beals, Carleton. *Brass-Knuckle Crusade: The Great Know-Nothing Conspiracy, 1820–1860.* New York: Hastings House Publications, 1960. Fillmore does not fare well in this colorful but helter-skelter narrative against nativism.

2072. Berger, Mark L. *The Revolution in the New York Party System, 1840–1860.* Port Washington, DC: Kennikat Press, 1973. Analysis of political realignments in the nativist movement that led to later Republican success.

2073. Billington, Ray Allen. *The Protestant Crusade, 1800–1860: A Study of the Origins of American Nativism.* Chicago: Quadrangle Books, 1964 [1938]. Still a valuable work on antebellum nativism and political Know-Nothings. Extensive notes and bibliography on contemporary sources.

2074. ———. "Tentative Bibliography of Anti-Catholic Propaganda in the United States (1800–1860)." *Catholic History Review* 18 (January 1933): 492–513. Unannotated list of anti-Catholic literature and serial publications widely circulated in the United States.

2075. ———. "The Know-Nothing Uproar." *American Heritage,* February 1959, 58–61, 94–97. Illustrated history of nativism and the American Party.

2075a. Bladek, John David. "America for Americans: The Southern Know Nothing Party and the Politics of Nativism, 1854–1856." Ph.D. diss., University of Washington, 1998. Southern Know-Nothings were unionist, nativists, and committed to slavery. Fillmore Whigs lost the south as they narrowed the movement into a unionist party.

2075b. Blades, Gene Granville. "The Politics of Sectional Avoidance: Maryland and the American Party." Ph.D. diss., The Catholic University of America, 1990. A genuine nativism made it a successful state party and gave Fillmore the state's electoral vote in 1856.

2076. Bowers, Douglas. "Ideology and Political Parties in Maryland, 1851–1856." *Maryland Historical Magazine* 64 (Fall 1969): 197–217. Examines the political instability and nativist opportunism that led to Fillmore's only state majority.

2077. Broussard, James H. "Some Determinants of Know-Nothing Electoral Strength in the South, 1856." *Louisiana History* 7 (Winter 1966): 5–18. The American Party was based on old Whig majorities, Union sentiment, old rivalries with Democrats, and the fear of immigrants.

2078. Brownson, Orestes. "The Know-Nothing Platform." *Brownson's Quarterly Review* 17 (October 1855): 473–98. Argues that American Catholics did not use politics to spread a religious empire.

2079. ———— . "The Know-Nothings." *Brownson's Quarterly Review,* 16 (October 1854): 447–87. Assures readers that time will integrate Catholic immigrants into Americans.

2080. ———— . "The Know-Nothings, Message of the President of the United States, December 1854." *Brownson's Quarterly Review* 17 (January 1855): 114–35. Defends Catholics against Know-Nothing attacks.

2081. ———— . "Native Americanism." *Brownson's Quarterly Review* 16 (July 1854): 328–54. Describes the reemergence of secret societies against Catholics.

2082. ———— . "The Presidential Election, Parties and Their Candidates." *Brownson's Quarterly Review* 18 (October 1856): 504–13. This influential independent Catholic editor respected Fillmore but could not support him or the Know-Nothings.

2083. Burgess, John W. *Reminiscences of an American Scholar.* New York: Columbia University Press, 1934. Remembers the violent confrontations in Tennessee between Fillmore Whigs and Buchanan Democrats.

2084. Burlingame, Michael. *The Inner World of Abraham Lincoln.* Chicago: University of Illinois Press, 1994. Mrs. Mary Lincoln preferred Fillmore in 1856. She believed he would keep foreigners in check and probably be elected with southern support in 1860.

2085. Cantrell, Greg. "Southerner and Nativist: Kenneth Rayner and the Ideology of 'Americanism' " *North Carolina Historical Review* 69 (April 1992): 131–47. Rayner hoped to split electoral tickets and throw the election into the House of Representatives.

2085a. Carey, Anthony Gene. "Too Southern to be Americans: Proslavery Politics and the Failure of the Know-Nothing Party in Georgia, 1854–1856." *Civil War History* 41 (March 1995): 22–40. Limited to anti-Democrat and pro-slavery positions they had little in common with their northern counterparts.

2086. Carlson, Adina Cheree. "Order, The Secret, and the Kill: The Rhetoric of the Know-Nothing Party." Ph.D. diss., University of Southern California, 1985. Know-Nothings created compelling public drama by stressing threatened American values.

2087. Carman, Harry J., and Reinhard H. Luthin. "Some Aspects of the Know-Nothing Movement Reconsidered." *South Atlantic Quarterly* 39 (April 1940): 213–34. Political review.

2088. Carroll, Anna Ella. *A Review of Pierce's Administration: Showing Its Only Popular Measures to Have Originated with the Executive of Millard Fillmore.* New York: Miller, Orton & Mulligan, 1856. Praise for Fillmore and the compromise measures.

2089. ———. *Which? Fillmore or Buchanan!* Boston: James French and Company, 1856. American Party campaign pamphlet praising Fillmore and damning Buchanan.

2090. Cassidy, Vincent H., and Amos E. Simpson. *Henry Watkins Allen of Louisiana.* Baton Rouge: Louisiana State University Press, 1964. Allen campaigned for Fillmore. He asked his audiences to remember the calm at the end of his presidency.

2091. Chamberlain, Ivory. *Biography of Millard Fillmore.* Buffalo: Thomas & Lathrop, 1856. An American Party campaign biography. Enhanced by the aid of Thomas M. Foote, Fillmore's friend, political colleague, and editor of the Buffalo *Commercial Advertiser.*

2092. Comfort, W. W. "Thomas Garrett's Letters to Two Ladies in Britain." *Delaware History* 4 (March 1950): 37–47. This antislavery Quaker called Fillmore a cipher and unable to get a majority in any state.

2093. Coryell, Janet L. "Anna Ella Carroll and the Historians." *Civil War History* 35 (June 1989): 120–37. Review essay on Carroll's partisan publications for Fillmore.

2094. ———. "Duty with Delicacy: Anna Ella Carroll of Maryland." In *Women and American Foreign Policy Lobbyists, Critics, and Insiders,* ed. Edward P. Crapol. Westport, CT: Greenwood Press, 1987. Examines her 1856 campaign material promoting the American Party and Fillmore.

2095. Curran, Thomas Joseph. "Know-Nothings of New York." Ph.D. diss., Columbia University, 1963. Fillmore Whigs believed they could use nativism to defeat Seward Whigs.

2096. ———. "Seward and the Know-Nothings." *New-York Historical Society Quarterly* 51 (April 1967): 141–59. Fillmore Know-Nothings failed to defeat Seward's reelection to the Senate in 1855.

2097. Dalzell, Robert F., Jr. *Enterprising Elite: The Boston Associates and the World They Made.* Cambridge: Harvard University Press, 1987. The mercantile group settled on Fillmore as the only candidate to sustain the Union and north-south commerce.

2098. Farnham, Wallace D. "The 'Religious Issue' in American Politics: An Historical Commentary." *Queen's Quarterly* 68 (Spring 1961): 47–65. Places the Know-Nothings and the American Party within the historical context of American anti-Catholic sentiment.

2099. *Fillmore and Donelson, Songs for the Campaign.* New York: Robert M. DeWitt, 1856. Rallying songs for the American Party and Fillmore. Includes extracts from Fillmore's Albany campaign speech.

2100. Fischer, Roger A. *Tippecanoe and Trinkets Too: The Material Culture of American Presidential Campaigns, 1828–1984.* Urbana: University of Illinois Press, 1988. States that the Fillmore-Donelson ticket generated over two dozen ribbons and badges devoted to Unionism.

2101. Godwin, Parke. *Political Essays.* New York: Dix, Edwards & Co., 1856. Set of essays denouncing the Kansas-Nebraska Act and reviewing the demise of the Whig party which was "useless for good and painful to behold."

2102. Guenter, Scot M. *The American Flag, 1777–1924: Cultural Shifts from Creation to Codification.* Rutherford: Fairleigh Dickinson University Press, 1990. Know-Nothings were the first to appropriate the American flag as a symbol for an ethnically pure elite.

2103. Hales, Jean Bartlett Gould. " 'Co-Laborers in the Cause': Women in the Antebellum Nativist Movement." *Civil War History* 25 (June 1979): 119–38. Popular sentiment about women's innate moral superiority and patriotism compelled nativists to recruit them for anti-immigrant crusades.

2104. ———. "The Shaping of Nativist Sentiment, 1848–1860." Ph.D. diss., Stanford University, 1973. Examines partisan newspapers and literature.

2105. Hesseltine, William B. *The South in American History.* New York: Prentice-Hall, Inc., 1947 [1936]. Southern Know-Nothings and Whigs trusted Fillmore but they feared a Republican President more. As the campaign drew to a close they deserted his candidacy for the security of the pro-Southern Democratic party.

2106. Hill, Benj. H., Jr. *Senator Benjamin H. Hill of Georgia: His Life, Speeches and Writings.* Atlanta: H. C. Hudgins & Co., 1891. Supported the American Party in 1856 in order to save the Union. Defended Fillmore against accusations that he had nothing to do with the Compromise of 1850.

2107. Hilliard, Henry W. *Politics and Pen Pictures at Home and Abroad.* New York: G. P. Putnam's Sons, 1892. Alabama Whig remembered Fillmore as an intelligent and dignified statesman. He campaigned for Fillmore in 1856 because of his national perspective and character.

2108. Hollcroft Temple R. "A Congressman's Letters on the Speaker Election in the Thirty-fourth Congress." *Mississippi Valley Historical Review* 43 (December 1956): 444–58. Edwin B. Morgan wrote a series of acrimonious letters against Fillmore Know-Nothings who were obstructing the Speaker elections in February 1856.

2109. Holt, Michael F. "Another Look at the Election of 1856." In *James Buchanan and the Politics of Crisis of the 1850s.*, ed. Michael J. Birkner. Selinsgrove: Susquehanna University Press, 1996. Analysis of intricate political efforts during the campaign gives credibility to Fillmore capturing the 1856 election.

2110. ———. "The Politics of Impatience: The Origins of Know-Nothingism." *Journal of American History* 60 (September 1973): 309–31. The convergence of national antipartyism and a disruptive economy aided the quick rise and fall of the Know-Nothings.

2111. Horrocks, Thomas. "The Know-Nothings." *American History Illustrated* 17 (January 1983): 22–29. Illustrated review of nativist organizations and Fillmore's 1856 campaign.

2112. Hurt, Peyton. "The Rise and Fall of the Know-Nothings in California." *California Historical Society Quarterly* 9 (March June 1930): 16–49, 99–128. Includes Fillmore's campaign appeal to former Whigs.

2113. Knobel, Dale T. *"America for the Americans: " The Nationalist Movement in the United States.* New York: Twayne Publishers, 1996. Nativists appreciated Fillmore's concern about immigrant voting abuses and commended his noninterventionist foreign policy while expanding American commerce.

2114. ———— . *Paddy and the Republic: Ethnicity and Nationality in Antebellum America.* Middletown: Wesleyan University Press, 1986. Examines language patterns that shaped popular nativist attitudes.

2115. "The Know-Nothings." *Whig Almanac, 1855.* New York: New York Tribune, 1855. 9–10. Analysis of the Know-Nothing party and the possibility that Fillmore would be its presidential candidate.

2116. Kraut, Alan M. "Nativism." In *Encyclopedia of American Political History: Studies of the Principal Movements and Ideas,* ed. Jack P. Greene. New York: Charles Scribner's Sons, 1984. 3 vols. 2: 863–77. Fillmore received 22% of the vote in 1856, but the American party could not broaden its appeal due to increasing sectionalism.

2117. Krout, John A. "The Maine Law in New York Politics." *New York History* 17 (July 1936): 260–72. The politicization of liquor in the 1850s crossed party lines and further weakened the Whig party before 1856.

2118. Kruschke, Earl R. "American Party (Know-Nothing)." *Encyclopedia of Third Parties in the United States.* Santa Barbara: ABC-CLIO, 1991. Review of the party's national politics.

2119. Latham, Frank B. *The Dred Scott Decision, March 6, 1857: Slavery and the Supreme Court's 'Self-Inflicted Wound.'* New York: Franklin Watts Inc., 1968. Contains an 1856 cartoon showing Fillmore settling sectional hostilities between Frémont and Buchanan.

2120. Leonard, Ira M., and Robert D. Parmet. *American Nativism, 1830–1860.* New York: Von Nostrand Reinhold Company, 1971. Substantial essay on nativism. Includes contemporary readings and historical evaluations.

2121. *Life of Millard Fillmore.* New York: R. M. DeWitt, 1856. Thirty-two-page pamphlet containing biographies of Fillmore and Donelson with Unionist rhetoric ascendant over nativism.

2122. Menendez, Albert J. *Religious Conflict in America.* New York: Garland Publishing, Inc., 1985. Contains a ten-page unannotated bibliography on nativism.

2123. "Monthly Report of Current Events—United States." *Harper's Monthly* 13 (August 1856): 402. Mentions Fillmore accepting the American Party nomination with a summary of his Albany campaign speech.

2124. "Monthly Report of Current Events—United States." *Harper's Monthly* 13 (November 1856): 839. Report on Fillmore's nomination at the Whig National Convention.

2125. Neely, Mark E., Jr. "Richard W. Thompson: The Persistent Know-Nothing." *Indiana Magazine of History* 72 (June 1976): 95–122. Prominent Midwest nativist.

2126. Nevins, Allen, and Frank Weitenkampf. *A Century of Political Cartoons and Caricature in the United States from 1800 to 1900.* New York: Octagon Books, 1975. Contains an American Party cartoon depicting Fillmore as an honest farmer watching the other candidates, shown as rats, scurrying for office.

2127. Overdyke, W. Darrell. *The Know-Nothing Party in the South.* Baton Rouge: Louisiana State University Press, 1950. Reviews the Southern strategy to elect Fillmore in 1856.

2128. Owsley, Harriet Chappell. "Andrew Jackson and His Ward, Andrew Jackson Donelson." *Tennessee Historical Quarterly* 41 (Summer 1982): 124–39. Like Andrew Jackson, Fillmore's running mate was trying to preserve the Union.

2129. Prendergast, William B. *The Catholic Voter in America Politics: The Passing of the Democratic Monolith.* Washington, DC: Georgetown University Press, 1999. Fillmore's faction of the American party fraternized with voting Catholics. Ironically, Maryland, the only state he carried, was the cradle of American Catholicism.

2130. Rawley, James A. *Race & Politics: "Bleeding Kansas" and the Coming of the Civil War.* Philadelphia: J. B. Lippincott Company, 1969. Kansas violence was the crucial issue in 1856 and Fillmore's silence on slavery demonstrated his failure to cope with the new sectional politics.

2131. Robertson, Alexander F. *Alexander Hugh Holmes Stuart 1807–1891.* Richmond: William Byrd Press, Inc., 1925. Includes twelve 1856 speeches supporting Fillmore and the American Party.

2132. Sacher, John M. "The Sudden Collapse of the Louisiana Whig Party." *Journal of Southern History* 65 (May 1999): 221–48. After Scott's nomination over Fillmore in 1852, Southern Whigs distrusted their Northern counterparts on the slavery question. They found the Know-Nothing party more attractive for the South in a national arena.

2133. Schelin, Robert C. "A Whig's Final Quest: Fillmore and the Know-Nothings." *Niagara Frontier* 26 (1979): 1–11. Fillmore wanted to use the American party as a vehicle for conservative Whigs to preserve the Union. He was not a militant nativist but he did want to stop the corrupt manipulation of naive immigrant voters.

2134. Scisco, Louis Dow. *Political Nativism in New York State.* New York: A M S Press Inc., 1968 [1901]. Dated but sound study on New York nativism and Know-Nothing factions in 1856.

2135. Sherman, John. *Recollections of Forty Years in the House, Senate and Cabinet*. Chicago: Werner Company, 1895. 2 vols. In Volume One Fillmore is credited with taking a strong campaign position against sectional politics.

2136. Shover, Kenneth B. "Another Look at the Late Whig Party: The Perspective of the Loyal Whig." *Historian* 48 (August 1986): 539–58. Conservative Whigs were reluctant to join in the fusionist politics of the American Party.

2137. ———. "The Free State Whigs and the Idea of a Conservative Strategy." *Mid-America* 54 (October 1972): 251–66. After 1852, Northern Whigs failed to revitalize their party and reluctantly accepted the Know-Nothing or Republican alternatives.

2138. Silbey, Joel H. "Parties and Politics in Mid-Nineteenth Century America: A Quantitative and Behavior Examination." In *The Rise and Fall of Political Parties in the United States, 1789–1989: The Congressional Roll Call Record*, ed. Joel H. Silbey. Brooklyn: Carlton Publishing Inc., 1991. Fillmore did well in the border states and Mississippi. He demonstrated that Whigs and anti-Democrats could still unite against the old Jacksonian forces.

2139. Snyder, Charles McCool. "Anna Ella Carroll, Political Strategist and Gadfly of President Fillmore." *Maryland Historical Magazine* 68 (Spring 1973): 36–63. Fillmore never read Carroll's campaign material and remained distant toward her.

2140. Soulé, Leon C. "Know-Nothing Party." In *The Encyclopedia of Southern History*, ed. David C. Roller and Robert W. Twyman. Baton Rouge: Louisiana State University Press, 1979. 692–93.

2141. Southwick, Leslie H., comp. "Andrew J. Donelson." In *Presidential Also-Rans and Running Mates, 1788–1980*. Jefferson, NC: McFarland & Company Inc., 1984. A Democrat whose personal prejudices led him into the Know-Nothing party.

2142. Stampp, Kenneth A. *America in 1857, A Nation on the Brink*. New York: Oxford University Press, 1990. Conservative Whigs were willing to vote for Fillmore, but Northern hatred for the Kansas-Nebraska Act gave most Whigs a bridge to the Republican party.

2143. Thompson, D. G. Brinton. *Ruggles of New York: A Life of Samuel B. Ruggles*. New York: A M S Press, 1968. This New York Whig wrote the party's resolutions nominating Fillmore.

2144. Whisker, James Biser, ed. *Anna Ella Carroll (1815–1893): American Political Writer of Maryland*. Lewistown, NY: Edwin Mellon Press, 1992. Collection of

Carroll's American party campaign pamphlets. She said Fillmore was the most illustrious President since Washington.

2145. Williams, Edwin. *The Life and Administration of Ex-President Fillmore.* New York: Edward Walker, 1856. A 50-page campaign pamphlet emphasizing Fillmore's dedication to the Constitution and Union. Includes extracts from speeches and a biographical sketch of Donelson.

2146. Winthrop, Robert C. *Addresses and Speeches on Various Occasions from 1852 to 1867.* Boston: Little, Brown and Company, 1867. 244–57, 292–308. Speeches for Fillmore by the Massachusetts Whig.

E. THE AMERICAN PARTY IN BUFFALO

2147. Gerber, David A. "Ambivalent Anti-Catholicism: Buffalo's American Protestant Elites Face the Challenge of the Catholic Church." *Civil War History* 30 (June 1984): 120–43. Protestant elites, including Fillmore, were apprehensive about the political influence of the Roman Catholic Church yet appreciated its charitable work, immigrant education, and social control.

2148. ———. *The Making of an American Pluralism: Buffalo, New York 1825–60.* Urbana: University of Chicago Press, 1989. Parts Three and Four describe the rise of ethnic diversity and nativist reaction in Buffalo. Fillmore was never an ideologue but at the urging of friends he used nativist organizations and their political party to run for President. Bibliography on local sources.

2149. Glasco, Lawrence Admiral. "Ethnicity and Social Structure: Irish, Germans and Native-Born of Buffalo, N.Y., 1850–1860." Ph.D. diss., State University of New York at Buffalo, 1973. A demographic study of Know-Nothing voting.

2150. Gredel, Stephen. "Immigration of Ethnic Groups to Buffalo Based upon Censuses of 1850, 1865 and 1892." *Niagara Frontier* 10 (Summer 1963): 42–56. Numerical breakdown of ethnic groups by ward and occupation.

2151. Horton, James Oliver, and Hartmut Keil. "African Americans and Germans in Mid-nineteenth Century Buffalo." In *Free People of Color, Inside the African American Community,* ed. James Oliver Horton. Washington, DC: Smithsonian Institution Press, 1993. Finds a more harmonious relationship between African Americans and Germans than between African Americans and the Irish. The study gives context to German support for the Republicans and Irish support for the Democrats in 1856. Neither group supported Fillmore.

2152. Lord, John C. "The Times of Men in the Hands of God: " *Quarter Century Sermon Delivered in the Central Presbyterian Church on Sabbath, November 8th,*

1860. Buffalo: Commercial Advertiser Steam Press, 1860. Reverend Lord admits publicly arguing against "the arrogant champions of popery" who want to use politics for sectarian goals. Fillmore attended this discourse and wished it published.

2153. O'Driscoll, M. Felicity. "Political Nativism in Buffalo, 1830–1860." *American Catholic Historical Society of Philadelphia, Records* 47 (1937): 279–319. Uses contemporary newspapers to describe anti-Catholic nativism, its poor electoral showing, and Fillmore's inability to carry Buffalo in 1856.

2154. Yox, Andrew P. "Bonds of Community: Buffalo's German Element, 1853–1871." *New York History* 66 (April 1985): 141–63. Reviews German immigrant visibility, their unity against nativism, and Fillmore's inability to get their votes.

F. THE DEMOCRATIC PARTY

2155. "The Claims of the Opposition." *Democratic Review* 38 (September 1856): 137–44. Claims there's a Fillmore-Frémont conspiracy to advance Federalist-Whig-Antimasonic principles.

2156. Davis, William C. *Breckinridge, Statesman: Soldier, Symbol.* Baton Rouge: Louisiana State University Press, 1974. Breckinridge, the Democratic Vice Presidential candidate, believed he might end up as Fillmore's Vice President or possibly the President if the election was thrown into the House of Representatives.

2157. DeBruhl, Marshall. *Sword of San Jacinto: A Life of Sam Houston.* New York: Random House, 1993. Houston was a good friend of Andrew Donelson, Fillmore's running-mate, but he did not publicly support their candidacy.

2158. (Democratic party). *The Agitation of Slavery: Who Commenced and Who Can End It? Buchanan and Fillmore Compared from the Record.* n. p. 1856. Anti-Fillmore pamphlet contending he was antislavery.

2159. Eaton, Clement. "Henry A. Wise and the Virginia Fire Eaters of 1856." *Mississippi Valley Historical Review* 21 (March 1935): 495–512. Governor Wise and the Democratic press thrashed the American Party and Fillmore Whigs.

2160. Klein, Philip S. *President James Buchanan, A Biography.* University Park: Pennsylvania State University Press, 1962. Standard political biography of the President.

2161. "Know-Nothingism." *Democratic Review* 37 (June 1856): 486–96. A Democratic analysis lumping the Seward and Fillmore partisans into a northern antislavery conspiracy.

2162. Kurian, George Thomas, ed. *The Encyclopedia of the Democratic Party.* Armonk, NY: M. E. Sharpe Inc., 1997. 2 vols.

2163. Milton, George Fort. *The Age of Hate: Andrew Johnson and the Radicals.* New York: Coward-McCann, Inc. 1930. The Tennessee Democrat and future President warned that Fillmore was a greater abolitionist than Frémont.

2164. Nichols, Roy F. *The Disruption of American Democracy.* New York: Macmillan Company, 1948. Follows the strategy and tactics of Buchanan's nomination and election.

2165. "The Present Condition of Parties in the United States." *Democratic Review* 38 (August 1856): 1–9. Fillmore's American Party is in a conspiracy with Frémont and Seward to defeat the Democrats.

2166. Rorabaugh, W. J. "Rising Democratic Spirits: Immigrants, Temperance, and Tamminy Hall, 1854–1860." *Civil War History.* 22 (June 1976): 138–57. Background on New York City immigrant opposition to prohibition and their related resistance to the Whig and Republican parties.

2167. Sears, L. M. "Slidell and Buchanan." *American Historical Review* 27 (July 1922): 709–30. John Slidell was Buchanan's campaign manager.

2168. Simpson, Craig M. *A Good Southerner: The Life of Henry A. Wise of Virginia.* Chapel Hill: University of North Carolina Press, 1985. Governor of Virginia and radical Southern Democrat who derided the Know-Nothings and wanted to discuss secession if Frémont was elected.

2169. Sloan, Irving J. *James Buchanan, 1791–1868: Chronology, Documents, Bibliographical Aids.* Dobbs Ferry, NY: Oceana Publications Inc., 1968.

2170. Trefousse, Hans L. *Andrew Johnson, A Biography.* New York: W. W. Norton & Company. 1989. The future President campaigned against the "antislavery" Fillmore in 1848 and against the "abolitionist" Fillmore in 1856.

2171. "The Union—The Dangers Which Beset It." *Democratic Review* 37 (February 1856): 89–104. Republican sectionalism and American Party nativism are dangers to the country.

2172. Wise, John S. *Recollections of Thirteen Presidents.* New York: Doubleday, Page & Company, 1906. Remembers the increased visibility of political cartoons in the 1856 election. One had Fillmore as an abolitionist walking arm in arm with a African American woman.

G. THE REPUBLICAN PARTY

2173. Abbott, Robert H. *Cobbler in Congress: The Life of Henry Wilson, 1812–1875.* Lexington: University Press of Kentucky, 1972. Massachusetts Senator worked to fuse Know-Nothings and Republicans.

2174. Allen, Stephen M. *The Old and New Republican Parties.* Boston: D. Lothrop & Co., 1886. Brief mention of the Fillmore administration and the 1856 election.

2175. Bancroft, Frederic., ed. *Speeches, Correspondence and Political Papers of Carl Schurz.* New York: G. P. Putnam's Sons, 1913. 5 vols. 1: 25, 30. After the election of Buchanan, Schurz predicted his administration would end the Democratic party as Fillmore's had ended the Whig party.

2176. Bartlett, Ruhl J. *John C. Frémont and the Republican Party.* New York: Da Capo Press, 1970 [1930]. Examines Frémont's political career.

2177. Basler, Roy P., ed. *The Collected Works of Abraham Lincoln.* New Brunswick: Rutgers University Press, 1953. 8 vols. Volume Two covers Lincoln's campaign to recruit Fillmore men into the Republican party. In Volume Three there is a reference to Fillmore refusing to become a Republican.

2178. Billotta, James D. "Race and the Rise of the Republican Party, 1848–1860." Ph.D. diss., State University of New York at Buffalo, 1985. Pervasive belief in the inferiority of African Americans motivated most Republican politicians to adopt policies of slave containment in the South and the colonization of free African Americans.

2179. Booraem, Hendrick, V. *The Formation of the Republican Party in New York: Politics and Conscience in the Antebellum North.* New York: New York University Press, 1983. Uses local sources to narrate the party's development.

2180. Bryant, William Cullen., II., comp. *Power for Sanity: Selected Editorials of William Cullen Bryant, 1829–1861.* New York: Fordham University Press, 1994. After Buchanan's election, the Republican Bryant dismissed Fillmore to "obscurity and contempt."

2181. Byrne, Frank L. *Prophet of Prohibition: Neal Dow and His Crusade.* Madison: University of Wisconsin, 1961. The temperance reformer subordinated his anti-liquor campaign to highlight the election of Republicans.

2182. Crandall, Andrew Wallace. *The Early History of the Republican Party.* Boston: Richard G. Bodger, Publisher, 1930. Substantial narrative on the nominations and campaigns of the 1856 election.

2183. Crouthamel, James L. *Bennet's* New York Herald *and the Rise of the Popular Press.* Syracuse: Syracuse University Press, 1989. James Gordon Bennet supported Frémont because he was uncontaminated by the corruption and sectionalism of the old parties.

2184. ——— . *James Watson Webb, A Biography.* Middletown: Wesleyan University Press, 1969. The editor of the New York *Courier and Inquirer* ridiculed Fillmore's campaign.

2185. Davis, William C. "John C. Fremont: A Profile of the 'Pathfinder'." *American History Illustrated* 5 (May 1970): 4–11, 44–47.

2186. Donald, David Herbert. *Lincoln.* New York: Simon & Schuster, 1995. Lincoln made it his mission to sway Fillmore Whigs and Know-Nothings to the Republican party.

2187. Fehrenbacher, Don E. "The Origins and Purpose of Lincoln's House-Divided Speech." *Mississippi Valley Historical Review* 46 (March 1960): 615–43. Lincoln's famous speech originated in his 1856 campaign against the Fillmore forces in Illinois.

2188. Field, Phyllis F. *The Politics of Race in New York: The Struggle for Black Suffrage in the Civil War Era.* Ithaca: Cornell University Press, 1982. High property qualifications limited free African American suffrage. African American conventions supported the Republican ticket because its views were closer to their petitions for total male suffrage.

2189. Fischer, Roger A. "The Republican Presidential Campaigns of 1856 and 1860: Analysis Through Artifacts." *Civil War History* 27 (June 1981): 123–37. Republicans inherited the Whig inclination for mass promotional campaign materials. Many anti-Fillmore items claimed he was controlled by the South.

2190. Foner, Eric. *Free Soil, Free Labor, Free Men: The Ideology of the Republican Party before the Civil War.* New York: Oxford University Press, 1970. Republicans made a great effort to attract Fillmore Whigs and those nativists disenchanted with old politicians leading their new party.

2191. Gienapp, William E. "The Crime Against Sumner: The Caning of Charles Sumner and the Rise of the Republican Party." *Civil War History* 25 (September 1979): 218–45. The emotional response to Sumner's caning by a proslavery congressman increased Republican strength, solidified the Democratic South, and crippled Fillmore's campaign in both sections.

2192. ———— . "Nativism and the Creation of a Republican Majority in the North before the Civil War." *Journal of American History* 72 (December 1985): 529–59. In order to succeed, Republicans needed nativists to combine in a single opposition against the Slave Power and Catholicism.

2193. ———— . *The Origins of the Republican Party, 1852–1856.* New York: Oxford University Press, 1987. Major work on the formation of the Republican and Know-Nothing parties. Uses the Fillmore Papers and numerous other primary sources to enhance its description of the political maneuvering within the two parties to find common ground and win elections. Bibliographic essay and appendix on voting behavior.

2194. Ginsberg, Judah B. "Barnburners, Free Soilers, and the New York Republican Party." *New York History* 57 (October 1976): 475–500. Examines antislavery Democrats who entered the Republican party.

2195. Greeley, Horace. *The American Conflict: A History of the Great Rebellion in the United States of America, 1860–65.* Hartford: O. D. Case & Company, 1867. 2 vols. 1: 248. Fillmore's campaign began the gross misapprehension that a Republican success would bring a Southern rebellion.

2196. Harrington, Fred Harvey. *Fighting Politician: Major General N. P. Banks.* Philadelphia: University of Pennsylvania Press, 1948. Speaker of the House from Massachusetts, he helped organize the Republican party and sponsored Frémont for President.

2197. ———— . "Frémont and the North Americans." *American Historical Review* 44 (July 1939): 842–48. Describes how Frémont obtained support from antislavery Know-Nothings without antagonizing ethnic voters.

2198. Hesseltine, William B., and Rex G. Fisher, eds. *Trimmers, Trucklers & Temporizers: Notes of Murat Halstead from the Political Conventions of 1856.* Madison: State Historical Society of Wisconsin, 1961. Halstead, a journalist for Greeley, ridiculed the American Party and Fillmore's nomination.

2199. Hoffert, Sylvia D. "The Brooks-Sumner Affair." *Civil War Times Illustrated,* October 1972, 35–40. Illustrated essay on the caning of Senator Sumner.

2200. Isely, Jeter Allen. *Horace Greeley and the Republican Party 1853–1861.* Princeton: Princeton University Press, 1947. Greeley was incredulous that Fillmore accepted the American Party nomination.

2201. Keil, Hartmut. "German Immigrants and African-Americans in Mid-Nineteenth Century America." In *Enemy Images in American History,* ed. Ragnhild

Fiebig-von Hase and Ursula Lehmkuhl. Providence RI: Berghahn Books, 1996. Republicans influenced German-Americans by reprinting the distinguished German scientist Alexander von Humbolt's recently published condemnation of American slavery.

2202. Kurian, George Thomas, ed. *The Encyclopedia of the Republican Party.* Armonk, NY: M. E. Sharpe Inc., 1997. 2 vols.

2203. Lyman, Darius. *Leaven for Doughfaces; Or, Threescore and Ten Parables Touching Slavery.* Cincinnati: Bangs and Company, 1856. Satire using a Fillmore-like Presidential candidate for the "ignoramus" party.

2204. Mickey, Earnest. *Henry Wilson: Practical Radical, a Portrait of a Politician.* Port Washington, DC: Kennikat Press, 1971. Senator helped to fuse the Massachusetts Know-Nothings and Republicans for the presidential election.

2205. Nevins, Allen. *Frémont, Pathmarker of the West.* New York: Frederick Ungar Publishing Co. 1961. 2 vols. Highlights Frémont's explorations and military career.

2206. "Party Platforms in 1856." *Tribune Almanac, 1857.* New York: New York Tribune, 1857. 42–43. Reprints the Republican platform and the substance of the Democratic and American parties.

2207. Potter, David M. *Lincoln and His Party in the Secession Crisis.* New Haven: Yale University Press, 1942. Republicans disregarded Fillmore's warning that the Union might dissolve after a Republican victory.

2208. Rankin, Henry B. *Personal Recollections of Abraham Lincoln.* New York: G. P. Putnam's Sons, 1916. Recalls Lincoln persuading a young Fillmore partisan to vote for Frémont.

2209. Renda, Lex. "Slavery, Law, Liquor, and Politics: The Case of *Wynehamer v. The People.*" *Mid America* 80 (Winter 1998): 35–53. Kansas violence and Sumner's beating subordinated prohibition in New York State.

2210. Schwartz, Thomas F. "Lincoln, Form Letters, and Fillmore Men." *Illinois Historical Journal* 78 (Spring 1985): 65–70. Lincoln urged Fillmore men to vote for Frémont.

2211. Silbey, Joel H. " 'The Undisguised Connection', Know Nothings into Republicans: New York as a Test Case." In Silbey, *The Partisan Imperative: The Dynamics of American Politics Before the Civil War.* New York: Oxford University Press, 1985. Describes Republican success at soliciting Know-Nothings.

2212. Southwick, Leslie H., comp. "John Charles Frémont." In *Presidential Also-Rans and Running Mates, 1788–1980.* Jefferson, NC: McFarland & Company Inc., 1984. Chronology and biography.

2213. Thomas, John L. *The Liberator: William Lloyd Garrison, A Biography.* Boston Little, Brown and Company, 1963. Unexpectedly told his readers that if one were to vote, it should be for Frémont.

2214. Ulm, Aaron Hardy. "Third Parties We Have Known." *Collier's,* February 14, 1920, 18, 40, 42, 44. Mentions Fillmore's candidacy as the probable cause for Frémont's defeat.

2215. Upham, Charles Wentworth. *Life, Explorations and Public Services of John Charles Frémont.* Boston: Ticknor and Fields, 1856. Frémont's campaign biography.

2216. Wesley, Charles H. "The Participation of Negroes in Anti-Slavery Political Parties." *Journal of Negro History* 29 (January 1944): 32–74. Northern African Americans who could vote favored Frémont.

2217. Wilson, Henry. *History of the Rise and Fall of the Slave Power in America.* New York: Negro Universities Press, 1969 [1872]. 3 vols. Volume Two describes his participation in the organization of the Republican party. He says Fillmore was a man of ability with conservative tendencies and under the influence of the Slave Power.

2218. Zabriskie, George A. "The Pathfinder." *New York Historical Society Quarterly* 31 (January 1947): 5–17. A brief biography with photographs and memorial.

H. FILLMORE AND THE CIVIL WAR

2219. Baringer, William E. *A House Divided: Lincoln as President Elect.* Springfield: Abraham Lincoln Association, 1945. Mentions Lincoln's visit with Fillmore in February 1861.

2220. Basler, Roy P., ed. *The Collected Works of Abraham Lincoln.* New Brunswick: Rutgers University Press, 1953. 8 vols. Volume Five and Volume Six refer to Fillmore writing Lincoln on behalf of his nephew. First, to appoint him a lieutenant. Second, to reevaluate his dismissal for intemperance.

2221. Blaisdell, Thomas C., Jr., and Peter Sely. *The American Presidency in Political Cartoons, 1776–1976.* Santa Barbara: Peregine Smith Inc., 1976. Contains an 1861 cartoon lampooning a fictional gathering of former Presidents trying to settle the secession crisis.

2222. Brummer, Sidney David. *Political History of New York State During the Period of the Civil War.* New York: A M S Press Inc., 1967 [1910]. Mentions Fillmore supporting the Union party and his early support for the war.

2223. Burlingame, Michael, ed. *Lincoln Observed: Civil War Dispatches of Noah Brooks.* Baltimore: Johns Hopkins University Press, 1998. Fillmore mentioned as a compromise candidate at the 1864 Democratic Presidential Convention.

2224. Cox, Samuel S. *Union-Disunion-Reunion: Three Decades of Federal Legislation, 1855–1885.* Providence: J. A. & R. A. Reid, Publishers, 1885. On July 26, 1861, Cox proposed a committee of seven citizens, including Fillmore, to organize a larger peace commission.

2225. De Bow, J. D. B. "Presidential Candidates and Aspirants." *De Bow's Review* 29 (July 1860): 92–103. Reports Fillmore as a possible candidate.

2226. Dix, Morgan. *Memoirs of John A. Dix.* New York: Harper & Brothers, 1883. 2 vols. Volume Two reports on the "Pine Street Meeting" in New York City to find a peaceable means to quell secession. Fillmore, though not present, endorsed the meeting and was appointed to a committee to visit the South. He was unable to go.

2227. Dudley, Harold M. "The Election of 1864." *Mississippi Valley Historical Review* 18 (March 1932): 500–18. Includes a letter from Fillmore giving his support to the Democratic presidential candidate Gen. George B. McClellan.

2228. Dyer, Thomas G. *Secret Yankees: The Union Circle in Confederate Atlanta.* Baltimore: Johns Hopkins University Press, 1999. Letters from a local unionist to the Atlanta *Intelligencer* in 1860 condemn abolitionists and fire-eaters while promoting men like Fillmore.

2229. "Ex-President Fillmore Opposes Lincoln." *Journal of the Illinois State Historical Society* 46 (Autumn 1953): 302. Fillmore wanted an administration that stressed peace and union. He also complimented the battle courage of naturalized citizens.

2230. Harris, William C. "Conservative Unionists and the Presidential Election of 1864." *Civil War History* 38 (December 1992): 298–318. Fillmore refused consideration as a presidential candidate or to campaign for McClellan, though he believed the Democrat was the last hope to restore the Union.

2231. Johannsen, Robert W. *Lincoln, the South, and Slavery: The Political Dimension.* Baton Rouge: Louisiana State University Press, 1991. After Lincoln's election in 1860, some southerners appealed for restraint because he would be no worse than Fillmore.

2232. Lang, H. Jack. *Letters in American History: Words to Remember, 1770 to the Present.* New York: Harmony Books, 1982. In April, 1861, the former Presidents thought to gather and advise Lincoln on ways to avert war.

2233. Lewis, Lloyd. *Myths After Lincoln.* New York: Harcourt, Brace and Company, 1929. An angry crowd demanded that Fillmore adorn his house in black crape to mourn the death of Lincoln. He explained his wife had been sick and he had no time. Days later he served on the reception committee for Lincoln's funeral train.

2234. "Lincoln Train Spans New York." *New York State and the Civil War* 1 (February 1962): 2–15. Lincoln stayed at Fillmore's home during his journey to Washington. Includes picture of Fillmore's house.

2235. Neely, Mark E., Jr. *The Abraham Lincoln Encyclopedia.* New York: McGraw-Hill Book Company, 1982. Summary of differences between Fillmore and Lincoln after 1856.

2236. Oliver, Doris, and Francis J. Walter. "The United States Sanitary Commission and the United Christian Commission in Buffalo During the Civil War." *Niagara Frontier* 11 (Summer 1964): 44–53. In February 1864, Fillmore headed a commit-tee to raise money for the Christian Commission's war relief work.

2237. Phisterer, Frederick., comp. *New York in the War of the Rebellion, 1861 to 1865.* Albany: J. B. Lyon Company, 1917. Volume One records Fillmore heading the ceremonial Buffalo Home Guard in April 1861.

2238. Riforgiato, Leonard R. "Bishop Timon, Buffalo, and the Civil War." *Catholic Historical Review* 73 (January 1987): 62–80. The Catholic bishop of Buffalo and Fillmore helped to unite the city in defense of the Union.

2239. Searcher, Victor. *The Farewell to Lincoln.* New York: Abingdon Press, 1965. News reports exaggerated an incident involving Fillmore's unadorned house after Lincoln's death. Fillmore led the ceremonies honoring Lincoln when his funeral train passed through Buffalo.

2240. ———. *Lincoln's Journey to Congress: A Factual Account of the Twelve-Day Inaugural Tour.* Philadelphia: John C. Winston Company, 1960. Fillmore hosted Lincoln during his stay in Buffalo.

2241. Staudenraus, P. J., ed. *Mr. Lincoln's Washington: Selections from the Writings of Noah Brooks, Civil War Correspondent.* New York: Thomas Yoseloff, 1969. Fillmore is mentioned as a presidential candidate by the Peace Democrats at the 1864 convention.

2242. Villard, Henry. *Lincoln on the Eve of '61.* New York: Alfred A. Knopf, 1941. Eyewitness account of Fillmore escorting Lincoln during his three-day stay in Buffalo.

2242a. Wilson, Clyde, Jr. "Five Men in a Dilemma." *Civil War Times Illustrated* 9 (October 1970): 20–27. Fillmore's initial support for the war devolved into disappointment that the country was moving toward bankruptcy, military despotism, and intractable sectionalism.

2243. Winthrop, Robert C., Jr. "Memoir of Robert M. Mason." *Proceedings of the Massachusetts Historical Society* 18 (1881): 302–17. Mason was a Boston businessman living in England who believed Lincoln's reelection looked doubtful. He preferred a safe man like Fillmore who would lead the country back to the Constitution.

2244. Wright, William C. *The Secession Movement in the Middle Atlantic States.* Rutherford: Fairleigh Dickinson University Press, 1973. Fillmore's former cabinet members tried to mediate peace in 1860–61.

Chapter 11

Personal Life of Millard Fillmore

A. THE FILLMORES IN THE WHITE HOUSE

2245. Aikman, Lonnelle. "The Living White House." *National Geographic* 130 (November 1966): 593–643. Fillmore acquired the first stove for the White House.

2246. Ampere, J. J. "M. Ampere in Washington." *Eclectic Review* 30 (October 1853): 239–53. Translation of an article from the *Revue des Deux Mondes*. Describes the President as modest, prudent, honest, and worthy of his unexpected station. The republican simplicity of a presidential dinner was in the manner of the President himself.

2246a. Anthony, Carl Sferrazza. *America's First Families: An Inside View of 200 Years of Private Life in the White House.* New York: Simon and Schuster, 2000. Use index to find many glimpses of the family. Excellent photographs of family and Fillmore's father Nathaniel.

2247. Barnum, P. T. *Struggles and Triumphs; or, Forty Years Recollections of P. T. Barnum.* Buffalo: Warren, Johnson & Co., 1873. At Fillmore's invitation, singer Jenny Lind spent several hours with his family. She was charmed by the President's unaffected manner and the kindness of his wife and daughter.

2248. Cable, Mary. *The Avenue of the Presidents.* Boston: Houghton Mifflin Company, 1969. The Fillmores were able hosts.

2249. Carosso, Vincent P. "Music and Musicians in the White House." *New-York Historical Society Quarterly* 48 (April 1964): 101–29. Describes the Fillmores' enjoyment of family musicals and Jenny Lind's presence at the White House.

2250. Ehrenpreis, Anne Henry, ed. "A Victorian Englishman on Tour: Henry Arthur Bright's Southern Journal, 1852." *Virginia Magazine of History and Biography* 84 (July 1976): 333–61. Describes Fillmore's Tuesday levees.

2251. Ellet, E. F. *The Court Circle of the Republic, or the Beauties and Celebrities of the Nation.* Hartford: Hartford Publishing Co., 1869. Complimentary review of the family's White House routine.

2252. *Gleason's Pictorial Drawing-Room Companion,* May 10, 1851. Illustration of the carriage and horses presented to Mrs. Fillmore by the citizens of New York City and Albany.

2253. Hitchcock, Ethan Allen. *Fifty Years in Camp and Field.* New York: G. P. Putnam's Sons, 1909. Description of the Fillmores.

2254. Jeffries, Ona Griffin. *In and Out of the White House.* New York: Wilfred Funk, Inc., 1960. Mentions Fillmore's care for the White House and the family's attendance at ceremonies.

2255. Katz, Irving. "Confidant at the Capital: William W. Corcoran's Role in Nineteenth-Century American Politics." *Historian* 29 (August 1967): 546–64. Fillmore knew and dined with the Washington banker. He corresponded with him during retirement.

2256. Kirk, Elise K. *Music at the White House: A History of the American Spirit.* Urbana: University of Illinois Press, 1986. The Fillmores were devoted to family musicals, enjoyed Jenny Lind's Washington concerts, and welcomed her to the White House.

2257. ———. "Nightingales at the White House: Divas Who Charmed Presidents." *Opera News* 45 (November 1980): 16–22, 42–43. The family enjoined the performances of popular singers.

2258. Lynch, Anne C. "A Sketch of Washington City." *Harper's Monthly,* December 1852, 1–15. Mentions the routine of Fillmore's levees.

2259. McClure, Alexander K. *Recollections of Half a Century.* Salem: Salem Press Company, 1902. Flattering description of Fillmore's appearance and an atypical recollection of a severe manner toward associates.

2260. Moore, John L. *Speaking of Washington.* Washington, DC: Congressional Quarterly, Inc., 1993. A good exposé of H. L. Mencken's fictional story about Fillmore installing the first bathtub in the White House.

2261. Moore, Joseph West. *Picturesque Washington: Pen & Pencil Sketches.* Providence: J. A. & R. A. Reid, 1887. Brief description of the Fillmores.

2262. Poore, Ben: Perly. "Waifs from Washington, No. I." *Gleason's Pictorial Drawing-Room Companion,* January 1, 1853. Describes the President as a tall, portly gentleman with a stolid but pleasant look.

2263. ———. "Waifs from Washington, No. IV." *Gleason's Pictorial Drawing-Room Companion,* January 22, 1853. Describes Fillmore and his family at a White House levee.

2264. ———. "Waifs from Washington, No. VII." *Gleason's Pictorial Drawing-Room Companion,* February 19, 1853. Fillmore's farewell levees were simple affairs and marked by their intellectual interest.

2265. Powers, Cyrus. "The Life and Times of Millard Fillmore." Cyrus Powers, Papers. Powers Library, Moravia NY. Read before the Cayuga County Historical Society on October 18, 1879. Cyrus Powers was Abigail Fillmore's nephew and visited the family many times. He describes the family and recounts conversations with Fillmore.

2266. Pryor, Mrs. Roger A. *Reminiscences of Peace and War.* New York: Macmillan Company, 1904. Recalls Washington in the early 1850s and the literary socials at the White House.

2267. "Reminiscences of Washington." *Atlantic Monthly* 47 (May 1881): 658–66. Describes White House receptions and Webster's ambition to be president.

2268. Rhoads, Samuel. *The Non-Slaveholder.* Westport: Negro Universities Press, 1970. 5 vols. 5: 215. The September 1850 issue reports Fillmore helping his coachman retrieve his abducted family from fugitive slave catchers. Fillmore and others in the administration collected donations for their release.

2269. Rosenback, A. S. W. "The Libraries of the Presidents of the United States." *Proceedings of the American Antiquarian Society,* 44 (1939): 337–64. Abigail Fillmore installed the first White House library. Includes brief remarks on their home library.

2270. Rosenberg, C. G. *Jenny Lind in America.* New York: Stringer & Townsend, 1851. In December 1850, the Fillmores' received Lind twice and twice saw her in concert.

2271. Seale, William. *The White House: The History of an American Idea.* Washington, DC: American Institute of Architects Press, 1992. Fillmore asked landscape architect Andrew Jackson Downing to redesign the White House public grounds. Includes a rendering of an unfinished design.

2272. Stegmaier, Mark J. "The Case of the Coachman's Family: An Incident of President Fillmore's Administration." *Civil War History* 32 (December 1986): 318–24. The new President started a fund to purchase the freedom of his coachman's family who where seized as fugitive slaves. At the time, Fillmore was lodging in Georgetown for protection from Washington's summer diseases.

2273. Traill, David A. *Schliemann of Troy: Treasure and Deceit.* New York: St. Martin's Griffin, 1995. Schliemann's account of meeting Fillmore was probably a lie.

2274. Weber, Shirley H., ed. *Schliemann's First Visit to America, 1850–1851.* Cambridge: Harvard University Press, 1942. The German archaeologist who later discovered the ancient city of Troy met Fillmore in 1851. He thought the President plain and friendly even when 800 people attended his levee.

2275. Wharton, Anne Hollingsworth. *Social Life in the Early Republic.* Williamstown, MA: Corner House Publishers, 1970 [1902]. Revealing portrayal of Fillmore's family and social life. Enhanced by the observations of Mary Abigail's friend who stayed at the White House.

2276. White House. *An Historical Guide.* Washington, DC: White House Historical Association, 1963. Illustrated history of the White House, including the first library arranged by Abigail Fillmore.

2277. Wingate, P. J. "The Philosophy of H. L. Mencken." *Proceedings of the American Philosophical Society* 127 (1983): 95–98. In 1917, Mencken playfully wrote that Fillmore was the first occupant to install a bathtub in the White House. Despite later denials by Mencken, the story would not wash away.

B. PUBLIC SERVICE

2278. Bowers, Claude G. *The Tragic Era: The Revolution After Lincoln.* Cambridge: Houghton Mifflin Company, 1929. Mentions a series of newspaper articles on foreign policy written by Fillmore in 1869. Includes Greeley's comment on their insignificance.

2279. Bryan, George J. "Biography of Mrs. John C. Lord." In *Biographies and Journalism.* Buffalo: Courier Company, Printers, 1886. 147–60. Fillmore was the first Buffalo branch president of the American Society for the Prevention of Cruelty to Animals.

2280. Carr, Clarke E. *My Day and Generation.* Chicago: A. C. McClurg & Co., 1908. Journalist recalls anecdote about Fillmore reconciling with a rich African American who had refused to shake his hand after signing the Fugitive Slave Law.

2281. *The Dedication of the Washington National Monument with the Oration by Hon. Robert C. Winthrop and Hon. John W. Daniel, Feb. 21, 1885.* Washington, DC: Government Printing Office, 1885. Fillmore was a guest at the laying of the cornerstone on July 4, 1848. He later became the ex-officio president of the Monument Society.

2282. Everett, Edward. "The Importance of Agriculture." In *Orations and Speeches on Various Occasions.* Boston: Little, Brown, and Company, 1897. 4 vols. 3: 537–67. Fillmore attended this speech at the New York State Agricultural Society's Annual Fair at Buffalo, October 9, 1857.

2283. Fess, Margaret Richmond. *The Grosvenor Library and Its Times.* Buffalo: Grosvenor Reference Division of the Buffalo and Erie County Public Library, 1956. Sketch of Fillmore's tenure as president of the library from 1870 to 1874.

2284. "The First Book Policy of the Grosvenor Library, 1863–1871." *Grosvenor Library Bulletin* 17 (March 1935): 62–70. Fillmore participated in the library's first major acquisitions.

2285. Glover, W. H., and Frank W. Copley. "Spaulding as Mayor of Buffalo." *Niagara Frontier* 7 (Spring 1960): 1–8. Fillmore addressed the Buffalo delegates to the Chicago Internal Improvement Convention of 1847. He talked on the history of federal support for harbor building.

2286. Goldberg, Arthur. *The Buffalo Public Library: Commemorating its First Century of Service to the Citizens of Buffalo . . . 1836–1936.* Buffalo: Privately Printed, 1937. Fillmore always favored circulating libraries. He supported the Buffalo Lyceum in the 1830s, followed by the Young Men's Association and the Buffalo Public Library, where he was a board member in 1854–55.

2287. Grey, David. "The Last Indian Council on the Genesee." *Scribner's Monthly* 14 (July 1877): 338–50. Recalls Fillmore's minor role in the last great council of the Seneca Indians.

2288. Hawes, Evelyn. *Proud Vision: The History of the Buffalo General Hospital, the First Hundred Years.* New York: Thomas Y. Crowell Company, 1964. Fillmore spoke at the dedication of the new hospital in June 1858. As chancellor of the University of Buffalo medical school he influenced hospital policies.

2289. Hermstadt, Richard L., ed. *The Letters of A. Bronson Alcott.* Ames: Iowa State University Press, 1969. In December 1857 Fillmore attended Alcott's Buffalo parlor meetings. Alcott wrote that the ex-President was a genial gentleman who was "sincere in his timidities" and conscientiously for the Union.

2290. Hibbard, George. "The Prince of Wales and Buffalo—1860." *Grosvenor Library Bulletin* 3 (December 1920): 14–19. Fillmore participated in an unsuccessful attempt to have the Prince of Wales visit Buffalo.

2291. Hill, Henry Wayland. "Historical Address." *Publications of the Buffalo Historical Society Volume 17.* Buffalo: Buffalo Historical Society, 1913. 84–111. Recalls Fillmore's role in founding the Buffalo Historical Society and his tenure as its first president.

2292. ———— . *An Historical Review of Waterways and Canal Construction in New York State. Publications of the Buffalo Historical Society Volume 12.* Buffalo: Buffalo Historical Society, 1908. Fillmore was a Vice President to the 1870 State Canal Convention.

2293. Hillery, Joseph D. "Gen. Daniel D. Bidwell and Buffalo's 74th Regiment." *Niagara Frontier* 11 (Winter 1964): 121–24. Fillmore was the guest of honor at the 1857 Washington Birthday Military Ball in Buffalo.

2294. Howland, Henry R. "From the Society of Natural Sciences." *Publications of the Buffalo Historical Society Volume 17.* Buffalo: Buffalo Historical Society, 1913. 80–83. Fillmore was one of the founders of the society in 1861.

2295. ———— . "Old Caneadea Council House and Its Last Council Fire." *Publications of the Buffalo Historical Society Volume 6.* Buffalo: Buffalo Historical Society, 1903. 97–123. Fillmore addressed the last council of Senecas in October 1872.

2296. Hulett, T. G. "The Old Niagara Car." *Publications of the Buffalo Historical Society Volume 25.* Buffalo: Buffalo Historical Society, 1921. 69–76. Fillmore helped a frightened woman cross the Niagara Gorge in a suspended metal basket.

2297. Ketchum, William. *An Authentic and Comprehensive History of Buffalo.* Buffalo: Rockwell, Baker & Hill, Printers, 1864. 2 vols. The work is dedicated to Fillmore, President of the Buffalo Historical Society. Mentions Glezen Fillmore's contribution to local Methodism.

2298. Learned, Henry Barret. *The President's Cabinet: Studies in the Origin, Formation and Structure of an American Institution.* New Haven: Yale University Press, 1912. In 1862 Fillmore was listed as an honorary member of the U.S. Agricultural Society.

2299. "The Lincoln Relics." *Publications of the Buffalo Historical Society. Volume 25.* Buffalo: Buffalo Historical Society, 1921. 257–62. On May 3, 1872, Fillmore presided over the dedication of a Civil War soldiers and sailors memorabilia case at the Grosvenor Library.

2300. Massachusetts Historical Society. *Proceedings of the Massachusetts Historical Society* 5 (1864): 26, 100, 102. Fillmore was elected an honorary member of the society in April 1863. He accepted in May.

2301. *Minutes of the Council of the University of Buffalo, 1846–1962.* Archives. State University of New York at Buffalo. Contains Fillmore's subscription donations to the university, his attendance as Chancellor at commencements, and the council's memorial address after his death in 1874.

2302. Nevins, Allen. *Grover Cleveland, A Study in Courage.* New York: Dodd, Mead & Company, 1962 [1932]. The future President was familiar with Fillmore's associates and a friend of his son, Powers Fillmore.

2303. *Nineteenth Annual Report of the Executive Committee of the Young Men's Association of the City of Buffalo.* Buffalo: Democracy Office, 1855. Fillmore was a life member and on the library committee.

2304. Overfield, Joseph M. "Baseball in Buffalo Before the Civil War." *Niagara Frontier* 11 (Summer 1964): 53–61. There was a Fillmore baseball club in 1860.

2305. Park, Julian. "The Beginning of the University of Buffalo," *Niagara Frontier* 9 (Spring 1962): 7–26. Includes Fillmore's early support and position as Chancellor.

2306. ———. "Highlights of One Hundred Years." *Niagara Frontier* 9 (Summer–Autumn 1962): 37–44. A history of the Buffalo Historical Society, with references to Fillmore's tenure as president from 1862 to 1868.

2307. ———. "Medicine Starts the University." *Niagara Frontier* 8 (Summer 1961): 48–58. Contains excerpts from Fillmore's dedication and commencement addresses as Chancellor of the University of Buffalo.

2308. Rathbun, Benjamin. "The Case of Benjamin Rathbun." *Publications of the Buffalo Historical Society. Volume 17.* Buffalo Historical Society, 1913: 227–70. Rathbun was a major financial figure in Buffalo when his 1836 bankruptcy rocked the city's economy. This is his defense against accusations of forging signatures to renew loans. Though not mentioned, Fillmore served as a trustee during his bankruptcy.

2309. "Recreational and Cultural Interest in Buffalo in 1846 as Seen in the Buffalo *Express.*" *Grosvenor Library Bulletin* 17 (December 1934): 39–49. Contains an announcement of a Fillmore lecture on February 1, 1847. No title or description, but probably on internal improvements.

2310. *Report of the Board of Trustees of the Buffalo Orphan Asylum for the Seventeenth Asylum Year, June 1853 to June 1854.* Buffalo: Democracy Association, 1854. Fillmore was a life member and donated $10.00 that year through the Unitarian Church.

2311. Schoonover, Thomas. "Mexican Minister Describes Andrew Johnson's 'Swing Around the Circle.' " *Civil War History* 19 (June 1973): 149–61. Mentions President Johnson's September 1866 meeting with Fillmore in Buffalo.

2312. Sellstedt, Lars Gustaf. *From Forecastle to Academy, Sailor and Artist.* Buffalo: Mathews-Northrup Works, 1904. Buffalo portrait-painter reveals some of Fillmore's personable character and charm during his later years.

2313. Severance, Frank H. "Historical Sketch of the Board of Trade, the Merchant's Exchange and the Chamber of Commerce." *Buffalo Historical Society Publication, Volume 13.* Buffalo: Buffalo Historical Society, 1909. 237–329. In 1862, Fillmore attended the dedication of the new quarters for the Buffalo Board of Trade.

2314. "Sheldon's Notes on the Early Book Collections of the Grosvenor Library." *Grosvenor Library Bulletin* 18 (March 1936): 38–57. Recalls Fillmore's participation in the library's first acquisitions.

2315. Smith, H. Perry. *History of the City of Buffalo and Erie County.* Syracuse: D. Mason & Co. Publishers, 1884. 2 vols. 2: 534–36. Fillmore helped to organize the Buffalo Historical Society in 1862. He was its first president and leading fundraiser.

2316. ———— . *History of the City of Buffalo and Erie County.* Syracuse: D. Mason & Co. Publishers, 1884. 2 vols. 2: 546. In 1867 the Buffalo Club was organized with Fillmore as its first president.

2317. Snyder, Charles M. "Harriet Prewett of Yazoo City and Ex-President Millard Fillmore: She Carried a Torch with a Sense of Humor." *Journal of Mississippi History* 39 (Summer 1977): 193–204. A newspaperwoman and Southern Unionist who supported Fillmore and wrote personable letters to him from 1855 through Reconstruction.

2318. Steele, Oliver G. "The Origins and Progress of the Buffalo Historical Society." *Publications of the Buffalo Historical Society Volume 1.* Buffalo: Buffalo Historical Society, 1879. 131–38. Fillmore was the Society's first President.

2319. Viele, Chase. "And the House Fell Upon the Lords." *Niagara Frontier* 4 (Spring 1957): 1–6. Fillmore's name was forged to guarantee loans in the scandalous Rathbun bankruptcy that devastated Buffalo in 1836.

2320. Warren, Joseph. "Address." *Buffalo Medical & Surgical Journal* 13 (March 1874): 306–14. Mentions Chancellor Fillmore's attendance at the University of Buffalo commencement ceremonies.

2321. Whitman, Roger. *The Rise and Fall of a Frontier Enterprise: Benjamin Rathbun, "Master Builder and Architect."* ed. Scott Eberle and David A. Gerber. Syracuse: Syracuse University Press, 1996. Fillmore, one of the trusted elites of the city, became a trustee of Rathbun's bankrupt empire in 1836. Excellent description of Buffalo's growth in the 1830s.

2322. Wilner, Merton M. *Niagara Frontier: A Narrative and Documentary History.* Chicago: S. J. Clarke Publishing Co., 1931. 4 vols. Volume One mentions Fillmore's many services to Buffalo.

C. RELIGION

2323. Boller, Paul F., Jr. "Religion and the U.S. Presidency." *Journal of Church and State* 21 (Winter 1979): 5–22. Fillmore attended Unitarian services but not regularly.

2324. Bonnell, John Sutherland. *Presidential Profiles: Religion in the Life of American Presidents.* Philadelphia: Westminster Press, 1971. After being snubbed by abolitionist Boston Unitarians, he gradually limited his attendance and later went to Baptist and Episcopalian services in Buffalo. Little evidence remains of Fillmore's intimate thoughts on religion.

2325. Gohdes, Clarence. "Some Notes on the Unitarian Church in the Ante-Bellum South: A Contribution to the History of Southwest Liberalism." in *American Studies in Honor of Wm. Kenneth Boyd,* ed. David Kelly Jackson. Durham: Duke University Press, 1940. 327–66. Fillmore was shown no disrespect at the Washington Unitarian Church despite antagonizing some members by signing the Fugitive Slave Law.

2326. Jones, Olga. *Churches of the Presidents in Washington.* New York: Exposition Press, 1954. Fillmore attended the First Unitarian Church at Sixth and D. Streets.

2327. McCollister, John. *"So Help Me God: " The Faith of American Presidents.* Bloomington, IN: Landmark Books, 1982. Fillmore never publicized his religious feelings but appeared to be content with a reasoned Unitarianism.

2328. Stange, Douglas C. *Patterns of Antislavery among American Unitarians, 1831–1860.* Rutherford: Fairleigh Dickinson University Press, 1977. With the exception of Unitarian abolitionists, Unitarians tolerated the Compromise and considered Fillmore a decent church member.

D. BUFFALO HOMES AND PROPERTY

2329. "The Changing Town.*" Publications of the Buffalo Historical Society. Volume 25* Buffalo: Buffalo Historical Society, 1921. 391–97. Brief history on the mansion Fillmore occupied after his second marriage. Pictures of its exterior and interior are shown in the section "Pictures of the Changing Town."

2330. Hibbard, George. "The Library of Millard Fillmore." *Grosvenor Library* 3 (September 1920): 2–18. Survey of the 5,000 volumes in Fillmore's home. Judged to be a fine gentleman's library but not a valuable collection.

2331. Jones, Cranston. *Homes of the American Presidents.* New York: McGraw-Hill Book Company, Inc., 1962. Pictures of Fillmore's Buffalo residences during and after his Administration.

2332. Severance, Frank H., ed. *The Picture Book of Earlier Buffalo, Publication of the Buffalo Historical Society, Volume 16.* Buffalo: Buffalo Historical Society, 1912. 384, 385. Picture of the family home occupied from 1830 to the end of his Presidency and a picture of the home he occupied after his second marriage.

2333. "Survey of Historical Activities." *Wisconsin Magazine of History* 2 (September 1918): 107–26. The John Hubbard Tweedy Papers contain deeds for land in Wisconsin signed by Fillmore. Probably acquired for their quick resale and profit.

E. HEALTH

2334. Bumgarner, John R., M.D. *The Health of the Presidents, the 41 United States Presidents Through 1993, from a Physician's Point of View.* Jefferson: McFarland & Company, Inc., 1994. Fillmore was in good health throughout his life and Presidency. He neither drank nor smoked but was overweight despite a diet of simple food. He suffered a stroke in February 1874 and died after a second stroke in March.

2335. Harding, Warren G., II, and J. Mark Stewart. *Mere Mortals: The Lives and Health Histories of American Presidents*. Worthingham, OH: Renaissance Publications, 1992. 66–69. Fillmore was in good health throughout his life and was possibly the first health addict in the White House. He was overweight in his later years but felt healthy until his first stroke on February 13, 1874. A second stroke on March 8, left him unconscious. He died hours later at the age of 74.

F. DEATH, FUNERAL, AND MEMORIALS

2336. "A Brief History of Forest Lawn Cemetery." *Gate* 15 (Summer 1999): 2–5. Describes Fillmore's family burial plot and obelisk. His former law partners, Nathan Hall and Solomon Haven, are buried near-by.

2337. Beecher, Henry Ward. "Charles Sumner." In *Plymouth Pulpit: Sermons Preached in Plymouth Church, Brooklyn*. Boston: The Pilgrim Press, 1875. 4 vols. 2: 7–22. Uses the "extraordinary conjunction" of the deaths of Fillmore and Sumner to contrast the respective weakness and honor of the nation. Fillmore represents weakness.

2338. Evans, Charles. *History of St. Paul's Church, Buffalo N. Y., 1817–1888*. Buffalo: The Matthews-Northrup Works, 1903. 116–17, 337. On March 12, 1874 Fillmore's body was removed from his residence to the Church vestibule where he lay in state. Thousands crowded the Church and surrounding streets to pay their last respects.

2339. Garrison, William Lloyd. *Fillmore and Sumner: A Letter from William Lloyd Garrison, From the Boston Journal, March 19th, 1874*. Boston: n. p., 1874. Claims Fillmore's "evil administration" served the slave power and kept millions in bondage. The friends of freedom throughout the world abhorred him and he deserved to be "unwept, unhonored and unsung."

2340. *Harper's New Monthly Magazine* 48 (May 1874): 906, 907. Fillmore is given a two-line obituary notice beside a description of Congress's memorial to Sumner.

2341. Hazard, George S. Papers. Buffalo and Erie County Historical Society. Scrapbook contains article from the March 12, 1874, Buffalo *Commercial Advertiser* reporting the Fillmore memorial arrangements by the Council of the University of Buffalo. Also includes a poetic tribute, *In Memoriam,* by Mrs. M. E. Mixer.

2342. *New York Times. The New York Times Obituary Index*. 2 vols. New York: New York Times, 1970. 1: 324. Obituary on March 9, 1874.

2343. Putnam, James O. *Addresses, Speeches, and Miscellanies*. Buffalo: Peter Paul & Brother, 1880. Contains memorial remarks to the Buffalo Historical Society immediately after Fillmore's death. Considered Fillmore an American statesman and, like Lincoln, an inspiration to American youth of humble origins.

2344. Winthrop, Robert C. "Fillmore and Sumner." In *Addresses and Speeches on Various Occasions from 1869 to 1879.* Boston: Little, Brown and Company, 1879. 307–11. Memorial praising Fillmore to the members of the Massachusetts Historical Society.

G. WILL

2345. Collins, Herbert R., and David B. Weaver. *Wills of U.S. Presidents.* New York: Communications Channels Inc., 1976. Includes the will, codicils, and a legal assessment of its technical features. Fillmore took particular care to provide for his wife Caroline, son, brothers, and sisters. The original will was dated December 8, 1865, with two codicils in 1868 and 1873 to increase yearly legacies because of increases in the cost of living.

H. ABIGAIL POWERS FILLMORE

2346. *African Repositor* 30 (February 1854): 46. Still mourning Abigail's, death in 1853, Fillmore sent a letter regretting his absence at the annual meeting of the American Colonization Society.

2347. Anthony, Carl Sferrazza. *First Ladies: The Saga of the Presidents' Wives and Their Power, 1789–1961.* New York: William Morrow and Company Inc., 1990. 2 vols. Volume One contains a substantial account of Abigail's invaluable assistance to Fillmore. Includes an account of her unexpected death in Washington following Pierce's Inauguration.

2348. ———. "Skirting the Issue: First Ladies and African Americans." *American Visions* 7 (October/November 1992): 28–32. Abigail pleaded with Millard not to sign the Fugitive Slave Law.

2349. Barzman, Sol. *The First Ladies: Intimate Biographical Portraits of the Presidents' Wives from Martha Washington to Pat Nixon.* New York: Cowles Book Company, Inc., 1970. Barzman is alone in his indifferent assessment of Abigail as a First Lady.

2350. Bassett, Margaret. *Profiles & Portraits of American Presidents & Their Wives.* New York: Grosset & Dunlap, 1969. An informative profile of Abigail and a brief notice on Fillmore's second wife Caroline Carmichael McIntosh.

2351. Caroli, Betty Boyd. "America's First Ladies." *American History Illustrated* 24 (May 1989): 26–31; 48, 50. Summary of Caroli's larger work.

2352. ———. *First Ladies*. New York: Oxford University Press, 1987. Sympathetic description of Abigail's White House tenure, including her feigning illness to stay away from social events. She is ranked 28th among White House wives, which is slightly higher than Fillmore's presidential ranking.

2353. Cole, Donald B., and John J. McDonough, eds. *Benjamin Brown French, Witness to the Young Republic: A Yankee's Journal, 1828–1870*. Hanover: University Press of New England, 1989. Records Washington's mourning the death of Abigail. She died just weeks after attending the inauguration of Pierce where she became ill from the damp and cold.

2354. "Fillmore, Abigail Powers." *The National Cyclopedia of American Biography*. New York: J. T. White & Company, 1929. Brief sympathetic biography.

2355. Gerlinger, Irene Hazard. *Mistresses of the White House: Narrator's Tale of a Pageant of First Ladies*. Freeport: Books for Libraries Press, 1970. Admires Abigail for her teaching career and for her performance in the White House despite poor health.

2356. Hampton, Vernon B. *Religious Background of the White House*. Boston: Christopher Publishing House, 1932. Abigail was raised a Baptist.

2357. Hannaford, Phebe A. *Daughters of America; Or Women of the Century*. Cincinnati: Forshee & McMakin, 1883. Romantic sketch of a loving, supportive wife.

2358. Hay, Peter. *All the Presidents' Ladies: Anecdotes of the Women Behind the Men in the White House*. New York: Viking, 1988. Abigail turned the Oval Room into the first White House library.

2359. Hoganson, Kristen. "Abigail (Powers) Fillmore." In *American First Ladies: Their Lives and Their Legacy*, ed. Lewis L. Gould. New York: Garland Publishing, Inc., 1996. 154–65. Using recently recovered Fillmore papers this study reveals Abigail's love for Fillmore, her devotion to their children, and her manner as first lady despite health problems. Also describes her death in Washington and the nation's mourning. Annotated bibliography.

2360. Holloway, Laura C. *The Ladies of the White House, or in the Home of the Presidents*. Philadelphia: A. Gorton & Co., 1882. Attractive sketches of Abigail and daughter Mary Abigail.

2361. Logan, Mrs. John A. *Thirty Years in Washington: or Life and Scenes in Our National Capital*. Hartford: A. D. Worthington & Co., 1901. Sentimental portrait of an able and intelligent first lady, including a sketch of daughter Mary Abigail.

Contains a late-19th-century photograph of the White House Library started by Abigail.

2362. McConnell, Jane, and Burt McConnell. *Our First Ladies, From Martha Washington to Pat Ryan Nixon.* New York: Thomas Y. Crowell Company, 1969. Biography of Abigail and her contributions to Fillmore's career.

2363. Melick, Arden Davis. *Wives of the President.* Maplewood, NJ: Hammond Incorporated, 1985. Brief sketch of Abigail.

2364. Prindiville, Kathleen. *First Ladies: Stories of the Presidents' Wives.* New York: Macmillan Company, 1964. 2d ed. Romantic portrait of the family's domestic relationships.

2365. Rayback, Robert J. "Fillmore, Abigail Powers." In *Notable American Women, 1607–1950: A Biographical Dictionary,* ed. Edward T. James, Janet Wilson James, and Paul S. Boyer. Cambridge: Belknap Press, 1971. 3 vols. I: 617. Good vignette by Fillmore's biographer.

2366. Rienow, Robert, and Leona Train Rienow. *The Lonely Quest: The Evolution of Presidential Leadership.* Chicago: Follett Publishing Company, 1966. Abigail was Fillmore's chief asset. His own humility allowed people to believe him unworthy.

2367. Risley, Marius. "Forest Lawn's First Lady Was First White House Librarian." *Gate* 7 (Fall 1991): 1. Account of Abigail's participation in the creation of the first permanent White House library. Contains a portrait of Abigail.

2368. Snow, Mrs. Julia. "Early Recollections of Buffalo." *Publications of the Buffalo Historical Society Volume 17.* Buffalo: Buffalo Historical Society, 1913. 127–64. Recalls her friend Abigail, their social circle, and Mary Abigail's desire to be a teacher.

2369. Watson, Robert P. "The First Lady Reconsidered: Presidential Partner and Political Institution." *Presidential Studies Quarterly* 27 (Fall 1997): 805–18. Reviews the recent literature and concludes Abigail was a life partner and confidante to the President.

I. CAROLINE CARMICHAEL McINTOSH FILLMORE

2370. "Caroline C. Fillmore's Music Album." Rare Book Room, Buffalo and Erie County Public Library. Contains numerous selections of popular sheet music.

2371. Risley, Marius. "Caroline Carmichael, The Second Mrs. Fillmore." *Gate* 9 (Autumn 1993): 1–2. Sketch of Fillmore's 16-year second marriage, including problems with Caroline's 50-page will. Contains a portrait of Caroline.

J. THE FILLMORE CHILDREN: MARY ABIGAIL AND MILLARD POWERS

2372. Bergson, Paul H. *The Papers of Andrew Johnson Volume 14, April–August 1868.* Knoxville: University of Tennessee Press, 1997. 14 vols. 14: 274–75. Letter mentions a spiritualist contacting Mary Fillmore who spoke on political matters.

2373. Chester, Alden. *Courts and Lawyers of New York: A History, 1609–1925.* New York: American Historical Society, Inc., 1925. 3 vols. 3: 1273. Mentions a law partnership between Powers and Eben Carleton Sprague, a well-known Buffalo lawyer.

2374. Evans, Charles. *History of St. Paul's Church, Buffalo N.Y., 1817–1888.* Buffalo: Matthews-Northrup Works, 1903. 116–17, 337. 176. Powers Fillmore subscribed $500.00 to the rebuilding of the church after a fire in 1888.

2375. Fillmore, Millard Powers. Papers. State University of New York at Oswego. 2 boxes (1830–1890). Papers from his legal career, financial records, and a small collection of copies of family correspondence.

2376. Mathews, Sylvester J. "Memoirs of Early Days in Buffalo." *Publications of the Buffalo Historical Society. Volume 17.* Buffalo Historical Society, 1913. 193–226. Growing up, Powers Fillmore never guessed he would be a President's son.

2377. Nevins, Allen, ed. *Letters of Grover Cleveland, 1850–1908.* Boston: Houghton Mifflin Company, 1933. Contains a letter describing the President's son as a man of reticent and private behavior.

2378. *Nineteenth Annual Report of the Executive Committee of the Young Men's Association of the City of Buffalo.* Buffalo: Democracy Office, 1855. M. P(owers) Fillmore was chairman of the law committee, which reported on property insurance and a charter change to help finance the Association.

2379. Perling, J. J. *Presidents' Sons, The Prestige of Name in a Democracy.* New York: Odyssey Press, 1947. An informative chapter on Powers Fillmore whose will requested the destruction of his father's private papers.

2380. Quinn-Musgrave, Sandra L., and Sanford Kanter. *America's Royalty: All the Presidents' Children.* Westport, CT: Greenwood Press, 1995. Reviews Power's legal career and the contention over his father's will with Caroline Fillmore.

Description of Mary Abigail's education, White House life, and her tragic death by cholera.

2381. Risley, Marius. "Two White House Children Repose in Forest Lawn." *Gate* 14 (Winter 1998): 1–2. Brief biographies with portraits.

2382. Sadler, Christine. *Children in the White House.* New York: G. P. Putnam's Sons, 1967. Informative section on Mary Abigail and Powers, neither of whom married.

2383. Smith, H. Perry. *History of the City of Buffalo and Erie County.* Syracuse: D. Mason & Co. Publishers, 1884. 2 vols. 1: 486. Powers is listed as a practicing attorney in Buffalo during 1883–84.

2384. Spragens, William C. "White House Staffs (1789–1974)." In *Organizing and Staffing the Presidency,* ed. Bradley D. Nash et al. Washington, DC: Center for the Study of the Presidency, 1980. Powers Fillmore served as his father's secretary.

2384a. Wood, John., ed. *America and the Daguerreotype.* Iowa City: University of Iowa Press, 1991. Clear daguerreotype of Mary Abigail.

Chapter 12

Historiographical Materials

A. CONTEMPORARY EVALUATIONS

2385. Barrows, John Henry. *Henry Ward Beecher: The Shakespeare of the Pulpit.* New York: Funk & Wagnalls Co., 1893. Believed Fillmore was without a political conscience because he compromised with Southern slavery and Northern commerce.

2385a. Blaine, James K. *Twenty Years of Congress: from Lincoln to Garfield.* Norwich, CT: Henry Bill Publishing Company, 1886. 2 vols. As President, Fillmore passed from the antislavery to the pro-slavery wing of the Whig party. His administration's disappointing support for Scott in 1852 gave the Democrats a victory while Fillmore barely escaped dishonor.

2386. Duberman, Martin. *James Russell Lowell.* Boston: Houghton Mifflin Company, 1966. In March 1855, Lowell met Fillmore and unaccountably described him as one of the stupidest-looking men imaginable.

2387. Fladeland, Betty. *James Gillespie Birney: Slaveholder to Abolitionist.* Ithaca: Cornell University Press, 1955. Birney believed Fillmore was a man of respectable talents but nonetheless odious for signing the Fugitive Slave Law.

2388. Frothingham, Octavius Brooks. *Theodore Parker: A Biography.* Boston: James R. Osgood and Company, 1876. Frothingham, like Parker, dismisses Fillmore as a tool of the slave power.

2389. Knowled, Wm. Edward. "Autographs and Autography of Distinguished Individuals, No. V." *Gleason's Pictorial Drawing-Room Companion,* October 2, 1852. Analysis of Fillmore's signature reveals a distinct, clear, and legible hand evincing regularity and careful habits. Also analyses cabinet members.

2390. Merriam, George S. *The Life and Times of Samuel Bowles.* New York: Century Company, 1885. Bowles, a contemporary journalist, believed Webster dominated Fillmore's administration.

2391. Poore, Ben: Perly. "Types of Mind: or Fac-similes of the Hand Writing of Eminent Persons." *Gleason's Pictorial Drawing-Room Companion,* January 8, 1853. Satirical analysis of Fillmore's signature, which smacked of the Comptroller's office. Reports Fillmore's virtues endeared him to the country.

2392. "Reminiscences of Washington." *Atlantic Monthly* 47 (April 1881): 538–47. Fillmore showed ability, but his intellect lacked heart. He felt no loyalty to Northern antislavery sentiments.

2393. Schurz, Carl. *Henry Clay.* Boston: Houghton, Mifflin and Company, 1887, 1899. 2 vols. Schurz, a German immigrant and antislavery Republican, described Fillmore as a man who preferred the politically safe middle course.

2394. "The State and Statesmanship." *Christian Examiner* 51 (July 1851): 36–53. Characterizes Fillmore as an agreeable man not suffering from pride.

B. HISTORIANS' EVALUATIONS

2394a. Brent, Robert A. "Failure of Executive and Legislative Leadership During the Decade of the 1850's." *Southern Quarterly* 9 (October 1970): 51–66. Better than Zachary Taylor, Fillmore showed some early promise. But his overall inept political actions demote him to a below-average chief executive.

2395. Burlingame, Michael, and John R. Turner Ettlinger, eds. *Inside Lincoln's White House: The Complete Civil War Diary of John Hay.* Carbondale: Southern Illinois University Press, 1997. Hay recalled a disparaging anecdote about Fillmore's reputation for wisdom.

2396. Ellis, Richard J., and Aaron Wildavsky. *Dilemmas of Presidential Leadership from Washington through Lincoln.* New Brunswick: Transactions Publishers, 1989. His failed Presidency is credited to the unsolvable slavery conflict, dissension in the Whig party, and not to any lack of political skill.

2397. Filler, Louis. "The Lady and the President: The Letters of Dorothea Dix & Millard Fillmore. By Charles M. Snyder." *Journal of American History* 63 (December 1976): 720–21. Filler believes Fillmore represented the majority middle position in the sectional crisis during the early 1850s.

2398. Fish, Carl Russell. *The Development of American Nationality.* New York: American Book Company, 1929. Fillmore was the docile instrument of Webster and Clay.

2399. Goldsmith, William M. *The Growth of Presidential Power: A Documented History.* New York: Chelsea House Publications, 1974. 3 vols. In Volume Two, Fillmore's Whig principles and his conciliatory manner place him with presidents who weakened the executive office.

2400. Hamilton, Holman. *White House Images & Realities.* Gainesville: University of Florida Press, 1958. Fillmore was an average mainstream politician.

2401. Hughes, Emmet John. *The Living Presidency: The Resources and Dilemmas of the American Presidential Office.* New York: Coward, McCann & Geoghegan, Inc., 1973. Fillmore contributed nothing helpful to avoid the Civil War.

2402. Link, Arthur S., ed. *The Papers of Woodrow Wilson.* Princeton: Princeton University Press, 1966–1990. 63 vols. 4: 143. In 1885 Wilson accepted the consensus that Webster overshadowed Fillmore's administration.

2403. Park, Julian. "Address of the President. "*Niagara Frontier* 6 (Autumn 1959): 65–66. Report on the gratifying revival of interest in Fillmore because of Robert J. Rayback's biography.

2404. Rossiter, Clinton. *The American Quest, 1790–1860: An Emerging Nation in Search of Identity, Unity and Modernity.* New York: Harcourt Brace Jovanovich, Inc., 1971. More resolute men than Fillmore were needed to advance America into modernity.

2405. Smith, Elbert B. "Review of Benson Lee Grayson, *The Unknown President: The Administration of President Millard Fillmore.*" *American Historical Review* 87 (February 1982): 257. Despite a critical review, Smith agrees that Fillmore's foreign policy was admirable.

2406. Snyder, Charles M. "Could Fillmore Have Saved the Union?" In *Six Presidents from the Empire State,* ed. Harry J. Sievers. Tarrytown: Sleepy Hollow Restorations, 1974. Fillmore was incapable of allowing passion to override reason, the compromise, or the Union.

2407. Stanwood, Edward. *A History of the Presidency from 1788 to 1897.* Boston: Houghton, Mifflin & Company, 1926. Considered Fillmore an active agent for compromise in the 1850s.

2408. Summers, Mark W. *The Plundering Generation: Corruption and the Crisis of the Union, 1849–1861.* New York: Oxford University Press, 1987. Using Democratic sources, the study claims Fillmore lacked moral leadership in the presence of political and business corruption.

2409. Sundquist, James L. *Dynamics of the Party System: Alignment and Realignment of Political Parties in the United States.* Washington, DC: Brookings Institute, 1983. Categorizes Fillmore as a displaced centrist during the polarizing realignments of parties during the 1850s.

2410. Wilson, Clyde. "The Lady and the President: The Letters of Dorothea Dix & Millard Fillmore. By Charles M. Snyder." *North Carolina Historical Review* 53 (July 1976): 332–33. The reviewer was taken by the moderation and decency of Dix and Fillmore.

2411. Woodward, C. Vann, ed. *Responses of the Presidents to Charges of Misconduct.* New York: Dell Publishing Co., 1974. No serious allegations were made against Fillmore's administration.

C. RATING EVALUATIONS

2412. Bailey, Thomas A. *Presidential Greatness, The Image and the Man: From George Washington to the Present.* New York: Appleton-Century-Crofts, 1966. Fillmore's presidential rating should be raised from below average to average.

2413. ———. *Presidential Saints and Sinners.* New York: Free Press, 1981. Fillmore is given a high rating for presidential integrity.

2414. ———. *The Pugnacious Presidents: White House Warriors on Parade.* New York: Free Press, 1980. Fillmore receives a low pugnacious rating but is credited as a conciliator.

2415. Goldman, Ralph M. "The American President as Party Leader: A Synoptic History." In *Presidents and Their Parties: Leadership or Neglect,* ed. Robert Harmel. New York: Praeger Publishers, 1984. Fillmore's party identification was weak and ambiguous.

2416. Holmes, Jack E., and Robert E. Elder, Jr. "Our Best and Worst Presidents: Some Possible Reasons for Perceived Performance." *Presidential Studies Quarterly* 19 (Summer 1989): 529–57. Ranking indicators for the Presidents from 1848 to 1871 are suppressed by the overwhelming drama of sectionalism and the Civil War.

2417. Klein, Mary, ed. *Viewpoints: The Presidency, The Power and Glory.* Minneapolis: Winston Press, 1973. Includes abstract of Maranell's low rating of Fillmore.

2418. Lonnstrom, Douglas A., and Thomas O. Kelly, II. "Rating The Presidents: A Tracking Study." *Presidential Studies Quarterly* 27 (Summer 1997): 591–98. Fillmore's below average rating is not likely to change.

2419. Lurie, Leonard. *Party Politics: Why We Have Poor Presidents.* New York: Stein and Day, 1980. Fillmore was a loyal party man and mediocre President.

2420. Maranell, Gary M. "The Evaluation of Presidents: An Extension of the Schlesinger Polls." *Journal of American History* 57 (June 1970): 104–13. Fillmore receives a poor evaluation in this random polling from the Organization of American Historians.

2421. Miller, Nathan. *Star-Spangled Men: America's Ten Worst Presidents.* New York: Scribner, 1998. Fillmore is not one of the ten. His low evaluations are not for his administration but reflect his later association with Know-Nothings, his original low ranking in the 1948 Schlesinger pole, and historians knowing nothing about him.

2422. Murray, Robert K., and Tim H. Blessing. "The Presidential Performance Study: A Progress Report." *Journal of American History* 70 (December 1983): 535–55. Fillmore is rated higher by southern historians than their northern counterparts.

2423. Riddings, William J., Jr., and Stuart B. McIver. *Rating the Presidents: A Ranking of U.S. Leaders From Great and Honorable to the Dishonest and Incompetent.* Secaucus NJ: Citadel Press Book, 1997. Fillmore ranks 36th of 41 Presidents. However he is given a sympathetic analysis by the authors.

2424. Schlesinger, Arthur M. "Historians Rate United States Presidents." *Life,* November 1, 1948, 65–66, 68, 73–74. The first assessment by professional historians gave Fillmore a below-average rating.

2424a. Schlesinger, Arthur M., Jr. "Rating the Presidents: Washington to Clinton." *Political Science Quarterly* 112 (Summer 1997): 179–90. His 1996 poll of historians reaffirms the longstanding assessment of Fillmore as a below-average President.

2425. Simonton, Dean Keith. *Why Presidents Succeed: A Political Psychology of Leadership.* New Haven: Yale University Press, 1987. Fillmore does not fare well in this behavioral analysis.

2426. *U.S. News and World Report* 92 (January 25, 1982): 29. Fillmore is ranked one of the ten worst Presidents in a poll of 49 scholars conducted by the *Chicago Tribune.*

D. OTHER EVALUATIONS

2427. Agar, Herbert. *The People's Choice: From Washington to Harding, A Study in Democracy.* Boston: Houghton Mifflin Company, 1933. Contends Fillmore was a political nonentity.

2428. Brady, Eric. "Millard & Me: Happy Birthday, Mr. Fillmore, from Your Biggest Fan." Buffalo *News, First Sunday*, January 2, 2000. It's good to be Fillmore's number one fan in Buffalo.

2429. Gallen, David, comp. *The Quotable Truman.* New York: Carroll & Graf Publishers, Inc., 1994. In 1960, Truman said Fillmore was a do-nothing President. He mistakenly says Fillmore was twice governor of New York.

2430. Holland, Barbara. "Millard Fillmore Was My Kind Of Guy." *Smithsonian* 20 (October 1989): 238. Humor. Fillmore got everything wrong but being born in a log cabin.

2431. Hollister, Frank M. " 'Millard Fillmore': Address at Unveiling of the Fillmore Memorial Tablet." *Publications of the Buffalo Historical Society Volume 17.* Buffalo Historical Society, 1913: 112–20. Mentions Fillmore's political luck until he signed the Fugitive Slave Law for which history set him aside. He was a public servant who rose to the required level of every public office he filled.

2432. *Millard Fillmore Anniversary Ceremonies.* Archives of the State University of New York at Buffalo. Annual birthdate memorial speeches held at Fillmore's grave site in the middle of Buffalo winters. They are sponsored by the University of Buffalo. The speeches date from 1960 to the present. While favorable, they emphasize Fillmore's contribution to the City of Buffalo.

2433. *Millard Fillmore Miscellany.* Archives. State University of New York at Buffalo. Three folders of 20th-century newspaper clippings ranging from ridicule to sincere memorials.

2434. Ritz, Joseph P. "From Here to Obscurity." *Buffalo Magazine,* February 12, 1995. 14–15. Surveys the ridicule directed at Fillmore stemming from his signing the Fugitive Slave Law.

2434a. Shenkman, Richard. *Presidential Ambition: How the Presidents Gained Power, Kept Power, and Got Things Done.* New York: Harper Collins, *Publishers*, 1999. Fillmore is considered inconsequential, yet credited with a bold move to open Japan.

2435. Siggelkow, Richard A. "Let's Hear It for Millard." *Buffalo Magazine,* January 6, 1991. 7–11. Good description of Buffalo's annual commemoration of Fillmore's birthday. Highlights the complimentary assessments made by many of the speakers. Article contains full page picture of the bronze statue of Fillmore standing in front of Buffalo's City Hall

2436. Tugwell, Rexford G. *How They Became Presidents: Thirty-Five Ways to the White House.* New York: Simon and Schuster, 1964. Uncomplimentary assessment of Fillmore.

E. BIBLIOGRAPHIES ON THE PRESIDENCY

2437. Cimbola, Diane J., Jennifer Cargill, and Brian Alley. *Biographical Sources: A Guide to Dictionaries and Reference Works.* Phoenix: Oryx Press, 1986. Annotated references to sources on political biography and the Presidency.

2438. Davidson, Kenneth E. *The American Presidency, A Guide to Information Sources.* Detroit: Gale Research Company, 1983. A compilation of sources, some annotated, on the Presidency, Presidents, and elections.

2439. Fehrenbacher, Don E. *Manifest Destiny and the Coming of the Civil War.* New York: Appleton-Century-Crofts, 1970. Dated but useful bibliography of the era.

2440. Foster, William Eaton. *References to the History of Presidential Administrations, 1789–1885.* Economic Tracts, no. 17. New York: Society for Political Education, 1885. Bibliography on the Taylor and Fillmore administrations. Contains 19th-century magazine sources.

2441. Gerber, David A. *The Making of an American Pluralism: Buffalo, New York 1825–60.* Urbana: University of Chicago Press, 1989. Useful footnotes on the City of Buffalo, Fillmore, and his local associates.

2442. Gienapp, William E. *The Origins of the Republican Party, 1852–1856.* New York: Oxford University Press, 1987. Informative footnotes and bibliographic essay.

2443. Goehlert, Robert U., and Fenton S. Martin. *The Presidency, A Research Guide.* Santa Barbara: ABC-Clio Information Services, 1985. Annotated references and research formats.

2444. Holt, Michael F. *The Rise and Fall of the American Whig Party: Jacksonian Politics and the Onset of the Civil War.* New York: Oxford University Press, 1999. Extraordinary footnoting with bibliography.

2445. Larned, J. N. *The Literature of American History: A Bibliographic Guide.* Boston: Houghton, Mifflin & Co., 1902. Interesting annotated reference to nineteenth-century historical scholarship.

2446. Martin, Fenton S., and Robert U. Goehlert. *American Presidents, A Bibliography.* Washington, DC: Congressional Quarterly, Inc., 1987. Little on Fillmore.

2447. Menendez, Albert J. *Religion and the U.S. Presidency: A Bibliography.* New York: Garland Publishing, Inc., 1986. Few sources on Fillmore.

2448. Miles, William. *The Image Makers: A Bibliography of American Presidential Campaign Biographies.* Metuchen, NJ: Scarecrow Press, 1979. Biographies for the 1856 campaign.

2449. Mugridge, Donald H. *The Presidents of the United States, 1789–1962: A Selected List of References.* Washington, DC: Library of Congress, 1963. A dated work.

2450. Prucha, Francis Paul. *Handbook for Research in American History: A Guide to Bibliographies and Other Reference Works.* Lincoln: University of Nebraska Press, 1987. Annotations on bibliographies.

2451. Rayback, Robert J. *Millard Fillmore, Biography of a President. Publications of the Buffalo Historical Society, Volume 40.* Buffalo: Buffalo Historical Society, 1959. 447–57. Dated but excellent reference on 19th and early 20th century sources.

2452. Sayler, James, comp. *Presidents of the United States: Their Written Measure.* Washington, DC: Library of Congress, 1996. Lists eight works on Fillmore. Includes Mathew Brady photo.

2453. Schlachter, Gail. *The American Presidency, A Historical Bibliography.* Santa Barbara: ABC-Clio Information Services, 1984. Abstracts of articles published between 1973 and 1982, containing two Fillmore citations.

2454. Severance Frank H., ed. *Millard Fillmore Papers, Publications of the Buffalo Historical Society, Vol. 11.* Buffalo: Buffalo Historical Society, 1907. Contains a useful 1907 bibliography.

2455. Smith, Elbert B. *The Presidencies of Zachary Taylor & Millard Fillmore.* Lawrence: University Press of Kansas, 1988.

2456. Stegmaier, Mark J. *Texas, New Mexico, and the Compromise of 1850: Boundary Dispute & Sectional Crisis.* Kent, OH: Kent State University Press, 1996. Informative footnotes and bibliographic essay

2457. Stetler, Susan L., ed. *Biographical Almanac.* 3d ed. Detroit: Gale Research Company, 1987. 3 vols. Volume One has biographical items on Fillmore, his first wife Abigail, and his second wife Caroline.

2458. Whitnah, Donald R. *Government Agencies.* Westport, CT: Greenwood Press, 1983. Descriptions, histories, and bibliographies of government departments, bureaus, agencies, commissions, and quasi agencies.

2459. Wise, W. Harvey, Jr., and John W. Cronin. *A Bibliography of Zachary Taylor, Millard Fillmore, Franklin Pierce, James Buchanan.* Presidential Bibliographic Series, no. 7. Washington, DC: Riverford Publishing Company, 1935. Good source for 1848 and 1856 campaign literature, portrait references, and important congressional speeches.

2460. Woodworth, Steven E., ed. *The American Civil War: A Handbook of Literature and Research.* Westport, CT: Greenwood Press, 1996. Contains three bibliographic essays on the causation of the war.

F. MEMORIALS

Burial Place

2461. Forest Lawn. "Millard Fillmore." Buffalo: Forest Lawn Cemetery, n. d. Pamphlet includes brief history, picture of the Fillmore obelisk, and the dedication on his memorial plaque.

Counties

Fillmore County, Minnesota

2462. Neill, Rev. Edward D., ed. *The History of Fillmore County.* Minneapolis: Minnesota Historical Society, 1882.

Fillmore County, Nebraska

2463. Gaffney, Wilber G., ed. *The Fillmore County Story.* Geneva, NE: Geneva Community Grange No. 403, 1968.

Millard County, Utah

2464. Daughters of Utah Pioneers. *Milestones of Millard: A Century of History of Millard County.* Springville, Utah: Art City Publishing Company, 1951.

Fort Fillmore, New Mexico Territory

2465. Baldwin, P. M. "Fillmore, Fort." In *Dictionary of American History,* ed. James Truslow Adams. New York: Charles Scribner's Sons, 1940. 5 vols. 2: 274. Established in honor of Fillmore, it was 36 miles north of El Paso in New Mexico Territory and first occupied on September 23, 1851.

2466. Barnett, Louise. *Touched by Fire: The Life, Death, and Mythic Afterlife of George Armstrong Custer.* New York: Henry Holt and Company, 1996. The southwest was desolate country for soldiers and their wives. One wife recalled seldom experiencing such a dreary place as Fort Fillmore.

2467. Crimmins, M. L., Col. "Fort Fillmore." *New Mexico Historical Review* 6 (October 1931): 327–33. Brief history of the fort, emphasizing its surrender to secessionist troops in 1861.

2468. Foote, Shelby. *The Civil War: A Narrative.* New York: Random House, 1958. 3 vols. 1: 295–97. The surrender of Fort Fillmore in 1861 led to the establishment of the Confederate Territory of Arizona.

2469. Frazer, Robert W. *Forts of the West, Military Forts and Presidios and Posts Commonly Called Forts West of the Mississippi River to 1898.* Norman: University of Oklahoma Press, 1965. Description and map of Fort Fillmore.

2470. Grant, Bruce. *American Forts, Yesterday and Today.* New York: E. P. Dutton & Co., 1965. Brief description.

2471. Gregg, Andy. *Drums of Yesterday: The Forts of New Mexico.* Santa Fe: Press of the Territories, 1968. History, map, and directions to the old site of Fort Fillmore.

2472. Josephy, Alvin M., Jr. *The Civil War in the American West.* New York: Alfred A. Knopf, 1992. Narrates the federal surrender of Fort Fillmore to secessionists in July 1861.

2473. Staski, Edward, and Joanne Reiter. "Status and Adobe Quality at Fort Fillmore, New Mexico: Old Questions, New Techniques." *Historical Archaeology* 30 (3): 1–19. Reviews history of the Fort and contains bibliography on military occupation in the southwest.

Hospital

Millard Fillmore Hospital

2474. Ulrick, Helen E. *Then and Now.* Buffalo: Millard Fillmore Hospital, 1983. Reprints series of articles published in the *Reporter.*

2475. ———— . "Then and Now." *The Reporter* 16 (January–December 1979). The history of Buffalo's Millard Fillmore Hospital is recorded in this series of the hospital newsletter. The hospital is associated with the Millard Fillmore Foundation which helps support its health system.

Museum

2476. Millard Fillmore House/Museum. 24 Shearer Avenue, East Aurora, NY., 14052. Restored house that Fillmore and Abigail lived in before they moved to Buffalo in 1830. The house is a National Historic Landmark restored and operated by the Aurora Historical Society. Open to the public.

Park

Fillmore Glen State Park, New York

2476a. Bailey, Bill. *New York State Parks.* Saginaw, MI: Glovebox Guidebooks of America, 1997. Fillmore Glen State Park is a family park near Morovia, New York.

2477. Haas, Irvin. *A Traveler's Guide: Historic Homes of the American Presidents.* New York: David McKay Company, Inc., 1976. Directions to Fillmore Glen State Park and photo of the replica of Fillmore's childhood home.

2478. New York State. "Welcome to Fillmore Glen State Park." Trumansburg, NY: Finger Lakes State Parks, Recreation and Historic Preservation Region (Flier). Established in 1921, it is located near Auburn, New York about five miles from Fillmore's birthplace. Contact: Box 283, R. D. 3, Trumansburg, NY 14886–0721, (607) 387–7041

School

2479. Millard Fillmore College. The Division of Continuing Education at the State University of New York at Buffalo.

Ships

2480. Niven, John. *The American President Lines and Its Forebears, 1848–1984: From Paddlewheelers to Containerships.* Newark: University of Delaware Press, 1987. There have been three ships named *President Fillmore.* All were named in the twentieth century and were cargo vessels.

Society

Society for the Preservation and Enhancement of the Recognition of Millard Fillmore, Last of the Whigs (SPERMFLOW)

2481. Daniels, Peggy Kneffel, and Carol A. Schwartz, eds. *Encyclopedia of Associations. Volume 1, Part 2, National Organizations,* Detroit: Gale Research Inc., 1993. 4 vols. Also known as the Millard Fillmore Society. Founded: 1975. Members: 400. Publications: *Fillmore Bugle,* annual. Members are dedicated to the celebration of mediocrity in American culture, as epitomized by Millard Fillmore.

Street Name, Buffalo

Fillmore Avenue

2482. *Index to Records of Streets, . . . of the City of Buffalo, from 1814 to 1896.* Buffalo: Bureau of Engineering, 1896. Former Avenue A renamed Fillmore Avenue. No date shown.

2483. Whitcomb, George, comp. *Buffalo City Directory for the Year 1894.* Buffalo: Courier Company, 1894. Avenue A renamed Fillmore Avenue by order of the Council in 1889.

Town

Fillmore, Utah

2484. Utah Writers Project. *Origins of Utah Place Names.* 3d ed. Salt Lake City: Utah State Department of Public Instruction, 1940. Fillmore is the county seat of Millard County. It was the Utah Territorial capital from 1851 to 1856.

Chapter 13

Iconography

2485. Abbott, Shirley. *The National Museum of American History.* New York: Harry N. Abrams Inc., 1981. The museum contains a lock of Fillmore's hair and a dress worn by his first wife Abigail.

2486. Bassett, Margaret. *Profiles and Portraits of American Presidents and Their Wives.* New York: Grosset & Dunlap, 1969. Photographic portrait from a daguerreotype.

2487. Brown, Richard C., and Bob Watson. *Buffalo: Lake City in Niagara Land.* Woodland Hills, CA: Windser Publications, 1981. Oversized illustrated history of Buffalo with pictures of Fillmore and the city during his lifetime.

2488. Buffalo and Erie County Historical Society, Iconography Department. Selection of Fillmore photographs and the City of Buffalo.

2489. Buffalo and Erie County Library, Central Library, Rare Book Room. "Photograph Album, Fillmore" (WNYD 1870 p. 47). Contains a photograph of Fillmore as Chancellor of the University of Buffalo. It is titled "Buffalo Medical School, the Faculty and Members of the Class of 1872."

2490. Cirker, Hayward, and Blanche Cirker, eds. *Dictionary of American Portraits: 4045 Pictures of Important Americans from Earliest Times to the Beginning of the Twentieth Century.* New York: Dover Publications, Inc., 1967. Photographs of Fillmore, his daughter, and paintings of his first wife Abigail and second wife Caroline.

2491. Craven, Wayne. *Sculpture in America.* New York: Cornwall Books, 1984. Photograph of a plaster copy of a 32-inch marble bust of Fillmore by Edward Sheffield Bartholomew sculpted in Italy in 1856.

2492. Cunningham, Noble E., Jr., *Popular Images of the Presidency.* Columbia: University of Missouri Press, 1991. Wonderful collection of antebellum images of Presidents. Includes engravings of Fillmore's 1851 trip on the New York and Erie Railroad from *Gleason's* Magazine.

2493. Durant, John, and Alice Durant. *Pictorial History of American Presidents.* New York: A. S. Barnes and Company, Inc., 1964. Photographs of Fillmore, his first wife Abigail, and his second wife Caroline.

2494. Duyckinck, E. A. *National Portrait Gallery of Eminent Americans: From Original Paintings by Alonzo Chappel with Biographies by E. A. Duyckinck.* New York: Johnson, Fry & Company, 1861–1864. 2 vols. Full-page portrait with an excellent biographical sketch by E. A. Duyckinck.

2495. Freidel, Frank. *The Presidents of the United States of America.* 9th ed. Washington, DC: White House Historical Association, 1982. Contains the official White House portrait of Fillmore by George P. A. Healy.

2496. *Gleason's Pictorial Drawing-Room Companion,* June 11, 1853. Portrait of Fillmore with all the former U.S. Presidents.

2497. *Grosvenor Library Bulletin* 14 (September–December 1931): 15–16. A note on the competition to design the Fillmore statue to be placed in front of Buffalo's City Hall.

2498. Gustaitis, Joseph. "A Presidential Gallery." *American History Illustrated* 24 (April 1989): 20–34. Portrait in the "oval office collection: " a subscription series of miniature porcelain portraits commemorating the 200th anniversary of the Presidency.

2499. Herring, James. *The National Portrait Gallery of Distinguished Americans: With Biographical Sketched. Supplementary Volume* (to the 1852 volume). Philadelphia: Rice, Rutter & Co., 1867. Engraved portrait with a 12-page biography.

2500. Jones, A. D. *The American Portrait Gallery: Containing Correct Portraits and Brief Notices of the Principal Actors in American History.* New York: Henry Miller, 1869. Portrait engraved on wood from original drawings by S. Wolin. Includes short biography.

2501. Lane, William Coolidge and Nina E. Brown. *A L A Portrait Index: Index to Portraits Contained in Printed Books and Periodicals* New York: Burt Franklin, 1964 [1906]. 3 vols. 2: 513. Contains references to over twenty nineteenth-century portraits and daguerreotypes of Fillmore in magazine and portrait collections.

2502. Lee, Cuthbert. *Portrait Register.* Ashville, NC: Biltmore Press, 1968. Records three portraits, including George P. A. Healy's White House portrait.

2503. Leish, Kenneth W., ed. *The American Heritage Pictorial History of the Presidents of the United States.* New York: American Heritage Publishing Co. Inc., 1968. 2 vols. Volume One contains an even-handed description of Fillmore's administration with lavish illustrations and a chronology.

2504. Loubat, J. F. *The Medalic History of the United States of America, 1776–1876.* New York: J. F. Loubat, 1878. 2 vols. Engraving of an 1850 Fillmore medal.

2505. Meredith, Roy. *Mr. Lincoln's Camera Man: Mathew B. Brady.* 2d ed. New York: Dover Publications, Inc., 1974. A lithograph of Fillmore appeared in Brady's 1850, *Gallery of Illustrious Americans.*

2506. ———. *Mr. Lincoln's Contemporaries: An Album of Portraits by Mathew Brady.* New York: Charles Scribner's Sons, 1951. Contains a photographic portrait of Fillmore.

2507. Mogavero, J. Frank. "Report of the Committee on Markers." *Niagara Frontier* 20 (Spring 1973): 12–16. Item on the dedication of a Fillmore marker for the Millard Fillmore Hospital in Buffalo.

2508. New-York Historical Society. *Catalogue of American Portraits in the New-York Historical Society.* New Haven: Yale University Press, 1974. 2 vols. 1: 265–66. Contains an oil portrait of Fillmore by Peter Kohlbeck in the 1850s.

2509. Pfister, Harold Francis. *Facing the Light: Historic American Portrait Daguerreotypes.* Washington, DC: Smithsonian Institution Press, 1978. 222–28, 317–18. Portraits of Fillmore and many of his contemporaries. Short essay on the Fillmore-Seward rivalry.

2510. Vail, R. W. G. "The Society Grows Up." *New-York Historical Society Quarterly* 38 (October 1954): 384–477. Fillmore and Nathan Hall are included in a large group painting of distinguished Americans who supported the Society.

Chapter 14

Periodicals

African Repository
Afro-Americans in New York Life and History
Alabama Review
American Archivist
American Benedictine Review
American Catholic Historical Society of Philadelphia
American Ecclesiastical Review
American Heritage
American Historical Review
American History Illustrated
American Journal of International Law
American Literature
American Neptune
American Quarterly
American Review of Canadian Studies
American Visions
American West
Armed Forces and Society
Asian Profile
Atlantic Monthly

Brownson's Quarterly Review
Buffalo Magazine
Buffalo Medical & Science Journal

California Historical Society Quarterly
California Western Law Review
Canadian Historical Review

Catholic History Review
Civil War History
Civil War Times Illustrated
Clio
The Collector
Collier's
Consortium on Revolutionary Europe 1750–1850: Proceedings
Cosmopolitan
Current History

De Bow's Review
De Bow's Southern and Western Review
Delaware History
Diplomatic History

The Eclectic Review
E S Q: Journal of the American Renaissance
Essex Institute Historical Collections
Ethnohistory

Filson Club Historical Quarterly

The Gate—(Forest Lawn Cemetery, Buffalo)
Gleason's Pictorial Drawing-Room Companion
Golden Book Magazine
Grosvenor Library Bulletin

Harper's Monthly
Harvard Law Review
Hastings Law Journal
Hispanic American Historical Review
The Historian
Historical Archaeology
Historical Journal of Massachusetts
Historical New Hampshire

Illinois Historical Journal
Indiana Magazine of History
Iowa Journal of History and Politics

Journal of American History
Journal of American Studies
Journal of Church and State
Journal of Mississippi History
Journal of Mormon History
Journal of Negro History
Journal of Presbyterian History
Journal of Southern History

Journal of the Illinois State Historical Society
Journal of the Rutgers University Library
Journal of the West

Kansas Quarterly

Life
Lincoln Herald
Louisiana Historical Quarterly

Maryland Historical Magazine
Melville Society Extracts
Michigan History
Mid-America
Military History of the West
Minnesota History
Minnesota Law Review
Mississippi Valley Historical Review
Missouri Historical Review

National Geographic
Nebraska History
New England Historical & Genealogical Register
New England Quarterly
New Mexico Historical Review
New-York Historical Society Quarterly
New York History
New York State and the Civil War
Niagara Frontier
Niles National Register
North American Review
North Carolina Historical Review

Ontario History
Opera News
Oregon Historical Quarterly

Pacific Historian
Pacific Historical Review
Pennsylvania Magazine of History and Biography
Phylon Quarterly
Plantation Society in the Americas
Political Science Quarterly
Polity
Presidential Studies Quarterly
Proceedings of the American Antiquarian Society
Proceedings of the American Philosophical Society
Proceedings of the Massachusetts Historical Society

Prologue

Quarterly Journal of Speech
Quarterly Publication of the Historical and Philosophical Society of Ohio
Queen's Quarterly

Register of the Kentucky Historical Society
The Reporter (Newsletter of Millard Fillmore Hospital, Buffalo)
Revista de Historia de America

Sartain's Union Magazine of Literature and Art
Saturday Evening Post
Scientific American
Scribner's Magazine
Senior Scholastic
Smithsonian
Social Science History
South Atlantic Quarterly
South Carolina Historical Magazine
Southern California Quarterly
Southern Literary Messenger
Southern Quarterly
Southern Quarterly Review
Southern Speech Communication Journal
Southwestern Historical Quarterly

Tennessee Historical Quarterly
Transactions—The American Lodge of Research, Free and Accepted Masons
Transactions of the Royal Historical Society
Tribune Almanac

United States Magazine and Democratic Review
U.S. Naval Institute Proceedings
U.S. News and World Report
Utah Historical Quarterly

Virginia Magazine of History and Biography

Western Historical Quarterly
Whig Almanac
Wisconsin Magazine of History

Yale Law Journal

Author Index

Fish, Hamilton, 91
Fisher, Louis, 315
Fisher, Marvin, 1421
Fisher, Rex G., 2198
Fishlow, Albert, 933
Fiske, John, 298, 1598, 1830
Fitch, Charles Elliott, 276, 493, 1682, 1914, 1929
Fladeland, Betty, 1291, 2387
Flanders, Carl N., 571, 1565, 1625
Flanders, Stephen A., 571, 1565, 1625
Flanigan, William H., 377, 379
Flexner, Eleanor, 623
Flick, Alexander C., 1169
Flint, Allan, 1919
Floan, Howard R., 624
Flora, Joseph M., 1609
Folkman, David I., Jr., 1374
Folwell, William Wates, 1046
Foner, Eric, 278, 522, 2190
Foner, Philip S., 625, 792, 1397, 1398, 1896
Foote, Andrew H., 1153–1155, 1242
Foote, Shelby, 2468
Ford, Lacy K., 872, 1736, 1961
Forbes, Ella, 854a
Fordham, Monroe, 793
Foreman, Edward R., 1629
Forgie, George B., 626
Formisano, Ronald P., 404, 405
Fornell, Earl W., 896
Forness, Norman O., 1174
Foster, Charles H., 1948
Foster, Herbert Darling, 1630
Foster, William Eaton, 2440
Fowler, Dorothy Ganfield, 1588
Fox, Dixon Ryan, 429
Frank, Douglas, 452
Franklin, John Hope, 627, 1997
Frazer, Robert W., 1091, 1092, 2469
Fredman, Lionel E., 1476
Fredrickson, George M., 960
Freehling, William W., 628
Freidel, Frank, 309, 310, 2495
French, Benjamin Brown, 2351
Friedman, Jean E., 430
Friedman, Leon, 1861
Friend, Llerena, 1772

Frierson, William Little, 1677
Fritz, Christian G., 980
Frost, Elizabeth, 12
Frost-Knappman, Elizabeth, 13
Frothingham, Octavius Brooks, 1956, 2388
Frothingham, Paul Revere, 1567
Fry, Joseph A., 1723
Fuess, Claude M., 760
Fuller, George W., 1009
Fuller, (Rev.), 961
Furniss, Norman F., 737

Gaffney, Wilber G., 2463
Gage, Matilda Joselyn, 664
Gale, Robert L., 277, 629
Gall, Susan B., 1383
Gallen, David, 2429
Gallman, Robert E., 618a
Galloway, John Debo, 934
Galpin, W. Freeman, 843
Ganaway, Loomis Morton, 731
Gann, L. H., 1240
Gantz, Richard A., 467
Gara, Larry, 536, 630, 762–764, 794, 795, 1834
Gardiner, O. C., 523
Gardner, John Cooper, 681
Garraty, John A., 269, 278, 279, 398, 481, 1132, 1561, 1568, 1600, 1615, 1621, 1670, 1674, 1699, 1700, 1706, 1720, 1767, 1778, 1786, 1819, 1835, 1863, 1867, 1964, 1972, 2012
Garrett, Franklin M., 2033
Garrison, William Lloyd, 2339
Gatell, Frank Otto, 508
Gates, Charles M., 1013
Gates, Paul W., 708, 935
Gatzke, Hans W., 1438
Gay, Sydney Howard, 570
Gazley, John Gerow, 1439
Gerber, David A., 431, 2147, 2148, 2321, 2441
Gerlinger, Irene Hazard, 2355
Gerring, John, 432
Ghent, W. J., 1053, 1075
Gibson, Florence E., 1292
Gibson, Patricia, 709

Subject Index

About the Compiler

JOHN E. CRAWFORD is a clerk at the Mirand Library, Roswell Park Cancer Institute in Buffalo, NY. He received his MS in Social Science from SUNY Buffalo.

**Bibliographies of the
Presidents of the United States**

Series Editor: Mary Ellen McElligott